10 X 10 / 3

100 Architects

10 Critics

Phaidon Press Limited
Regent's Wharf
All Saints Street
London N1 9PA

Phaidon Press Inc.
180 Varick Street
New York, NY 10014

www.phaidon.com

First published 2009
Reprinted in paperback 2011
© 2009 Phaidon Press Limited

ISBN: 978 0 7148 6252 1

A CIP catalogue record for this book
is available from the British Library.

Designed by Julia Hasting
Printed in China

Acknowledgments
The publisher would like to extend thanks to
the 100 architects in 10 x 10_3 and the ten critics:
Shumon Basar, Mercedes Daguerre, Luis Fernández-
Galiano, Bart Goldhoorn, Joseph Grima, Carlos
Jimenez, Kengo Kuma, Andrew Mackenzie, Peter
Cachola Schmal, and Ai Weiwei.
    We would also like to thank the following
individuals, institutions, and publishers for permission
to reproduce images of works: Claude Parent and
Paul Virilio for an image of the Church of Sainte-
Bernadette du Banlay; Alejandro Leveratto and
Mondadori Electa S.p.a. for an image of the Church
of Christ the Worker; Luis Fernández-Galiano for an
image of El Escorial; Ateliers Jean Nouvel and DR
for images of the Tokyo Opera House; Walter De
Mulder for images of House Vandenhoute-Kiebooms;
Renzo Piano Building Workshop and Paul Hester for
an image of the Menil Collection; Eiji Mima for an
image of Bruno Taut's box; Renzo Piano Building
Workshop and Michel Denancé for an image of the
Centre Georges Pompidou; Elemental and Cristobal
Palma for images of Quinta Monroy; and Ai Weiwei
for an image of the aftermath of the May 2008
earthquake in Sichuan, China.

Preface

The world of building is changing: green architecture has gone from novelty to necessity, walls have become optional rather than necessary. Conceptual statements have taken physical shape and interstitial spaces offer a new focus. Building materials have been re-imagined, landscape has become increasingly precious, and the specifics of locale are a more powerful determinant than ever.

10x10_3 features 100 architectural practices from around the world chosen by ten widely respected architecture critics, practitioners, and curators. The 100 architects featured in this volume, all of whom have emerged internationally in the last five years, are pushing the boundaries of design and constantly revising our understanding of architecture.

The book is the latest volume in Phaidon's ground-breaking series on contemporary architecture. Like its predecessors *10x10* and *10x10_2*, it is arranged alphabetically by practice name. The work of each of these architects is featured on four pages, and each of their projects are presented in detail and accompanied by an insightful text by the selecting critic. The curators were also asked to choose one seminal building or influential architect, from any period, which they believe has made a profound impact on the development of architecture.

10x10_3 introduces the reader to the architects who are redefining what it means to design today, and to the architecture that will forever change the way we think about what is possible: the architecture of tomorrow.

10 Critics

Shumon Basar

is a London-based architecture writer and curator. He worked for Zaha Hadid Architects from 1996 until 1999, when he co-founded the experimental journal *sexymachinery*. He directs the prestigious Cultural Programme at the Architectural Association, London, and is a contributing editor to *Tank*, the U.K. fashion, art, and architecture magazine, and *Bidoun*, the U.S.–based magazine dedicated to contemporary Middle Eastern arts and culture. He is the author of several publications, including *Did Someone Say Participate?* and *Cities from Zero*.

Mercedes Daguerre

is the author of several publications on the history of contemporary architecture and is a writer for the Italian-based architecture magazine *Casabella*. Born and raised in Argentina, Daguerre moved to Italy to pursue her architecture studies at the University Institute of Architecture in Venice (IUAV) in 1984. Her publications include *Architectural Guide Switzerland: 20th Century*, *Latin American Houses*, and *Eladio Dieste 1917–2000*.

Carlos Jimenez

is the principal of Carlos Jimenez Studio and a professor at Rice University School Architecture in Houston, Texas. Born in San Jose, Costa Rica, he trained as an architect at the University of Houston College of Architecture and has taught at numerous prominent universities. Jimenez is a frequent lecturer, critic and jury member at national and international architectural venues, as well as a long-term jury member of the Pritzker Architecture Prize.

Kengo Kuma

is an internationally renowned architect, and a professor at Keio University in Tokyo. After studying at the University of Tokyo and Columbia University in New York, Kuma established his practice Kengo Kuma & Associates in Japan in 1990. Among Kuma's major works are the Kirosan Observatory, Lotus House, and the Suntory Museum of Art. He is currently working on the development of the Sanlitun District in Beijing.

Luis Fernández-Galiano

is an architect, a professor at the School of Architecture of Madrid's Universidad Politécnica, editor of the journals *AV Monografías* and *Arquitectura Viva*, and architecture critic for the leading national newspaper *El País*. President of the jury of the 2004 Architecture Biennale in Venice, and juror of the Mies van der Rohe European Award, he has taught at renowned universities and institutes around the world. Among his books are *Fire and Memory: On Architecture and Energy*, and *Atlas: Global Architecture circa 2000*.

Andrew Mackenzie

is the editor-in-chief of *Architectural Review Australia* and *(Inside) Australian Design Review*, Australia's leading architecture magazines. He studied fine art at London's Goldsmiths College and was a practicing artist before turning to architecture and becoming the exhibition director at The Architectural Association, London from 1995–2000. Mackenzie now lives in Melbourne.

Bart Goldhoorn

is the founder and publisher of *Project International*, *Project Baltia*, and *Project Russia*, the country's leading architecture journal published in English and Russian. Based in Amsterdam and Moscow, Goldhoorn has lectured and published extensively on post-communist architecture. In 2008 he was curator of the first Moscow Architecture Biennale.

Peter Cachola Schmal

is the Director of the Deutsches Architektur-museum (DAM) in Frankfurt. Raised in Pakistan, Germany, and Indonesia, he was trained as an architect and worked at Behnisch Architekten in Stuttgart. Schmal is a professor and curator, and was the German Commissary to the 2007 International Architecture Biennale in São Paulo.

Ai Weiwei

is one of the most interesting artists/architects working in China today. Based in Beijing, he is also an author, curator, and critic. His multidisciplinary studio, Fake Design, has created such iconic works as the Yiwu River Embankment and Jinhua Architecture Park, both in Jinhua, China. Weiwei collaborated with the Swiss architecture firm Herzog & De Meuron as an artistic consultant for the Beijing National Stadium.

Joseph Grima

is a New York-based architect, writer, and critic. He is the current Director of Storefront for Art and Architecture, a gallery and events space in New York City devoted to the advancement of innovative positions in architecture, art, and design. He is a special correspondent for the Italian architecture magazine *Abitare*, the author of *Instant Asia*, a critical overview of the recent work of emerging architecture practices across Asia, and co-editor of *Shift: SANAA and the New Museum*.

100 Architects

2012Architecten
Allmann Sattler Wappner Architekten
Amateur Architecture Studio
Andrade Morettin Architects
Antón García-Abril & Ensamble Studio
Aranda\Lasch
Arctangent Architecture & Design
at 103
Atelier Kempe Thill
Bernaskoni
Bevk Perović Arhitekti
BIG Architects
Tatiana Bilbao
Ueli Brauen + Doris Wälchli architectes
Brückner & Brückner
Bureau Alexander Brodsky
Candalepas Associates
Cassandra Complex
CEBRA
CJ Lim/Studio 8 Architects
Paulo David
Dellekamp Arquitectos
Durbach Block Architects
Durisch + Nolli Architetti
Keller Easterling
ecosistema urbano
Estudio Teddy Cruz
FAR frohn&rojas
FAT
Didier Fiuza Faustino/Bureau des
    Mésarchitectures
Gramazio & Kohler
Guedes + de Campos
Hiroshi Nakamura & NAP Architects
Information Based Architecture (IBA)
International Festival
Sebastián Irarrázaval
James Carpenter Design Associates

Jan De Vylder Architecten
Jarmund/Vigsnæs
JDS Architects
Johnston Marklee
Jun Igarashi Architects
junya.ishigami+associates
K2S Architects
Kavakava
Diébédo Francis Kéré
Klein Dytham architecture
Totan Kuzembaev Architectural Workshop
LAR/Fernando Romero
m3architecture
MAD Office
Francisco Mangado
Matharoo Associates
McBride Charles Ryan
Meixner Schlüter Wendt Architekten
Miller & Maranta
Minsuk Cho/Mass Studies
Miró Rivera Architects
Mount Fuji Architects Studio
Nendo
Neville Mars/Dynamic City Foundation
NEXT architects
Nieto Sobejano Arquitectos
Kenichiro Niizeki/Niizeki Studio
NO.MAD–Eduardo Arroyo
Office Kersten Geers David Van Severen
Satoshi Okada architects
Onix
Patkau Architects
Paul Morgan Architects
Pedrocchi Meier Architects
Pezo von Ellrichshausen Architects
Bill Price
Productora
Project Meganom

Smiljan Radic
Philippe Rahm Architectes
Randić-Turato
raumlaborberlin
REX
Rojkind Arquitectos
savioz meyer fabrizzi architectes
SeARCH
selgascano
Shim+Sutcliffe Architects
Srdjan Jovanovic Weiss/NAO
Studio Gang Architects
studio mk27
Studio Mumbai
SYSTEMarchitects
Terroir
Thomas Heatherwick/Heatherwick Studio
Thomas Phifer and Partners
TNA Takei Nabeshima Architects
Werner Tscholl
UnSangDong Architects Cooperation
Guillermo Vázquez Consuegra
Wandel Hoefer Lorch + Hirsch
Eyal Weizman
WORK Architecture Company

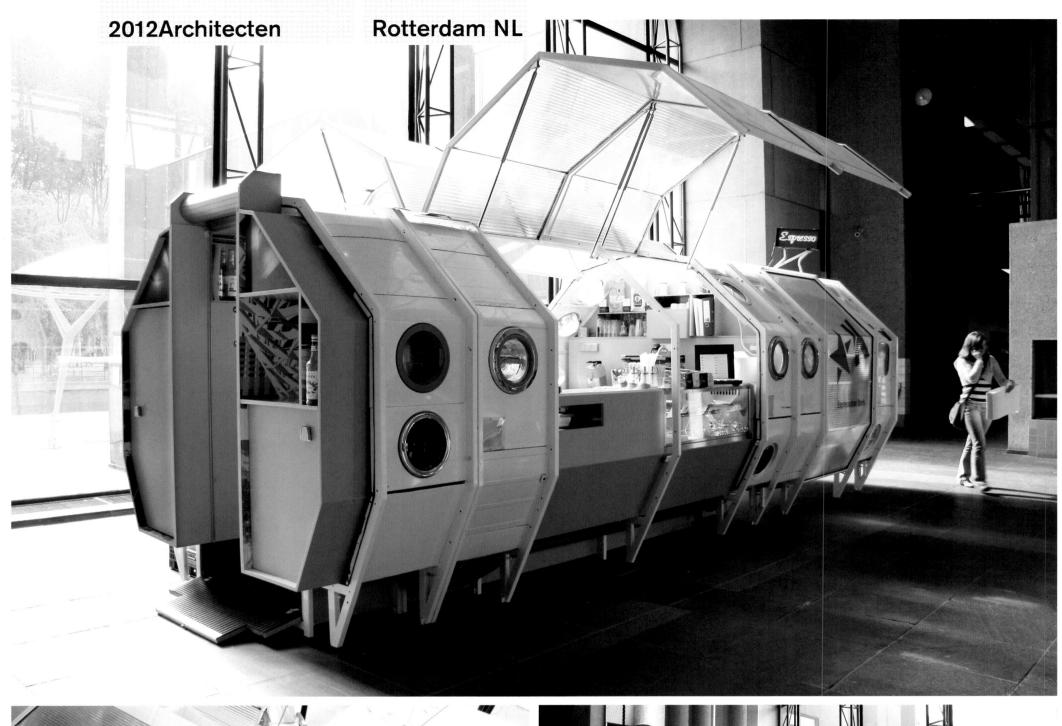

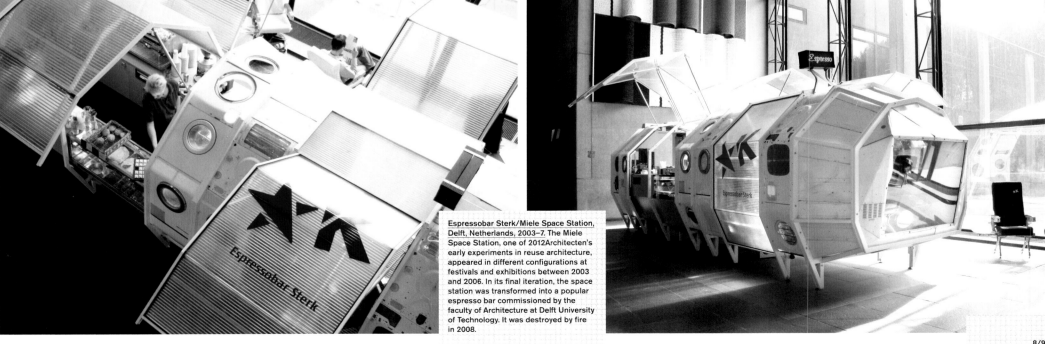

Espressobar Sterk/Miele Space Station, Delft, Netherlands, 2003–7. The Miele Space Station, one of 2012Architecten's early experiments in reuse architecture, appeared in different configurations at festivals and exhibitions between 2003 and 2006. In its final iteration, the space station was transformed into a popular espresso bar commissioned by the faculty of Architecture at Delft University of Technology. It was destroyed by fire in 2008.

Just as there are one-issue parties in politics, 2012Architecten can be called a one-issue architectural firm. This would not be very interesting if the issue did not concern a theme that is increasingly gaining importance: sustainability in general and the use of recycled materials in particular. The mission of 2012Architecten is to build all of its projects by reusing old stuff. With this the firm does not mean new products made of recycled materials but rather materials with a history. For each project, the office organizes a hunt for used materials in the vicinity of the project's location. This is not only an ecologically motivated principle; the architects also intend that these materials add to the aesthetic value of a project.

Unlike in art, in architecture the use of old materials is virtually taboo. The common practice is to use the newest available materials, which are usually standardized and can be easily ordered. In this respect one could call the position of 2012Architecten marginal: they do not create "traditional" architecture, which requires watertight guarantees and precision. But this position is not as uncommon as it seems, since architects are not usually invited to make prototypes but rather to create unique objects that are not intended to be reproduced. The only reason for their reproducibility is the fact that they are created in the context of a market economy where contractors have to compete. By actually searching for materials themselves, 2012Architecten reclaim a position the architect once had, that of the provider of construction materials. Doing this, they not only get more control over the result, they also eliminate the need for making reproducible objects.

Many people are reticent toward modernist architecture because of its perceived sterility—in comparison with the hands-on work of visual artists there seems to be a lack of spirit. The projects of 2012Architecten are developed in accordance with the materials they happen to find at the moment they start designing. These accidental findings actually influence the design, just as the *objets trouvés* of the surrealists were instrumental in generating their art. Consequently, the aesthetic effect of their projects is very close to surrealism. 2012Architecten is much more than just a project by do-gooders to make the world better, or to give a face to the rubbish piled up in our backyards—it introduces architecture to a new form of aesthetics.
// Bart Goldhoorn

WORM@VOC, Rotterdam, Netherlands, 2005–7. This project was conceived as a flexible and transportable tool that allows any available building to be adapted to temporary use, including, in this case, the monumental VOC building in Rotterdam. Nothing could be altered here because of the building code, so the design had to be adapted to the existing structure.

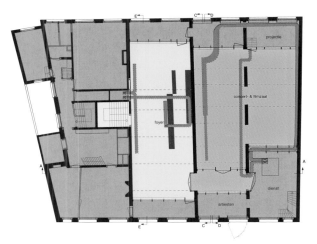
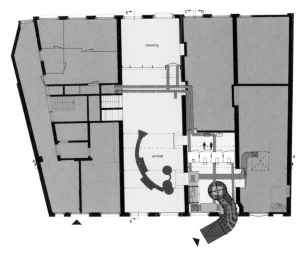

Playground, Rotterdam, Netherlands, 2007–8. The design is based on the layout of the site's former playground, with the addition of a composition of five "broken" polyester windmill wings. Within this pile of wings a labyrinth is created, with four towers connected by a climbing net surrounding a central concrete play surface. All four towers have their own character, signifying different activities.

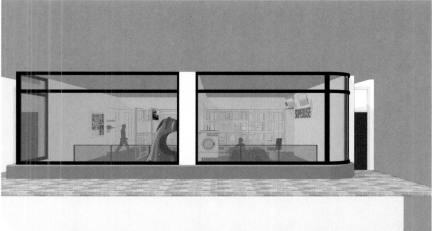

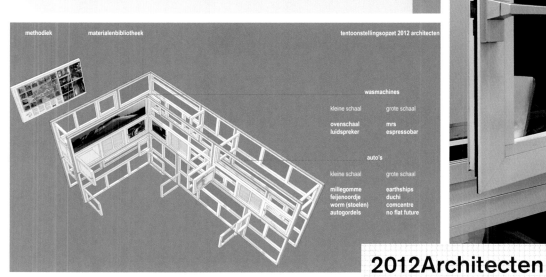

methodiek   materialenbibliotheek   tentoonstellingsopzet 2012 architecten

wasmachines

kleine schaal   grote schaal

ovenschaal   mrs
luidspreker   espressobar

auto's

kleine schaal   grote schaal

millegomme   earthships
feijenoordje   duchi
worm (stoelen)   comcentre
autogordels   no flat future

2012Architecten

"OmBouwen/ReStructure" exhibition design, Den Haag, Netherlands, 2007. Sponsored by *Superuse*, a publication devoted to adaptive reuse, the gallery Stroom Den Haag invited 2012Architecten to design the exhibition, which proposed that the three approaches to building intelligently—reuse, lightweight construction, and "cradle-to-cradle"—are different but complementary. The project employed window frames salvaged from a social housing block which will be used again in future projects.

Allmann Sattler Wappner Architekten   München D

Sports Hall, Tübingen, Germany, 2002–4. The sports hall's concept accommodates the requirements of professional sports, amateur sports clubs, and school sports, as well as a variety of more trendy sports, all within one building. Here traditional sports can be intelligently combined with one another, while at the same time the exterior facades are activated through additional functions such as climbing, skateboarding, and streetball.

It was twenty years ago that three graduates of München's Technical University, Markus Allmann, Amandus Sattler, and Ludwig Wappner, set up their own practice, which has recently come to be regarded as one of the most innovative architecture firms in Germany. Their brand buildings for Audi will soon be familiar to design aficionados around the world; they conceived the new brand pavilion for inner-city locations in a wide range of metropolises, from München to London, Tokyo to Sydney, where they collaborate with local architects. The first ten "Audi Terminals" are already completed, and around 350 such buildings will be realized in the coming years, adapted to the local context and developed in line with a basic vocabulary. The München terminal will serve as a template through its precise metallic look, curving shapes and slanting surfaces with large display windows, multiple levels connected by escalators, and a strikingly urban profile. This is no longer simply an auto dealer on the arterial road.

Two more structures in München demonstrate the architects' sensitivity for residential buildings: The Nymphenburger Straße complex, with its six-story new building in front of a converted factory, makes consistent use of the same light-colored material from the base through to the roof to give the building an innovative profile despite the considerate approach the architects took toward the existing context. By contrast, the Haus der Gegenwart (House of the Present, 2005) is an experimental project. A magazine had asked architects for their positions on how people will live in the future. The winning design was realized as a pilot project. The architects cast a critical look at the state of society: four individuals live separately on the ground floor, where they have their own entrance, bathroom, and garden access, while on the upper floor they share a kitchen, living room, and lounge with everything intelligent building systems currently permit. By contrast, the Sports Hall in Tübingen demonstrates that the firm can also produce sustainable architecture on a tight budget while creating a fascinating layering of uses and spaces. The southwestern facade serves as a complete photovoltaic solar system, a side facade merges into an integrated halfpipe, another consists of a covered climbing wall, a niche indent in the main facade creates a covered forecourt, and the roof is landscaped to create a green "fifth facade." // Peter Cachola Schmal

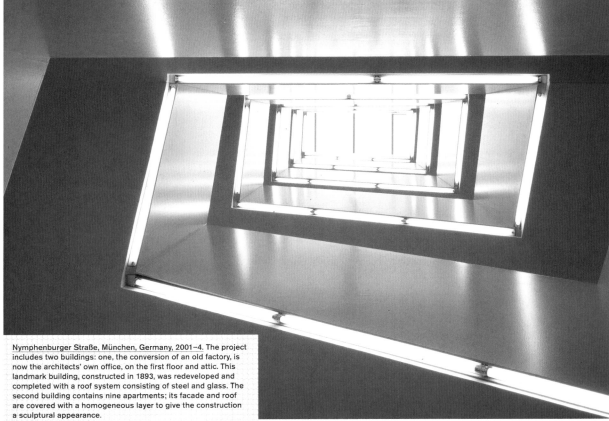

Nymphenburger Straße, München, Germany, 2001–4. The project includes two buildings: one, the conversion of an old factory, is now the architects' own office, on the first floor and attic. This landmark building, constructed in 1893, was redeveloped and completed with a roof system consisting of steel and glass. The second building contains nine apartments; its facade and roof are covered with a homogeneous layer to give the construction a sculptural appearance.

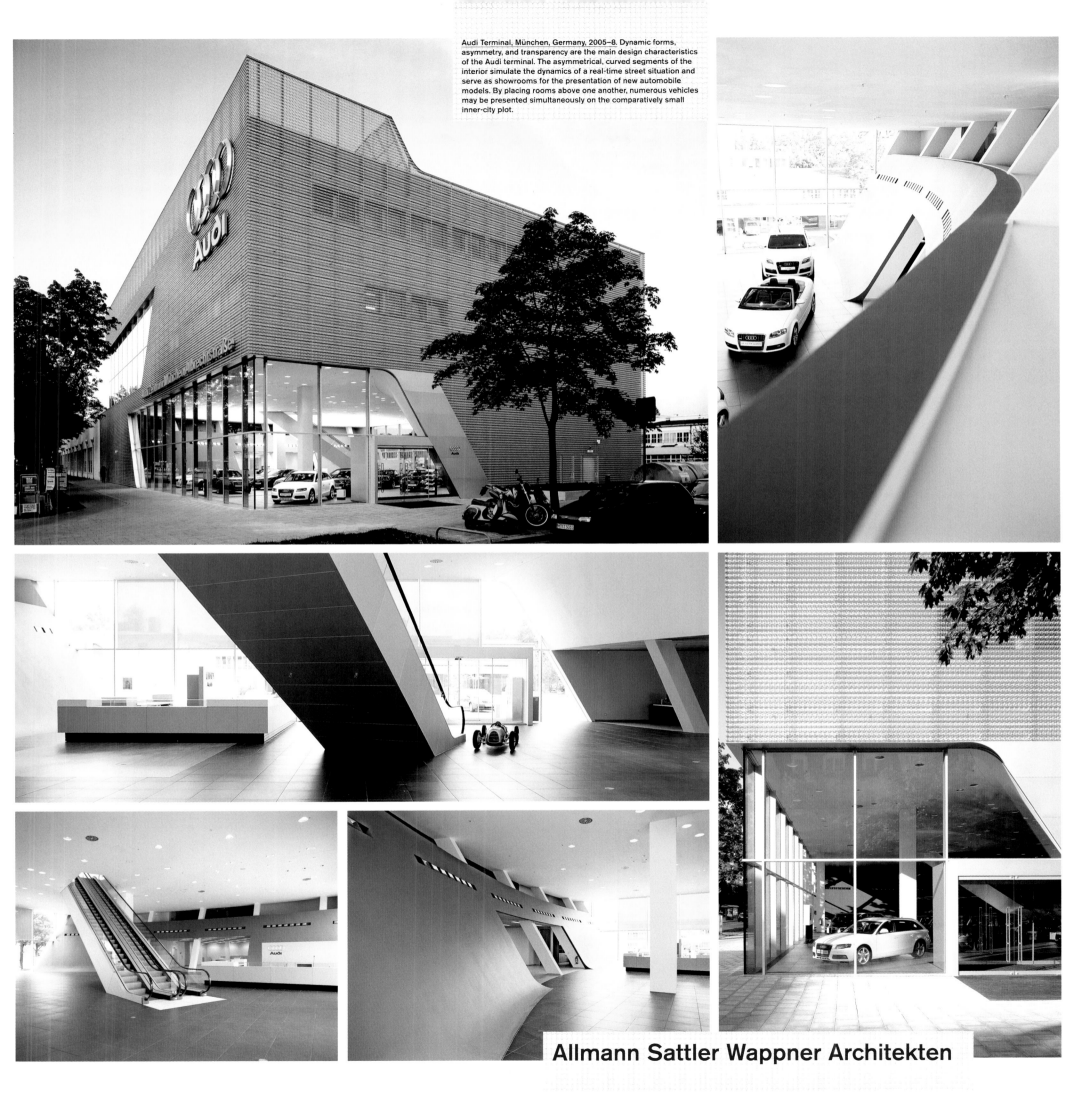

Audi Terminal, München, Germany, 2005–8. Dynamic forms, asymmetry, and transparency are the main design characteristics of the Audi terminal. The asymmetrical, curved segments of the interior simulate the dynamics of a real-time street situation and serve as showrooms for the presentation of new automobile models. By placing rooms above one another, numerous vehicles may be presented simultaneously on the comparatively small inner-city plot.

Allmann Sattler Wappner Architekten

Wang Shu approaches anonymous architecture —be it temporary or even illegal—with great respect. For this reason, Wang and his wife, Lu Wenyu chose a programmatic name for the office they founded in 1998 in Hangzhou, China: Amateur Architecture Studio. For their first projects, to cut costs, they primarily chose recycled materials from demolished buildings in the vicinity. Over six million used bricks and tiles were collected for the rambling campus of the China Academy of Art in Hangzhou, where Wang is currently the dean of the architecture school. According to Wang, the tactile properties of these used gray bricks play a decisive role in the overall design: "They hide the buildings in the scene. The buildings can breathe with the hill." In 2006, Amateur Architecture Studio created another sea of gray brick as the official contribution to the Chinese pavilion of the Architecture Biennale in Venezia with their poetic intervention, the Tile Garden. The reuse of traditional construction materials and the deliberate resonance of the curved roof of the traditional tea house are intended to reconcile millennia-old shapes and typologies with the rapid pace of contemporary change. This stance is unique in China and runs counter to the usual concept of sweeping the slate clean. In the process, Wang does not eschew contemporary forms, layouts, and materials, but he also offers his users an emotional home within contemporary architecture.

A beautiful example of this is the Ceramic House coffee pavilion in the Jinhua Architecture Park in Zhejiang Province. Its walls are coated on both sides with specially glazed ceramic tiles in the traditional colors of Chinese porcelain-making. In this building, where one can physically experience nature, Wang—who at the beginning of his career planned to be an architect part-time and otherwise continue working as a poet—has dedicated himself to his original vocation.
// Peter Cachola Schmal

Ceramic House, Jinhua, Zhejiang, China, 2003–6. As one of sixteen architects commissioned to create projects for the Jinhua Architecture Park, Amateur Architecture Studio designed a 1076-sq.-ft. (100-sq.-m) coffee house. The shape of the house is inspired by traditional Chinese inkstones. Pieces of porcelain made by artists were used to cover the inner and outer walls of the building. Arranged irregularly to colorful effect, they represent the traditional hues of Chinese ceramics.

Contemporary Art Museum, Ningbo, Zhejiang, China, 2001–5.
The old port control building and tower of the former port in
Ningbo were converted and rebuilt into a large contemporary
art museum. The museum's materials reflect the site's rich
historical context: the blue brick in the foundation is the main
building material of the existing urban fabric; the steel and
timber in the upper part echo the materials used to construct
the docks as well as those employed in the construction of ships.

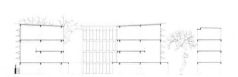

Xiangshan Campus, China Academy of Art, Hangzhou, Zhejiang, China, 2002–4. The campus is situated around a small hill in the southwest of Hangzhou. The first phase of the renovation added about 700,000 sq. ft. (65,000 sq. m) with ten buildings including a library, classrooms, workshop and studio spaces, galleries, and a small stadium. Over three million pieces of recycled tiles were used on the roofs of the new buildings.

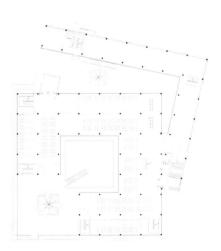

Gallery in Five Scattered Houses, Ningbo, Zhejiang, China, 2003–6.
One of five structures built by Amateur Architecture Studio in the
Yinzhou Park in Ningbo, this small building is located close to
the back entrance of the park, facing a lake. The curving, tent-like
roof echoes traditional roofs of the region—a response to the
rainy climate. Recycled bricks and roof tiles were used throughout,
as was an innovative, low-cost technology: thick cast-in-place
concrete planks eliminate the need for beams inside the gallery.

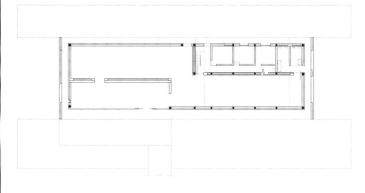

Amateur Architecture Studio

São Paulo-based Vinicius Andrade and Marcelo Morettin worked with prominent Brazilian architects, including Paulo Mendes da Rocha and Joaquim Guedes, before opening their own office in 1997. Heirs of the Paulista School, they demonstrate an increasingly confident mastery of their craft through strict geometrical design, a penchant for structural experiments, and an unflagging interest in environmentally sustainable solutions.

Their House B is the most recent of a successful series of houses built in the environs of São Paulo, in which formal and constructional ideas are articulated around the contrast between nature and technology (antithetical volumes, slender decks, lightweight structures of timber or steel, cement blocks, sheet metal, glass membranes, and translucent polycarbonate panels). Here the architects focus on the relationship between interior and exterior. The spatial fluidity of the living areas provides a counterpoint to the glass box suspended over the garden, which contains the upper floor with the sleeping quarters. Its effect is heightened by the silkscreened pattern covering its surface, which echoes images of the surrounding park.

The architects went on to address collective housing with the design of an apartment complex on São Paulo's Rua Aimberê, consisting of twelve morphologically independent units stacked on top of one another. The building is integrated into the urban fabric and the functional versatility of the apartments reflects changes in city living.

Their Living Steel project (2008) responded to the request for environmentally sustainable solutions to address the housing shortage in the tropical town of Recife. The brief for the competition was a work firmly embedded in its context, rational construction, energy efficiency, and recycling. The architects tackled these issues in a number of ways—by using the free plan of buildings set on columns to favor natural ventilation; the design of the roof as a large umbrella; shaded balconies which also keep out the rain; and devices to control solar radiation—while also reflecting on the role of architecture in coping with global challenges. Similar principles guided their design of the Comperj Information Center at Itaboraí. It elaborates on the idea of a pavilion resting delicately on the ground, minimizing its footprint. The clear articulation of the volumes copes successfully with the large scale, while the choice of materials and use of water and forestation as compositional elements enhance its ties with the landscape. Andrade Morettin Architects' ability to achieve a synthesis between simplicity and sophistication, and to combine traditional and industrial elements in innovative solutions based on sustainability, offers a stimulating jolt for architecture in South America.
// Mercedes Daguerre

House B, São Paulo, Brazil, 2006–8. The spaces of this house maintain a clear relation with the surrounding 16,000-sq.-ft. (1,500-sq.-m) park. The translucent glass box, apparently floating above the garden, houses the rooms that require greater privacy, while providing shade to the open spaces and the deck located on the ground floor. The pattern printed on the glass facade represents an abstract image of the park.

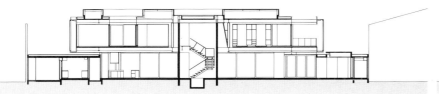

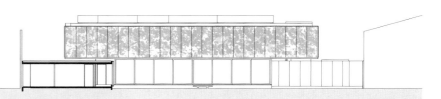

Comperj Information Center, Itaboraí, Brazil, 2008–11. This new visitor's center will be the gateway to a major petrochemical complex in Rio de Janeiro State, close to an important archaeological site. It was designed to land delicately on the ground, integrating itself into the landscape without altering the topography significantly. The simple but powerful shape, the design of the open spaces, and the chosen materials are intended to reveal the features of the surrounding East Basin of Guanabara Bay.

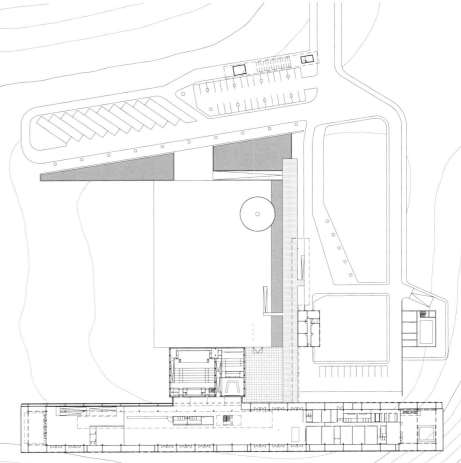

Residential Complex, Rua Aimberê, São Paulo, Brazil, 2005–8.
This nine-story building consists of twelve autonomous units, each
with a specific morphology. The volume is cut in order to bring in
natural light. Most apartments have two levels, featuring two-story
open spaces, as well as large balconies that serve as garden porches.
The interiors are adaptable: spaces can be further integrated or
divided, and the location of kitchens and bathrooms is flexible.

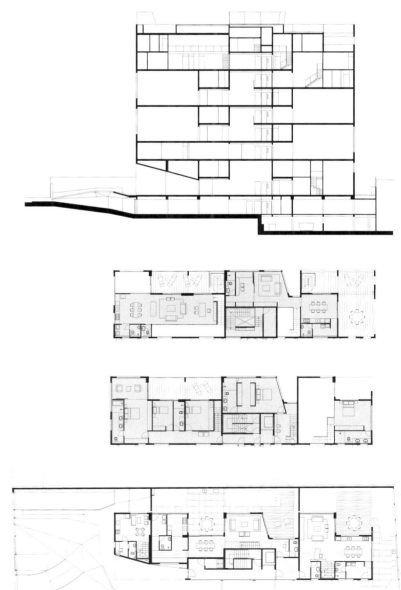

Andrade Morettin Architects

SGAE Central Office, Santiago de Compostela, Spain, 2005–8.
The new headquarters for the General Society of Authors and
Publishers sits at the edge of a former private garden, defining
the boundary between park and street. Its three walls offer
distinctive construction, materials, and visual scales that work
as filters, delimiting and organizing the program. The building
arches, widens, and narrows, generating fluid multivalent spaces
and an urban space inside the garden.

Antón García-Abril is a prominent member of the emerging generation of Spanish architects. Prior to establishing the firm Antón García-Abril in 1995, the architect worked in the offices of two of Spain's most celebrated designers, Alberto Campo Baeza and Santiago Calatrava. In 2000, García-Abril appended the title Ensamble Studio/Materia Inorgánica to the name of his firm, an emphatic reminder of how much the architect values materials and construction as the critical equation for creating architecture.

There have been few practitioners in recent contemporary architecture whose professional life has been characterized by the confidence and boldness of construction that can be found in García-Abril's sparse yet memorable works. From the beginning of his independent practice, the architect has created buildings that manifest the visceral power of materials, often embracing their rawness and abrasiveness as an alluring enterprise. These works remind us of the physicality of architecture, as if chiseled by the most immediate of hands. García-Abril's Musical Studies Center (2002), located in the fabled Galician city of Santiago de Compostela, is a case in point: a work that probes the awe-inspiring properties of weight, mass, and scale while adding to the city's lineage of granite constructions. In this fortress-like work we find an architect unafraid to mobilize this ancient material to great effect and surprising freedom, an alchemist intent on harnessing the virtues of granite for its structural and thermal qualities.

The Hemeroscopium House in Las Rozas, a town on the outskirts of Madrid, is a fascinating merger of architecture and engineering, or rather a still life that incorporates large structural and infrastructural fragments as primary compositional devices. The result is a work of dynamic coherence, though its singular pieces might hint otherwise. The precise yet fluid floor plan is an effective contrast to the gravity-defying and massive structural pieces suspended over a common field.

The SGAE (General Society of Authors and Publishers) Central Office, another work in Santiago de Compostela, is an intriguing work of architecture as installation, yet one farthest from the latter's transient connotation. The SGAE is a porch-like building whose elongated screen wall is a marvelous concoction of tumbling and irregular granite pieces, all held captive in a resilient dance of weight, light, and gravity.
// Carlos Jimenez

Berklee Tower of Music, Valencia, Spain, 2006–11. The Tower of Music is a vertical campus for the Berklee College of Music. The project is composed of two basic elements: a plinth, and a tower standing on top of it. The tower is generated by an ascending double helix of blocks that rotate and pile up to form elevated plazas, which offer views to the city, an orchard, and the sea. The building balances volumes and voids and is enclosed by a structural wall made of precast concrete beams.

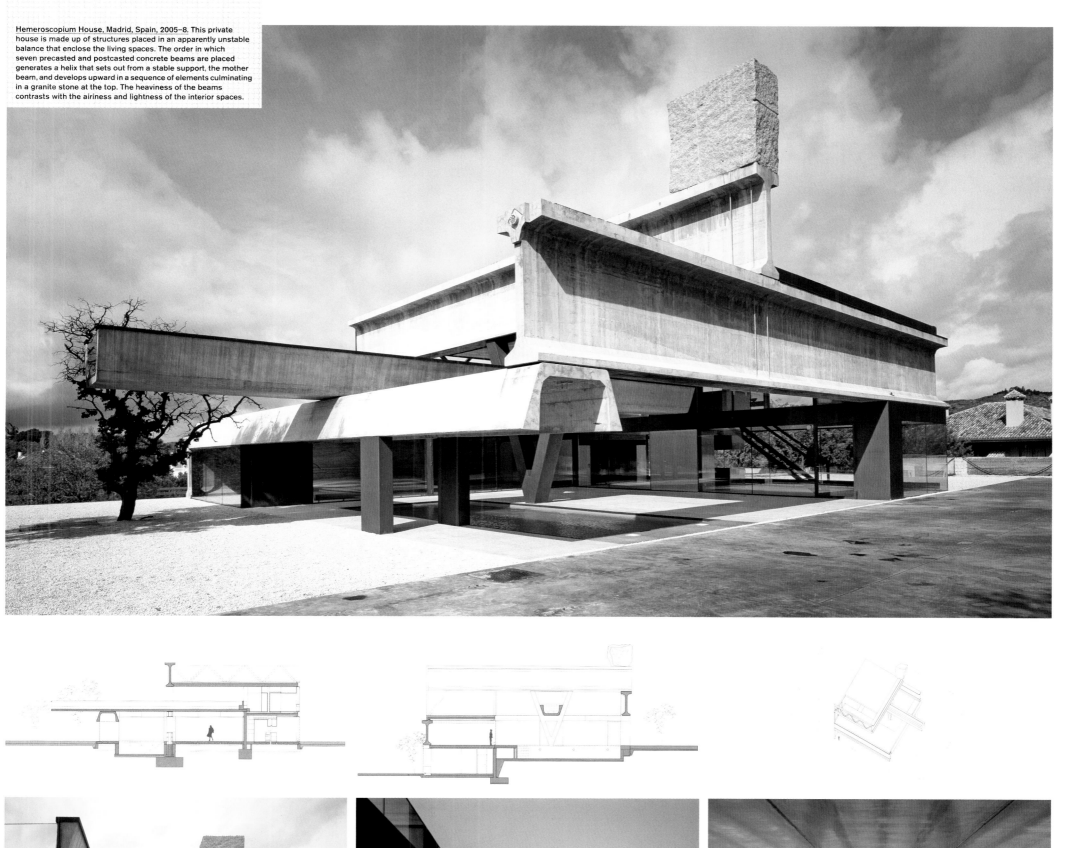

Hemeroscopium House, Madrid, Spain, 2005–8. This private house is made up of structures placed in an apparently unstable balance that enclose the living spaces. The order in which seven precasted and postcasted concrete beams are placed generates a helix that sets out from a stable support, the mother beam, and develops upward in a sequence of elements culminating in a granite stone at the top. The heaviness of the beams contrasts with the airiness and lightness of the interior spaces.

Antón García-Abril & Ensamble Studio

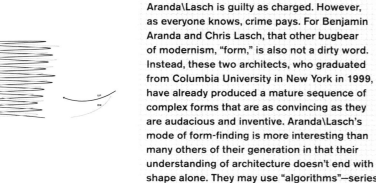

If ornament remains a crime, exactly 100 years after Adolf Loos made the accusation, then Aranda\Lasch is guilty as charged. However, as everyone knows, crime pays. For Benjamin Aranda and Chris Lasch, that other bugbear of modernism, "form," is also not a dirty word. Instead, these two architects, who graduated from Columbia University in New York in 1999, have already produced a mature sequence of complex forms that are as convincing as they are audacious and inventive. Aranda\Lasch's mode of form-finding is more interesting than many others of their generation in that their understanding of architecture doesn't end with shape alone. They may use "algorithms"—series of procedural steps or calculations—and they may program their own computer code to generate said algorithms, but once their software has spluttered out some wondrous riff on patterns found in nature, Aranda\Lasch invests it with intelligent, witty, and innovative functions.

Their 10-Mile Spiral, proposed as a gateway for Las Vegas, was a condensed montage of Sin City's best bits, conceived as composing the view from a hurtling car. In other projects the only narrative is simply the stunning beauty of the surfaces. Furniture pieces act as small-scale test sites for aggregate patterns—reminiscent of flocks of birds frozen in time—which can also operate at larger scales, as in their laser-cut white drapery for the 2008 Design Miami venue. An ambitious collaboration with artist Matthew Ritchie and the engineering firm Arup, the building culminated in an ectoplasmic black "anti-pavilion" that could, potentially, expand forever.

Aranda\Lasch also has an artsy alter-ego called Terraswarm. Here, they explore their fascination with technologies of surveillance, feedback, and communication: monitoring pigeons in flight or drenching Queens and Brooklyn, New York, with shifting colored light. If the alleged dream of computation is deterministic predictability, the resulting world would prohibit human dreaming to take place. It is not a divide between man and machine that we should fixate on but the vital potential that lies in the schism between the two. When asked how they intended to distinguish their burgeoning practice from the pack, Ben Aranda said, "We're going to do something different precisely because we excel at making very elaborate mistakes." Elaborate mistakes: not exactly what one would expect a couple of ardent programmers to valorize. // Shumon Basar

Aranda\Lasch   New York USA

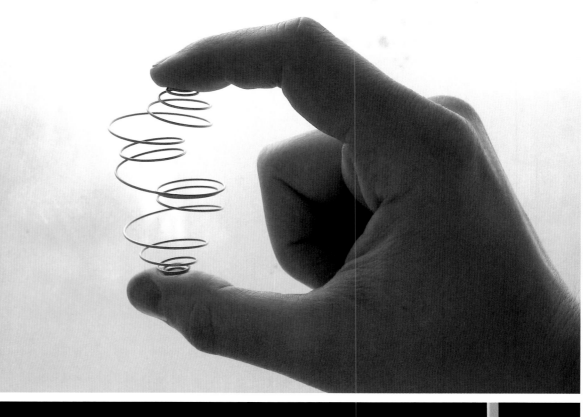

10-Mile Spiral, Las Vegas, Nevada, USA, 2004. This gateway to Las Vegas is a long spiral in which one can play the slots, get married, see a show, get a carwash, and ride through a tunnel of love, all without ever leaving the car. It is a compact Vegas, experienced at fifty-five miles per hour and topped off by a towering observation ramp offering views of the valley floor below.

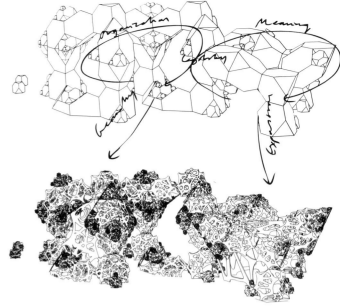

The Morning Line, Sevilla, Spain, and London, England, UK, 2006–8. Commissioned by Thyssen-Bornemisza Art Contemporary to explore the interplay between art, architecture, cosmology, and music, the Morning Line was created in collaboration with Matthew Ritchie and the Arup Advanced Geometry Unit. It is conceived as a drawing in space, where each line connects to other lines to construct a spatial picture. Within this space, composers and musicians perform. It is made from epoxy-coated aluminum units, geometrically based in a three-dimensional fractal, which are modular, stackable, and transportable for future sites.

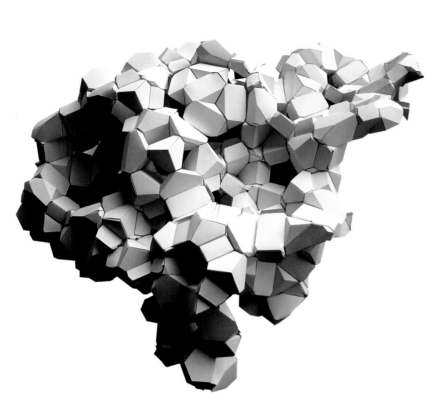

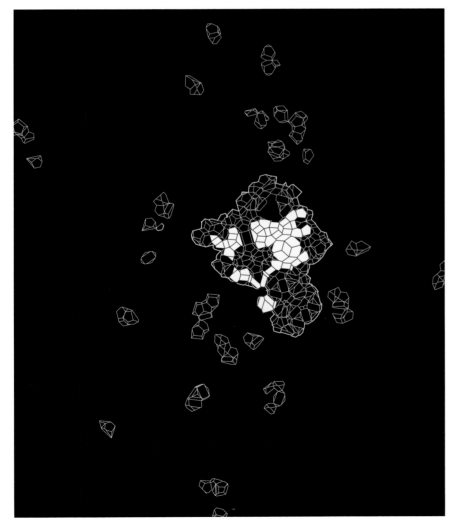

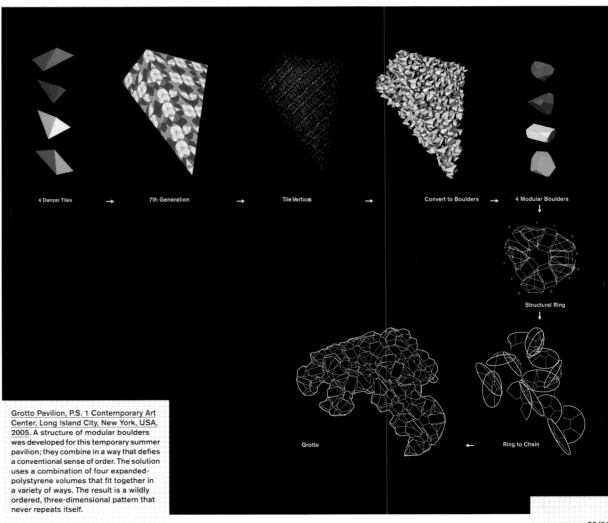

4 Danzer Tiles → 7th Generation → Tile Vertices → Convert to Boulders → 4 Modular Boulders

Structural Ring

Grotto

Ring to Chain ←

Grotto Pavilion, P.S. 1 Contemporary Art Center, Long Island City, New York, USA, 2005. A structure of modular boulders was developed for this temporary summer pavilion; they combine in a way that defies a conventional sense of order. The solution uses a combination of four expanded-polystyrene volumes that fit together in a variety of ways. The result is a wildly ordered, three-dimensional pattern that never repeats itself.

Design Miami Temporary Structure, Miami, Florida, USA, 2008. This structure houses over twenty-five design galleries in a single 43,000-sq.-ft. (4,000-sq.-m) space. The modular structural system can easily be packed, stored, and reassembled for use in other locations and in alternate configurations. Natural light is modulated through an external mesh scrim. The structure sits on a prominent corner in Miami's Design District, so the highly customized facade allows for a layered transition from the public space into the galleries.

Aranda\Lasch

Arctangent Architecture & Design

New York USA / Taipei RC

Kyle Chia-Kai Yang is an architect of connections. By looking at his unique career, one can see what it is that he wants to connect. Born in Taiwan, he studied architecture at Columbia University in New York and later was employed at an architect's office in the city before founding his own practice, Arctangent Architecture & Design. He is an architect who links Asia and the United States, and his works show the special characteristics of both.

It is interesting that Yang studied not only architecture in the United States but also civil engineering, the field in which he earned his first master's degree from Columbia. During the twentieth century, architecture and engineering were largely separate, occupying two different spheres that rarely interacted. This distance existed despite the fact that they had originally been one field. In the nineteenth century, architectural projects and engineering for structures such as bridges proved mutually inspiring and led to many new designs. But by the twentieth century, such interaction was rare.

Yang's study of both fields has had a major impact on his architectural designs. Look, for example, at the Far Eastern Telecom Building, with its highly amusing base. His rendering recalls the engineering of unfaced concrete structures as well as the modernism of Japanese architects Kenzo Tange and Kunio Maekawa and their creations of the 1950s and 1960s. At that time, Japan was recovering from the devastation and disorder of the war, and the Japanese were filled with an unbounded youthful enthusiasm as they opened the way to a new era. These powerful concrete forms, with their evocation of the discipline of engineering, symbolized this energy. In a similar manner, Yang's dynamic use of concrete may also be a symbol of the energy that fills the nation of Taiwan.

Another interesting structure by Yang is the Children's Storytelling Park in Taiwan (2006), which blends wood and steel. Here can be seen more than just the linking of engineering and architecture. There is also a dialogue between wood and steel, Asian and Western technology, and modern and traditional technology. In some cases the juxtaposition of materials remains rough, but the meeting of dissimilar textures and the union of divergent spheres generates stimulating results.
// Kengo Kuma

Stratus House, Aodi, Taiwan, 2007–10. This project is part of Taiwan's Next Gene 20 housing development, which features twenty homes designed by Taiwanese and international architects. The house features custom-made curved glass walls for the exterior, with horizontal and vertical "water channels"—when rain falls, it leaves a trail on the surface of the glass.

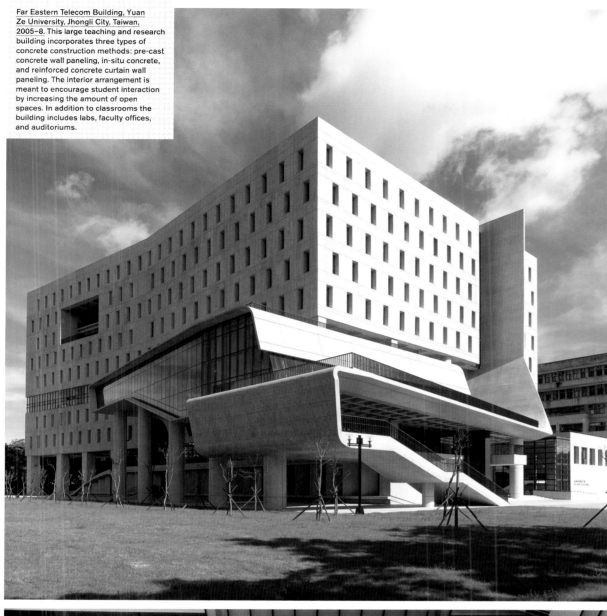

Far Eastern Telecom Building, Yuan Ze University, Jhongli City, Taiwan, 2005–8. This large teaching and research building incorporates three types of concrete construction methods: pre-cast concrete wall paneling, in-situ concrete, and reinforced concrete curtain wall paneling. The interior arrangement is meant to encourage student interaction by increasing the amount of open spaces. In addition to classrooms the building includes labs, faculty offices, and auditoriums.

Chong-ming Park, Taichung City, Taiwan, 2005–7. This urban landscape renewal project called for redesigning an existing park, bridge, and riverbank, and designing underground parking. The strategy was to transform the bridge, one of 398 in the city, into an outdoor seating area, which can serve as a viewing platform for street fairs and performances—an informal community living room.

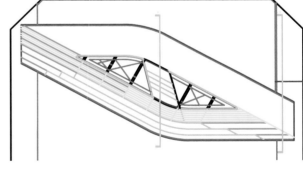

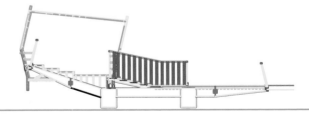

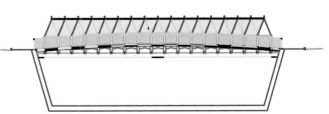

School of Liberal Arts, Tunghai University, Taichung City, Taiwan, 2004–8. The first phase of this university project includes the completion of the fine arts department and music school, which were designed as a dialogue with the church on campus by I.M. Pei. The intent was to break down traditional barriers between inside and outside, creating several courtyards for socializing and for holding classes. The green vegetation on the curved concrete walls helps to regulate the temperature inside the buildings.

Arctangent Architecture & Design

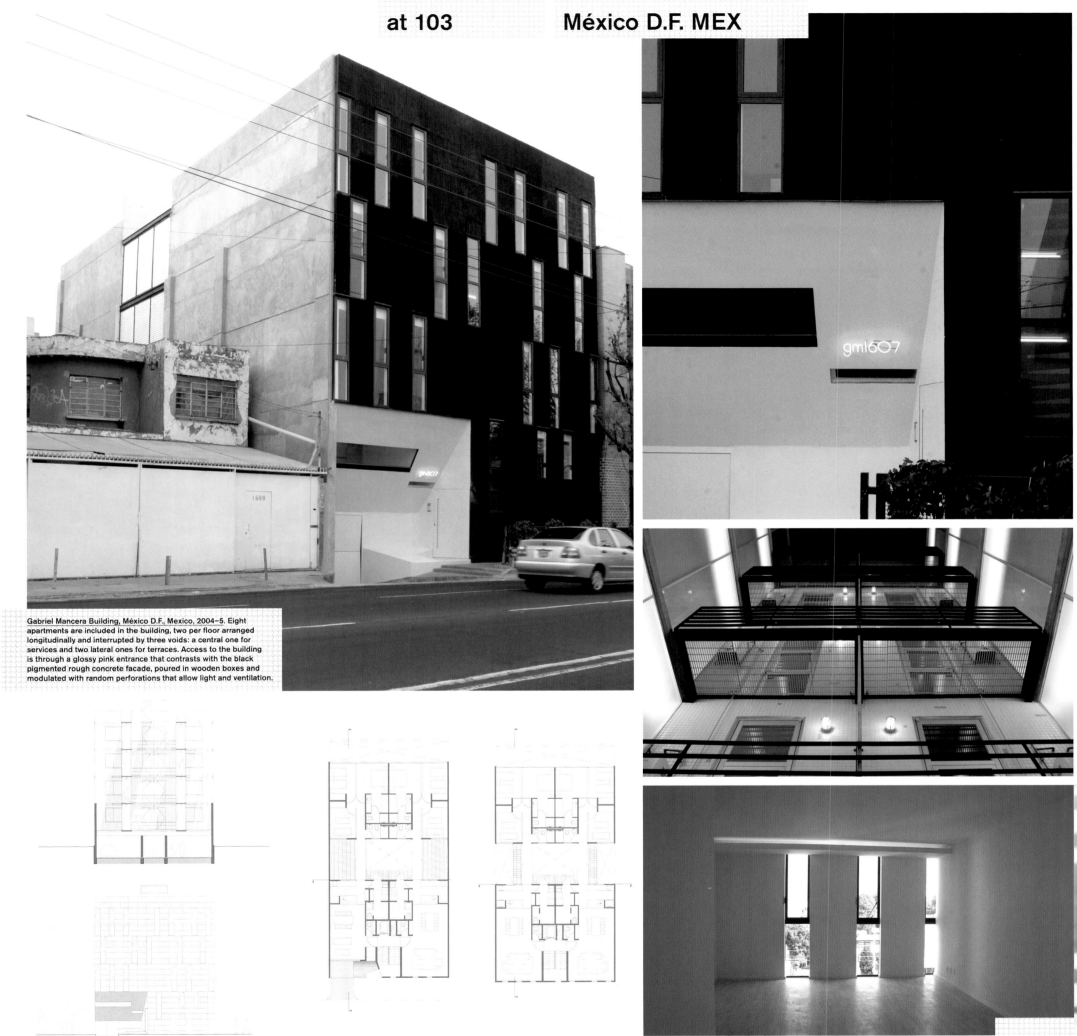

Gabriel Mancera Building, México D.F., Mexico, 2004–5. Eight apartments are included in the building, two per floor arranged longitudinally and interrupted by three voids: a central one for services and two lateral ones for terraces. Access to the building is through a glossy pink entrance that contrasts with the black pigmented rough concrete facade, poured in wooden boxes and modulated with random perforations that allow light and ventilation.

at 103, run by partners Julio Amezcua and Francisco Pardo, is located in México D.F. Their body of work—they have completed a wide range of projects, from fire stations to housing developments—reflects the dynamic and unstable nature of the expanding city in which they work. The emerging pair addresses the human and commercial need of architecture, with a sense of aesthetics that succeeds, to varying degrees, in delivering answers.

at 103 was chosen to participate in the Ordos 100 project, which invited 100 young architectural practices to the desert of Nei Mongol, China, to each design a 10,000-square-foot (1,000-square-meter) villa. The at 103 Villa raises the issue of human desire versus human need, while poviding a stimulating answer to the spatial questions posed by the project. The result is a program in which the spaces of necessity below ground are separated from the spaces of desire above ground. In addition to the separation between above and below ground activities, the project is divided into five volumes, each destined to house one of the subcategories of workers, guests, family, parents, and children—again demonstrating the building's clear articulation of function.

Ave Fenix Fire Station is a symbolic resurrection on a site previously razed by a terrible fire. The building houses training facilities for the fire department as well as programs for the general public. Inside the metal clad box, both uses alternate and complement each other. They are organized through planes with perforations that vary in size, providing light sources as well as offering communication between the levels.

at 103's varied approaches and varied degrees of success are testament to their development as young architects. At times delivering a high aesthetic, at times trendy, the pair continues to reach for a consistent style. This is apparent in the Gabriel Mancera Building. A straight-forward response to commercial need, this project efficiently provides relatively equal and spacious living quarters to each unit along with outside terraces. The overall volume of the building is interrupted by three voids, the first being a central core for services, while the remaining two provide green space and terraces to filter the city from the apartments. The housing project expresses at 103's ability to create practical form with competent execution. // Ai Weiwei

Ave Fenix Fire Station, México D.F, Mexico, 2004–7. The station presents itself like a simple elevated box that almost disappears behind a facade in a game of reflections. Both a proper working fire station and a space open to the public that includes a library, the station floats over an open area where the trucks are held on the ground floor.

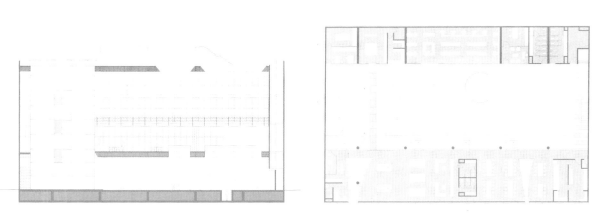

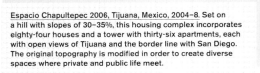

Espacio Chapultepec 2006, Tijuana, Mexico, 2004–8. Set on a hill with slopes of 30–35%, this housing complex incorporates eighty-four houses and a tower with thirty-six apartments, each with open views of Tijuana and the border line with San Diego. The original topography is modified in order to create diverse spaces where private and public life meet.

at 103 Villa, Ordos, Nei Mongol, China, 2008–9. The at 103 Villa is designed around the concepts of "need" and "want." The "need" spaces below ground reflect elements of the traditional house, while the "want" program above shows the house as the object of desire. The program consists of five connected houses, each for different users, and includes patios and gardens.

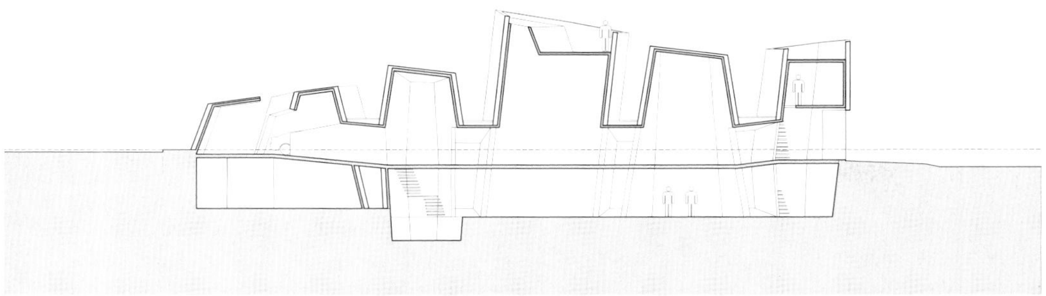

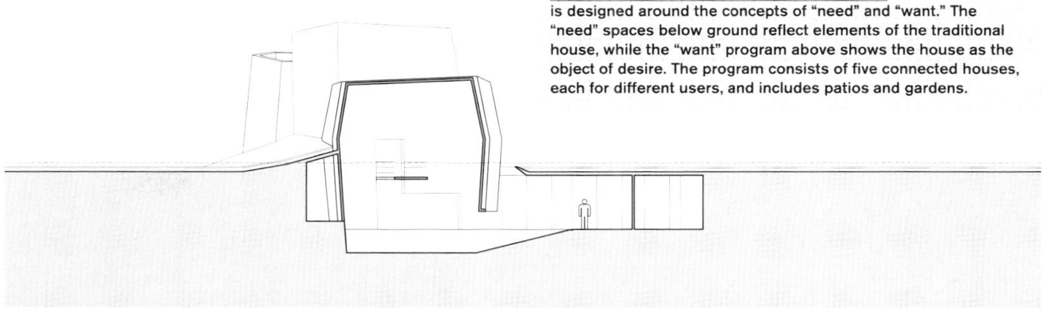

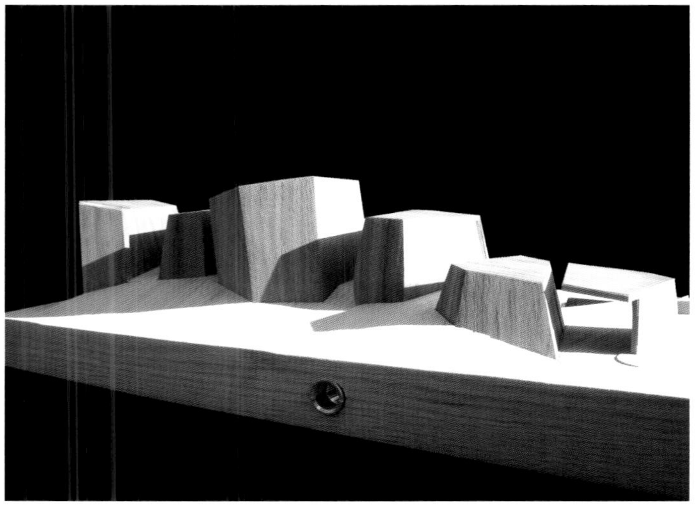

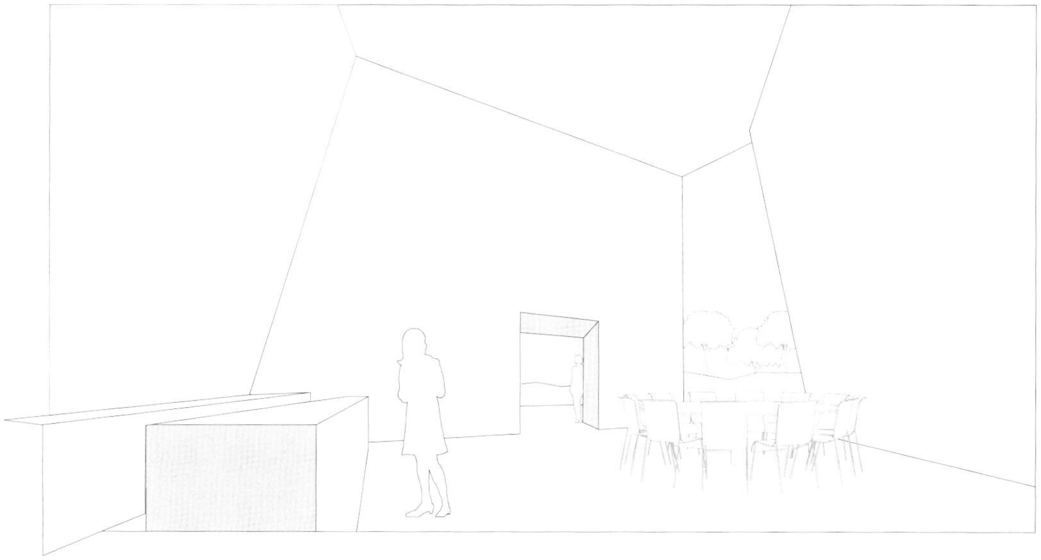

at 103

Atelier Kempe Thill   Rotterdam NL

Atelier Kempe Thill (AKT) represents an interesting case of the simultaneous maturation of two young architects who grew up in what was then East Germany, studied architecture in Dresden, ventured abroad together to learn from the architecture of Tokyo and Paris, and ultimately set up shop in Rotterdam in 2000. With their tenacity, Andre Kempe and Oliver Thill succeeded in winning multiple commissions and establishing a sound practice for themselves. The Town Houses in Amsterdam's Osdorp district are a good example of their continual method of working against schematic expectations. AKT subversively integrated the garages into the houses, expanding the spatial range—extending the depths and reducing the widths of the houses—and thus saving costs. The covered carports become private terraces on the second story as an extension of the residential area, while the kitchens become two-story halls in a configuration reminiscent of Le Corbusier's Unités d'Habitation. The minimal and economical solution creates a spacious and light sense of home.

One of the first public jobs AKT secured, through a competition, was for the Franz Liszt Concert Hall in Raiding, Austria, directly opposite the house in which the composer was born. There again, despite a tight budget, the architects created a distinctive project: a concert hall that, in terms of scale, fits into the rural village context but also distinguishes itself through its material properties. The shell is made of polyurethane, and the huge panes are acrylic glass. The hall, which has the proportions of a shoe box, is made completely of wood, with glue binder as the load-bearing structure and spherically milled bracing made of spruce, all in an effort to re-create acoustics that would be heard during Liszt's time.

Another public building to emerge in the Netherlands, the Museum Veenhuizen, is a crafts museum with a workshop for traditional handicrafts in a former prison complex, located in the hinterland known as the "Dutch Siberia." The "Classicist Romantics," as Kempe and Thill sometimes call themselves, gave the buildings back their original volumes, removed many extension wings, and introduced their own additions, such as glass entrances with black steel frames. The interiors were rendered in snow-white plaster in striking contrast to the external brickwork. ATK are currently working on an especially idiosyncratic public building, the council building for Belgium's German-speaking community, which has its seat in Eupen, Belgium.
// Peter Cachola Schmal

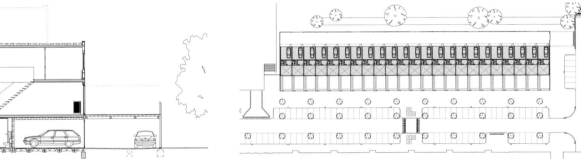

Town Houses in Osdorp, Amsterdam, Netherlands, 2005–8.
In order to build as many houses as possible, the width of each house is minimized, while the windows are maximized to bring in enough daylight. Storage and parking are integrated into the house on the ground floor. The accessing street is covered by terraces on the first floor, concealing the cars and maximizing privacy for the floors above.

Dutch Pavilion IGA, Rostock, Germany, 2002–3. The pavilion is an "instant pergola." The architectural starting point is a fascinating new building element: the "smart screen," an ivy hedge grown in Dutch greenhouses and normally used in gardens. Essentially an industrial product, the hedges can be deployed to build "green walls."

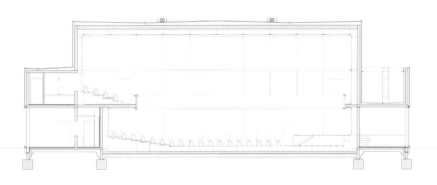

Franz Liszt Concert Hall, Raiding, Austria, 2005–6. Through its modest design and decent proportions, this building is designed to preserve the intimate character of the surrounding garden. On all four sides, acrylic windows between 49- and 59-ft. (15- and 18-m) long, and 13-ft. (4-m) high open the building to the landscape. Behind the windows are public foyers that enclose the concert hall. The hall itself is made out of wood; the grid of the beam construction creates good acoustics, with additional acoustic elements avoided.

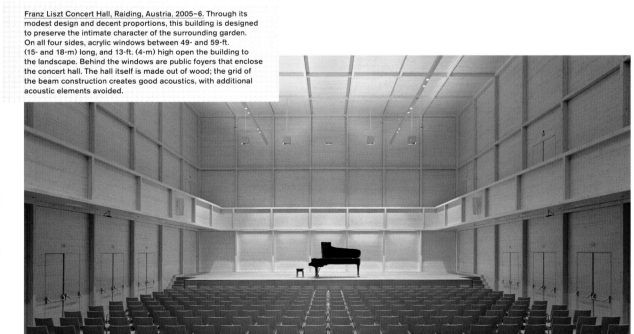

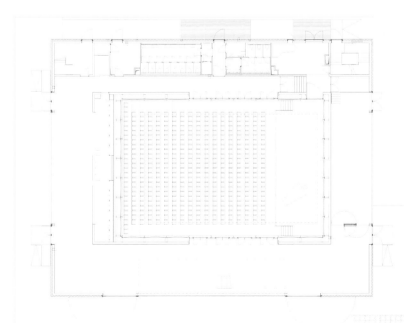

Museum Veenhuizen, Veenhuizen, Netherlands, 2005–8. The new museum, housed in a former prison complex, consists of an exhibition hall, several workshops for traditional crafts, an education center, and a retail outlet for historic building materials. The four existing structures, built circa 1900, were remodeled from the inside to accommodate their new function. In the main auditorium building, a large part of the ceiling is opened to show the beautiful wooden roof construction.

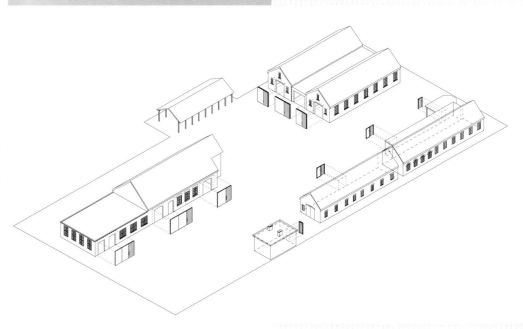

Atelier Kempe Thill

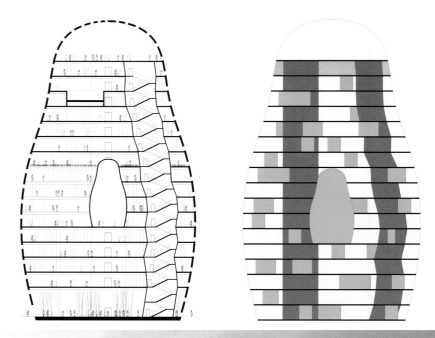

MATREX Building, Moskva, Russian Federation, 2000–2008.
Matreshka, or nesting dolls, are the inspiration for a new building
type for Moskva and a universal construction system for rapidly
growing metropolises around the globe. The proposal is for
matreshka, of various typologies and functions, to appear along
the Moskva River at different scales—from a super-construction
of 1,640 ft. (500 m) to a light transparent monolithic form for
a private house.

Boris Bernaskoni first received international attention at the age of thirty-one when he won the 2008 competition for the Perm Museum of Modern Art, located in the Russian city of Perm near the Ural Mountains. Judged by Peter Zumthor against such high-profile competitors as Coop Himmelbau, Zaha Hadid, and Asymptote, the young architect's design, which includes a railway station and mooring area, stood out. However, Bernaskoni had already been a well-known figure on the Russian architecture scene for over a decade thanks in part to a series of self-initiated projects that were often not purely architectural but hovered somewhere between architecture, visual art, and design. These include the journal *A_0* (published as a series of eight-page inserts in the Russian architecture journal *Project Russia*), a tomb for Kasimir Malevich, an office for the president, and a design for a new Russian flag. Some of these projects were unexpectedly transposed into the real world, for instance when Bernaskoni's flag became the basis for the background of the Russian government's new official press room.

Considering the turbulent development of contemporary Russian society, the fact that Bernaskoni is active in so many fields simultaneously should come as no surprise—the borders between the professions are very porous, and Bernaskoni has proven himself to be skilled in graphic design, visual communication, visual arts, interior design, and architecture. In this respect it is quite remarkable that Bernaskoni's work does not include private interiors, a major field of work for young Russian architects. Maybe this is due to the conceptual nature of the work, in which each detail has a specific place in the whole. This is hardly compatible with the banalities of the typical bourgeois Moskva apartment.

At first glance the work of Bernaskoni could be called minimalist, but it lacks minimalism's perfectionism and aesthetic asceticism. It would be better to relate his work to conceptual art, which Bernaskoni seems to grasp instinctively, and it is probably no coincidence that his main body of work is in the design of art exhibitions. A book with his projects and ideas on this theme, and of course his prize-winning project for Perm, was recently published—and, not surprisingly, written, designed, and produced by Bernaskoni himself. // Bart Goldhoorn

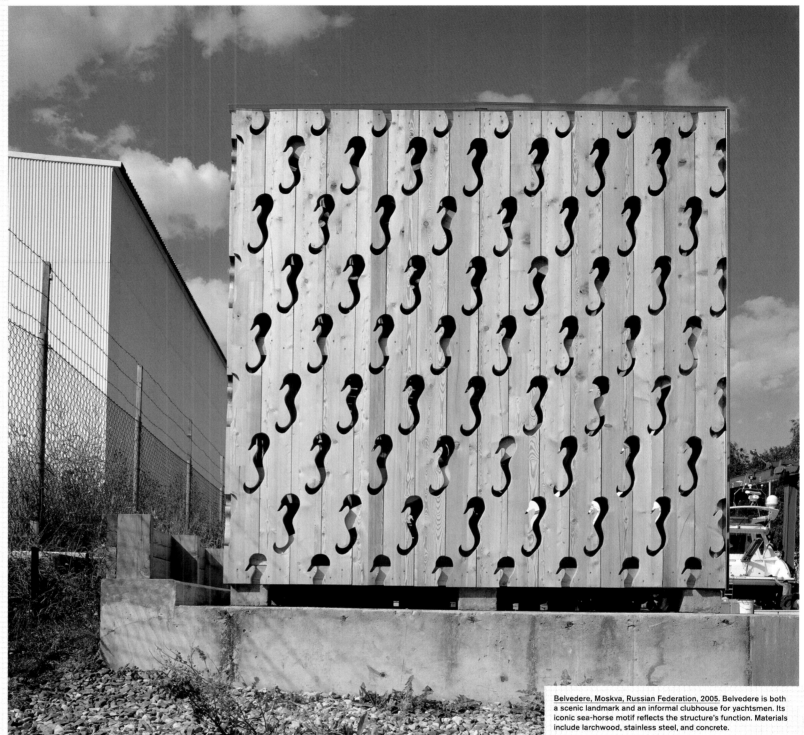

Belvedere, Moskva, Russian Federation, 2005. Belvedere is both a scenic landmark and an informal clubhouse for yachtsmen. Its iconic sea-horse motif reflects the structure's function. Materials include larchwood, stainless steel, and concrete.

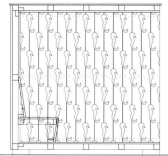
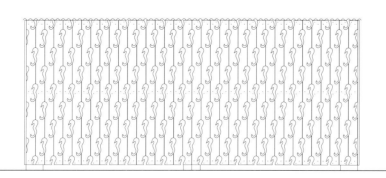
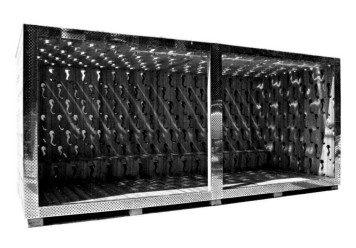

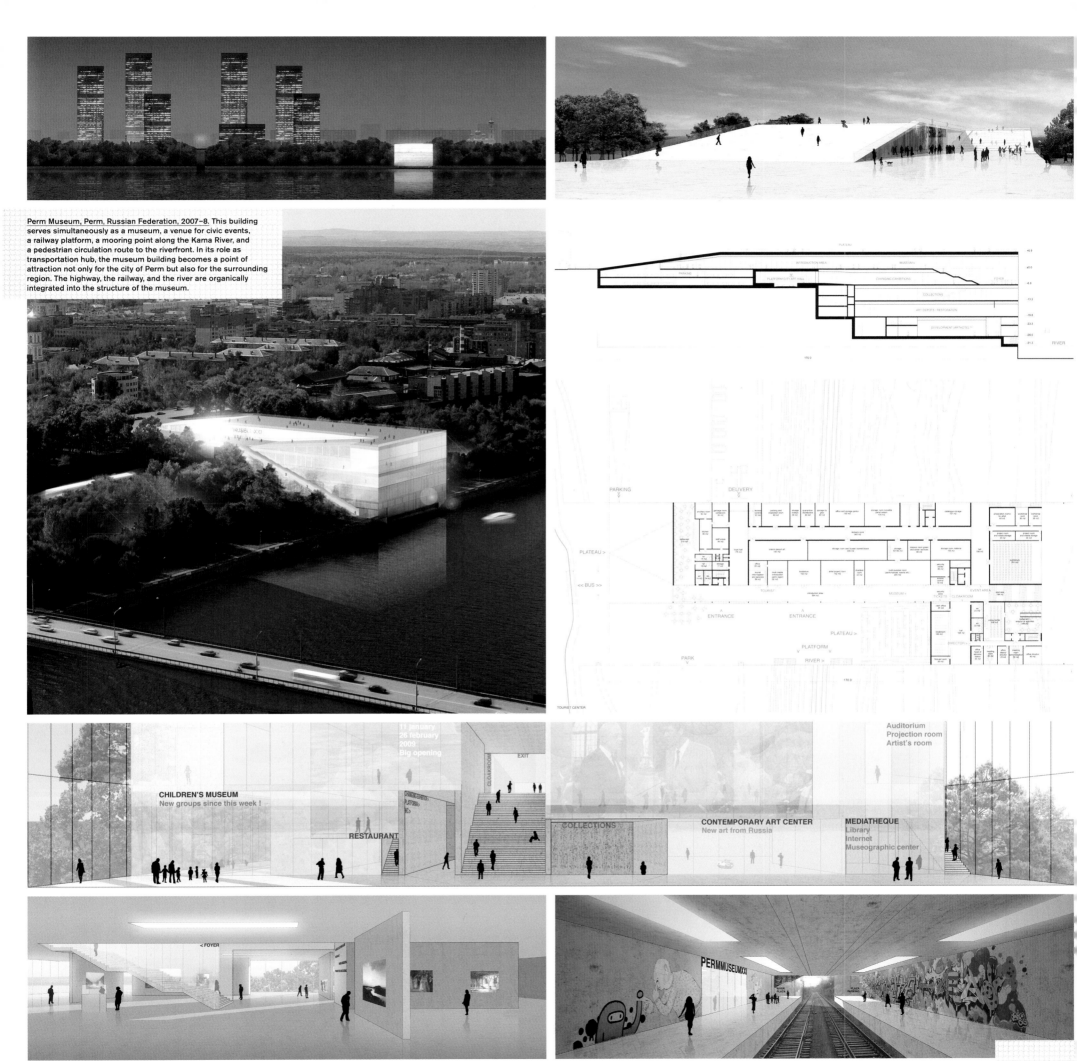

Perm Museum, Perm, Russian Federation, 2007–8. This building serves simultaneously as a museum, a venue for civic events, a railway platform, a mooring point along the Kama River, and a pedestrian circulation route to the riverfront. In its role as transportation hub, the museum building becomes a point of attraction not only for the city of Perm but also for the surrounding region. The highway, the railway, and the river are organically integrated into the structure of the museum.

Russia Pavilion, Shanghai, China, 2008. The Russia Pavilion represents a formal dialogue between China and Russia. The architecture of the pavilion is a combination of traditions and sign systems from both countries. The six volumes are a dual metaphor for the Russian Gold Reserve and the Chinese Book of Change (*I Ching*). The pavilion can be built quickly and simply without heavy vehicles on any number of sites.

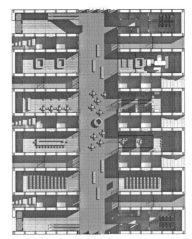

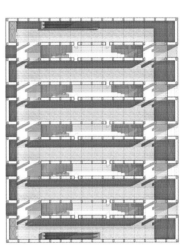

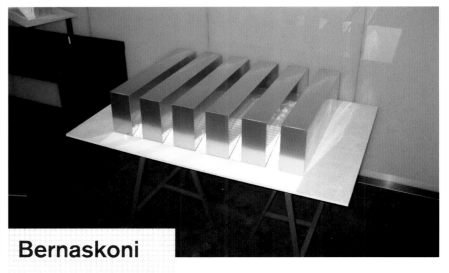

Bernaskoni

Faculty of Mathematics, Ljubljana University, Ljubljana, Slovenia, 2002–6. The Ljubljana University's Faculty of Mathematics is not a new building per se but an addition—a three-story volume built on top of the existing two-story building. Because the addition is elevated and does not allow for street level access to open meeting halls, a series of transparent rooms re-create a sense of public space, even at three or four stories high.

The Serbian Vasa J. Perović and the Slovenian Matija Bevk established their joint practice in Ljubljana in 1997, when Bevk had not yet graduated from architecture school, and Perović—seven years his senior—had recently completed a master's degree in architecture at the Berlage Institute in Rotterdam. Together with four other architects, they designed a primary school in Kočevje, Slovenia, that received the Plečnik Prize after its completion in 2002. Jože Plečnik does indeed cast a long shadow over Slovenian architecture, however, the work of Bevk Perović—in spite of having been distinguished several times with the eponymous prize—cannot be described as influenced by the mystical nationalism of the Ljubljana master, whose catholic version of the Wagnerschule is more admired than imitated by the new generations of Eastern European architects. The projects of this team belong rather to a conventional tradition of modernism, one that is polished and sophisticated, reflecting the wealthy and cultivated social milieu of Slovenia, the least troubled of the fragments into which the former Yugoslavia was split.

Since 2000, Bevk Perović has produced a body of work stamped as its own, which has been widely recognized. Both the apartment complex Zeleni Gaj in Šiška, Ljubljana (1999–2001), and the ambassador's residence for the Dutch Embassy in Ljubljana (2002–3) were nominated for the Mies van der Rohe Award, in 2003 and 2005, respectively. In 2007 the architects received the Emerging Architect Special Mention of the Mies van der Rohe Award for their elegant extension of Ljubljana University's Faculty of Mathematics, a three-floor addition clad in striped-printed glass, while their exquisitely detailed dormitory at Ljubljana University, Student Housing Poljane, earned Bevk Perović its fourth Plečnik Prize in ten years. All of this is an extraordinary record of achievement for a practice that is destined to become a reference point for the Balkans, Italy, and the Germanic countries. // Luis Fernández-Galiano

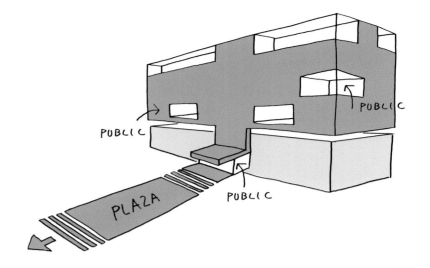

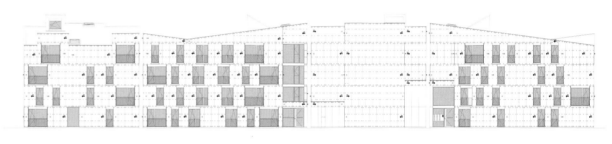

Housing Polje, Ljubljana, Slovenia, 2002–5. These six apartment blocks situated on the edge of the city are literally the last buildings of Ljubljana—facing open fields on one side, the built urban fabric on another, and busy railway tracks on a third side. Hanging balconies and a small park extend the private realm into the public.

House SB, Ljubljana, Slovenia, 2002–4. This private residence is located in a suburban settlement on the outskirts of Ljubljana, on a 5,380-sq.-ft. (500-sq. m) plot. A timber-clad facade faces the street, its ribbon window elevated to offer privacy but still provide light, while the custom-made glass facade looks out into the forest. The east wing of the L-shaped plan, located on the ground floor, contains intimate family rooms; the west wing, or cantilevered upper level, contains an open plan for communal spaces.

Bevk Perović Arhitekti

Maritime Youth House, København, Denmark, 2002–4. The project
was designed to accommodate the requirements of two very
different facilities: a youth center, which needed outdoor space
for children to play, and a sailing club, which required space for
mooring its boats. The building is the result of these two
contradictory demands. The deck is elevated high enough to
allow for boat storage underneath while providing an undulating
landscape for children to run and play above.

To understand the true measure of the accomplishments of Bjarke Ingels, founder of the Danish architecture practice BIG Architects, consider this: when was the last time reporters from every corner of the world were seen scrambling to cover the opening of a building by a thirty-three-year-old architect? As if that were not enough, the inauguration in question was not a museum, a library, or even a luxury condo, but a low-cost housing development. Architects long ago declared the housing sector to be in a state of crisis—which unquestionably it is—and have variously laid the blame for this on developers, government, and even public opinion. Yet as BIG Architects' work proves, it is a sector in which there is yet room for innovation, experimentation, profit, and even acclaim.

Mountain Dwellings (MTN), inaugurated in 2008, is the latest in a series of housing developments in the suburbs of København designed by BIG Architects. As is the custom among architects whose early formation occurred at the Office for Metropolitan Architecture (OMA), Ingels describes the building as the result of something more akin to a mathematical equation than a creative design process. Take an 86,000-square-foot (8,000-square-meter) site, eighty apartments, and four or five levels of parking spaces. Spread the housing on top of the parking like jam on bread. Tilt the resulting sandwich so you have a wedge-shaped block, orient the block for optimal exposure to light and sun, stagger the arrangement of the apartments, and presto! you have your Mountain Dwellings.

The reality is much more nuanced, and takes many of its cues from the surrounding urban fabric. MTN rises in a thoroughly suburban sector of København that is in part a weekend second-home destination for residents of the city's denser neighborhoods. Standing on the peak of MTN, an ocean of one- and two-story dwellings stretches out toward the port and shipyards to the south. Seen from the opposite perspective, it rises like a mountain on the horizon. "I liked the idea of suburban living with a view," says Ingels. "It's as though the suburbs crept across the canal and up the slope of the building." Each apartment—most are about 1,000 square feet (100 square meters)—has an exterior terrace, and despite the tightly packed arrangement of the residences each one enjoys almost total privacy from its neighbors.

All this could be just the incipit of even more radical experiments in the possibilities of metropolitan dwellings, with projects like Lego housing further pushing the boundaries of topographical urbanism. For the moment, having inspired a generation of architecture students to disregard premature proclamations of the death of housing in architecture is achievement enough. // Joseph Grima

Mountain Dwellings, København, Denmark, 2005–8. Mountain Dwellings merge the two functions of parking and housing into a symbiotic relationship. A mountain of 215,000 sq. ft. (20,000 sq. m) of parking forms the foundation for 108,000 sq. ft. (10,000 sq. m) of terraced houses: a pixelated mountainside of single-family homes resting on the colorful foundation of the parking levels.

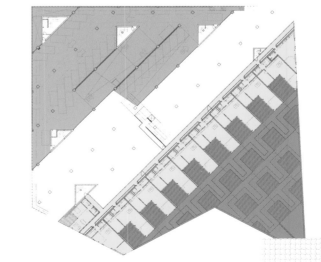

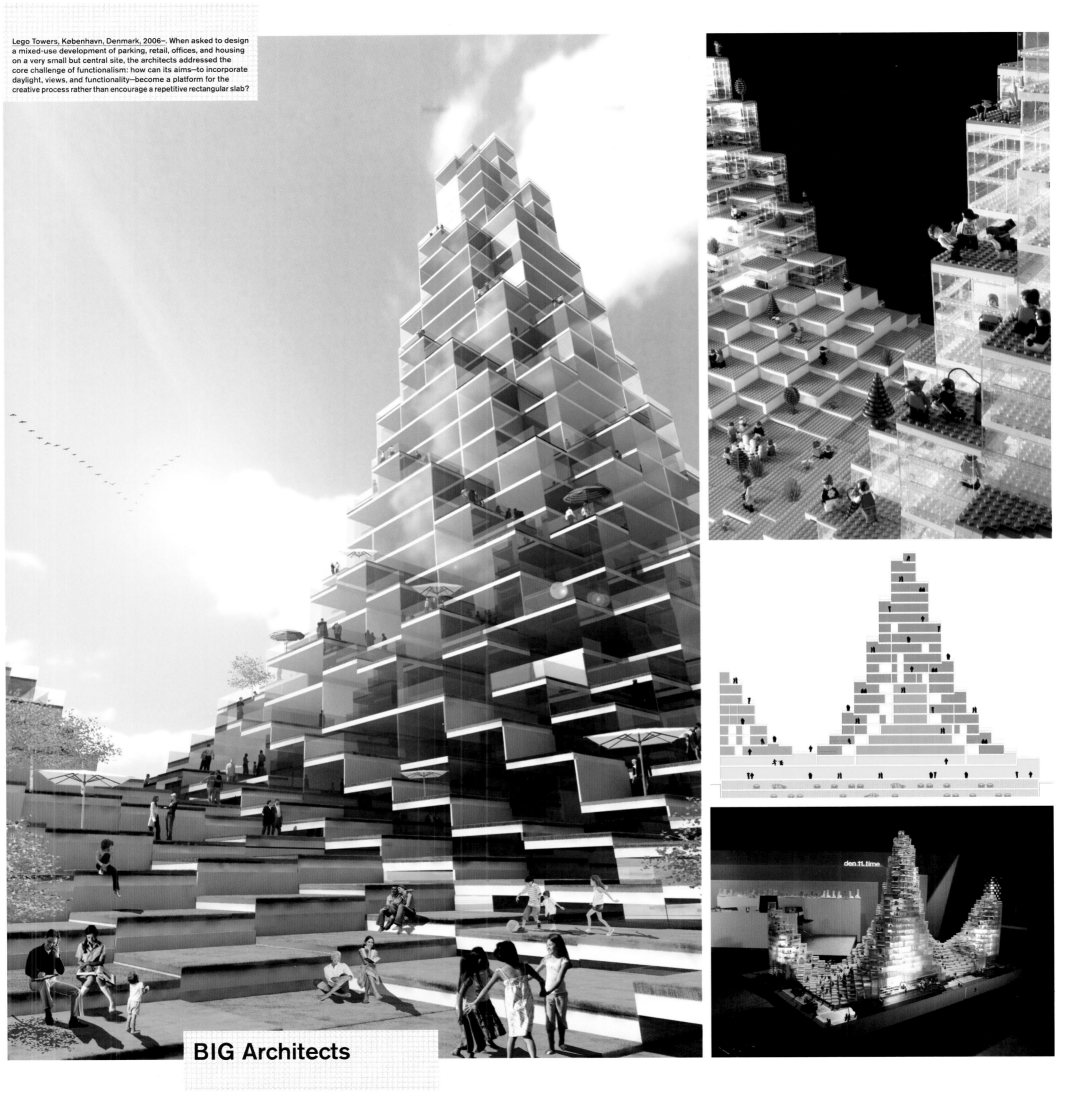

Lego Towers, København, Denmark, 2006–. When asked to design a mixed-use development of parking, retail, offices, and housing on a very small but central site, the architects addressed the core challenge of functionalism: how can its aims—to incorporate daylight, views, and functionality—become a platform for the creative process rather than encourage a repetitive rectangular slab?

BIG Architects

Casa Observatorio, Roca Blanca, Mexico, 2005–7. This 2,580-sq.-ft. (240-sq.-m) house overlooks the coast of Oaxaca. Designed for and with artist Gabriel Orozco, with local materials and local craft techniques, it is based on the design of the Jantar Mantar observatory in Jaipur, India.

Tatiana Bilbao established her office in 2004. She simultaneously co-founded MXDF Urban Research Center, which is focused on the production, occupation, and defense of space in México D.F. Since founding her firm, she has completed projects in Spain, China, and Mexico. With strong interests in urbanism and issues of city scale always on her mind, Bilbao makes architecture that speaks to the group of young Mexican architects with whom she collaborates, attempting to understand and respond to her rapidly changing nation.

Beginning with an archetypal house shape, Bilbao has developed variations on that recognizable profile and expressed them in House A, designed for the Ordos 100 project in Ordos, Nei Mongol, China. Bilbao sliced the project into seven varied profiles, each systematically subtracted from the total shape to respond to the functional requirements of the project, with each section serving different needs. Whether providing parking or offering terrace space and allowing light to bathe the interior, the synergy of form and function is successful.

Bilbao's often formalist approach to architecture is inherently feminine. With the addition of overhangs and orifices creating zones of comfort, her forms take on a subtle, but distinctive, feminine character. This is exemplified by the Casa Observatorio on the coast of Oaxaca, Mexico, a house designed for, and in collaboration with, the artist Gabriel Orozco. The project, built from a mixture of concrete and sand, has simple symmetry. The simplicity of the bold circular pool, coupled with the method of construction, expresses at once a classical and a contemporary solution to a unique program. The elegant reversal of the building's functions, locating the private functions in quadrants below the terrace and pool, gives the project a bold individuality.
// Ai Weiwei

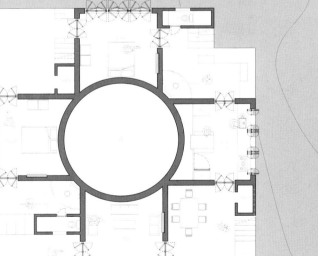

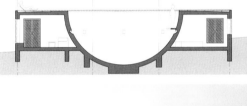

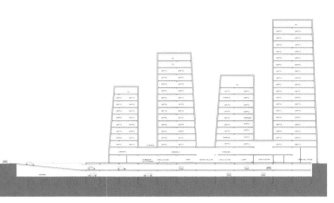

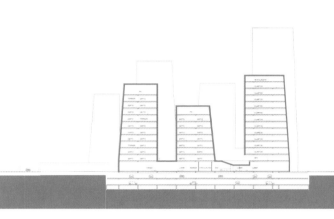

Housing and Cultural Center, Guadalajara, Mexico, 2007–12.
Built on a former factory site, this 645,000-sq.-ft. (60,000-sq.-m)
development is located in a residential neighborhood of Guadalajara.
The four rows of buildings will contain housing, a hotel, an art
gallery, and cinemas. They are designed to generate 45% of the
buildings' electricity, and clean 100% of their polluted water,
generating its own potable water.

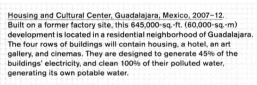

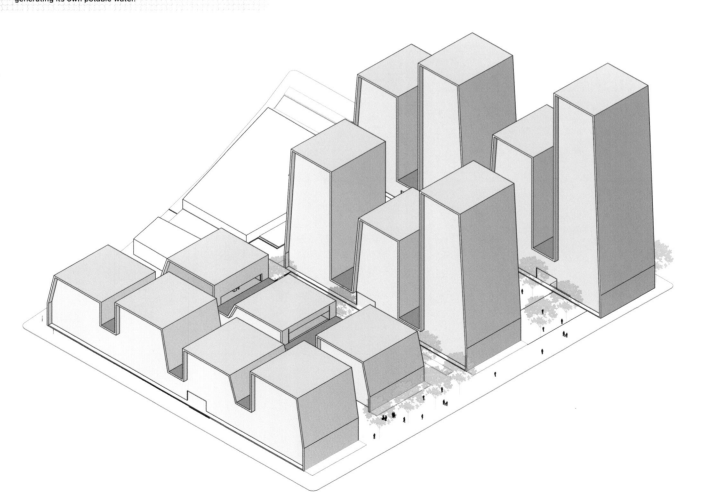

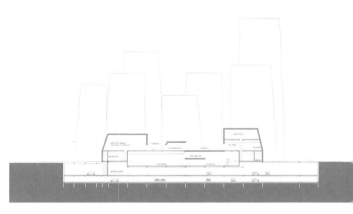

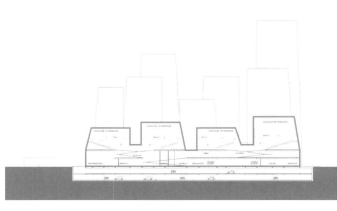

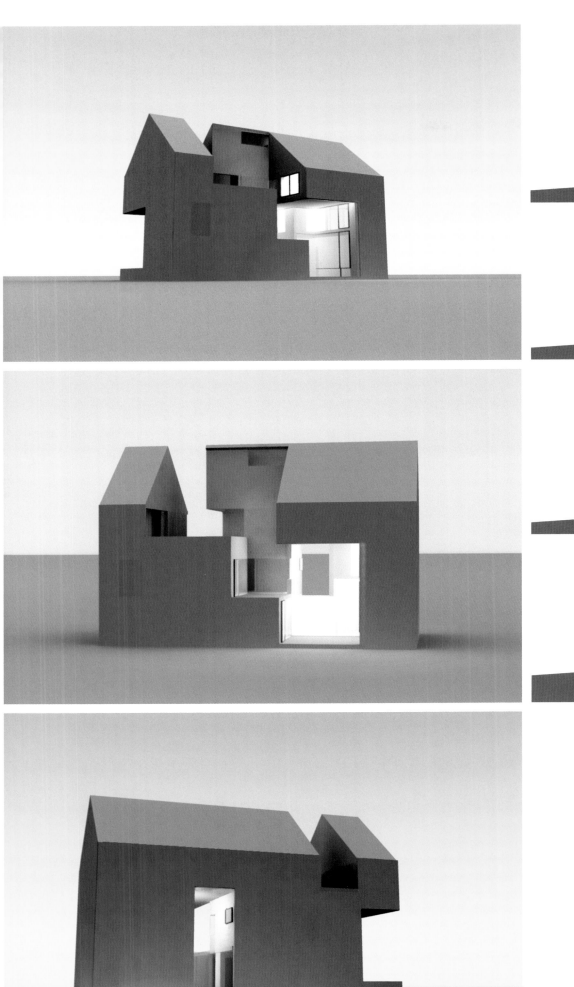

House A, Ordos, Nei Mongol, China, 2008—. Part of the Ordos 100 project, featuring 100 villas designed by international architects, this 10,700-sq.-ft. (100-sq.-m) villa plays on the archetypical form of a house and divides it vertically into seven parts according to function.

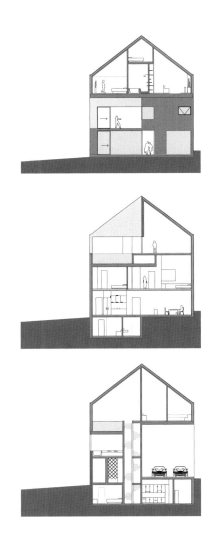

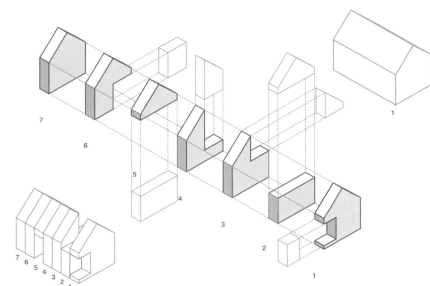

Tatiana Bilbao

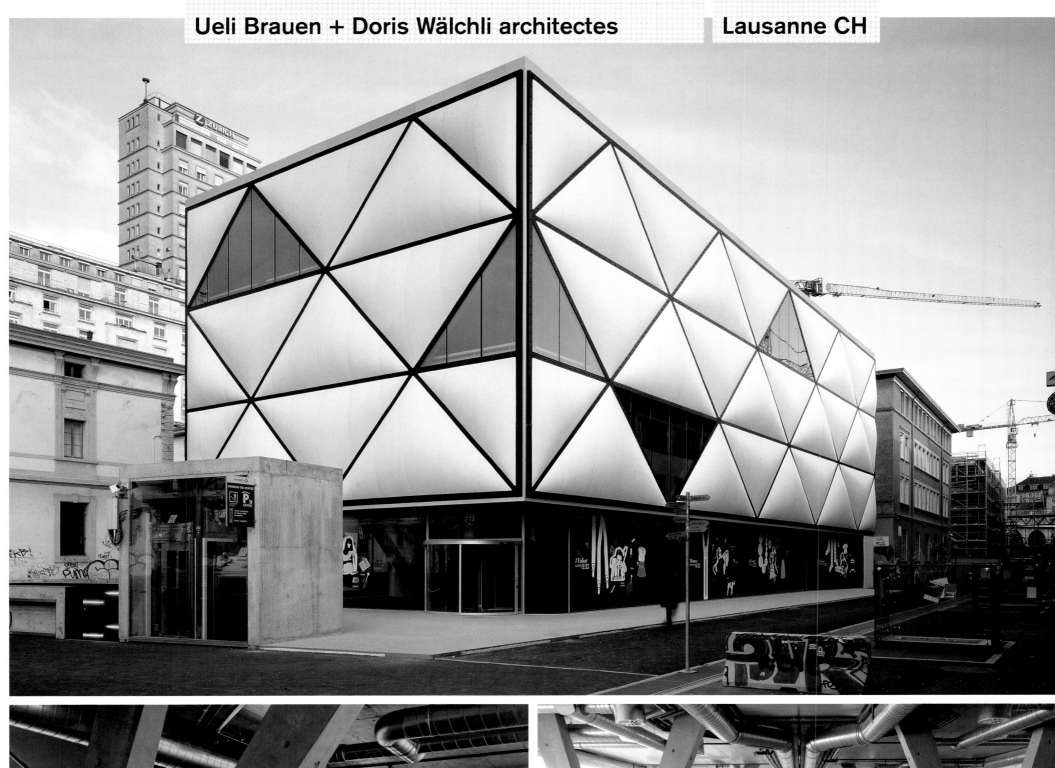

Ueli Brauen and Doris Wälchli suggest that we look at their work as a sort of "fractal" in which the dynamic of the overall order is reproduced identically in each of its individual components. This intriguing vision is combined with an analytic conception of the design process. Their buildings are the outcome of constant research, which, by juggling scale and contexts but without evident disruptions, explores the subjects closest to the architects' hearts.

Both Brauen and Wälchli graduated in architecture from the Swiss Federal Institute of Technology in Lausanne (EPFL) in 1988, and worked at the offices of various international architects, including Mario Botta, Herzog & de Meuron, and José Luis Mateo. In 1990 they founded their own practice in Lausanne. From their earliest projects to the more recent—the pavilion of the Multifunctional Center for International Olympic Committee (IOC) Headquarters and the elegant Langensand Bridge in Luzern (2007–9)—the architects' work has explored structural form as expressive of architectural vocabulary, as well as new materials and technologies. Other themes include an interest in vernacular architecture (as in their own house at Noville, 1994–7) and the topography of the site (CEPNV, Yverdon, 1999–2000); dialogue with existing buildings (Maison des Parlements, Genève, 2000–2002, and Swiss Embassy, La Paz, Colombia, 2001–3), while also drawing on valuable ideas from contemporary art.

In La Miroiterie commercial center, an ingenious tree-shaped structural system multiplies its "branches" to transmit the loads from top to bottom. A translucent fabric membrane enfolds the mall's volumes, forming large triangular pneumatic cushions. On the interior this creates a diaphanous atmosphere that heightens the playful effect of suspension in space. When night falls, artificial lighting transforms the building into an enigmatic urban landmark. This structural approach again emerges in the design for the Drize school, where a repeated ramified element, suggesting a row of trees, forms the supporting framework and articulates the entire facade. The architects' substantial oeuvre exhibits a continuity with a noble strain of Swiss modernism, but above all, Brauen and Wälchli's range of striking achievements reveal a formidable imagination at work: the confluence of precise calculations and designs; experimental and innovative systems of statics closely bound up with the configuration of space and use of light; careful assessment of color, rhythm, and the intrinsic qualities of materials; and the perennial relationship between technology and nature.
// Mercedes Daguerre

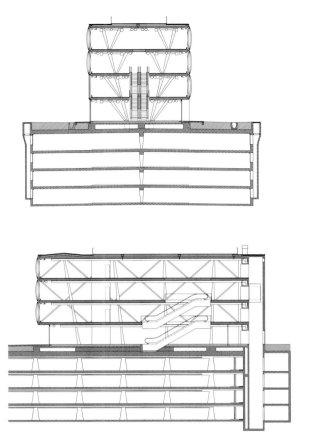

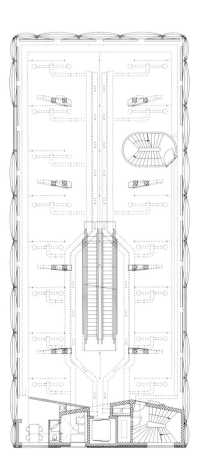

La Miroiterie, Lausanne, Switzerland, 2005–7. This commercial center is built on top of a parking garage used as the foundation for the building. Sitting above a glazed, ground-floor lobby, the top floors are supported by a branch-like system of beams that transfer the load to the structural spine of the parking garage. The translucent, pneumatic cushions spanning the facade give the impression of weightlessness, while also providing insulation.

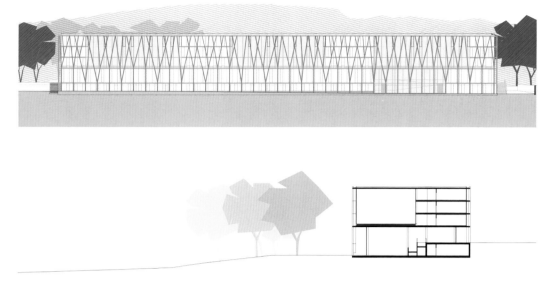

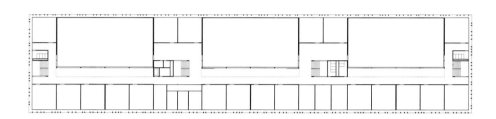

Drize School, Genève, Switzerland, 2005–9. This professional school is situated in a park on the outskirts of Genève. The supporting structure is reminiscent of a row of trees tapering at the top to form openings that offer views to the Salève and Jura Mountains. The service gangways and vertical solar blinds are located between the "branches" of the supporting structure and the recessed glass facade. The main entrance at the intermediate basement level opens via the ramp, offering transparent views through the student cafeteria.

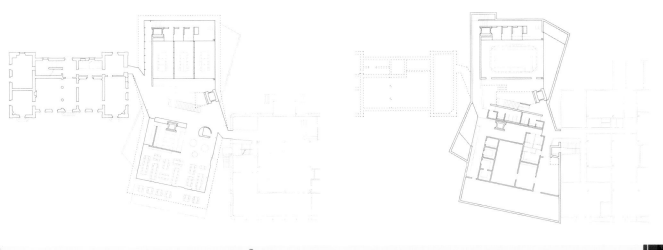

Multifunctional Center for International Olympic Committee (IOC) Headquarters, Lausanne, Switzerland, 2004–8. The transparent volume is encased by huge glass panels and a double folded roof, which is draped in ivy. The frameless building has a minimal supporting structure: in addition to the elevator shafts and a few walls, the construction is supported by a handful of chrome-plated cross-mountings. The front of the building, facing the lake, houses the restaurant; the rear stories house conference rooms and translation booths. The upper floor of the conference complex can be opened toward the restaurant via a sliding wall.

Ueli Brauen + Doris Wälchli architectes

Combined Heat and Power Plant, Würzburg, Germany, 2002–6. The extension and modernization of the coal-fired power station in Würzburg provided an opportunity to enclose the old and new plants with a curtain of sheet aluminium. The strong horizontality of the building is offset by the three new chimneys.

Family continuity, strong local roots, and the use of local materials are all strengths that can recharge contemporary architecture with new energy. Architects Peter and Christian Brückner joined the practice of their father, Klaus-Peter Brückner, in Tirschenreuth, Germany, after studying in München and Stuttgart. They won their first major competition in Würzburg for the conversion of a landmarked wheat silo into the Museum of Concrete Art in 1998. The Kulturspeicher building won numerous architecture prizes, and the young architects from provincial Bavaria were soon lecturing at architecture schools throughout Germany. For the Kulturspeicher, they added annexes of green ornamental glass to the long existing sandstone building and extended the edifice with a slatted membrane. The authentic feel of the industrial monument is enhanced by the exceptional quality of the new design, which adheres to the architects' credo of looking to tradition to create modern forms.

Their second major project was the extension of the village church in Wenzenbach, located outside Regensburg. Instead of tearing down the existing church, which had become too small, the architects extended it by adding a new hall, which they shrouded with a series of fifty-foot (fifteen-meter) high vertical larchwood rods. The violet-blue glazing of the new hall behind the wooden rods affords spectacular views from Kirchplatz, and the former nave now serves as a foyer and holds the new organ. The old building, with its classic plaster, and the new building, with its wall screen made of locally milled wood, enter into an exciting symbiosis of regional construction methods and materials. The "Like a Rock" Granite Center in Hauzenberg, in the Bavarian forest, sits on the edge of a disused granite quarry that has been transformed into a picturesque lake. Here the architects demonstrate the full expressive range of the natural stone, which was carefully split, sawed, polished, and finely finished by local craftsmen. The complex is in part below grade within the quarry's cliffs, and in part covered over by granite gravel that will in time disappear completely beneath vegetation to blend with the surrounding landscape. The architectural highlight in the region is the Cistercian abbey of Waldsassen, founded 875 years ago and whose main church is considered one of the high points of Bavarian Baroque architecture. The Brückners were commissioned to build a multiphase extension; the completed Art and Education Center attests to the sensitivity and respect the architects have when exposing the traces of the past and employing the same materials for new construction. // Peter Cachola Schmal

"Like a Rock" Granite Center, Hauzenberg, Germany, 2001–5. The form of the new built museum takes its cues from the natural rock structure. The main materials—granite, oak, iron, graphite, and concrete—originate in the region and merge into a unit that is integrated into the adjacent stone quarry.

Cistercian Abbey of St. Joseph, Waldsassen, Germany, 2006–8.
This reconstruction of a former malthouse is based on the interface
between the basilica and the Baroque monastery with its additions.
The interaction between the historical foundation and contemporary additions creates a straightforward and functional structure.

Brückner & Brückner

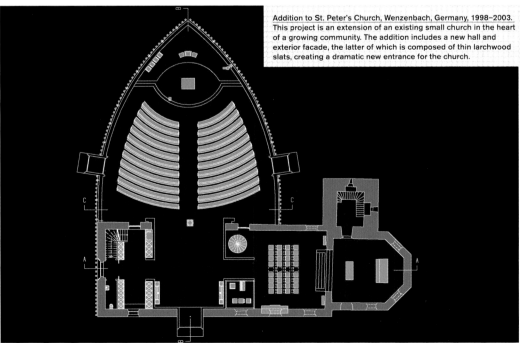

Addition to St. Peter's Church, Wenzenbach, Germany, 1998–2003. This project is an extension of an existing small church in the heart of a growing community. The addition includes a new hall and exterior facade, the latter of which is composed of thin larchwood slats, creating a dramatic new entrance for the church.

For a long time, Alexander Brodsky was better known internationally for his artworks than for his architecture. Still, he started his career as an architect. He was part of the avant-garde group of so-called paper architects in the Soviet Union in the 1970s, and together with Ilya Utkin won a number of competitions organized by the journal *Japan Architect* in the 1980s. After moving on to enjoy an internationally recognized career as an artist, he came back to architecture around 2000.

The realities of both Soviet and post-Soviet Russia can best be described as imperfect and disorganized, and this is certainly the case when talking about construction. The practice of erecting factory-produced buildings, which started in the 1960s, led to a complete erosion of professional construction skills. Practically the only custom-made buildings were the *dachas*— do-it-yourself holiday homes made of the leftovers from the centrally planned economy. Brodsky has made the aesthetic of imperfection his trademark, and in this respect he is one of a few architects whose work you could call typically Russian. At the same time it is unique. In nearly every other part of the Western world, architects have formalized their relationship with the construction industry by specifying the exact sizes and qualities in contract documents. In contrast, Brodsky's works are barely documented. Architectural journals and magazines have great difficulty obtaining drawings from him. Everything is decided on the spot. For Brodsky, architecture becomes a matter of instinct—or talent, or taste, if you wish—which is how he achieves the authenticity that makes the difference between kitsch and art.

Another thin line walked by Brodsky is his position between modernism and classicism— the Paper Architecture movement was in essence postmodernist, and many of Brodsky's colleagues from this group (including his former partner, Utkin) are now designing classicist buildings. With their archaic profiles, Brodsky's works are both classical and modern. They oppose the slick, sophisticated modernist experiment as well as the classicist palaces that are so popular with the Russian nouveaux riches, all the while relating to an archetypical sense of building.

The big question, of course, is whether these buildings can stand the test of time. Are they sustainable? Is this a responsible way of building? These buildings are extremely cheap, often made of degradable materials, and, in fact, look like they are temporary. It appears that they will not survive for a long time, especially in the Russian climate, and conserving them will certainly require large investments. Does their artistic value mean that they will have to be kept up for later generations? // Bart Goldhoorn

Bureau Alexander Brodsky   Moskva RUS

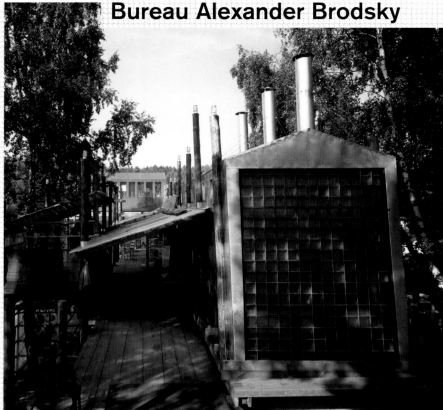

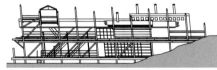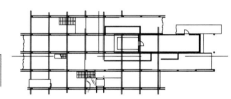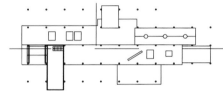

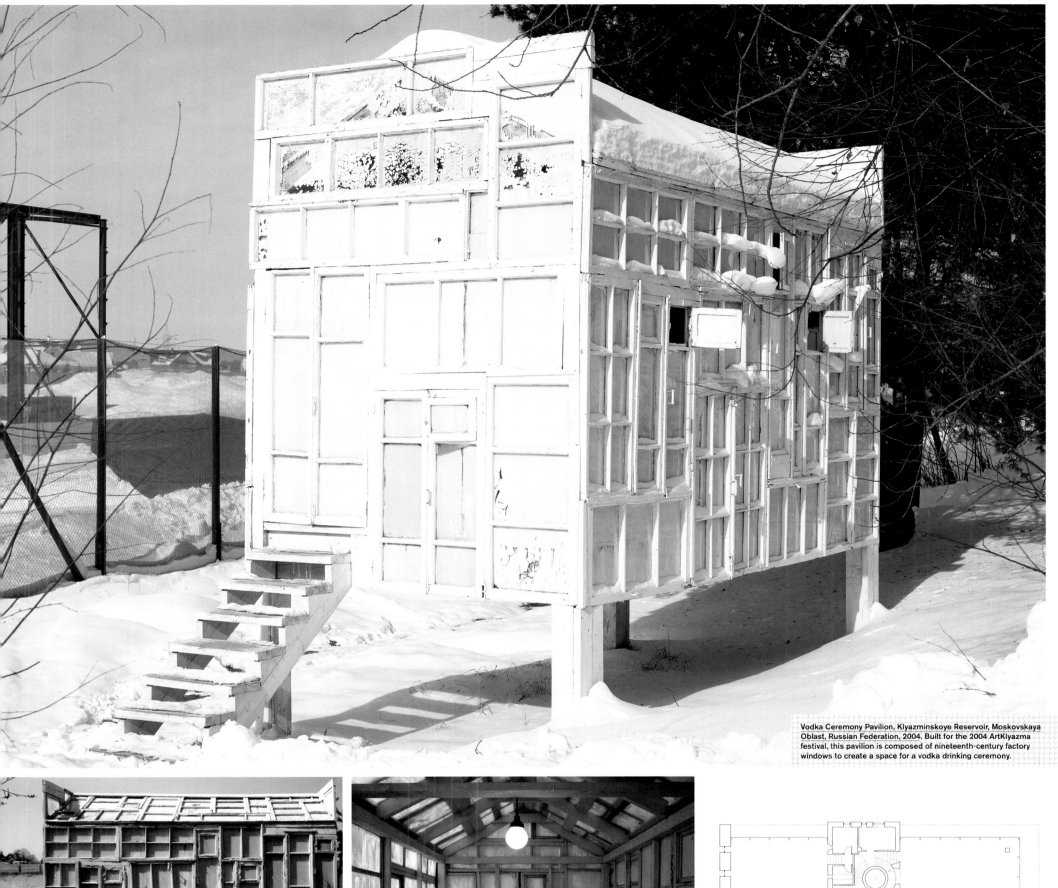

Vodka Ceremony Pavilion, Klyazminskoye Reservoir, Moskovskaya Oblast, Russian Federation, 2004. Built for the 2004 ArtKlyazma festival, this pavilion is composed of nineteenth-century factory windows to create a space for a vodka drinking ceremony.

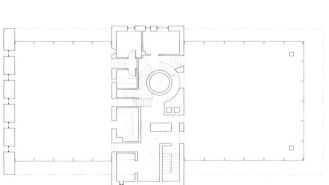

Guelman Apartment, Moskva, Russian Federation, 2002. For this project, Brodsky created custom furniture out of steel and glass built into the bare shell of an old apartment. An elaborate shelving system is suspended above the custom-designed kitchen island.

Green Cape House, Moskovskaya Oblast, Russian Federation, 2004–. This project is a meditation on the relationship between high-tech contemporary imagery, an antiquated core, strategies for adaptive reuse, and the contrast between vast living spaces and cluttered service spaces. Materials include concrete, concrete blocks, and timber.

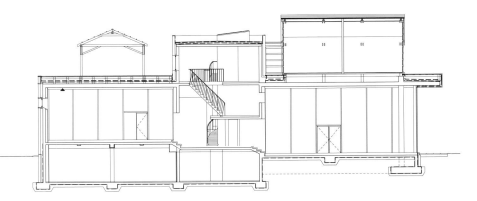

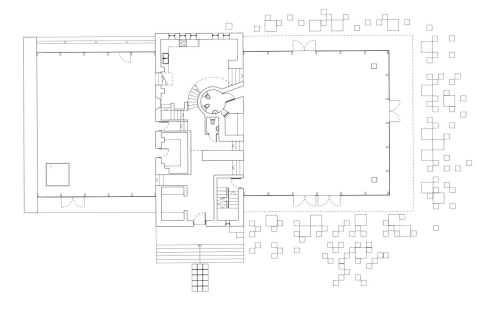

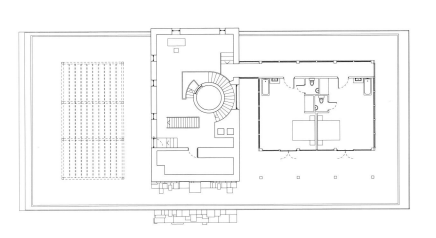

Bureau Alexander Brodsky

61 York St., Sydney, New South Wales, Australia, 2002–6. The facade's composition is defined by the familiar contemporary dimension of 8 ft. (2.4 m), which translates to all elements of the building. This arrangement is refined by a repetition of motive, both vertically and horizontally, inspired by a musical "rondo."

To write about architectural composition today is to risk being stereotyped as a formalist, disengaged from the fractured narratives of contemporary cultural meaning. So to say that Angelo Candalepas takes composition very seriously requires some qualification. Composition here refers to something that is allied to, but not solely, the arrangement of space, light, and materials. Within the work of Candalepas Associates, formal invention is umbilically linked to a shrewd understanding of forces that exert less visible though no less powerful influence on the composition of contemporary architecture— a combination of regulatory and commercial constraints, without an understanding of which it is hard to do much of value in Sydney besides houses in pretty locations.

The first observation to be made about this practice is its refusal to isolate the lyrical, the practical, and the cultural. A second observation is that this holistic approach to each new commission helps create a practice that is adaptable. There is a fluid confidence in each new project within an expanding portfolio of residential, commercial, educational, and, more recently, sacred spaces. Having earned his stripes winning an unusual number of competitions as a young architect, Candalepas is now in full command of his plan, section, program, and scale. As is evident when visiting an apartment building such as Pindari, a recent city office building, or a suburban grammar school, the projects are completely legible as a balanced whole—almost easy. They do not equivocate, nor do they use decorative surfaces to disguise a flawed parti. They hit you between the eyes with their clarity. But there is a third element to this work that makes it resonant: a commitment to the humanist project of architecture. Some spaces are designed for silence, others for bustle. Some render reflection, others interaction. If we accept that modern architecture failed at times to check its ideology against its commodity, no such criticism could be leveled at the modern cast of this work. These buildings are wholly designed for occupation, not for the vanity of either architect or client.

Modernist it is. A plastic quiddity ties it to Louis Kahn, Le Corbusier, and the like—concrete heft, plain unadorned brickwork, flush joins, recessive detail, often leaning toward the monumental. I am reminded of Sigfried Giedion's description of Henrik Berlage: "[H]e gave the wall—until then either chaotically dismembered or deceptively patched together—the reconquered unity of the flat surface." It is this desire for unity, embedded in the experiential and practical composition of design, rather than rekindled dogma, that keeps this work engaged and on its toes. // Andrew Mackenzie

All Saints Grammar School, Belmore, New South Wales, Australia, 2004–8. The design is based on a lineal spine of light and air, devised as a multi-level corridor that organizes the spaces while providing access to the rooms. Western light is shaded on the top floor by a large angled eave, and wide corridor spaces on each level allow students to congregate.

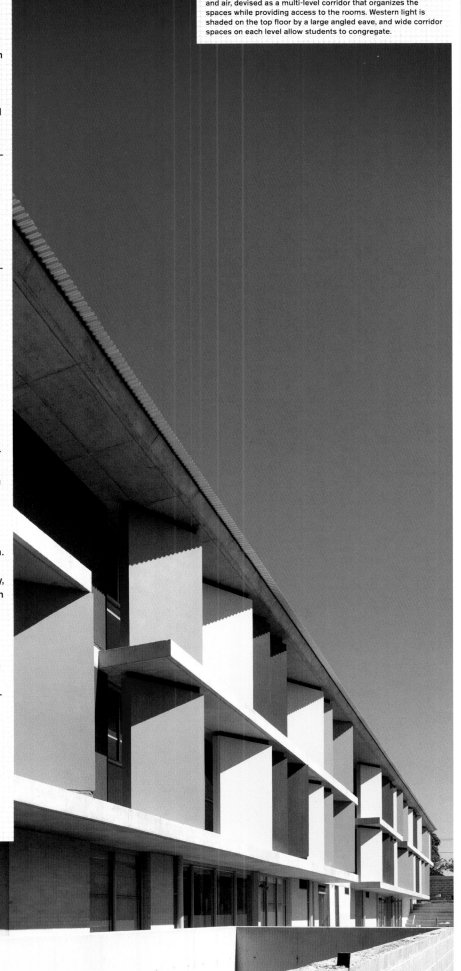

Pindari, Randwick, New South Wales, Australia, 2002–6.
The stepping and vertical junctures in the building's elevations
relate to the sloping site and vertical stand of trees, while materials
and colors refer to the local eucalyptus trees. White cement render,
fiber cement sheet, timber cladding, and clear glass establish the
building within the treescape.

Messy House, Glebe, New South Wales, Australia, 2003–7. This house was designed and built for the architect's family. The abundance of controlled natural light avoids the reliance on artificial lighting. Natural cross ventilation with operable walls, hatches, and vents reduces the need for cooling, further minimizing the environmental impact.

Candalepas Associates

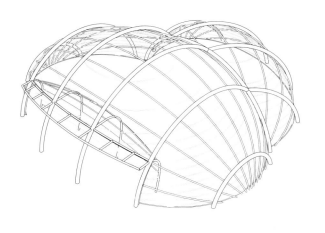

Platypusary, Healesville, Victoria, Australia, 2005. Nested in the Healesville Sanctuary, the Platypusary is an observation point for platypusses in their natural habitat. Two bright gold steel conjoined ovoid forms provide enclosure and protection from predators.

There is a theory that if you can name your demons, you are a long way to subduing them. Perhaps that is why Cassandra Fahey named her practice Cassandra Complex, after the Greek princess whom Apollo gave the power to see into the future but then cursed her by ensuring that no one would believe her warnings—an appropriate cautionary tale for architects, who believe they have much to offer the world if only the world would listen. So with the full intention of being heard, Fahey has filled her short career to date with culturally bold, sensually rich, and urbanistically mischievous architecture.

Perhaps her most unusual project is the rather Austin Powers–inspired Platypusary, a gold-colored, double-dome, woven steel pipe enclosure for Australia's bizarre little creature, the platypus. A scatter of gum leaf shapes simulate the forest canopy (and defend against passing birds of prey), while thousands of tiny marbles embedded into a playpool add to the exotic decoration of this animal enclosure.

The Smith Great Aussie Home is an exuberant, somewhat iconoclastic cornucopia of cultural influence, from its etched-glass, mildly erotic depiction of Aussie swimming legend Ian Thorpe to its cricket bat fencing and its baroque explosion of decorative motifs on wallpaper, tiles, glazing, and carpets. Another house, the Chameleon, transforms an old light industrial building into a new home for Fahey's partner. The building was once, with more than a pinch of poetic punch, a candy factory. A large curving candy-red form is a major interior component, as is an enlarged image of the client as a five-year-old child. Thus Fahey rejects modernism's machismo and replaces the "machine for living" with a "playground for living."

Alongside these residential projects Fahey has also completed a number of bars and restaurants, which have allowed her investment in delight to find rich expression. Of these, New Gold Mountain is her best, a tiny four-story building squeezed into a back lane of Melbourne's Chinatown, reinventing the opium dens of yesteryear. Surprisingly for a site so spatially constrained, the project's mix of exotic materials, colors, patterns, and forms serves to liberate the space. // Andrew Mackenzie

The Smith Great Aussie Home, Blackrock, Victoria, Australia, 2004–6. Situated opposite expansive Port Philip Bay, this private house contains a seemingly typical program: living and dining spaces, kitchen, three bedrooms, study, garage. But the house has some atypical elements, including a floor-to-ceiling high glass pane image of the swimmer Ian Thorpe, clamshell bathroom sinks, and patterned wallpaper everywhere, some with a so-called techno bunny motif.

New Gold Mountain, Melbourne, Victoria, Australia, 2005–6.
The proprietors' desired theme for this bar was an old-fashioined
opium den. The bar is a series of rooms divided by screens and
distinguished by color and patterning that covers every wall
and upholstered surface. All patterns consist of two layers: a
background image depicting a scene from the time of the Gold
Rush, and a foreground layer that is abstract to the point of being
purely geometric.

Chameleon, Melbourne, Victoria, Australia, 2003. This project comprised the conversion of a turn-of-the-century industrial warehouse into a residential space over three levels. The client is represented in the work through a series of digital laminate surfaces that feature slightly blurry images of him as a young boy. All of the spaces are independent and private while still being connected by light and openness.

Cassandra Complex

CEBRA | Århus DK

Bakkegaard School extension, Gentofte, Denmark, 2003–6.
The project added a sports complex, located on the old school
yard, that connects two existing buildings, creating a social
space. The architects recreated the yard as a garden roof on top
of the new building.

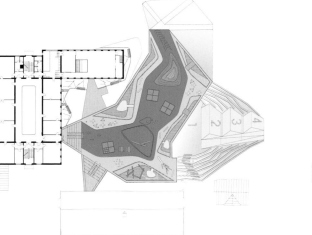

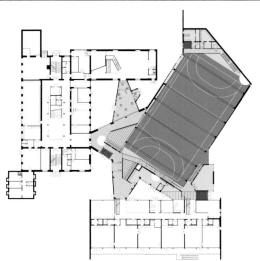

Isbjerget (The Iceberg), Århus, Denmark, 2008–11. In order to bring sunlight and views of the sea to as many apartments as possible, the apartment blocks are placed at parallel angles facing south and out to the harbor. Each building forms pointed mountain tops staggered with valleys, creating sculptural blocks reminiscent of an iceberg.

A decade ago, when reflecting upon Danish architecture, I imagined quiet, pipe-smoking, corduroy-clad men, a bit dull perhaps, producing responsible and ecologically sound architecture with a light postmodern touch. At best one could expect neat modernism. The architects of CEBRA, who recently received the prestigious Nykredit Architecture Prize, do not fit this image of Danish architects. Not only do they dress casually, their renderings appear unpolished and do not always do justice to the architecture.

In order to understand CEBRA's work, one must look at their realized projects. The most important is a relatively modest commission, a sports hall in the courtyard of an existing school complex. In the end, the hall itself is a simple rectangular box, defined by the sizes of the sport fields. From a traditional Danish architect one would have expected a plain, well detailed volume, connected to the other buildings via corridors similar to those at the Louisiana Museum of Modern Art in Humlebæk. Instead, CEBRA created a wild landscape in which the sports hall is not an isolated box but the termination point of an avalanche of stairs, bridges, ramps, and corridors. All materials and detailing are quite cheap, which only enhances the overall playground atmosphere. It is difficult to believe that such a spectacular and multi-faceted space could emerge from such a simple commission.

CEBRA is a rising star among Danish architects. "CEBRA is a name that the Danes can just as well start getting used to, alongside such icons as Jørn Utzon, Henning Larsen, Olafur Eliasson, and Lene Tranberg," says Kent Martinussen, managing director of the Danish Architecture Centre. Together with offices like BIG Architects, they form a new avant-garde that shows some similarities with the architecture scene in the Netherlands during the 1990s. As in the Netherlands, this seems to be the result of a large government investment in architecture, starting with the foundation of the Danish Architecture Centre in København and followed in 2007 by an official document outlining the policies of the Danish government on the advancement of architecture. If they experience the same success with their policies as the Dutch, Danish architects are bound to produce much more exciting work in the years to come. // Bart Goldhoorn

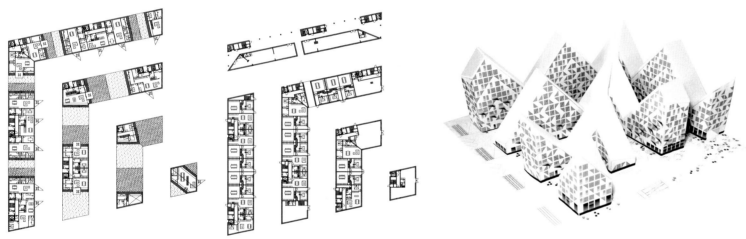

Ordrup School, Gentofte, Denmark, 2003–5.
This extension links the ends of an older
horseshoe-shaped school building to
create an inner atrium and new connections
and synergies while eliminating dead ends.

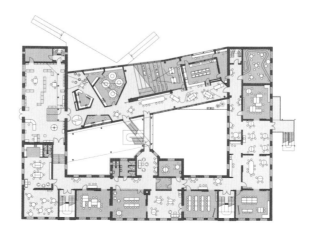

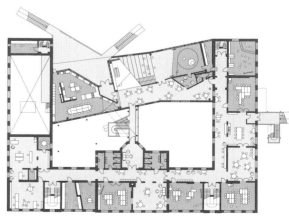

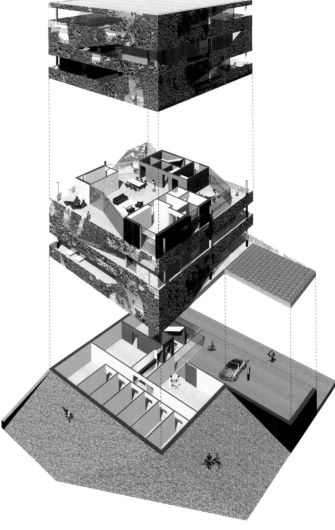

Villa Strata, Kolding, Denmark, 2005–9. The most popular housing form in Denmark is the detached house, which inspired the architects to compose this high-rise building as a stack of houses on top of each other—one house per floor. This removes the disadvantages of the detached house, such as time-consuming gardening, while retaining its advantageous qualities, such as light from all sides.

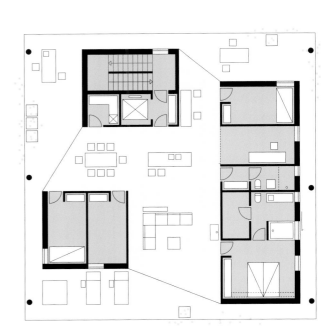

CEBRA

CJ Lim/Studio 8 Architects   London GB

"Seasons Through the Looking Glass," Victoria & Albert Museum, London, England, UK, 2008. An installation for the subway tunnel entrance at the Victoria & Albert Museum, this work evokes the adventures of Alice in Wonderland and her trip down the rabbit hole, which landed her on a heap of twigs and leaves. This multi-sensory intervention explores the spatial possibilities of a subterranean garden; a tree trunk and twigs are constructed from honey-combed cardboard panels, and flowers from rolled-up recycled fabric that change to reflect the seasons. A large mirror at the foot of the tunnel immediately beyond the entrance portal reflects the topiary structure, infinitely extending the museum in virtual space.

It is not just that CJ Lim's architecture does not limit itself to architecture; after all, Thomas Heatherwick's recent works also move beyond architecture. The issue is that Lim's goal appears to be architectural transcendence. Britain has a tradition of this sort of nonarchitectural architecture. Conservative methods rooted in Italian classicism and the French Beaux-Arts style are at the center of the Continental architectural tradition, but British architecture consistently stands apart. The British Architectural Association (AA) School of Architecture started in dissent against the traditional academy, and it is no coincidence that Lim taught at the AA School for many years. Still, Lim's submission to the Nam June Paik Museum competition in the Republic of Korea in 2003, in which the outer walls of the museum represent a cluster of butterflies that has been drawn to those walls, made it clear that the nonarchitectural qualities of this work could not be reduced to just these British roots.

British architecture maintains a deep relationship with British technological traditions. But Lim is exuberantly developing an independent, nonarchitectural game, no longer related to technology, that criticizes architectural conservatism. In it there is no right or wrong or good or bad, and there are no distinctions between what is technologically possible and what is not. He unfolds before us a world without gravity that has no east or west, no north or south. This is a magnificent game in which everything has been incorporated: nonarchitectural technology, Asian-style chaos, and laughter.

As a result of the magnificence of his game, Lim has long been known as an architect whose designs cannot be built. But now, the chance is at hand. Today architects are permitted bravura action according to their own rules of the game. At last the day has come when Lim can work in the real world, using real materials and the earth's surface. // Kengo Kuma

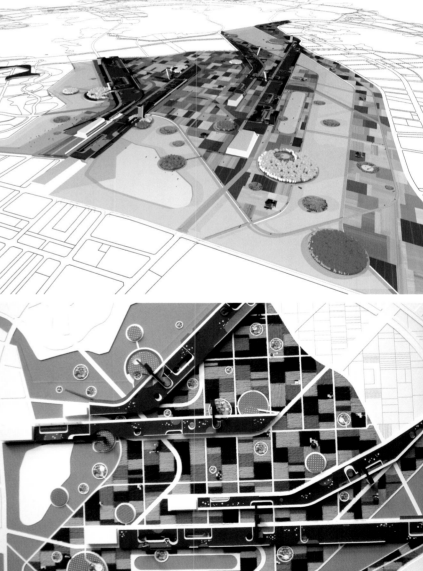

Central Open Space, MAC, Yeongi-gun, Republic of Korea, 2007. A competition entry for a public park in a Multi-functional Administrative City (MAC) in Korea, the 2.69-sq.-mile (6.98-sq.-km) Central Open Space is designed as an "arable kitchen-garden park." The concept for the park integrates the area's existing traditional farming activities and a freshwater lake with an artificial beach and lawn-covered "piers" that support artists' studios, sound gardens, and leisure activities.

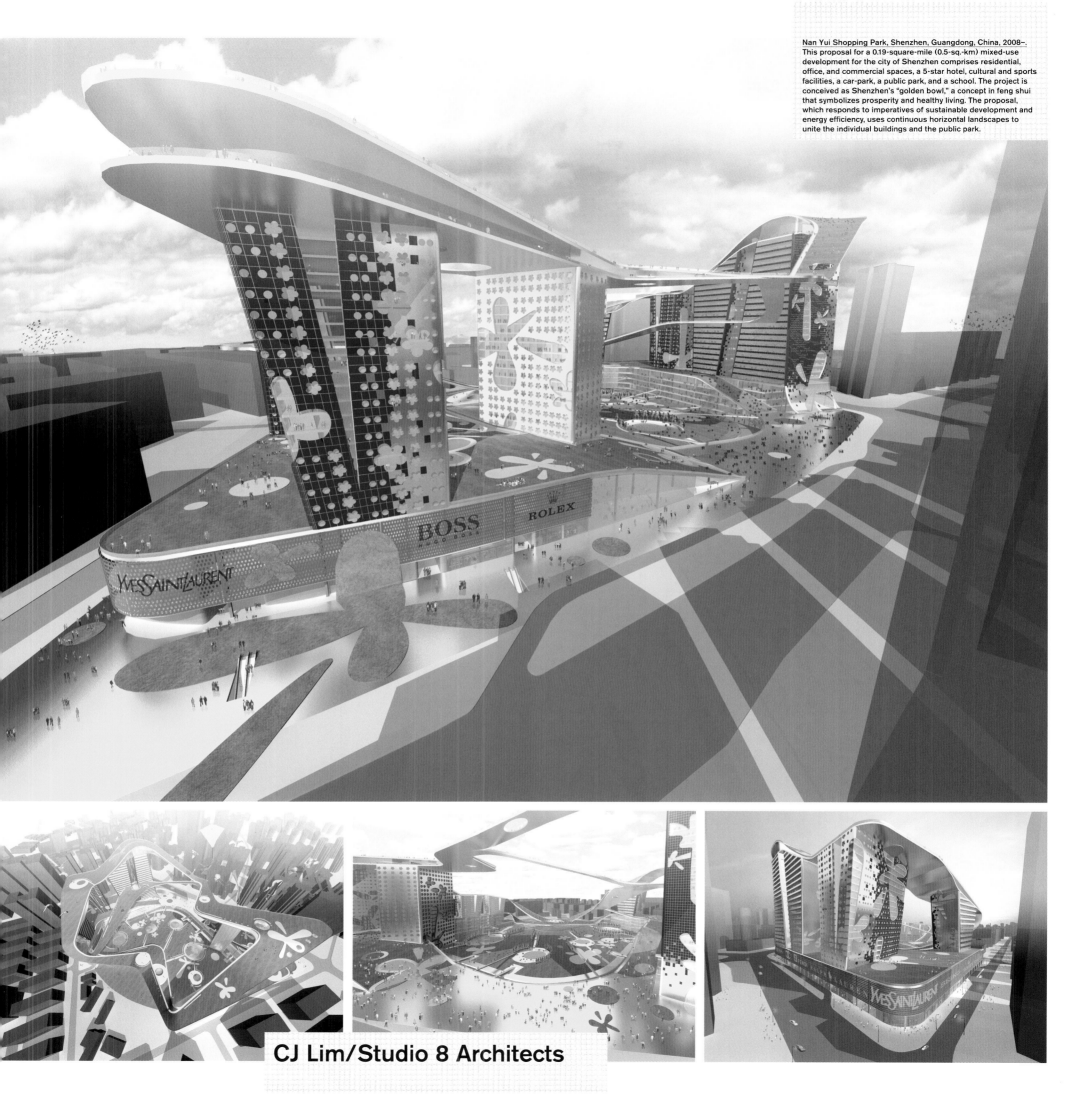

Nan Yui Shopping Park, Shenzhen, Guangdong, China, 2008–. This proposal for a 0.19-square-mile (0.5-sq.-km) mixed-use development for the city of Shenzhen comprises residential, office, and commercial spaces, a 5-star hotel, cultural and sports facilities, a car-park, a public park, and a school. The project is conceived as Shenzhen's "golden bowl," a concept in feng shui that symbolizes prosperity and healthy living. The proposal, which responds to imperatives of sustainable development and energy efficiency, uses continuous horizontal landscapes to unite the individual buildings and the public park.

CJ Lim/Studio 8 Architects

Paulo David | Madeira P

Born on the Portuguese island of Madeira, Paulo David graduated from Lisbon Technical University in 1989 and remained in Portugal's capital until 1996, acquiring professional experience in the office of Gonçalo Byrne. That year he returned to Madeira, opening his own firm in the island's capital, Funchal, where he also worked part-time as an urban planner for the local government.

Though David received a local prize for the design of a preschool, Creche Primaveras (Funchal, 1994), he did not receive international attention until the completion in 2004 of an arts center on a cliff overlooking the ocean in the township of Calheta. An abstract, sculptural addition in basalt to the already existing Casa das Mudas, the center became an instant icon that enhanced the dramatic scenery with its hermetic carved volumes. It received much recognition, including a nomination for the prestigious European Mies van der Rohe Award in 2005.

The architect's second major building, the Salinas Swimming Pools in Câmara de Lobos—also located on a magnificent site on the rugged coast of Madeira—was launched in 2007 by Marmomacc's International Award for Architecture in Stone, and was also distinguished by the Spanish FAD Award. David's Swimming Pools comprise an inspired landscape project that includes a seafront promenade; they gracefully introduce artificial geometries into the grand theater of nature on this majestic Atlantic island.

Continuing the tradition of Portuguese architecture that achieved international acclaim through figures like Álvaro Siza or Eduardo Souto de Moura, David pursues a demanding path of material elegance and tactile refinement with his tectonic works in the midst of the ocean. // Luis Fernández-Galiano

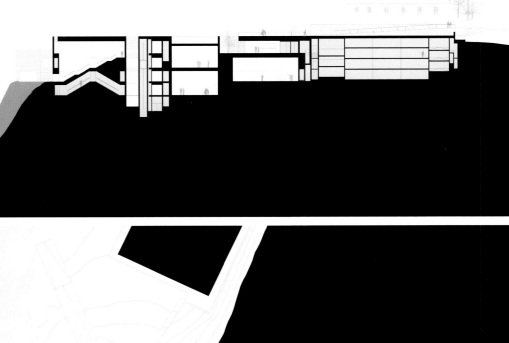

Casa das Mudas Art Center, Calheta, Madeira, Portugal, 2002–4.
The Art Center is situated 600 ft. (180 m) above the Atlantic Ocean,
on a volcanic basalt promontory. Two terraces of local black
basalt jut out from the cliff, with sunken patios and light wells
that allude to the stepped agricultural terraces common in rural
Madeira. The Center includes a museum, library, bookshop,
auditorium, and a restaurant.

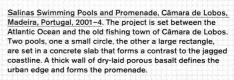

Salinas Swimming Pools and Promenade, Câmara de Lobos, Madeira, Portugal, 2001–4. The project is set between the Atlantic Ocean and the old fishing town of Câmara de Lobos. Two pools, one a small circle, the other a large rectangle, are set in a concrete slab that forms a contrast to the jagged coastline. A thick wall of dry-laid porous basalt defines the urban edge and forms the promenade.

Salinas Restaurant and Garden, Câmara de Lobos, Madeira, Portugal, 2004–6. The restaurant, part of the Salinas Swimming Pools and Promenade site, sits atop a cliff that juts out over the Atlantic Ocean. A glazed box clad in wooden slats to filter the strong sunlight, it offers panoramic views from its long terrace. A metal service core houses the kitchen and connects the restaurant to a rooftop garden.

Paulo David

Dellekamp Arquitectos   México D.F. MEX

AR 58, México D.F., Mexico, 1999–2002. This apartment building consists of three fronts on two small side streets and the busy Alfonso Reyes Avenue. The volume of each apartment is rendered visible on the facade with a distinct surface material—white or gray aluminum, smooth or corrugated. The living spaces face toward the streets, with balconies and open views, while the service areas of the apartments are distributed around an interior patio facing north.

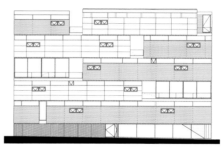

Dellekamp Arquitectos, located in the La Condesa neighborhood of México D.F., was founded by Derek Dellekamp in 1999. As a collective of related disciplines, the members of the studio are able to break down traditional barriers by integrating the design and construction processes. This allows them to provide intelligent, practical forms as a solution to architectural problems. With refreshing dignity, the firm achieve's the poetic dictation of a symbiotic relationship between use and form.

This symbiosis is well demonstrated in AR 58, Dellekamp's apartment building at number 58, Alfonso Reyes Avenue in México D.F. The design takes advantage of the site, which is opened on three sides, by creating a stunning exterior that commands attention to each of the three facades. The interplay of the rectilinear, stacked volumes—differentiated by varying materials and textures—creates negative spaces to beautiful effect, while allowing for exterior patios and necessary support functions. Dellekamp has a remarkable ability to derive form from practical considerations and distill it down to its purest shape.

This sensitivity to form is best expressed in the Villa 14 designed for the Ordos 100 project in Nei Mongol, China. Dellekamp Arquitectos's almost elliptical form has a simplicity that is evident in equal measure on the interior and in the poetic simplicity of the exterior. Circulation inside the building is redirected with reversing curves and, simultaneously, exterior spaces are created within the container.

A brilliant architect, Dellekamp designs with great intelligence, sensitivity, and humor. His designs are attuned to the user's need, while maintaining a bold dignity. A kind of physical poetry, Dellekamp's buildings integrate form, language, and meaning. // Ai Weiwei

CB 30, México D.F., Mexico, 2003–6.
This residential building consists of three
apartments facing the street, and a
two-story house in the back that opens
onto an interior patio. The public areas
are contained in a single space that
opens outward—to the street and the
patio. Obstructions were eliminated
through structural geometry that allowed
for a column-free space nearly 50-ft.
(15-m) long.

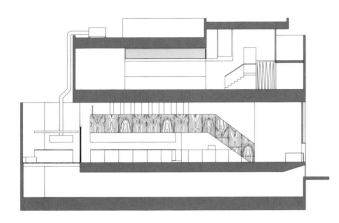

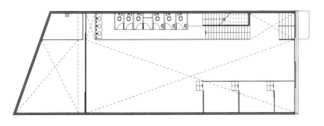

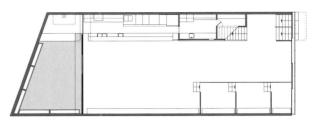

La Capital, México D.F., Mexico, 2008.
This building contains a bar, a restaurant,
and a music venue, each on one floor
organized as open, column-free spaces.
The style, while decidedly modern, plays
with retro influences from the fifties.

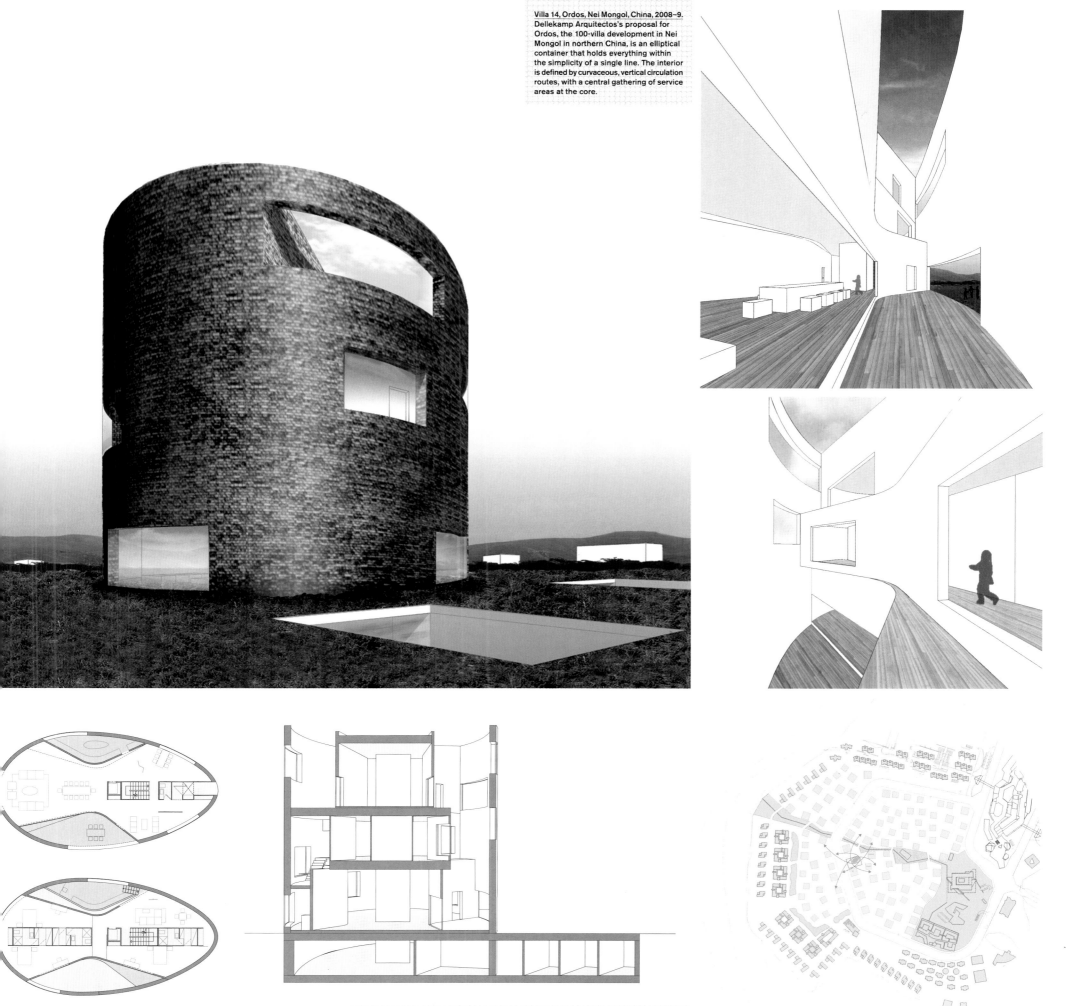

Villa 14, Ordos, Nei Mongol, China, 2008–9. Dellekamp Arquitectos's proposal for Ordos, the 100-villa development in Nei Mongol in northern China, is an elliptical container that holds everything within the simplicity of a single line. The interior is defined by curvaceous, vertical circulation routes, with a central gathering of service areas at the core.

Dellekamp Arquitectos

The American architecture critic Jeffrey Kipnis once described Frank Gehry's work as possessing a certain "singularity"—upon entering his work one is arrested by its sheer comprehensive resolution. It is a capacity not born of the digital revolution but of cardboard, Scotch tape, a soda can or two, and the occasional dab of super-glue—that is to say, the architectural model. Like Gehry, the Australian architecture firm Durbach Block Architects develops some of its best ideas in the process of moving relentlessly between models and drawings. One's spatial imagination seems to plug the gap between model and building so much better when that model exerts its own physical presence. A visit to the office of Durbach Block Architects, then, is not unlike a Lilliputian voyage through a cardboard world of compelling completed projects, as well as many more compelling uncompleted projects.

Within this oeuvre of apartments, houses, offices, and some recent civic-scale landscape projects, it is undoubtedly the residential designs of Durbach Block Architects that have received the most attention: luminescent works within which the cardinal elements of light, form, and space lyrically intersect. They have no "style," no signature parti or rhetorical gestures; no desperate appeals to the iconic or predictable materials or color palates. There are, however, allegiances. Traces of Alvar Aalto, Jørn Utzon, and Josep Antoni Coderch are discernible in works such as Spry House, Holman House, and the Sussan Sportsgirl Headquarters. But each project is invented anew. Each is an opportunity to pull, stretch, twist, and reconfigure the site, the brief, and indeed the practice, often literally. It is a supple process that begins each project with first principles.

Holman House, its plan an assembly of fluid parts honed to capture views but also to create dynamic interior spaces, represents Durbach Block Architects at its agile best. It reveals not only a figurative tension, between the dynamic plan and elastic volumes, but also an almost ethical tension between the virtues of accom-modation and site responsiveness: enclosure and view poised in balance.

In this manner, Durbach Block Architects registers a resistance to the picturesque topography of Sydney, to which many architects surrender. It is a city hostage to its virtues: the harbor, the bush, the wild rugged coast. In architecture, this landscape has promoted complacency: the meaningless elegance of a white box with a view. And while Melbourne architecture is often scorned for replacing the picturesque with constructed cultural narratives, Durbach Block Architects finds a balance that defies either extreme, making it not only one of Australia's best practices working today but also one that does so by defining its own creatively charged, architecturally fluid language.
// Andrew Mackenzie

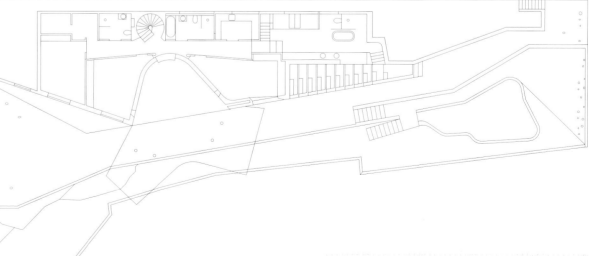

Holman House, Sydney, New South Wales, Australia, 2000–2004. Situated on the edge of a cliff 230-ft. (70-m) high, the house, in plan, refers to Picasso's painting *The Bather*. It contains a complex series of fluid living spaces set within a meandering perimeter that arcs and folds in response to sun, landscape, and views. Living and dining areas cantilever out over the ocean, allowing dramatic views along the coast. The lower floor forms a base that is built from rough stone walls like an extension of the cliff below.

Sussan Sportsgirl Headquarters, Melbourne, Victoria, Australia, 2006–7. This project is the renovation of a clothing company's corporate headquarters, for which the architects reconceived three existing buildings as one, planned around a new central garden. A new entry, reception area, and private art gallery become the public face on the street, while the 54,000 sq. ft. (5000 sq. m) of general offices face south, overlooking the river.

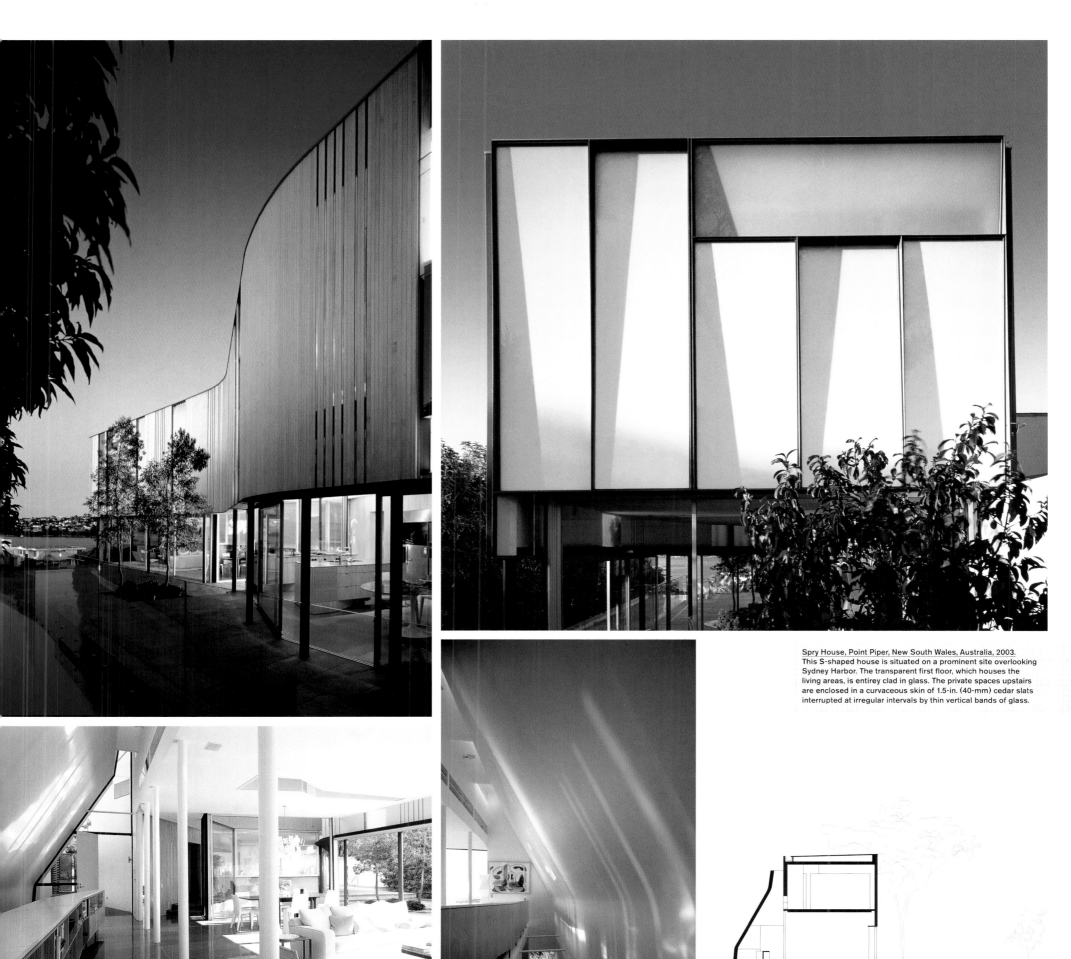

Spry House, Point Piper, New South Wales, Australia, 2003.
This S-shaped house is situated on a prominent site overlooking
Sydney Harbor. The transparent first floor, which houses the
living areas, is entirey clad in glass. The private spaces upstairs
are enclosed in a curvaceous skin of 1.5-in. (40-mm) cedar slats
interrupted at irregular intervals by thin vertical bands of glass.

Durbach Block Architects

Durisch + Nolli Architetti　Lugano CH

M.A.X. Museo, Chiasso, Switzerland, 2002–5. The museum is dedicated to the work of twentieth-century Swiss graphic designer Max Huber. It consists of a pre-existing hangar with four large roof lights, and a new building, with two stories and a basement, occupying a 30-ft. (9-m) wide site. A plaza, intended for outdoor exhibitions, leads to the main entrance under the cantilevered floor of the gallery.

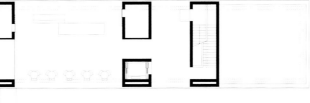

The term "living architecture" can be used to define Pia Durisch and Aldo Nolli's approach to design, as one that grows out of everyday life and is closely related to their own biographies. From the beginning their work lay between two precise frames of reference: the modern tradition of architecture in the canton of Ticino, Switzerland, and the tactile and minimalist architecture that came from north of the Alps. In the 1980s Durisch and Nolli trained at the Institute of Technology (ETH) Zürich, where they were influenced by important Swiss architects such as Dolf Schnebli, Flora Ruchat, and Fabio Reinhart. They subsequently worked first in the office of Santiago Calatrava, then in the practice of Durisch's father at Riva San Vitale in Ticino. Their work is nurtured by a concern for detail and precise construction. Another factor is the importance they gave to place, not only as a unique physical and cultural context, but also in Aldo Rossi's sense, as something inhabited and bound up with collective memory, made up of "encounters, impressions and images." This is an inseparable part of Ticinese architecture in recent decades, which is distinguished by a responsible attitude toward the management of the city and the environment. Since 1993, when the young architects established their own firm, their output has developed into a coherent oeuvre, rigorous and open to a wide range of influences.

For the M.A.X. Museo in Chiasso dedicated to the work of Swiss graphic designer Max Huber, Durisch + Nolli Architetti presented a "magic box" with dynamic, translucent facades, and a bright, transparent atmosphere on the interior. The work confronts the lackluster character of the suburb where it is located. For the SSIC Professional Center in Gordola, the architects transformed a topographical constraint—the need to elevate the construction to protect local residents from flooding—into a resource. They created a single building generated by the serial repetition of a small number of structures running lengthwise along a raised deck. This "ark," characterized by its thin copper skin and the sharp-edged profile of its shed roof, contains flexible classrooms and laboratories. A current project for the Federal Courthouse in Bellinzona guarantees the typological integrity of the existing building with a spatial solution enhanced by overhead lighting. Finally, in the Student Housing for the University of Luzern the articulation comes from the perfect "domino-like" sequence of the plan. The restraint evident in the interiors is the outcome of synthesizing conflicting demands, which makes the architectural features subtle, but clear to the residents themselves—this patient reconciliation is increasingly apparent in their work. The firm's approach is always balanced by solid competence, while their architecture, strongly committed to ensuring continuity with its roots, symbolically occupies a border area, and for this very reason contains unprecedented creative potential.
// Mercedes Daguerre

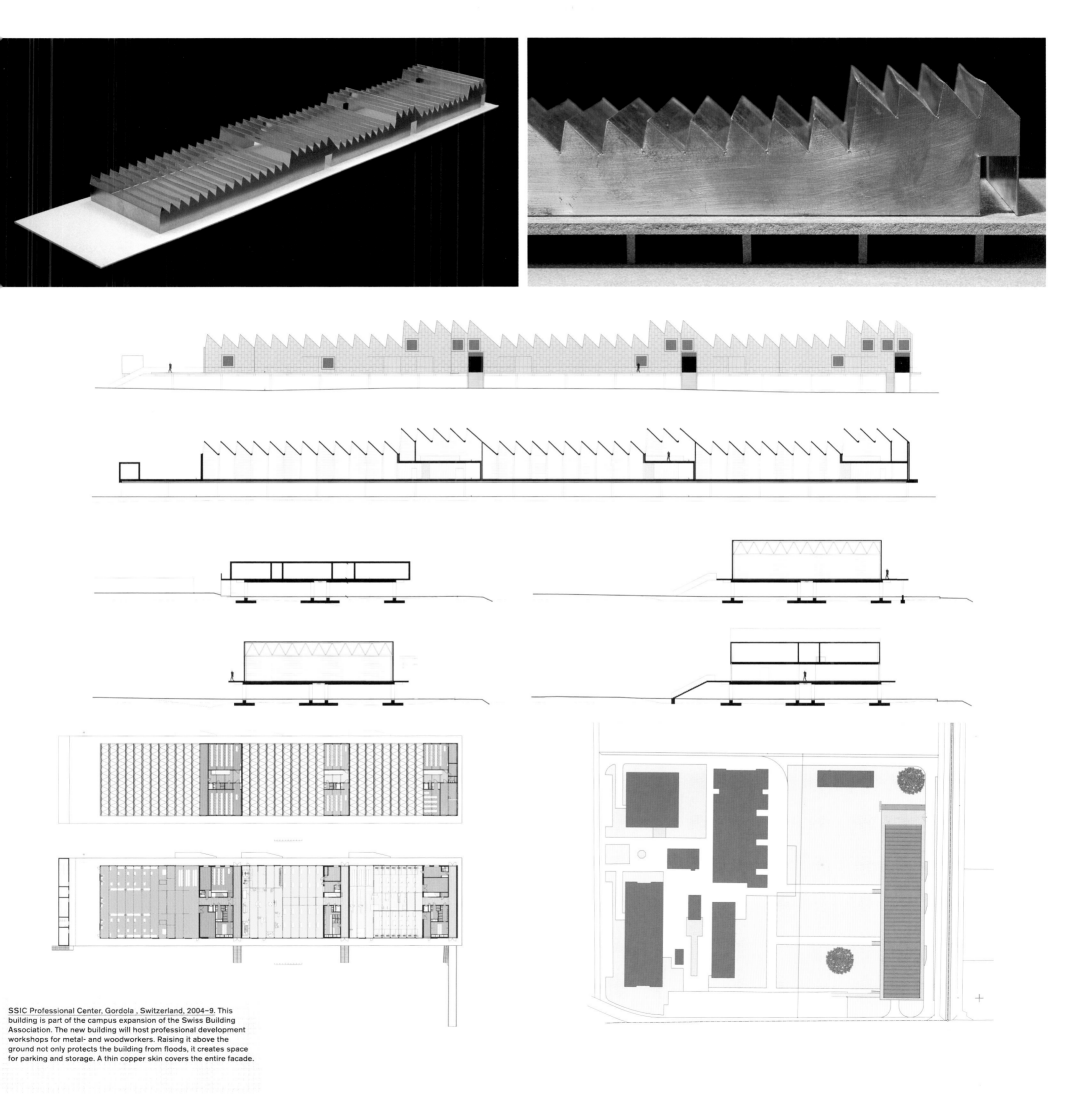

SSIC Professional Center, Gordola , Switzerland, 2004–9. This building is part of the campus expansion of the Swiss Building Association. The new building will host professional development workshops for metal- and woodworkers. Raising it above the ground not only protects the building from floods, it creates space for parking and storage. A thin copper skin covers the entire facade.

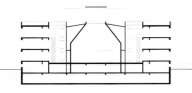
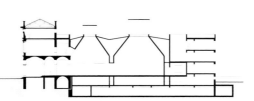
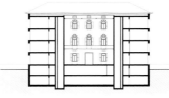
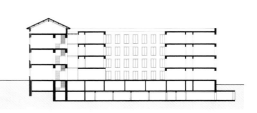

Federal Courthouse, Bellinzona, Switzerland, 2008–12. The project consists of an expansion and reconfiguration of two historic structures in Bellinzona, creating a new complex for the federal court.

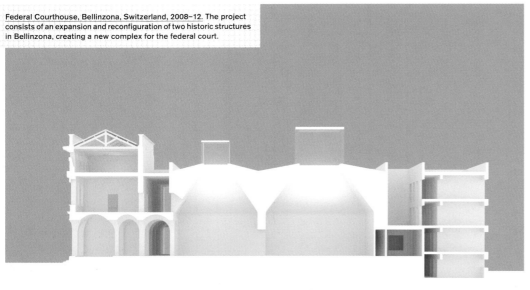
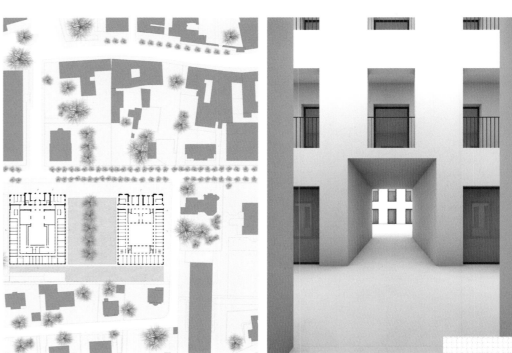

Student Housing, Luzern, Switzerland, 2008–12. In response to the high demand for low-cost housing, the private Luzern Student Mentor Foundation embarked on the construction of residences for 280 students and affiliates of the University of Luzern. The apartments, of various sizes, allow a high degree of adaptability to the needs and the requests of the inhabitants.

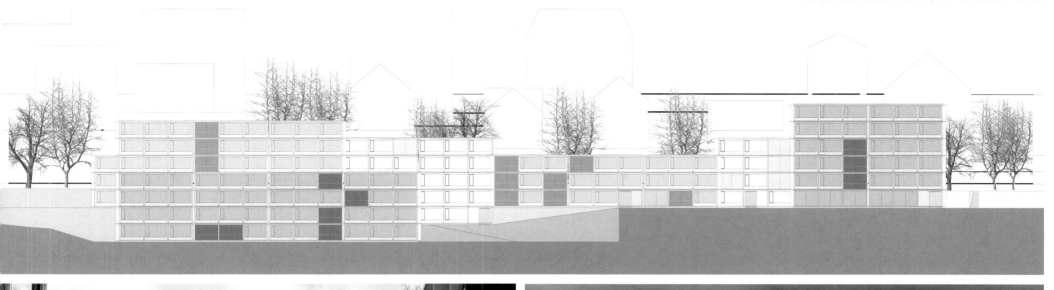

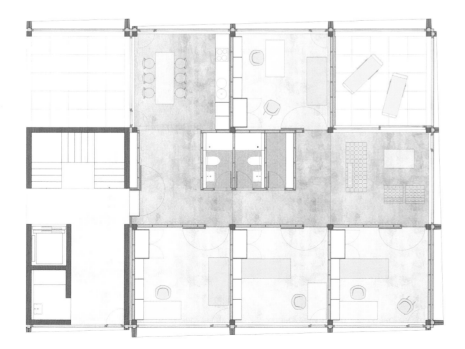

Durisch + Nolli Architetti

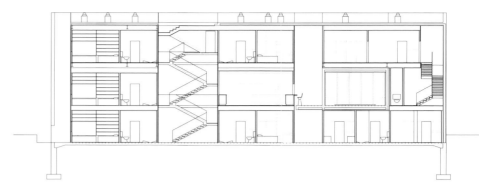

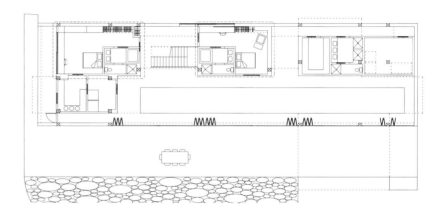

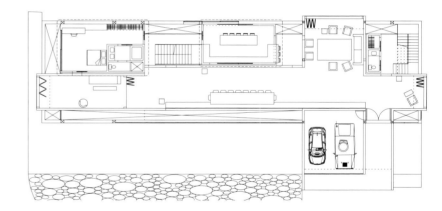

Ordos 100 Villa, Ordos, Nei Mongol, China, 2008—9. The Villa, one of a hundred to be commissioned for a new district in Ordos in northern China, is organized as a series of concentric boxes. An outer box handles passive heating and cooling, and an inner box serves as a large open space for events and exhibitions. Stacks of boxes in between these two layers provide identical apartments for family members and guests, as well as visiting artists, commissioned to alter the panelized components of the boxes.

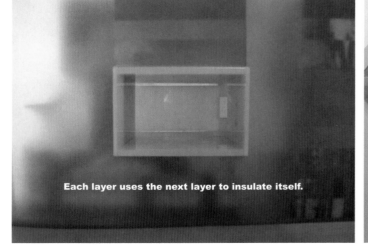

Each layer uses the next layer to insulate itself.

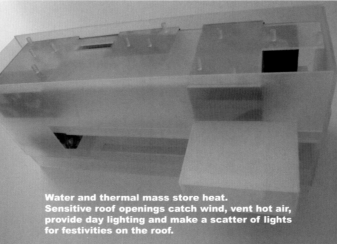

Water and thermal mass store heat. Sensitive roof openings catch wind, vent hot air, provide day lighting and make a scatter of lights for festivities on the roof.

Temperature regulation can be confined to an outer box equipped with radiant heating/cooling and super-insulated concrete.

The *Love Boat* cruise between South and North Korea; Maharishi Vedic City in Iowa; the urban-scale greenhouses of El Ejido, Spain; Dubai's media and technology "cities"; and the spectacular destruction of has-been resort hotels on Las Vegas's strip: This eclectic chain of destinations are not obvious objects of architectural criticism, since they are all but bereft of what one might conventionally call "significant buildings." But it is precisely this surreptitious significance that seems to captivate architect, writer, and educator Keller Easterling's attention in her ongoing research and proposals. She selects her subjects not for what they look like but for how they perform in early-twenty-first-century geopolitics and geo-economics.

Easterling refers to this wayward geography as a series of "difficult political situations." And rather than focus exclusively on architecture, as one might expect an architectural theorist to do, she prefers to look at "spatial products," a term that is at once assuredly anodyne and also opaquely capitalist. Golf courses become executive toys. Ten-million-dollar island retreats are weekend getaways. Easterling surfs closer to the rhetoric-cum-mantras of neoliberalism than the trusted anxiety of leftist Marxist critiques of the capitalist system. In this way, she is as contemporary as the world around us appears to be, where forms of resistance are instantaneously coopted by advertising campaigns for running shoes or sugar-free cola drinks.

It is interesting to note that Easterling's pre-architecture career was devoted to the theater and acting. Her interest in role-play, enunciation, and the politics of speech seem to come from these disciplines. The Western avant-garde in the twentieth century tried to kill aesthetic or symbolic obviousness, and replace it with the heroically *unobvious*. Easterling makes visible the return of obviousness in the burgeoning economy of symbolic and real capital. Shapes and outlines of man-made islands, elite villas, and business parks are defiantly Platonic, or even archetypal, in the Jungian sense. She locates the heroic transformational dimensions of our world not in modish architectural forms, but in the nameless masses who choreograph internet cabling under ocean beds. There is no easy prescription in Easterling's architecture parables, no clear moral waters to wade through in the knowledge that it's only a Disney ride, the sharks won't bite, and the mermaids will triumph. // Shumon Basar

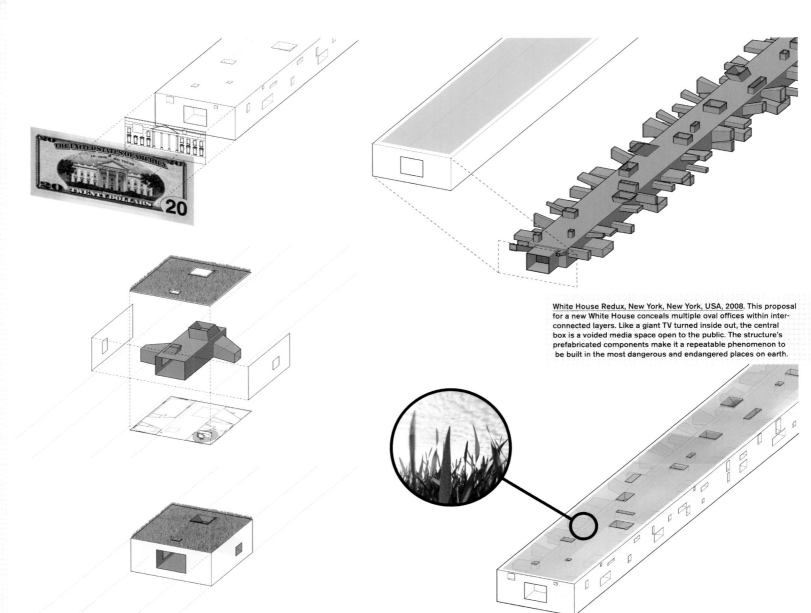

White House Redux, New York, New York, USA, 2008. This proposal for a new White House conceals multiple oval offices within interconnected layers. Like a giant TV turned inside out, the central box is a voided media space open to the public. The structure's prefabricated components make it a repeatable phenomenon to be built in the most dangerous and endangered places on earth.

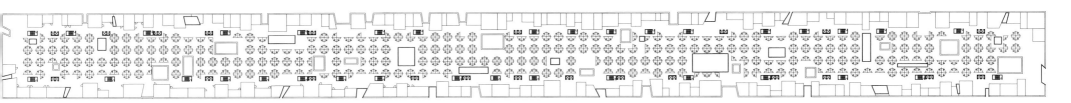

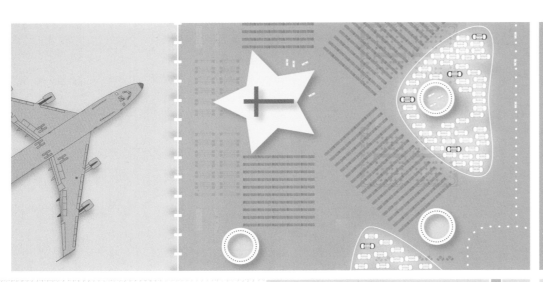

Floor, New York, New York, USA, 2008. Floor is a research project that investigates the impact of new vehicles on architectural morphology. Given the merger of cars and elevators in warehouses, ports, and other logistics environments, the research argues that the common floor, which provides navigational instructions for these automated vehicles, is the new germ of architectural design. Here, floors are horizontal elevator shafts and loud graphic surfaces, which are analogous with what used to be the exterior space of parking and roadway.

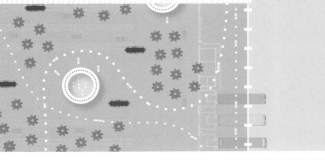

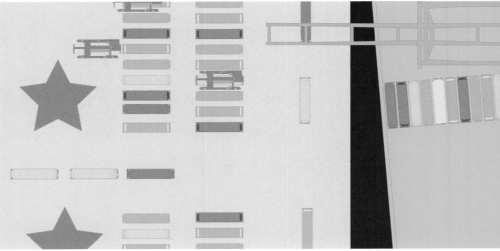

"I am not an architect, but you would probably want make the horizontal and vertical shafts like structure....like floors and columns."

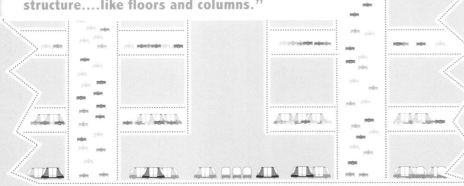

"New fuels and new vehicles have no exhaust and so no front or back. They can be stored anywhere, so there is not much difference between parking lot, elevator and road."

Floor: a few facts (excerpt)

"See, basically, the car and the elevator are merging.

Both are borrowing technology from automated vehicles used in warehouses and ports...

The floor is the most important surface.

Vehicles read graphic patterns on the floor or transponders embedded in the floor. Transponders use magnets, gps and lasers. Sometimes the floors have loud patterns. ...

There are a lot of new vehicles.
My favorite automated vehicle is the one that comes toward you really slowly with a giant roll of cellophane.

New fuels and new vehicles have no exhaust and so no front or back.
With new automated parking technology, they can be stored anywhere in a building.
New vehicles also move horizontally and vertically, so there is not so much separation between elevator, parking lot and road.

What I mean is that the floor is also a passageway, like a horizontal elevator shaft.
I am not an architect, but you would probably want to make the horizontal and vertical shafts act like the structure...floors and pillars."

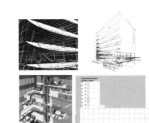

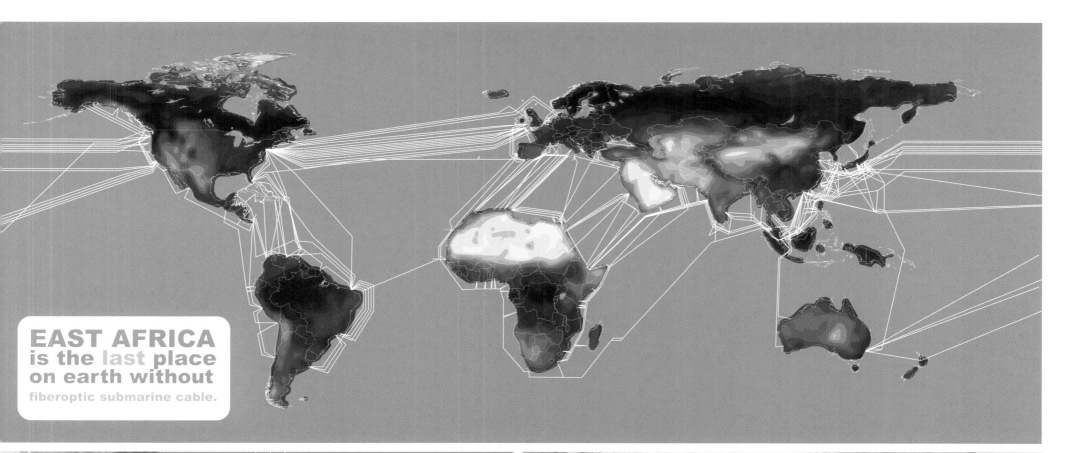

EAST AFRICA
is the last place on earth without
fiberoptic submarine cable.

Over a decade of planning has yet to deliver submarine cable to Kenya, but at the moment, several competing cable schemes are underway.

TEAMS

EASSy

Seacom

Mombasa

Broadband/Month

Kenya	$7500
US	$200

25 calling stations/mo.

Kenya	$17,500
competing countries	$600-900

 "We want to change this country to become a lion and fight the tigers."

—Dr. Bitange Ndemo

In Kenya, the road between Nairobi and Mombasa is lined with—virtually lit by— advertisements for mobile telecoms in the region. Along the same road, a billboard publishes a 40% unemployment rate.

Mombasa
Nairobi Road
The backhaul or terrestrial fiberoptic cables will follow the Mombasa Nairobi Road and parallel the 19th century rail of the British East Africa Company.

Mombasa

East Africa is already being considered as the new "best kept secret" in global offshoring.

THE (Athi River)
ANTI-ZONE
As Kenya vies for some of the world's BPO industry, the most predictable urban outcropping of fiberoptic cable is the free zone. Kenya's Athi River EPZ is something like an anti-zone. Far from forbidding strikes and labor organization, Athi River promotes labor unions and serves as a place for labor consolidation and exchange.

Nairobi

Cable, New York, New York, USA, 2008. East Africa, one of the most populous areas of the world, has no fiber-optic submarine cable link, and broadband costs twenty to forty times more than it does in the United States. Cable is a research drawing that imagines urban consequences linked to the three cable projects currently making their way to Mombasa, Kenya. It suggests techniques for leveraging global financing and free zone formation toward better labor conditions on the road between Mombasa and the Kenyan capital of Nairobi.

  IFC

RCIP
Africa Regional Communications Infrastructure Program is part of an initiative by the World Bank and the International Finance Corporation to provide "catalytic funding" to organize and leverage private money for ICT development in Africa. The program works on two fronts promoting the various undersea cable initiatives as well as the reach and position of terrestrial infrastructure.

Nairobi

"Africa comprises 20% of the world's land mass, contains 12% of its population, but accounts for only 2% of the world's telecommunications.

Keller Easterling

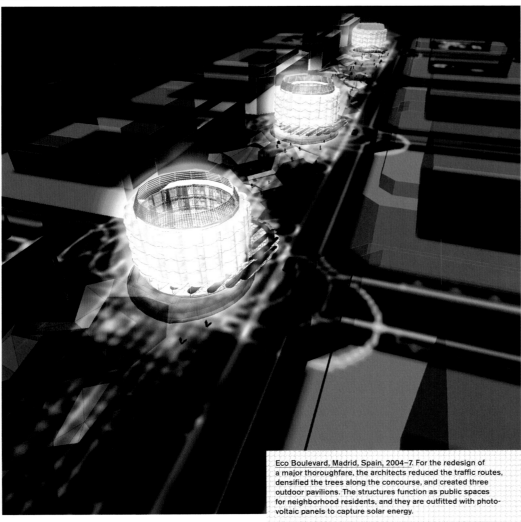

Eco Boulevard, Madrid, Spain, 2004–7. For the redesign of a major thoroughfare, the architects reduced the traffic routes, densified the trees along the concourse, and created three outdoor pavilions. The structures function as public spaces for neighborhood residents, and they are outfitted with photo-voltaic panels to capture solar energy.

Committed both to research and to alternative design, ecosistema urbano was launched in Madrid in 2000 by Belinda Tato and José Luis Vallejo; by 2008 the office had expanded to eight architects and engineers, working together in a way that reflects the collective nature of their name, which translates as "urban ecosystem." Theirs is no conventional "green architecture," however, as the name might imply, but rather a version of "action architecture," inspired by figures like the Brazilian Jaime Lerner or the French team of Lacaton & Vassal, in which sustainability issues intersect with strategic planning, cost effectiveness, and the reality of contemporary security issues.

In 2007 the firm completed what is its most significant work to date: the Eco Boulevard, a series of cylindrical towers with vertical gardens in a rather barren new district in the southern part of Madrid. The towers—freestanding structures in the main traffic and pedestrian thoroughfare—provide shade, informal meeting spaces, and a sense of identity for the inhabitants of the social housing around them, becoming both an environmental statement and an urban icon. Justly celebrated, the Eco Boulevard has received numerous awards and distinctions, and has given the young and socially engaged practice international visibility. Their many projects—some of them initiated by the firm—have twice earned the European Holcim Award, perhaps the most prestigious in the field of sustainable construction, which is the global goal of this unusual practice. // Luis Fernández-Galiano

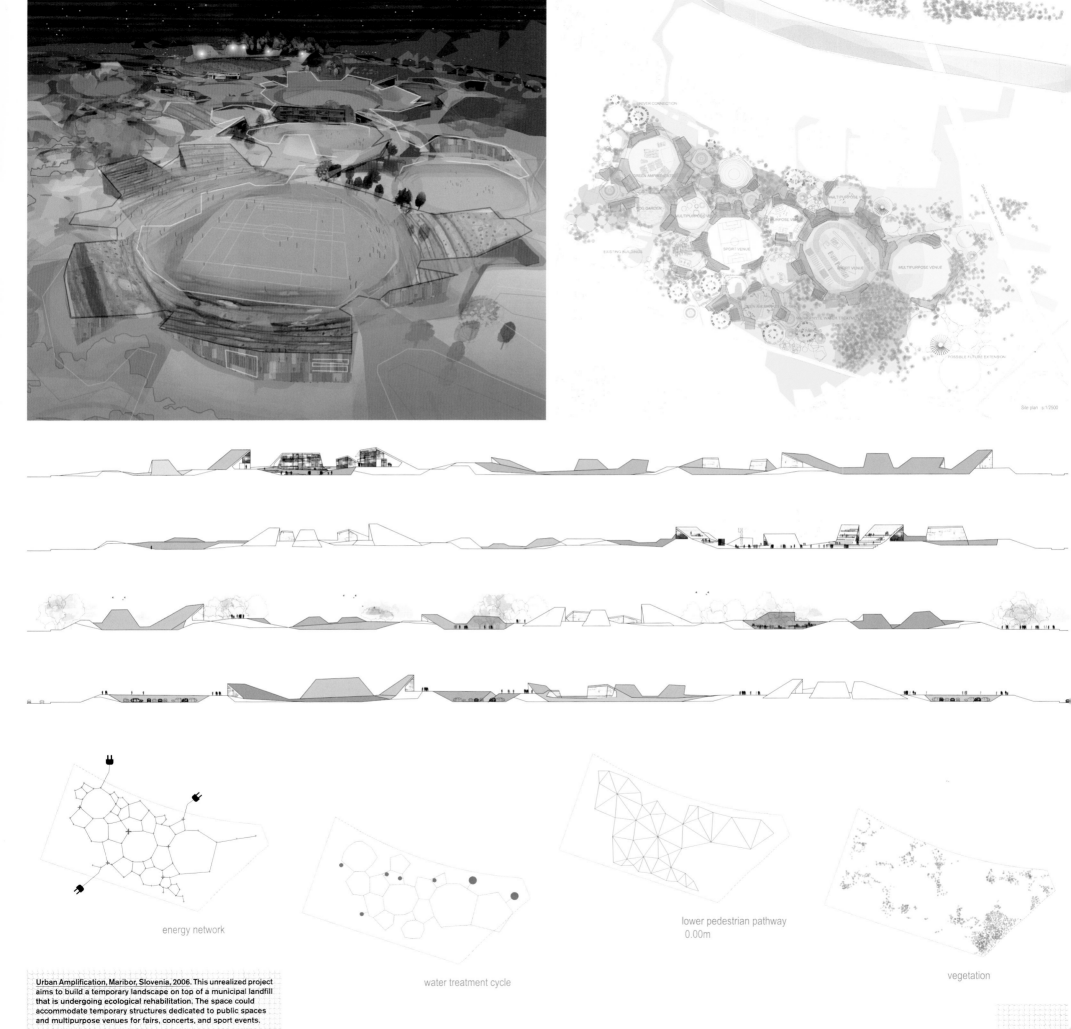

energy network

water treatment cycle

lower pedestrian pathway
0.00m

vegetation

Urban Amplification, Maribor, Slovenia, 2006. This unrealized project aims to build a temporary landscape on top of a municipal landfill that is undergoing ecological rehabilitation. The space could accommodate temporary structures dedicated to public spaces and multipurpose venues for fairs, concerts, and sport events.

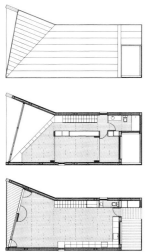

House of Steel and Wood, Ranón, Spain, 2003–5. This private house is a contemporary interpretation of the traditional vernacular architecture of northern Spain, which respects the forest environment and is adapted to local climatic conditions. A collapsible and recyclable structure, made of a mix of steel and local pine wood, the house is detached from the ground and is supported at only four points to minimize its impact on the environment.

ecosistema urbano

Estudio Teddy Cruz | San Diego USA

Hudson 2+4, Hudson, New York, USA, 2007–. This project, in collaboration with the PARC Foundation, conceives of housing as an economic and social engine that amplifies the role of communities in producing new forms of ownership, economies, and social organization. A series of housing prototypes will be distributed across downtown Hudson, reclaiming vacant sites and leftover easements. Each prototype comprises a mixture of social services, managed by a coalition of nonprofit organizations, as well as community gardens, collective kitchens, and shared tool sheds.

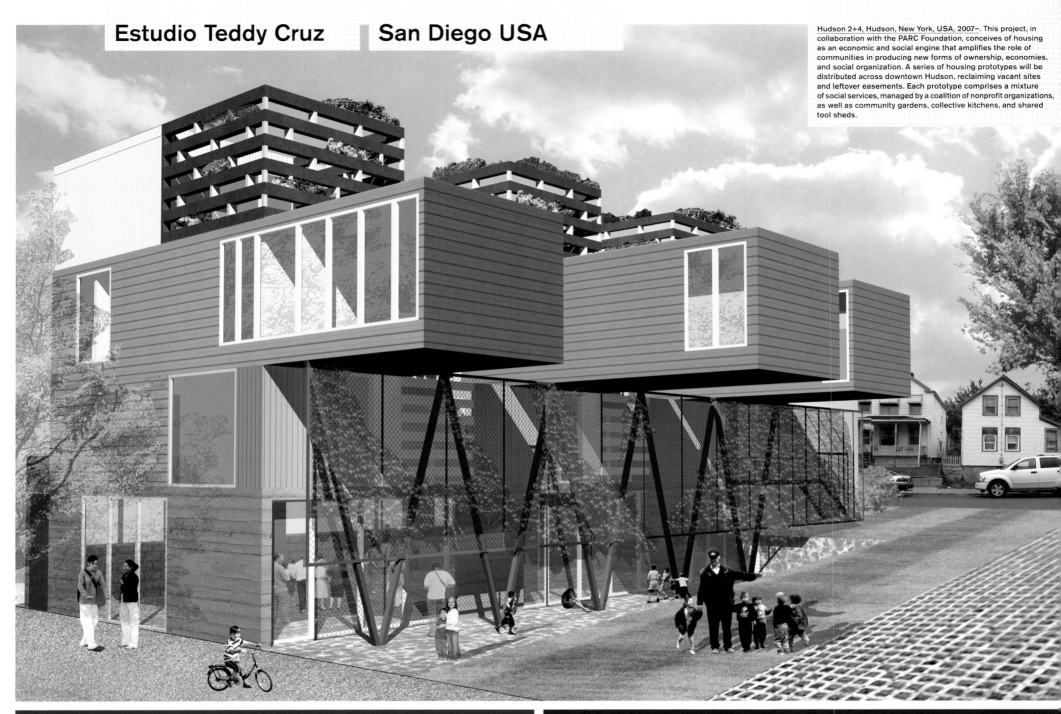

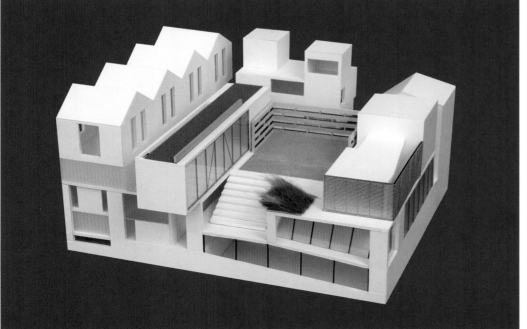

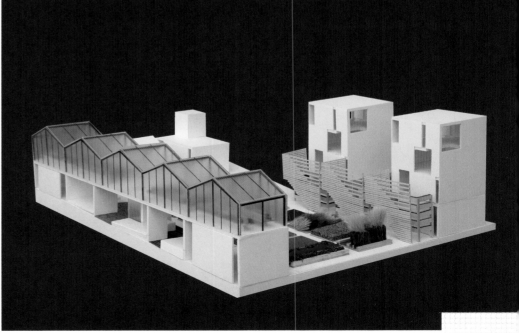

What will the role of architecture be in the twenty-first century? Will it be a manifestation of political activism? A form of artistic expression? The flashpoint of geopolitical tensions? A frontline combatant in the climate crisis? Most likely, all of these and more still. Teddy Cruz believes that in a post-9/11 society, "our institutions of architecture representation and display have lost their socio-political relevance." This is the premise on which Estudio Teddy Cruz, based in San Diego, California, is predicated: to remain relevant, it is the architectural practice itself— and not the architectural artifact—that must be reinvented from scratch. With the population concentrated in urban areas having finally surpassed those in rural (or, perhaps more accurately, exurban) areas, will architecture rise to the unequivocal challenges looming on the horizon?

The work of Estudio Teddy Cruz to date is inextricably tied to the spatial politics of the border between the United States and Mexico; what is background noise for the rest of America is a matter of day-to-day existence in San Diego. The Tijuana–San Diego border is the busiest land port of entry in the world, with more than 131,000 legal passages daily; trans-border labor is vital to the southern Californian economy. Informal architecture and informal economies have flourished, triggering bottom-up innovation. Cruz's research uses these as a starting point, seeking to engage and optimize preexistent tendencies. The office's design work, deeply rooted in day-to-day life both south and north of the border, pays as much attention to the socioeconomic, political, and infrastructural implications of buildings as to their formal manifestation. With Manufactured Sites, Cruz offers a model for densification in suburban areas; his intervention is little more than a framework that can be progressively adapted by the recipient to his or her needs for expansion. Instead of resisting the natural forces of perpetual change and adaptation, Manufactured Sites embraces these tendencies, transforming them into an effective and economical—albeit almost invisible—force for improvement of daily life. Such projects are driven less by the desire for formal innovation than a desire to embrace and empower the natural resourcefulness of these communities.

As Cruz points out, the most experimental work in housing in the United States is not in the hands of private development or government. Rather, it is being carried out by progressive, community-based nonprofit organizations such as Casa Familiar, working in the border neighborhood of San Ysidro, California. Cruz's collaboration with Casa Familiar led to the development of specific proposals for a number of new buildings in the San Ysidro area, but more importantly, it led to a strategy of socially integrated self-development that would ultimately empower the community to become a developer of alternative dwelling prototypes for its own housing stock. // Joseph Grima

Manufactured Sites, Tijuana, Mexico, 2005–. In collaboration with the NGO Casa Familiar, the firm designed an informal framework for affordable housing that addresses issues of the California–Mexico border. The goal is to get resources and structural support systems into Tijuana's impoverished neighborhoods by using recycled materials brought from San Diego that can be reassembled in Tijuana.

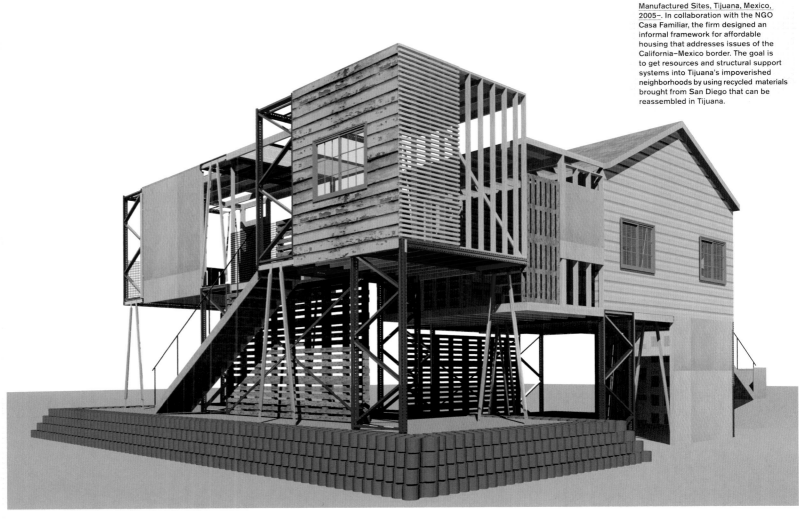

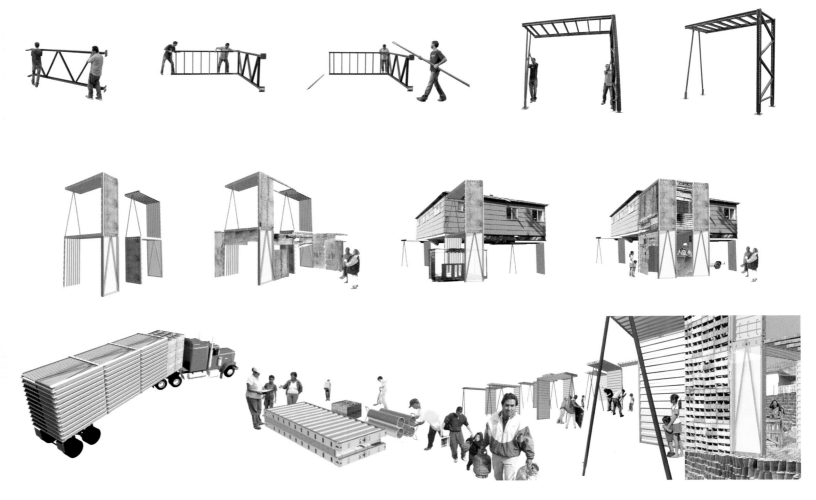

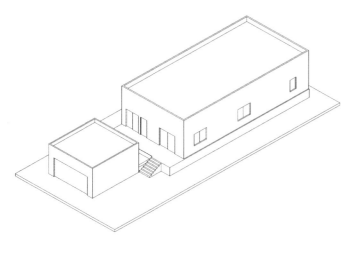

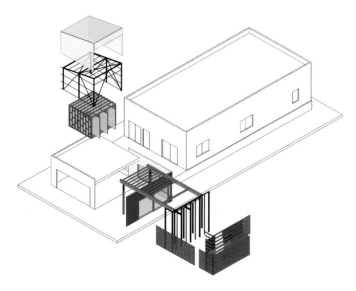

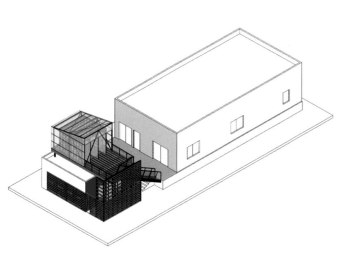

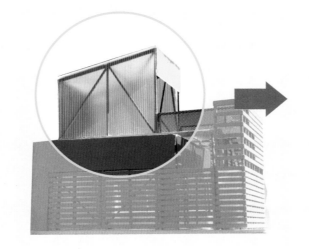

Mike Davis's Writing Studio, San Diego, California, USA, 2005.
Author Mike Davis, a frequent collaborator with Estudio Teddy
Cruz, commissioned the firm to transform his existing garage
into a writing studio and sleeping porch, and by doing so create
a viable prototype for advancing density in the city. The project
explores a formal organization that "breaks" the generic mass
of a building into a series of interstitial spaces or environments
that can accommodate a variety of uses and mediate between
inside and outside.

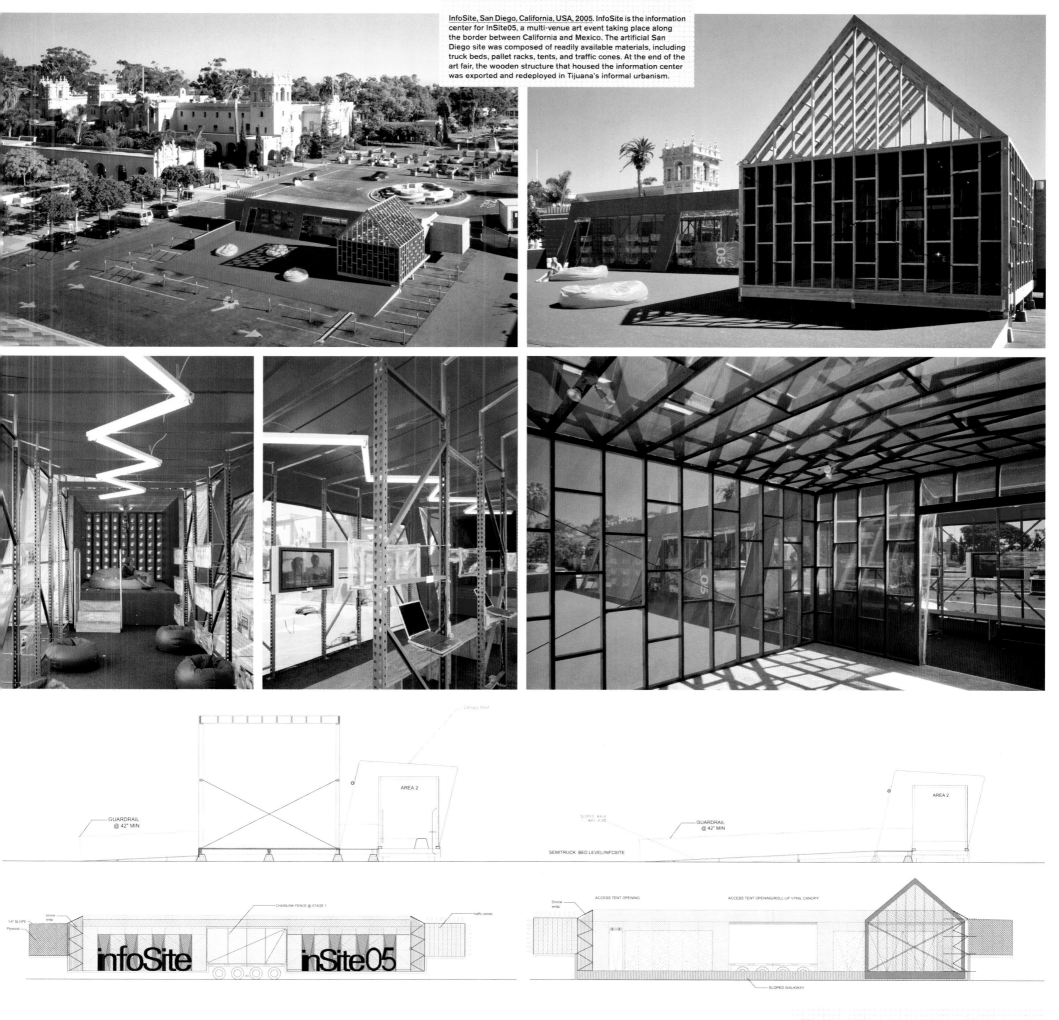

InfoSite, San Diego, California, USA, 2005. InfoSite is the information center for InSite05, a multi-venue art event taking place along the border between California and Mexico. The artificial San Diego site was composed of readily available materials, including truck beds, pallet racks, tents, and traffic cones. At the end of the art fair, the wooden structure that housed the information center was exported and redeployed in Tijuana's informal urbanism.

Estudio Teddy Cruz

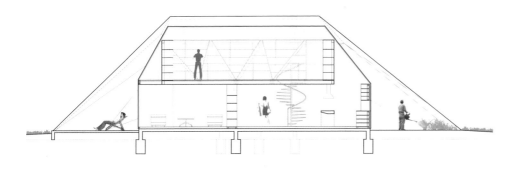

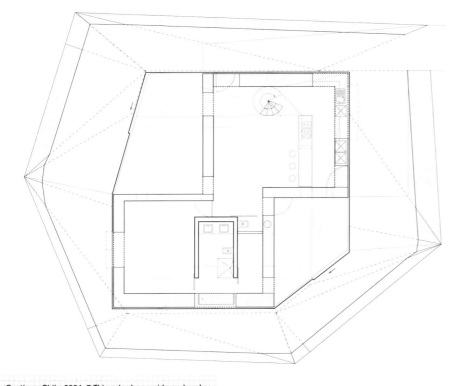

Wall House, Santiago, Chile, 2004–7. This suburban residence breaks down the traditional walls of a house into a series of four delaminated layers (concrete cave, stacked shelving, milky shell, soft skin) in between which the different spaces of the house slip, blurring the boundary between interior and exterior. The outermost layer, an energy screen that is more typically used in greenhouses, creates diffused lighting and climate control, while contributing to the tent shape of the structure.

Some people might want to live in a home that requires no more responsibility than a tent, but building a house that is as simple as a tent is not so easy. Most people's lives are much more fine-tuned than one might expect, and people are more vulnerable than we generally suppose. It would be difficult for most of us to bring the ease of tent living into our own lives.

The Wall House, by the international architecture firm FAR frohn&rojas, is an unusual dwelling that brilliantly overcomes such difficulties. Two techniques were used to make this prodigious achievement possible. First, containers to hold the household furnishings were pre-assembled in a factory and then placed on the building site with a crane, becoming the body of the structure. This method made it possible to eliminate most structural elements, such as pillars and beams, and construction time was significantly reduced. The second technique was the use of sheeting similar to a material used in greenhouses to block light. The sheeting was draped over the building like a roof, creating a graceful, tentlike structure as well as achieving an energy-friendly and sustainable house. In this way, an uncomplicated configuration consisting almost entirely of boxes was transformed into a grasslands tent.

Storage containers and greenhouse-type sheeting are both commonly used as independent construction elements. By pulling them together into one building, and by using the containers as interior units, FAR frohn&rojas presents new options for conventional architectural design. In addition to challenging the existing vocabulary of shapes, the firm uses innovative methods to achieve sustainability in a new way. Such creativity will enable the discovery of new possibilities for technique and design. // Kengo Kuma

2 in 1, Köln, Germany, 2007–. This project is a residence for two families. The design takes the idea of the traditional duplex, or *Doppelhaus*, a step further by allowing the two families to share their living environment in three zones which connect the two gable-roofed units: co-eating, children's play area, and greenhouse.

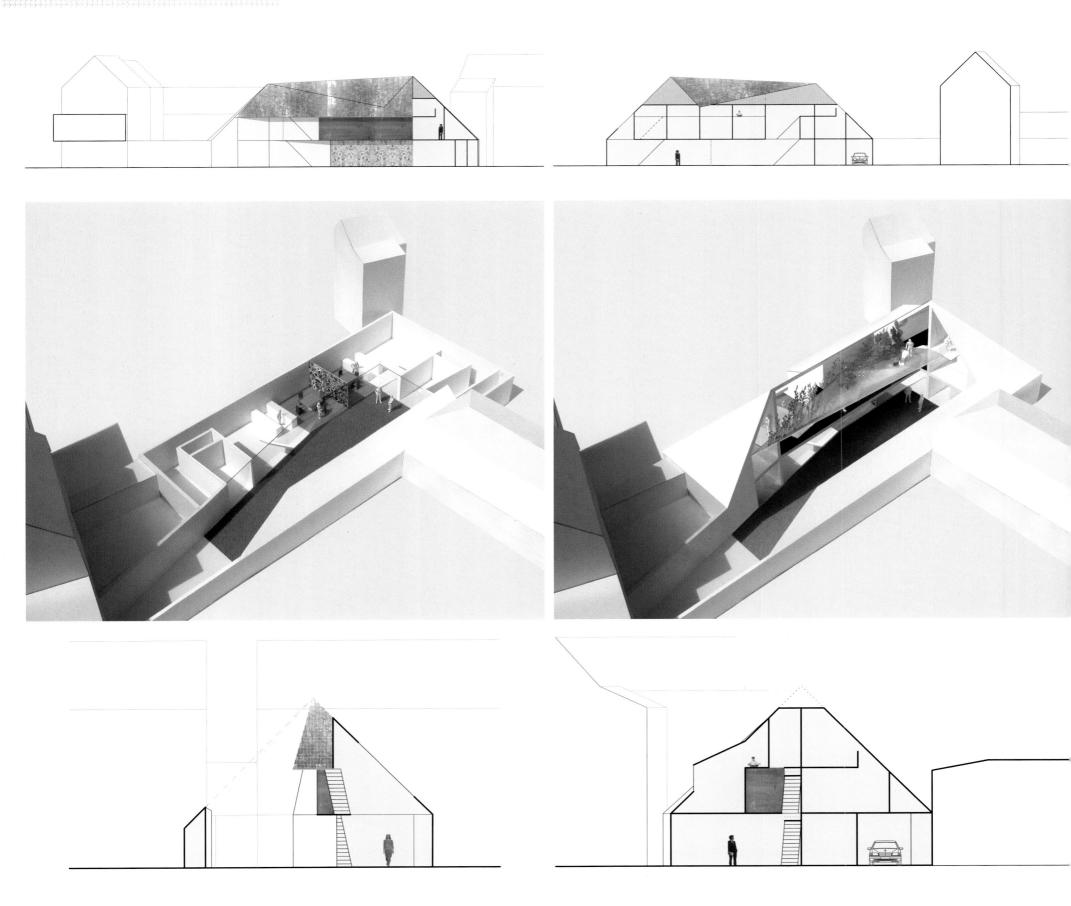

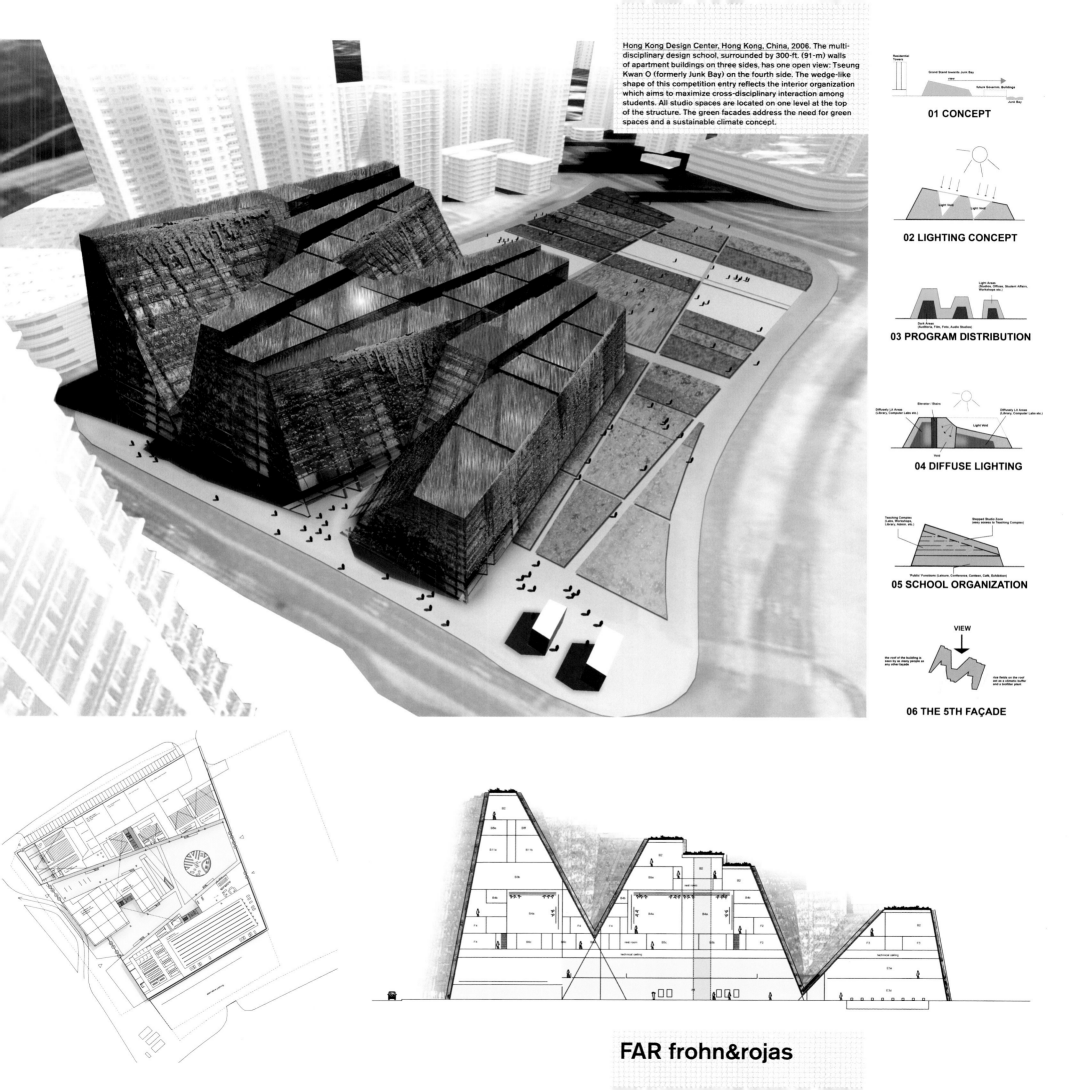

Hong Kong Design Center, Hong Kong, China, 2006. The multi-disciplinary design school, surrounded by 300-ft. (91-m) walls of apartment buildings on three sides, has one open view: Tseung Kwan O (formerly Junk Bay) on the fourth side. The wedge-like shape of this competition entry reflects the interior organization which aims to maximize cross-disciplinary interaction among students. All studio spaces are located on one level at the top of the structure. The green facades address the need for green spaces and a sustainable climate concept.

01 CONCEPT

02 LIGHTING CONCEPT

03 PROGRAM DISTRIBUTION

04 DIFFUSE LIGHTING

05 SCHOOL ORGANIZATION

06 THE 5TH FAÇADE

FAR frohn&rojas

Britain in the 1990s cheered up considerably. Bands like Pulp, Oasis, and Blur ushered in "Cool Britannia," an era of swaggering pop music and sensational, media-friendly artists such as Damien Hirst and Tracey Emin. Fed on a diet of *Wallpaper** magazine, home makeover programs, and IKEA furniture, the British public finally embraced modernism as a style. Among architects, a new breed of ascetic, "polite" minimalists emerged. They were pious, sincere, and rallied against the prevalent idiom of the 1980s and early 1990s: postmodernism. Fashion Architecture Taste (FAT) which has its roots in this transformational period of the 1990s, is pop and neo-postmodernist simultaneously. It made its name early on with satirical installations, artlike objects, and pop-collage interiors for "cool" advertising agencies. Its sensibility is akin to Richard Hamilton's love of American culture—which gave birth to English Pop in the 1950s—laced with a punkish spirit of irreverence and thrilling bad taste.

Postmodernism is now synonymous with camp historicism, but this hasn't stopped FAT from trying to resuscitate it as a legitimate style and subject of cultural archaeology. And the firm has taken a more serious twist in the past few years (evident in the new, more sober website that replaced a previous incarnation that allowed one to sing along with Rod Stewart). FAT now builds buildings such as a housing scheme for the northern British town of Manchester. It refuses the stripped-down faux-minimalism of the majority of developer-led projects and offers its residents quaint, decorative homes that are unashamedly pretty. A recurrent typology has emerged: simple boxes (containing interiors, programs, people, and things) fronted by ornamentally loud and intricate facades, summoning familiar historical precedents. Increasingly, though, what is most intriguing is the way in which odd and unrelated references are sampled to create something that is neither abstract nor figurative, but possibly both. The stern authority of Mies van der Rohe's Chicago Convention Center is evoked, but wrapped in a filigree table-cloth; the smart-stupid semiotics of Venturi Scott Brown are reemployed after decades of inactivity. If FAT's ardent desire to make postmodernism relevant again were merely an ironic posture, one would be tempted to dismiss it. But I believe that FAT represents a concerted, relevant effort to find a plausible exit from modernism's endgame.
// Shumon Basar

FAT   London GB

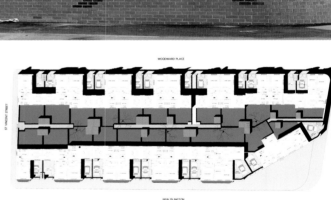

Islington Square, Manchester, England, 2004–6. Part of a 29-acre (12 ha) mixed-used development just east of Manchester's city center, this sustainable social housing project comprises 23 L-shaped, two- to four-bedroom houses with gardens organized around a city block.

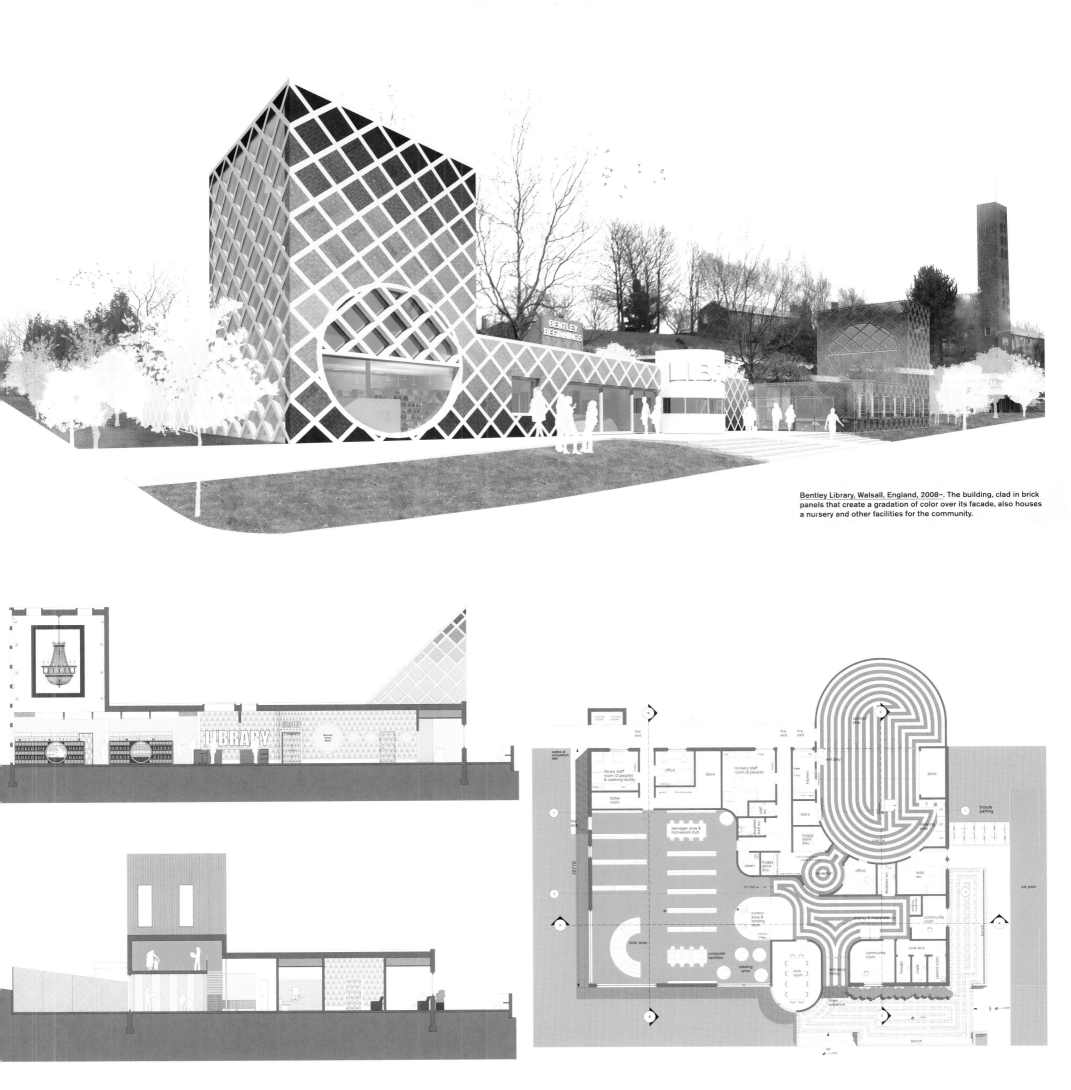

Bentley Library, Walsall, England, 2008–. The building, clad in brick panels that create a gradation of color over its facade, also houses a nursery and other facilities for the community.

Lingfield Point, Darlington, England, 2008–. Lingfield Point is a master plan for the regeneration of an old wool factory into a sustainable mixed-use scheme combining community center, retail spaces, restaurants, health care facilities, housing, and office space.

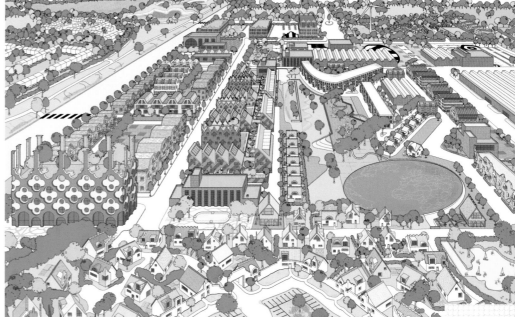

Heerlijkheid Hoogvliet, Rotterdam, Netherlands, 2002–8. This community building is part of a regeneration effort in the town of Hoogvliet, on the outskirts of Rotterdam. Surrounded by a 13-acre (5.4 ha) landscaped park, it includes a multi-use hall, offices, and a café.

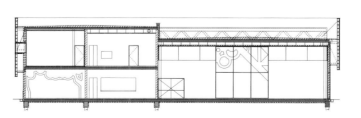

FAT

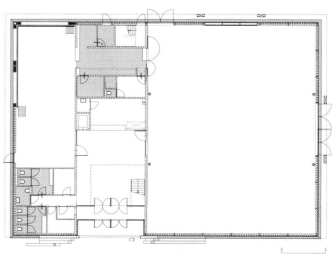

Deciding whether it is more appropriate to define Didier Fiuza Faustino as an artist whose medium is architecture or an architect whose expression is irrefutably artistic is a difficult—and ultimately pointless—exercise. His work attracts invitations from festivals of art and architecture alike; he has collectors and a gallery in Paris, but also a healthy roster of clients; his work is covered both in reviews of art exhibitions and architecture journals. Ultimately, much of it can be interpreted as a critique of contemporary architecture's failure to acknowledge its socio-political obligations, articulated through a forceful and conceptually sophisticated discourse.

The point of departure of many of Fiuza Faustino's works coincides with its point of arrival: the body. Many of the architect–artist's projects play on the body's inherent fragility, "packaging" it in a defensive skin capable of safeguarding it in extreme environments. The most drastic example of this approach is also one of the earliest: Body in Transit (2000) is literally a hard case for a single human being, not dissimilar to those used by musicians to transport large instruments; as a commentary on the status of the body as an object of trafficking and international commerce it needs little further explanation. From this starting point, Fiuza Faustino scaled up his ambitions, moving on to design a self-sustaining urban dwelling in the form of a habitable billboard. It was anticipated that with the revenue generated by advertising, the unit would not only be rent-free but would in fact pay for the occupant's living expenses. Another project, One Square Meter House, addresses the much-discussed issues of high-density urban living and skyrocketing land prices in cities by proposing a dwelling unit with an almost nonexistent footprint on the ground—a kind of capsule hotel-cum-affordable housing.

Ultimately, where Fiuza Faustino's work truly excels is in remixing existing building typologies to create new, mutant architectural species. His AMJ (Arteplage Mobile Jura), designed for Switzerland's Expo 02, is a floating theater composed of a steel container-like structure and a set of lighting masts spliced onto a recycled barge. Fiuza Faustino describes it as "a mutant, crossover body-machine, a series of grafts that amplify an existing object, a mere receptacle." It is ultimately proof that the architect-as-inventor can successfully devise new typologies: as a mobile receptacle for social functions of almost any kind, it could be considered vehicle design, architecture, or even sculpture. As with many architects of his generation, Fiuza Faustino sees the practice of architecture itself, as much as the commissions he receives, as a blank canvas in need of a new definition. // Joseph Grima

One Square Meter House, Porte d'Ivry, Paris, France, 2008. By reducing living space to its smallest unit, the square meter, this prototype promotes a critical view of land speculation. Beyond this, it subverts the notions of habitability, adaptability, and evolvement. Taking contemporary narcissism to its most absurd level, One Square Meter House makes public space the only possible terrain for social interaction.

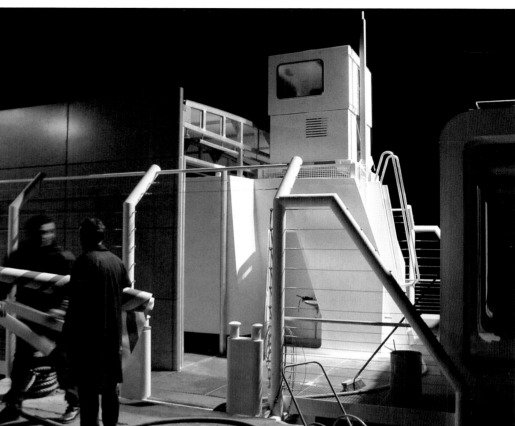

AMJ (Arteplage Mobile du Jura) Floating Theater, Expo 02, Switzerland, 2002. The autonomous, experimental territory created by this floating theater produces what the architect calls "a relational architecture." Designed for the sixth Swiss exposition, the drifting structure created from a recycled barge has towering, movable light fixtures resembling appendages of a living creature.

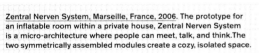

Zentral Nerven System, Marseille, France, 2006. The prototype for an inflatable room within a private house, Zentral Nerven System is a micro-architecture where people can meet, talk, and think.The two symmetrically assembled modules create a cozy, isolated space.

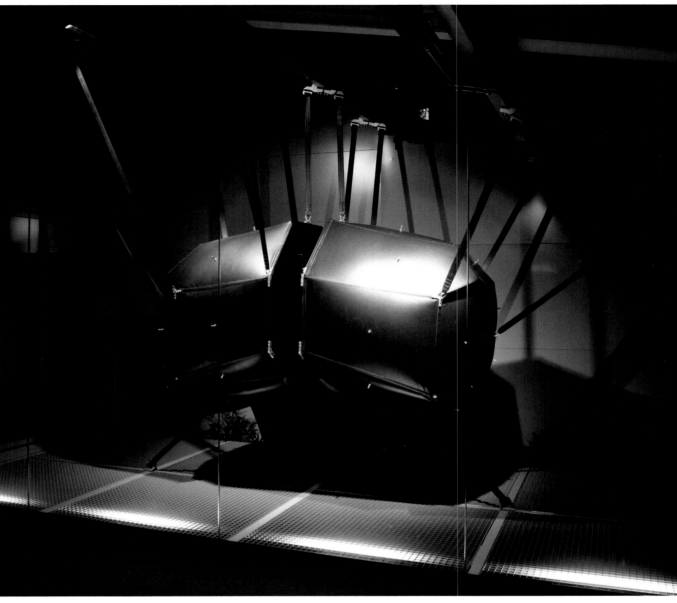

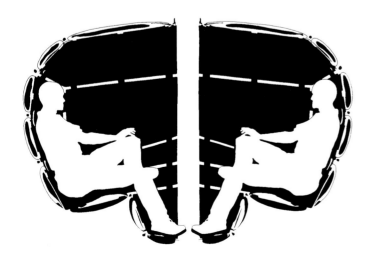

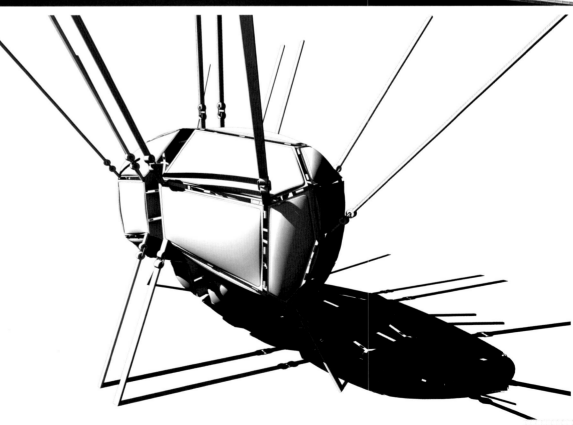

Sky Is the Limit, Yang Yang, Republic of Korea, 2008. Sky Is the Limit is a tea pavilion propulsed 65 ft. (20 m) above the ground, its two long rooms projected in a state of seeming weightlessness. The building's body appears as a fragile skeleton, its thin spider-like structure set beneath the tea rooms.

Didier Fiuza Faustino/Bureau des Mésarchitectures

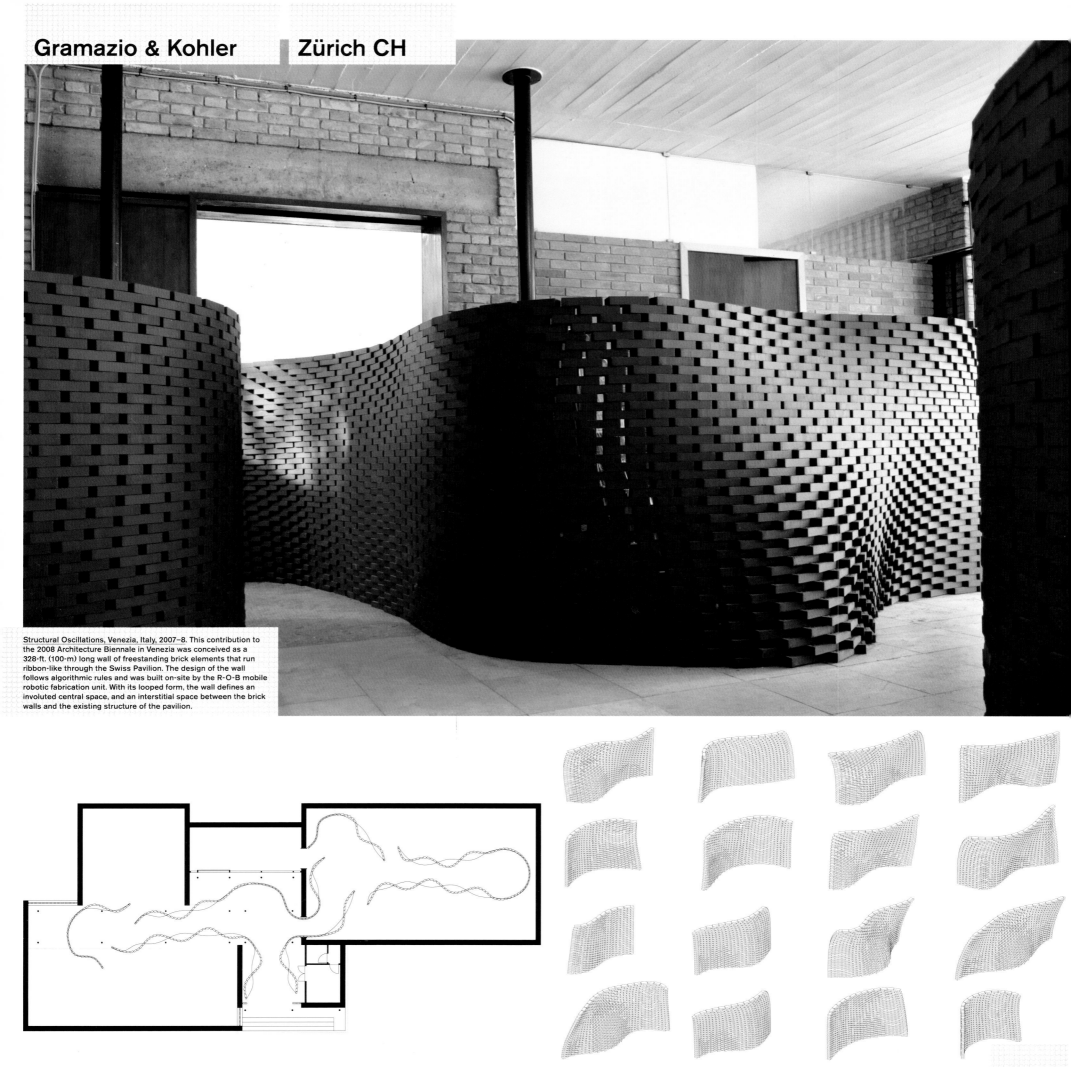

Structural Oscillations, Venezia, Italy, 2007–8. This contribution to the 2008 Architecture Biennale in Venezia was conceived as a 328-ft. (100-m) long wall of freestanding brick elements that run ribbon-like through the Swiss Pavilion. The design of the wall follows algorithmic rules and was built on-site by the R-O-B mobile robotic fabrication unit. With its looped form, the wall defines an involuted central space, and an interstitial space between the brick walls and the existing structure of the pavilion.

Fabio Gramazio and Matthias Kohler, who established their practice around a research laboratory at the Swiss Federal Institute of Technology (ETH) in Zürich, adopted a radically different approach to the use of computers in the construction process. Instead of using numerically controlled machinery to define the form and create a scale replica of a much larger artifact, they investigated the possibilities inherent in the use of computer-controlled equipment for the construction of buildings on a 1:1 scale. Much of their work is centered around the adaptation of robotics to the service of architecture: under the appropriate conditions, the speed and precision of a robot compared to a human is equivalent to that of a bubble-jet printer compared to a drafter. No architect would dream of drawing construction sets by hand; why are so few building components custom-built by robots?

As an aspiration, little of this is new: prefabrication has fascinated designers ever since the times of Archigram and the Metabolists in the 1960s, and mass-customization was the architectural fantasy *par excellence* of the late 1990s. Yet the work of Gramazio & Kohler is unique in that it utilizes relatively simple materials—bricks and mortar—and relies on the opportunities offered by highly developed, preexisting technologies such as robotics and automated assembly to open the window onto a new world of patterns and complex geometric arrangements. What is refreshing about this approach—which is in the very early stages of development—is that the building itself is the precision-crafted artifact, not a second-best to a seductive prototype that sits on the architect's desk.

One of Gramazio & Kohler's first real-life applications of the technique was in the facade of the Gantenbein Winery. The bricks are offset so as to allow precise modulation of the amount of daylight that penetrates the hall. The robotic production method developed at ETH enabled each one of the 20,000 bricks used in the facade to be laid precisely according to programmed parameters—at the desired angle and at exact prescribed intervals—defining the desired light and air permeability of each wall.

The Gantenbein Winery does not push the technology to its limits, but it is an interesting early testing ground for this innovative technique. Is this a new Fordist revolution in architecture? No, but it may be the beginning of a long-awaited diversification of the meaning—and expression— of parametric design. // Joseph Grima

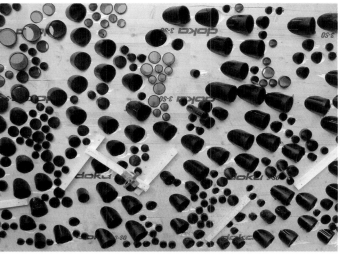

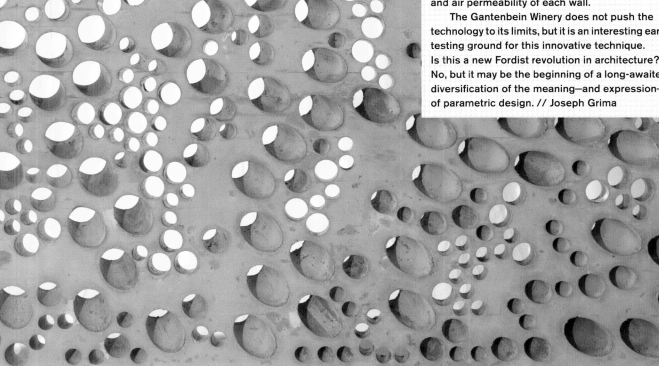

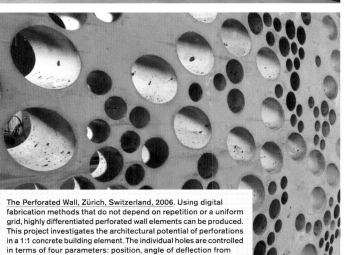

The Perforated Wall, Zürich, Switzerland, 2006. Using digital fabrication methods that do not depend on repetition or a uniform grid, highly differentiated perforated wall elements can be produced. This project investigates the architectural potential of perforations in a 1:1 concrete building element. The individual holes are controlled in terms of four parameters: position, angle of deflection from the surface, rotation around their center, and by size.

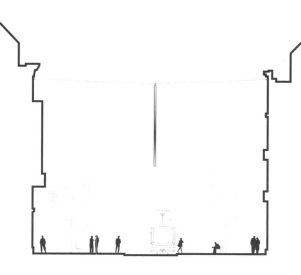

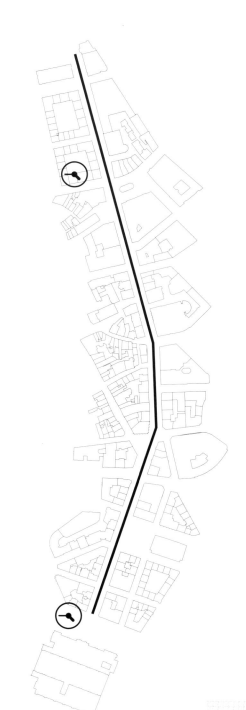

Bahnhofstrasse Christmas Lights, Zürich, Switzerland, 2003–5.
New Christmastime lighting for the famous Bahnhofstrasse in
Zürich spans a length of .68 mile (1.1 km) using 275 tubes of
light. Special software controls 8,800 LED bulbs, altering the
light patterns and ambiance continuously, depending on the
level of activity in the street and the progression of time during
the month of December.

Facade for Gantenbein Winery, Fläsch, Switzerland, 2006. The winery building consists of a large fermentation room for processing grapes, an underground cellar for storing wine barrels, and a roof terrace for receptions. Gramazio & Kohler was commissioned to design and construct the facade of the building. The bricks, laid according to precisely programmed parameters, are positioned to regulate light infiltration and air flow in the building.

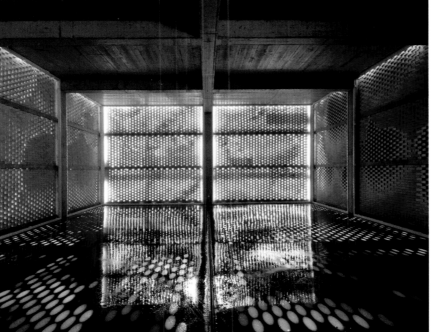

Gramazio & Kohler

INAPAL Metal Industrial Unit, Palmela, Portugal, 2006. This facility, dedicated to the production of metal components for the automobile industry, is composed of two volumes. One volume consists of two wings and a cantilever that combine material storage and production units; the other consists of two floors for the technical and social programs. One unique surface material—trapezoidal metal cladding—is used in two ways: revetment sheet for the closed spaces, and honeycomb-shaped cut metal-sheet for the spaces that require regulated light and ventilation.

If it is possible to define a unified "School of Porto" style among Portuguese architects, then Cristina Guedes and Francisco Vieira de Campos would seem to have developed from it, alongside iconic figures of contemporary Portuguese architecture. Guedes worked with Álvaro Siza in the early 1990s, while during the same period Vieira de Campos worked in the office of Eduardo Souto de Moura. In 1994 they founded their firm, also known as Menos é Mais (Less is More). While the work of the two architects reflects the minimalism that is conventionally identified with Porto architects, they have been especially interested in creating a rapport with existing buildings and specific places, but starting from an approach attuned to developments in the European avant-garde rather than local traditions.

A distinctive feature of Guedes + de Campos's work is their attempt to define an expressive vocabulary, which is reflected in an economy of means, standardized dimensions, clean lines, and lightness. A marked interest in experimental building through the use of new materials and prefabrication systems is accompanied by precision of design, abstraction in the composition, and meticulous control of detail. These working methods first appeared in the pavilion-like bars erected on the banks of the river at Vila Nova de Gaia (1999–2002).

They were taken further in the INAPAL facility for the manufacture of metal automobile components. Here the architects' conceptual approach focused on the definition of the envelope through the adoption of a unifying facade material (trapezoidal metallic sheets) applied in different ways depending on need and orientation. Inspired by the aerodynamic imagery of automobile design, the architects created a refined aesthetic based in a rigorous study of building procedures. In their design strategy, the first idea often contains the final concept. But as soon as they have fixed the ground rules for a project, they attempt to disrupt them by means of subtle gestures that contain the possibility of transformation.

In the Quinta do Vallado Winery (under construction) they create a respectful dialogue with the topography without subordinating the new architecture to it. The compositional matrix of the project establishes a close relationship with the landscape, reconciling technical and productive requirements with the ancient vaulted structure. In the Azores Contemporary Art Center, also under construction, the impact of the addition lies in the measured contrast between irregularity and volumetric clarity, the solids of the walls and the voids of the courtyards, the textures and colors of the surfaces, the opposing perceptual qualities evoked by the subtle interplay of light and shade. // Mercedes Daguerre

Azores Contemporary Art Center, Ribeira Grande, Portugal, 2007–.
The new art center prompts a dialogue with the site's former alcohol
and tobacco factory. The different scales and shapes of the buildings
are reflected in the contrast between the volcanic stone of the old
building and white mortar of the new buildings.

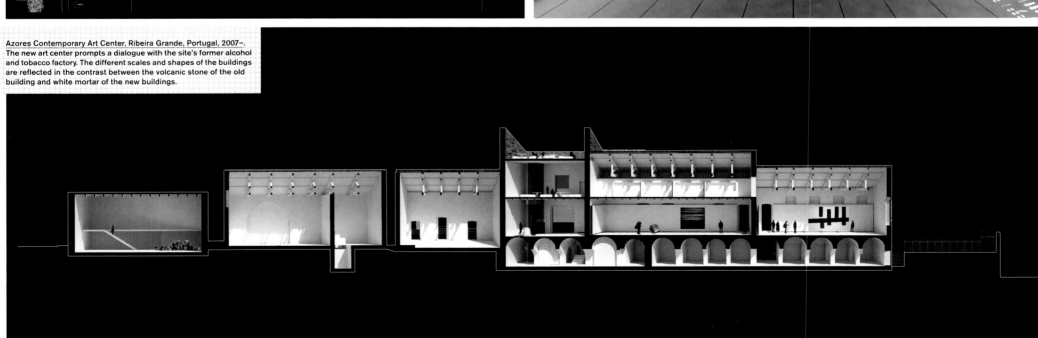

Quinta do Vallado Winery, Peso da Régua, Portugal, 2006–. This project includes the renovation of the existing winery buildings and construction of new buildings: a fermentation warehouse, and a barrel and reception warehouse. The enlargement of the winery calls for building on a pronounced slope. The project at once blends into the landscape and affirms its artificial nature.

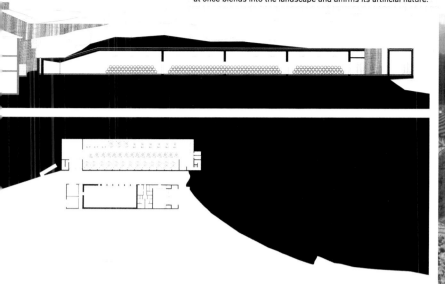

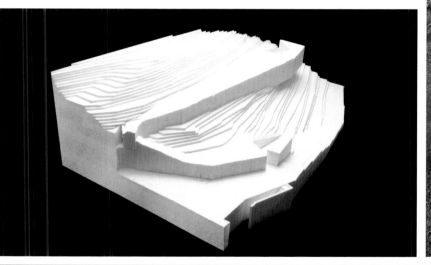

Guedes + de Campos

Dancing Trees, Singing Birds, Tokyo, Japan, 2007. This house was designed in a prime location in the Ebisu neighborhood of Tokyo, in the city center yet surrounded by trees. The aim was to create maximum volume while maintaining an environment where people and birds could live in harmony. Once the location of the tree roots was determined, a foundation wall and a snaking underground beam were constructed to avoid the roots. The house was then built around the trees.

Hiroshi Nakamura's architecture is diverse. Even though he is young, the variety of his work is remarkable. He uses many different materials and works with many different shapes. He makes adroit use of wood and takes on the challenge of steel with equal ease. Even so, there is no sense of inconsistency, and I have wondered why this is so.

The mystery of this diversity was solved when I saw the title of his book, *Koi suru Kenchiku* (The Architecture I Love): Nakamura falls in love with materials, and he is a man of many loves. Modernist architects often select their materials and use them according to the rules. But people who accept rules as fundamental truths restrict themselves. They, too, may be attracted to many different things, but the rules limit them. But Nakamura lives according to his own fundamental truth, the truth of love. He feels no need for rules or regulations. This is the source of his work's freshness, and because of this, many feel that Nakamura is the herald of a new era.

The approach he takes is neither lighthearted nor simple. The most important part of falling in love is not to explain why, but to sing the praises of one's beloved, and Nakamura does exactly that. When he fell in love with wood, for example, he built a gabled shape that resembles a wooden cottage on an island. This was because he knew that a love song for wood could best be expressed through shape. When Nakamura became enamoured with steel sheets, he made an infinite number of small holes in the steel out of love for the light that poured through the openings. He knew that his love for steel would be revealed in the resulting moment of unexpected exhilaration.

I wonder, however, whether love really is unrelated to rules. Love is made sweet by the very fact that regulation exists. Love's delight is not an exhilaration that occurs after a choice. Does it not exist, instead, in the tension-filled process before the choice? // Kengo Kuma

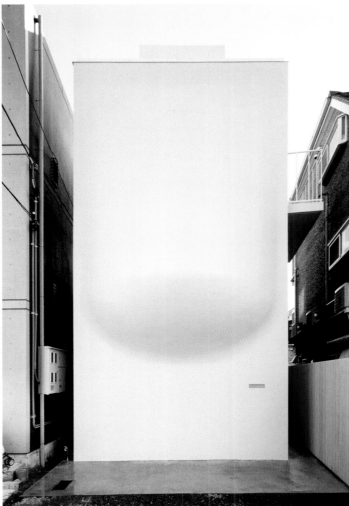

House SH, Tokyo, Japan, 2005. This small house in Tokyo, north-facing and surrounded by buildings on three sides, contains a large skylight and a vaulted ceiling to ensure daylight without windows. As a result of pushing the walls of the building to the site's edge, area is maximized and the residents physically interact with the architecture by lying and sitting on the walls.

Necklace House, Yamagata Prefecture, Japan, 2006. This house, located in the countryside, employs a C-shaped structural wall, around which a series of detached rooms, connected like beads on a necklace, are arranged. The style of each room varies greatly—there is a bathroom with 1,600 windows, a timber bedroom with large trusses, and a Japanese style room. The C-shape affords all rooms a garden view and avoids the need for blinds, while the white rooms' elevation is ideal for winters that can see 6 ft. (2 m) of snow accumulation.

Lanvin Boutique Ginza, Tokyo, Japan, 2004. The facade of this store, located on a main street in the Ginza shopping district, is composed of approximately 3,000 acrylic cylinders inlaid into steel plates using a new technique invented in collaboration with a boatbuilder. The inset holes create kaleidoscopic light effects during the day and cast a starry glow on the street at night.

Hiroshi Nakamura & NAP Architects

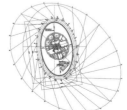

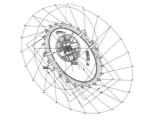
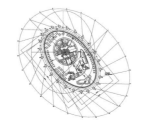
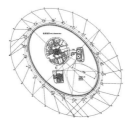

Guangzhou Television and Sightseeing Tower, Guangzhou, Guangdong, China, 2004–9. The form, volume, and structure of the tower are controlled by a rotation between a top and bottom ellipse. The tightening caused by the rotation between the two forms a "waist" where there is a densification of material. The lattice structure, which at the bottom of the tower is porous and spacious, becomes tighter at waist level, where transparency is reduced and views to the outside are limited.

While mass housing and offices in China are being built by local architecture practices under the strictest financial conditions, many of China's concert halls, museums, and stadiums have been commissioned through high profile international competitions. The map of China is scattered with cities building iconic forms that dazzle and bewilder in equal measure. Guangzhou, which sits on the coast of the South China Sea, 113 miles (182 kilometers) from Hong Kong, is no exception. It is China's largest and most prosperous southern city, an important seaport for foreign trade, and a cultural center for thousands of years.

The Dutch firm Information Based Architecture (IBA) won the competition to build the tallest structure in China, the 2,000-ft. (610-m) Guangzhou Television and Sightseeing Tower, close to Zaha Hadid's new opera house. Having built nothing of comparable scale or complexity, IBA entered headfirst into the fast-moving world of dizzying deadlines and Chinese construction culture. IBA also won the competition for Guangzhou Television's headquarters, an elegant, sharply faceted mass at the foot of the tower, perforated by a grid of curvaceous openings. Their design for a velodrome, also in Guangzhou, which has been especially welcoming to this young practice, looks like a massive pebble made from soft, white, pricked fabric.

But before anything else, it is the Guangzhou Television and Sightseeing Tower that will loom most imposingly and unforgettably. Here a slowly twisting steel structure connects an ellipsed perimeter outline at the top and the bottom. This steel mesh forms an environmental filter, which modulates light and frames extraordinary views. The profile narrows midway, giving the tower a lanky, "supermodel" hourglass figure. The interior of the tower is programmatically subdivided into climatic zones, such as Arctic, Tropical, Ocean, and Tundra, each with its own leisure or sightseeing program. Mark Hemel and Barbara Kuit, IBA's founding partners, have harnessed the unique inventiveness an emerging economy like China offers European architects and engineers, which is handsomely reflected in IBA's sculpturally imaginative and serious work. // Shumon Basar

610.0M

460.8M

7.4M

Velodrome, Guangzhou, Guangdong, China, 2008. The velodrome consists of a porous, monolithic 525-ft. (160-m) single-span shell that integrates the structural, spatial, and lighting requirements into one simple but rich solution. It is a representative example of IBA's biomorphic forms.

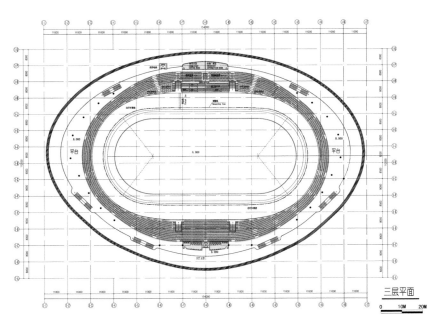

三层平面

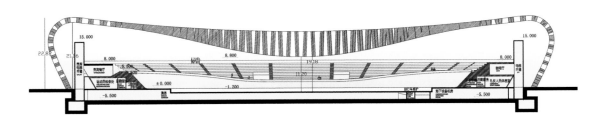

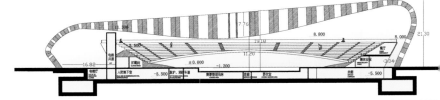

Guangzhou Television Headquarters, Guangzhou, Guangdong, China, 2006. This winning competition entry for Guangzhou Television Headquarters is a multifaceted volume sculpted from a mass of tubes. The resulting facades are all coherently formed, while each sculpted face has a different pattern: one is circular, another consists of stretched elliptical tubes. The screen around the building reduces glare and diffuses the light, creating bright, indirectly lit interior spaces.

Information Based Architecture (IBA)

Taxinge Plaza, Stockholm, Sweden, 2005–6. In collaboration with the design group Front and the gallery Tensta Konsthall, International Festival worked with local authorities and developers to transform a parking lot into a public square using easily sourced, ready-made products.

What would happen if serious European philosophy were to mate with a discotheque? If architecture disappeared completely, would people still be able to make love as though there were walls protecting their modesty? Is there more spatial richness in a cheerleading routine than there is in the Acropolis? These are some of the seriously absurd and absurdly serious questions that spring to mind when looking at the work of International Festival. Founded by architect Tor Lindstrand and choreographer Mårten Spångberg in Sweden in 2004, International Festival claims that "a theater audience, as well as museum visitors, are conventionally addressed as a single population . . . [We] challenge this notion by engaging the audience in the production of the work itself."

Their portfolio is a riotous and messy itinerary of events, dances, guerrilla performances, films, texts, and also physical interventions in public or institutional spaces. Duration is key. Rarely will anything last forever. The finite existence of a performance endows it with an existential urgency. International Festival is the pop-descendant of British architect Cedric Price (who married an actress and worked with theater director Joan Littlewood): Price too rejected architecture's "will to eternity"; he also programmed the end of his buildings into their fabrication.

Recently, all of International Festival's projects are named after Rolling Stones songs. They claim this is in part due to the fact that both Spångberg and Lindstrand were born in 1968; but, more acutely, they say that the Rolling Stones embody the myth of rock 'n' roll authenticity in an industry that is clearly and ruthlessly commoditized and corporate in nature. I also see productive potential in an architecture that is envious of music and of performance. Music and dance impact upon the senses in a strangely irrational yet direct way. International Festival rightfully focuses on the gamut of human reactions that situations can elicit rather than the perfect material envelope within which such actions take place. "I am for an architecture that is political-erotical-mystical, that does something other than sit on its ass," they say, paraphrasing Claes Oldenburg. Architecture can have theory, International Festival seems to be implying, if it is also prepared to risk failure and, in the process, look a little silly. Nothing will last forever, and nothing should even try. // Shumon Basar

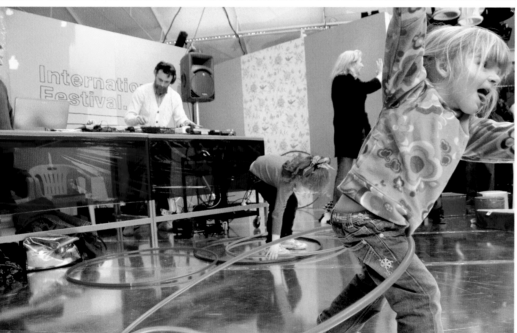

Start Me Up, Liverpool, England, UK, 2008–9. International Festival was commissioned to design a social space for the exhibition *The Fifth Floor: Ideas Taking Space* at Tate Liverpool. A modular and flexible film-set installation was modified and reconfigured to host a myriad of performances and events, from baby disco and seminars to stand-up comedy shows.

The Theatre, Graz, Austria, 2005–7. The Theatre is an interactive, collaborative project, originally designed for the Steirischer Herbst festival of new art, engaging groups and individuals to develop, design, and realize a fully functioning theater.

International Festival

Sebastián Irarrázaval | Santiago RCH

8x8x8 House, Marbella, Chile, 2004–6. The configuration of this weekend house, made of concrete, glass, and stone, proposes multiple ways of moving from one place to another; one can circulate through the house or around its perimeter. The space is defined by the play of shadows created by the lattice and pillars in the central patio.

A member of the most recent generation of architects to have given international prominence to Chilean architecture, Sebastián Irarrázaval approaches design as a conversation between theoretical principles and the reality of the construction site. In 1994 he started a professional practice (first with Guillermo Acuña and then independently) while also pursuing an academic career. The two activities have nurtured each other and decisively influenced his working method: a dynamic approach to the architectural project that tackles each problem starting from a thesis, which the design probes carefully, seeking continuously to enhance it. In his often simple volumes, materials are dominant and circulation through the building is of fundamental importance, creating the framework of the construction.

The principles underpinning his architecture are apparent in a number of houses completed over the past decade and in Irarrázaval's most recent works. La Reserva House is inspired by the idea of the "container," the prototype for a building that can be adapted to any site. Its cruciform plan distributes the functions of the home and the views it offers. The choice of materials stresses the tectonic conditions of the compositional elements, with the inevitable action of weathering seen as a variable that will enhance them. The 8x8x8 House explores the relationship between abstraction and construction. The irregular arrangement of the columns defines the space by multiplying the routes through it, blurring the boundaries between interior and exterior. The Indigo Patagonia Hotel is inspired by the process of discovery experienced by the traveler. A gradual and fragmentary interpretation of the building, articulated by a system of ramps, stairs, and catwalks, enriches the space of the atrium, while the rhythms of the windows and the use of nautical materials such as timber and sheet metal echoes local building practices.

In Irarrázaval's work, materials are instrumental to form. By using materials—from iron to vinyl siding—without preconceptions, the architect melds the craft of the building tradition with the innovative potential of advanced technologies. In his project for the PUC School of Design, he sets himself the challenge to provide unequivocally "pedagogical" answers to combine clearly functional spaces with a comb-shaped layout and an anti-seismic structure. This constant drive to explore the boundaries of the discipline and convey new architectural experiences— shared by other local designers now coming to prominence—bodes well both for Irarrázaval's own practice and for the vitality of contemporary Chilean architecture. // Mercedes Daguerre

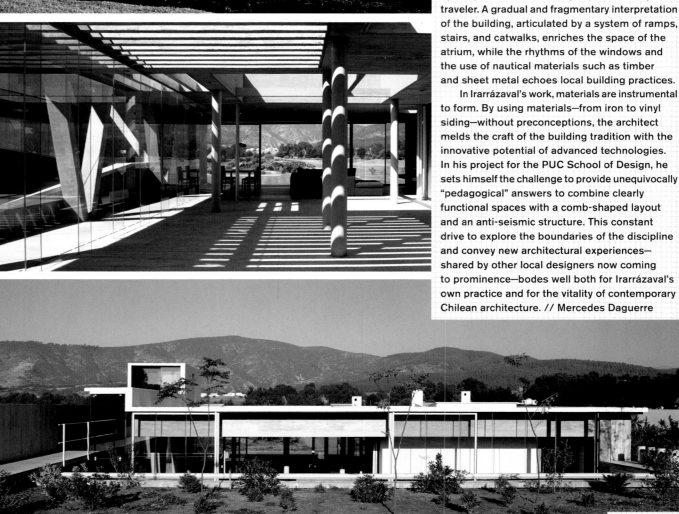

La Reserva House, Colina, Chile, 2004–6. This prototype for a low-cost housing module of 1,500 sq. ft. (140 sq. m), relates to the idea of the container that is not tied to a specific place. To reduce construction time, geometry is simple and the construction system is prefabricated.

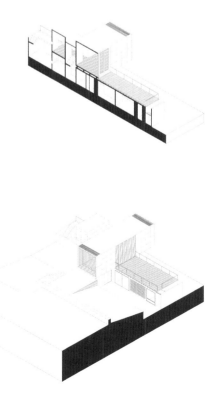

Indigo Patagonia Hotel, Puerto Natales, Chile, 2005–7. The project is organized around three main ideas: to discover the building as a voyager who experiences places, not at once, but through continuous steps; to be sensitive to the site's provincial character and quietude; and to radically differentiate the intimate space of the sleeping quarters from the monumental space of the public areas.

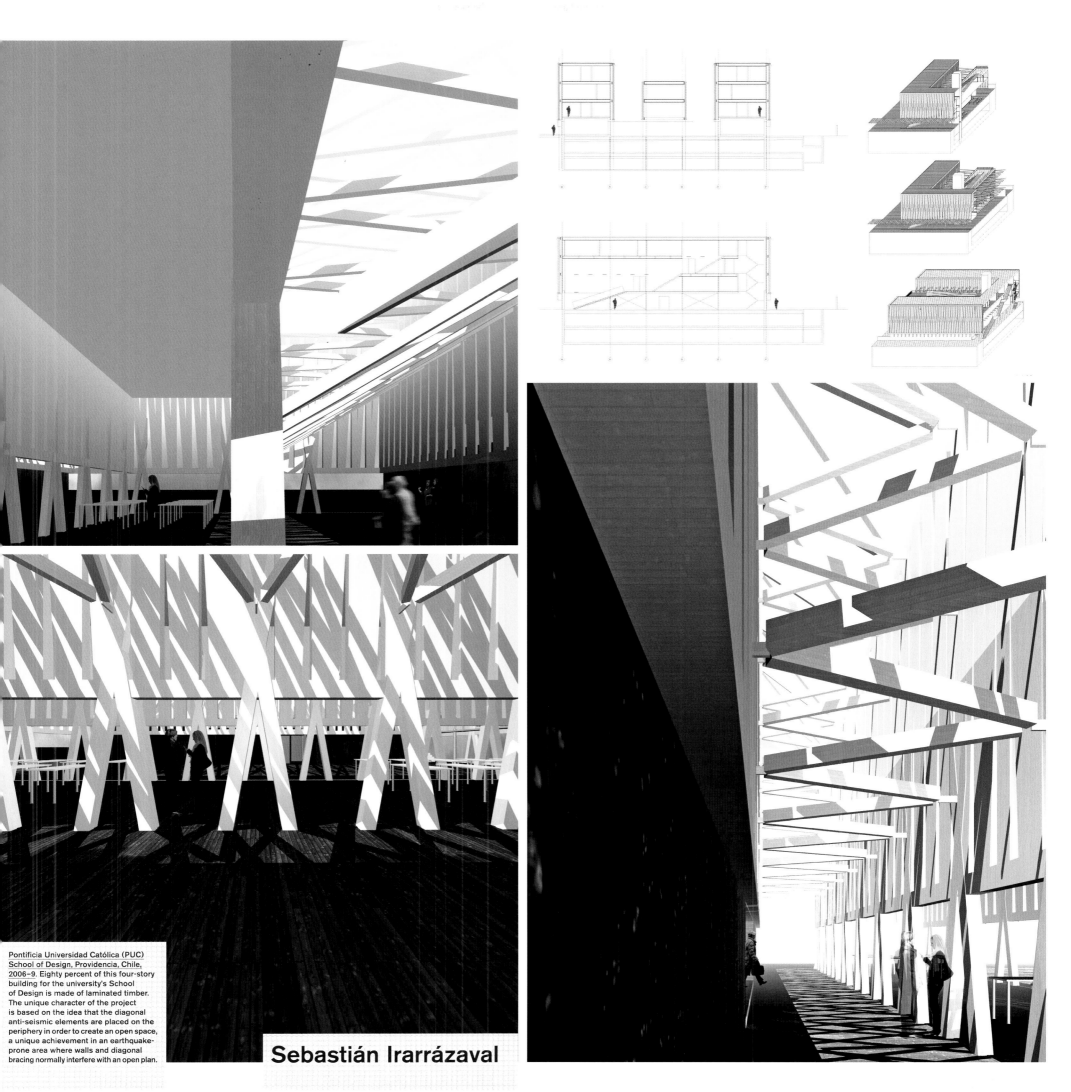

Pontificia Universidad Católica (PUC)
School of Design, Providencia, Chile,
2006–9. Eighty percent of this four-story
building for the university's School
of Design is made of laminated timber.
The unique character of the project
is based on the idea that the diagonal
anti-seismic elements are placed on the
periphery in order to create an open space,
a unique achievement in an earthquake-
prone area where walls and diagonal
bracing normally interfere with an open plan.

Sebastián Irarrázaval

7 World Trade Center, New York, New York, USA, 2003–6. In collaboration with Skidmore, Owings & Merrill, JCDA designed the podium wall at the tower's base, the curtain wall, and the lobby cable-net wall and canopy. The podium wall consists of two layers of prismatic stainless-steel wire with internal LED lighting. The curtain wall features a "linear lap" system with spandrel daylight reflectors.

After graduating from the Rhode Island School of Design, having studied architecture and sculpture, James Carpenter spent a formative decade as a consultant with Corning Glass Works in Corning, New York, where his interest in the technical, expressive, and prismatic qualities of plate glass thrived. Since founding James Carpenter Design Associates (JCDA) in New York in 1978 he has collaborated with numerous architects, engineers, technicians, and fabricators to create works in which glass becomes a versatile and phenomenal dimension of architecture. These works do not remain pure material installations or aloof environments, but rather active and integral participants in the life of the architecture. Often described as an artist or as a sculptor, Carpenter is a consummate design professional who has expanded the technical and artistic potential of glass through surprising applications. The artist's exacting sensibility in refining impressions, reflections, and visual narratives from glass has no equal.

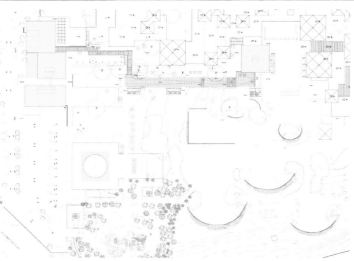

One of Carpenter's most accomplished recent works is 7 World Trade Center, the first building to be rebuilt at the World Trade Center site in New York. Collaborating with Skidmore, Owings & Merrill and its design partner David Childs, Carpenter was directly involved with three critical components of the 50-story tower: the curtain wall system, the lobby, and the high concrete base housing the enormous electrical transformers that power lower Manhattan. The building's lobby and the concrete base super-structure are fused into a continuously luminous plinth eight stories high. The ingenious solution addresses not only the transformers' ventilation needs but also camouflages their massive concrete shell via an exquisite screen made of stainless steel and LED lighting. At night this light "podium" becomes an uplifting and mesmerizing presence at the indelibly wounded site.

Another recent work is the expansion and renovation of the Israel Museum in Jerusalem. The fabled museum is one of the finest in the Middle East, home of the Dead Sea Scrolls and the setting of one of Isamu Noguchi's most memorable sculpture gardens. Carpenter's firm was faced with a daunting challenge: how to reconfigure the vast museum complex to become a legible and cohesive whole. The architects incisively clarified relationships between existing and isolated galleries, reconnected them to the site's distinct topography, and added public spaces. The latter include a formal front entrance, entry pavilion, a user-friendly network of circulatory routes, and a gallery entrance pavilion. The new pavilions provide a complementary contrast to the existing architecture, as their walls and light wells gently filter the harsh Mediterranean light, to the pleasure of countless visitors.
// Carlos Jimenez

Israel Museum, Jerusalem, Israel, 2005–10. The expansion and renovation of the museum involves 50,000 sq. ft. (4,600 sq. m) of new shaded glass buildings, a complete reorganization of visitor circulation, the renovation of the galleries, and a new underground passageway.

Gucci Ginza, Tokyo, Japan, 2004–6. For the facade of Gucci's flagship store in the fashionable Ginza district of Tokyo, beveled roller-patterned glass is layered with a crystalline skin of low-iron glass creating a deeply shimmering volume.

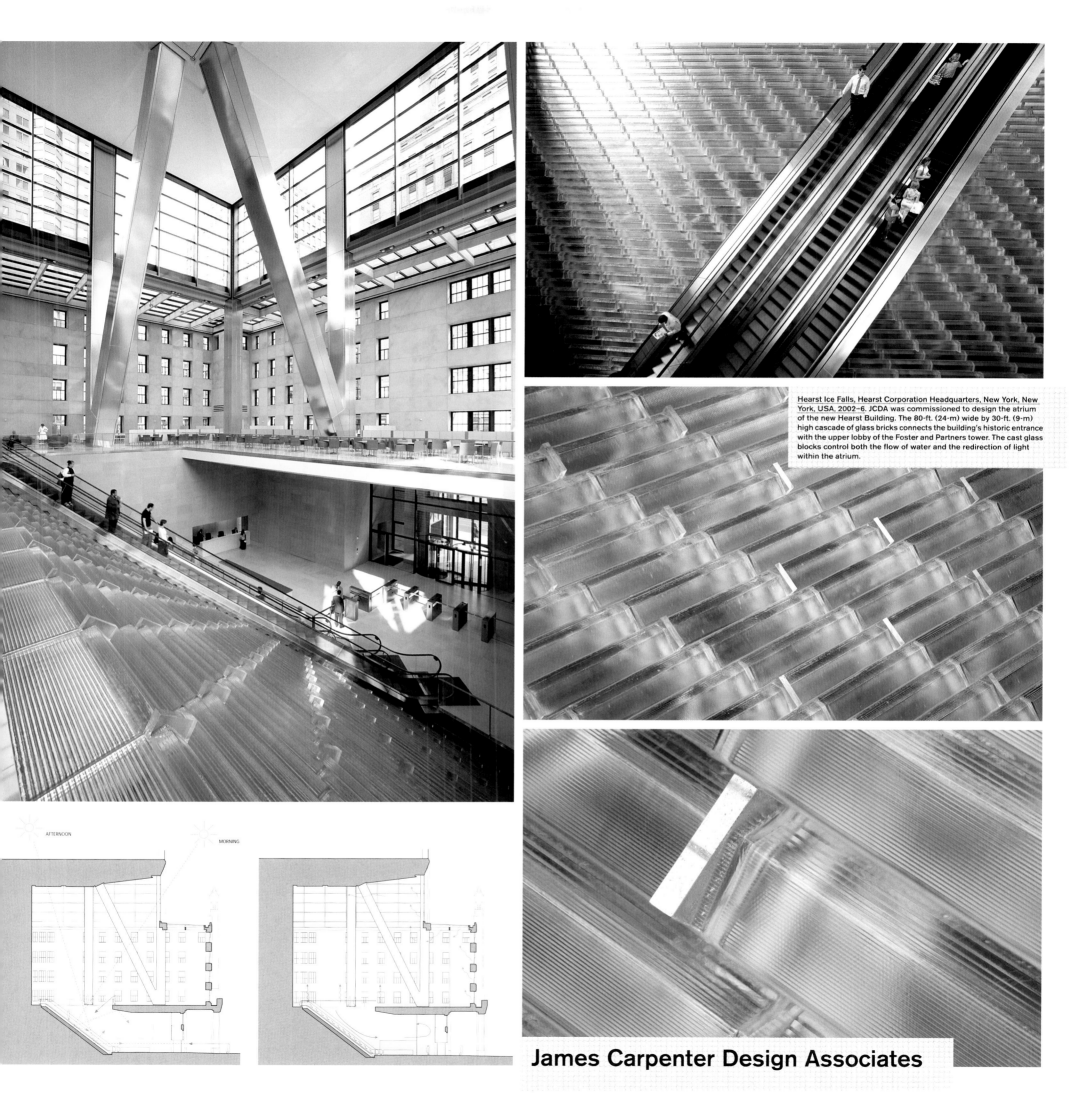

Hearst Ice Falls, Hearst Corporation Headquarters, New York, New York, USA, 2002–6. JCDA was commissioned to design the atrium of the new Hearst Building. The 80-ft. (24-m) wide by 30-ft. (9-m) high cascade of glass bricks connects the building's historic entrance with the upper lobby of the Foster and Partners tower. The cast glass blocks control both the flow of water and the redirection of light within the atrium.

AFTERNOON

MORNING

James Carpenter Design Associates

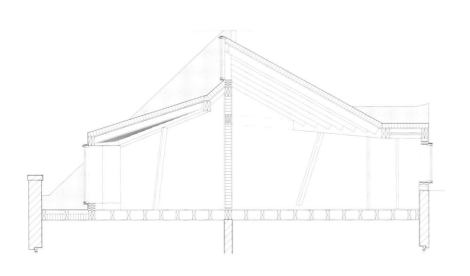

House Alexis, Gent, Belgium, 2005–8.
This extension is built on the roof of an
existing house. The interior finishing
reveals the light wooden construction
materials and wooden beams; the
exterior is covered with polymer panels
typically used for swimming pools.

Jan De Vylder Architecten, located in Gent, Belgium, delivers projects that play with existing conditions while directly relating to the user's needs. With his many renovations of vernacular Belgian houses, Jan De Vylder demonstrates his ability to communicate human desire within a framework of limitations. The playfulness with which he approaches smaller renovation projects is beautifully expressed as an awkward hand-shake between the old and the new.

Zooming in on HeL, De Vylder's largest project to date, offers the opportunity to become familiar with his character as a designer. This ground-up construction project has two production studios for dance and music theater. The structure consists of two closed buildings, each with one open glazed facade. The buildings are essentially mirror images of one another, and they stand back to back while appearing to look over their shoulders at each other. Brick walls and steel beams are set behind the two glazed facades as a backdrop of intrigue, hiding the interior functions. The bizarre surrealism and the layering of old and new that were developed in the renovation projects of Houses 43, Alexis, and H, are evident in HeL. De Vylder's peculiar character is embodied in the varying materials and details: The exposed green columns and the beams of steel and wood, plus the concrete and the brick masonry, all add up to a hallucinatory vision inscribed onto the building's facade.

De Vylder's humor and sensitivity mix to reveal another side of the world. With a school-girl-like stubbornness, De Vylder insists on a freedom and uniqueness of expression not common among architects. Like an artist, he applies his gentle touch to simplify situations into what he desires. His architecture bears witness to a relentless attempt to have fun. De Vylder designs projects that stand above any doctrine, telling the world what he wants, one blueprint at a time. // Ai Weiwei

House H, Oosterzele, Belgium, 2005–8. Just outside Gent, House H is a renovation of and extension to an existing house. The new addition utilizes concrete plates that are generally used for garden walls or sheds, and floor-to-ceiling glass panels create a lightness that contrasts with the older brick house.

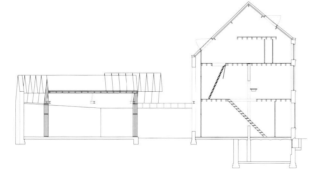

House 43, Gent, Belgium, 2004–5. The outstanding feature of this house renovation is the sliding glazed roof that covers a 172-sq.-ft. (16-sq.-m) garden. When the roof is closed, the grass below becomes a "carpet" and the space is transformed into an "indoor" room; when open, it becomes an outdoor garden in between the front and back of the house.

HeL, Gent, Belgium, 2003–8. This project consists of two production studios for a dance and theater company housed in two different buildings in close proximity to one another. Their glazed facades expose the materials used in the interiors. The rough finishing on the other facades is designed to promote the growth of greenery.

Jan De Vylder Architecten

Einar Jarmund and Håkon Vigsnæs founded their practice in Oslo in 1996 after studying in Seattle, Washington, and at the Architectural Association in London, and brought on a third partner, Alessandra Kosberg, in 2004. All three originally studied at the Oslo School of Architecture and Design, whose new building they later designed. It is a paradigmatic edifice that celebrates a carefully calibrated encounter between the existing building (a former factory) and the new structure, without the overtly aestheticized details of Sverre Fehn, Norway's most famous architect, under whom Vigsnæs himself once worked. Concrete supports or beams are cut through, sandblasted, and then left in place, while new glass facades have been positioned wherever needed; the new finds its way, the old remains where it was, and the two otherwise conflicting ages find a modus vivendi that is a warm, friendly, and unpretentious building.

The architects' most spectacular project is the Svalbard Science Center in Longyearbyen, the most northern university and research institute in the world, located on the island of Spitsbergen in the Arctic Ocean. In keeping with their motto that "every commission should be unique with reference to its site and circumstances," the architects created an unmistakable, hard-edged structure that crouches flat above the ground and, thanks to a form that was optimized through wind simulations, avoids the accumulation of high snowdrifts around it. Like a spaceship, the volume rests on tubular steel stilts in order not to heat the permafrost ground and all areas for work and leisure, as well as circulation routes, are housed indoors. The entire structure is made of wood and clad in copper on the outside to avoid thermal bridges.

Two other projects, exciting small houses that have just been completed, highlight the firm's talent for creating small-scale jewels. The Edge House in Kolbotn outside Oslo rests on stilts above a precipice. Access from the road below cuts through the layout of the house. Its steel structure is clad on the outside with fibrated concrete panels, on the inside with birch paneling. The charming Farm House in Toten is likewise located on a slope. It feels improvised, almost homemade, due to the reuse of wood cladding from the former barn that stood on its site.
// Peter Cachola Schmal

Edge House, Kolbotn, Norway, 2005–8. The house was built on a challenging site, which presents a 26-ft. (8-m) height difference between its point of access and the main surface on a plateau. To leave the plateau as untouched as possible, the building was pushed toward the eastern perimeter of the site and suspended above the slope on slender steel stilts. The access stairs rise along the slope through the house and up to the plateau.

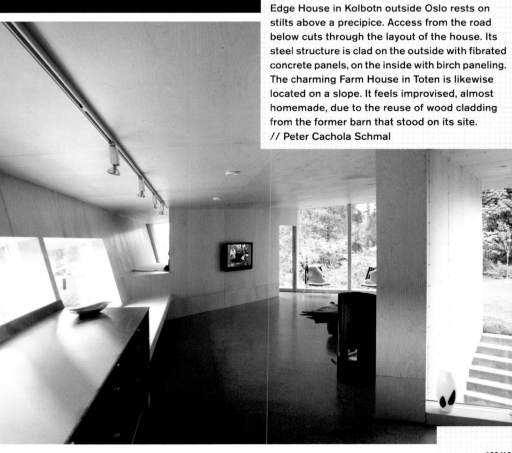

Farm House, Toten, Norway, 2005–8. The house echoes the adjacent old barn—which was eventually torn down—in terms both of spatial organization and wood cladding, which was salvaged and recycled. A continuous band of windows allows for natural light and expansive views.

Oslo School of Architecture and Design, Oslo, Norway, 1998–2001.
Based in an existing factory building from 1938, the school is
arranged around a new internal courtyard that is connected to
the adjacent riverside park. Parts of the old complex were torn
down to bring light into the deeper parts of the building, the
remnants of the construction sandblasted to expose the concrete,
and new building elements made transparent to reflect the social
transparency of the institution.

Svalbard Science Center, Longyearbyen, Spitsbergen, Norway, 2001–5. The new building, connected to a small existing university, is lifted off the ground on stilts and streamlined to minimize snowdrifts and weather high winds. All the functions of a campus are gathered indoors in a single, low impact building.

Jarmund/Vigsnæs

VM Houses, København, Denmark, 2002–5. This project, a collaboration between BIG Architects and JDS Architects, consists of two apartment buildings—the V building houses 114 apartments, the M, 95 apartments. By "bending" the buildings into V and M shapes, each unit obtains diagonal views. All apartments have a double-height space to the north and wide panoramic views to the south.

Founded in 2006 by Julien de Smedt—and with offices now in Denmark, Belgium, and Norway—JDS Architects approaches design with a strong affinity for the fantastical. With the majority of its work coming from international competitions, the firm engages in a wide range of projects. Whether designing small installations or small cities, it displays a madness that seems to disregard not only restraint but reality. But the function of their projects is clear, the spatial quality is interesting, and the construction carefully considered.

One example of JDS Architects' powerful ideas is the Big Brother House (2008–9), designed for the Ordos architectural district in Ordos, Nei Mongol, China. Featuring stacked boxes like containers piled in the desert, it demands very little from its construction, while providing introverted and extroverted spaces circling a central core. The VM Houses in København are another strong idea, accompanied by a bold silhouette. The two buildings are bent to form a "V" and an "M," the chevron shape maximizing inhabitants' views of the surrounding fields. In an attempt to increase these views even further, the balconies become exaggerated extrusions of the floor slab, giving the building a distinctive facade of saw-tooth-like severity.

The Architectural Moussaka in Athens bears a strong resemblance to the containers of the Big Brother House. JDS Architects has playfully arranged cubes into designs improved by the varying orientations and by negative and positive space. Unlike the rolled dice the cubes resemble, there is a controlled randomness to this project. The rectilinear volumes show no relationship to grid or order; instead, they begin to frame irregular courtyards and public spaces, which in turn create a connection between reality and fantasy.

JDS Architects is a firm that often attempts to bring fantasy to reality, and its designs have a no-holds-barred, "everything goes" craziness. But their projects also belong to the new trend of an architecture without individual style, in which postmodern knowledge is absorbed and regurgitated, then fused with other historical and artistic influences. // Ai Weiwei

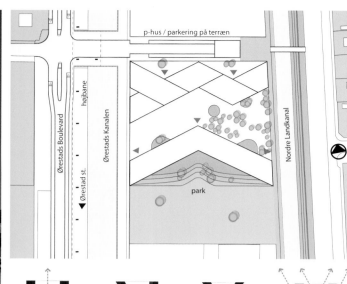

Architectural Moussaka, Athens, Greece, 2007–10. The program for these mixed-use buildings includes parking, commercial spaces, office spaces, and housing. Their angled placement at once maximizes inhabitants' views and privacy. Functions are stacked, starting with a parking cellar, then shops and galleries, followed by restaurants and more shops, and on top one floor of offices and two floors of housing. Thirty percent of the site is unbuilt land for public use.

THE HOUSING GRID GIVES EVERY APARTMENT LONG (CONTEXT) AND SHORT (COURTYARD) VIEWS.

WINDOW OPENINGS ARE ANGLED TO OPTIMIZE BETTER VIEW AND TO PROTECT PRIVACY.

M6B1 Housing, Paris, France, 2008–. Set within a developing neighborhood, this student housing contains an inner spiral for social activities and green space, linking the ground floor to the roof terrace. The exterior remains generic—a response to the yet-unknown aesthetic and function of the neighborhood.

JDS Architects

Johnston Marklee   Los Angeles USA

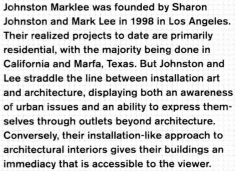

Johnston Marklee was founded by Sharon Johnston and Mark Lee in 1998 in Los Angeles. Their realized projects to date are primarily residential, with the majority being done in California and Marfa, Texas. But Johnston and Lee straddle the line between installation art and architecture, displaying both an awareness of urban issues and an ability to express themselves through outlets beyond architecture. Conversely, their installation-like approach to architectural interiors gives their buildings an immediacy that is accessible to the viewer.

The Hill House is a faceted form that creates a volume with bright, spacious interiors. Precariously seated on a hillside, with a very small footprint, it demonstrates a careful consideration of the local limitations and site conditions. By essentially allowing the form to be established by the conditions that limit it, the firm makes clear its ability to deal with the surroundings sensitively.

To understand Johnston Marklee in greater detail, we must also look at the art installation they created in response to urban sprawl in the fringe city of Tijuana, Mexico. Their *Critical Mass at the Fringe* exhibition, which steps outside the realm of architecture, is a reflection of the two housing types, formal and informal, that are shaping this sprawling city on the US/Mexican border. The installation expresses the pair's ability to distill issues down to their black and white—or in this case red and green—components, and to create an abstract installation and a powerful exhibition that enlighten the visitor and directs attention to the housing problem in Tijuana.

Johnston Marklee's approach to design has an inherent playfulness, though its architectural work sometimes does seem to fit into current trends. For the Hong Kong Design Institute, the firm proposed a simple building module, repeating and stacking it in a way that serves the concept, function, and structure of the project. The idea of essentially repeating one building unit, as this project does, is not unique but it is effective. // Ai Weiwei

Hong Kong Design Institute, Hong Kong, China, 2006. For the 650,000-sq.-ft. (60,000-sq.-m) Hong Kong Design Institute (HKDI) competition, Johnston Marklee designed an asymmetrical building that would hold its own against the backdrop of surrounding skyscrapers. The stacked and offset building modules provide structural stability with an economical means of construction and allow for unique configurations of indoor and outdoor spaces.

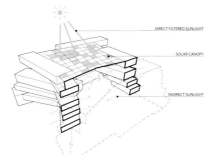
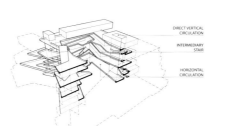

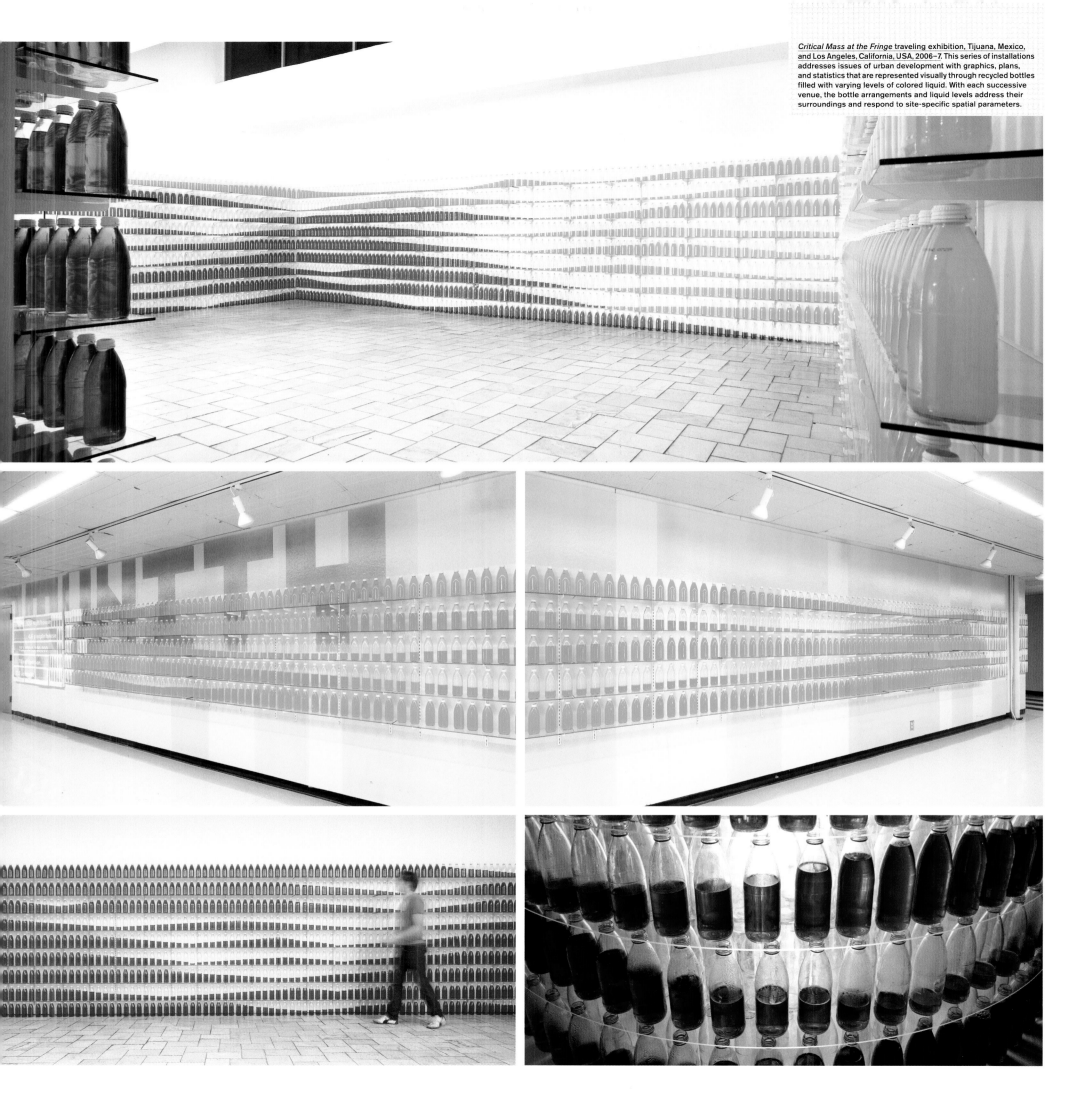

Critical Mass at the Fringe traveling exhibition, Tijuana, Mexico, and Los Angeles, California, USA, 2006–7. This series of installations addresses issues of urban development with graphics, plans, and statistics that are represented visually through recycled bottles filled with varying levels of colored liquid. With each successive venue, the bottle arrangements and liquid levels address their surroundings and respond to site-specific spatial parameters.

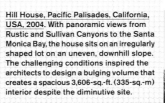

Walden/Wilson Studio, Culver City, California, USA, 2002. Built as a detached addition to a suburban house, this 900-sq.-ft. (84-sq.-m) studio and garage is devised as a sculptural assembly of three stacked objects—garage, studio, and skylight. Using cement fiberboard panels to clad the structure, the recessed windows punctuate each facade with zones for proposed built-in furniture and storage on the interior. The baffled skylight creates changing qualities of both diffused and reflected light.

Johnston Marklee

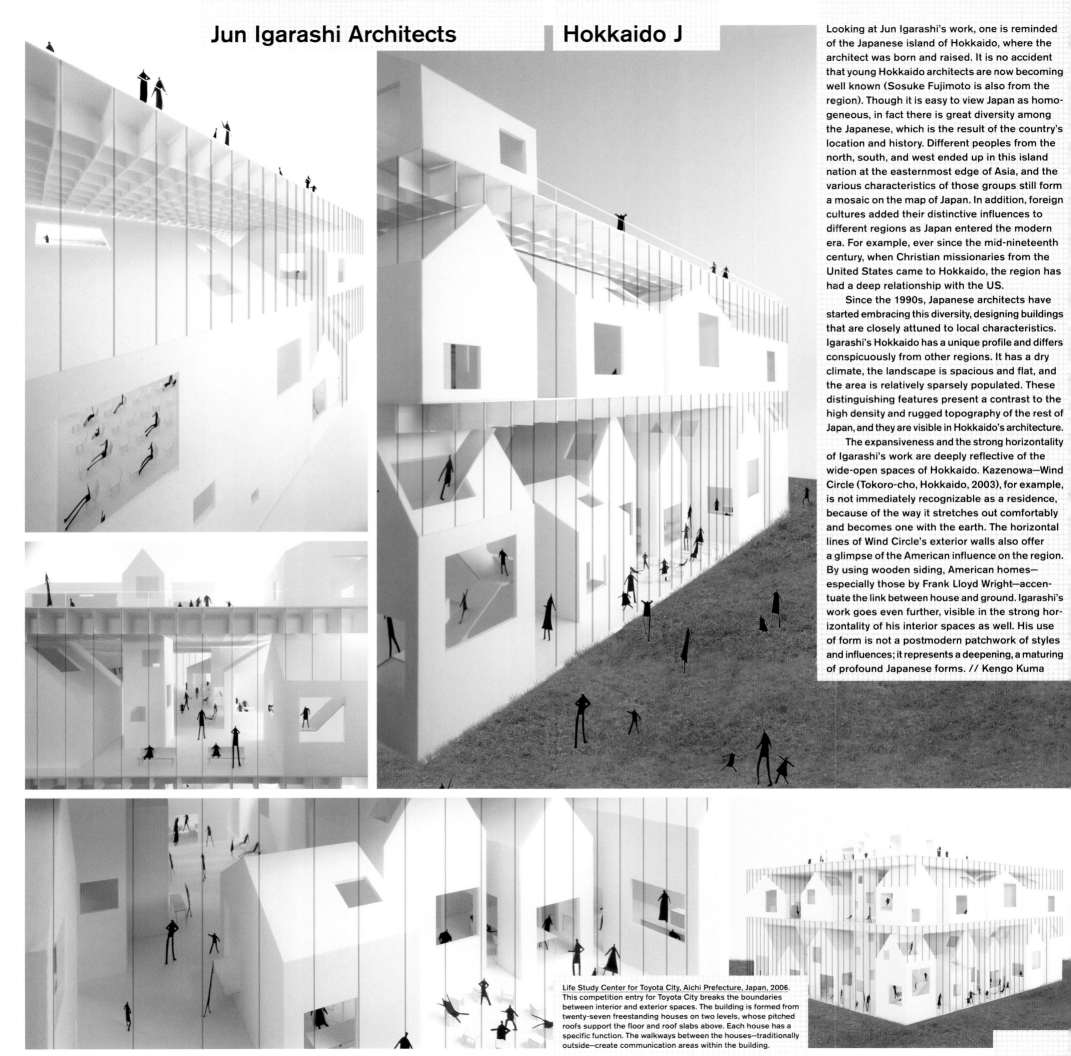

Jun Igarashi Architects

Hokkaido J

Looking at Jun Igarashi's work, one is reminded of the Japanese island of Hokkaido, where the architect was born and raised. It is no accident that young Hokkaido architects are now becoming well known (Sosuke Fujimoto is also from the region). Though it is easy to view Japan as homogeneous, in fact there is great diversity among the Japanese, which is the result of the country's location and history. Different peoples from the north, south, and west ended up in this island nation at the easternmost edge of Asia, and the various characteristics of those groups still form a mosaic on the map of Japan. In addition, foreign cultures added their distinctive influences to different regions as Japan entered the modern era. For example, ever since the mid-nineteenth century, when Christian missionaries from the United States came to Hokkaido, the region has had a deep relationship with the US.

Since the 1990s, Japanese architects have started embracing this diversity, designing buildings that are closely attuned to local characteristics. Igarashi's Hokkaido has a unique profile and differs conspicuously from other regions. It has a dry climate, the landscape is spacious and flat, and the area is relatively sparsely populated. These distinguishing features present a contrast to the high density and rugged topography of the rest of Japan, and they are visible in Hokkaido's architecture.

The expansiveness and the strong horizontality of Igarashi's work are deeply reflective of the wide-open spaces of Hokkaido. Kazenowa—Wind Circle (Tokoro-cho, Hokkaido, 2003), for example, is not immediately recognizable as a residence, because of the way it stretches out comfortably and becomes one with the earth. The horizontal lines of Wind Circle's exterior walls also offer a glimpse of the American influence on the region. By using wooden siding, American homes—especially those by Frank Lloyd Wright—accentuate the link between house and ground. Igarashi's work goes even further, visible in the strong horizontality of his interior spaces as well. His use of form is not a postmodern patchwork of styles and influences; it represents a deepening, a maturing of profound Japanese forms. // Kengo Kuma

Life Study Center for Toyota City, Aichi Prefecture, Japan, 2006. This competition entry for Toyota City breaks the boundaries between interior and exterior spaces. The building is formed from twenty-seven freestanding houses on two levels, whose pitched roofs support the floor and roof slabs above. Each house has a specific function. The walkways between the houses—traditionally outside—create communication areas within the building.

Tea House, Tokoro-gun, Hokkaido Prefecture, Japan, 2005–6. A private retreat in the client's back garden, this project is conceived as two small concrete huts, sunk in a concrete pit and accessible by a few stairs, capped by a sheet of rusted steel that functions as a table.

House of Trough, Shikaoi, Hokkaido Prefecture, Japan, 2007–8.
This introverted house is centered around the living room, which
is sheathed from the outside. It has just two small windows
to the exterior, but large rectangular openings to other rooms of
the house allow light to flow in the central space. Translucent
curtains can be closed for additional privacy.

Jun Igarashi Architects

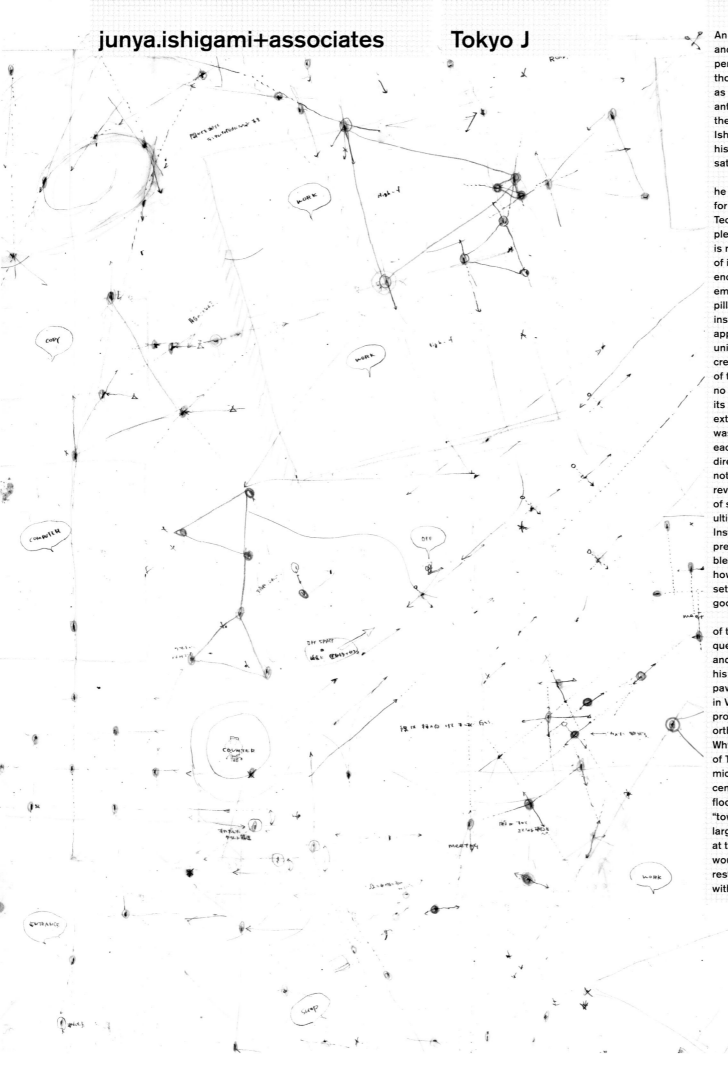

junya.ishigami+associates   Tokyo J

An age-old adage shared by design critics and horse-racing pundits dictates that expected performance, be the subject an architect or a thoroughbred steed, depends as much on lineage as individual track record. As a direct descendant of the Shinohara–Ito–Sejima bloodline, the stakes for young Japanese architect Junya Ishigami have been high; in its short existence, his Tokyo-based office appears to have already satisfied many of these expectations.

Ishigami founded his practice in 2005 when he received a commission to design a building for the campus of the Kanagawa Institute of Technology, located in a suburb of Tokyo. Completed in 2008, the building, a studio for students, is not quick to reveal the exceptional nature of its design: at a glance, it is a prismatic shed enclosed by glass curtain walls. The interior is empty except for plants, furniture, and slender pillars that support the roof slab. On closer inspection, however, subtle details become apparent. The distribution of the pillars is not uniform: their density is modulated so as to create enclosures and open areas, the equivalent of thickets and clearings in a forest. There are no diagonal braces on the facade: to preserve its purity and the continuity between interior and exterior, the task of bracing against wind loads was distributed across the 305 vertical pillars, each of which is flat and oriented in a different direction. The building's subtlety is hard-earned, not accidental, and required years of experiments, revisions, and research—even the development of special engineering software. Yet there is ultimately nothing spectacular about the Kanagawa Institute of Technology, and for many this is precisely what makes Ishigami's work remarkable. The tenacity to rigorously pursue an idea—however simple it may be—is ultimately what sets the few great architects apart from the many good architects.

As a natural consequence of inhabiting one of the world's densest cities, Ishigami frequently questions the conventions of metropolitan living and its architectural embodiments. Much of his unrealized work, showcased in the Japanese pavilion for the 2008 Architecture Biennale in Venezia, consists of seemingly outlandish proposals for dwellings that imply distinctly unorthodox lifestyles on the part of their inhabitants. Why purchase a spacious home in the suburbs of Tokyo when one could acquire several dozen micro-apartments, each on a different floor, in a centrally located tower block? By linking each floor to the one above with a spiral staircase, a "tower-apartment" is created. Most people in large houses only utilize a fraction of the space at their disposal; thus only a couple of floors would be used on a day-to-day basis. And the rest? "Weekend explorations," replies Ishigami, with an ironic glint in his eye. // Joseph Grima

Kanagawa Institute of Technology (KAIT) Workshop, Atsugi, Kanagawa Prefecture, Japan, 2005–8. A studio facility for students to casually drop in and work on individual creative projects, the KAIT Workshop was designed to evoke the feeling of strolling in the woods with sunlight filtering through the trees. The 305 columns erected as soft, ambiguous borders enable users to change spaces freely and quickly.

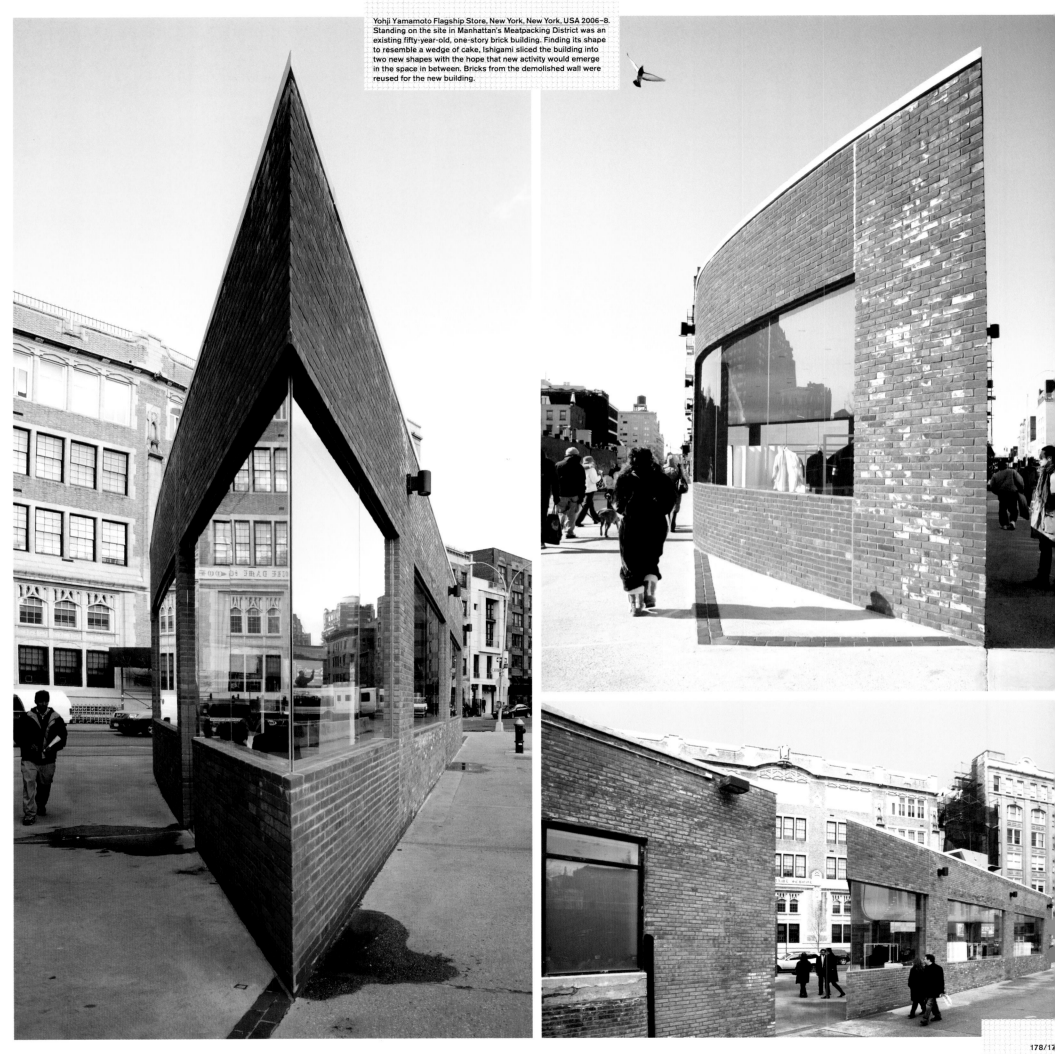

Balloon, Museum of Contemporary Art, Tokyo, Japan, 2007. This one-ton rectangular balloon, created for an exhibition at Tokyo's Museum of Contemporary Art, is built as a solid aluminum truss structure. As tall as a four-story building, it drifts through the museum's atrium, filled with helium, not attached to the building in any way.

junya.ishigami+associates

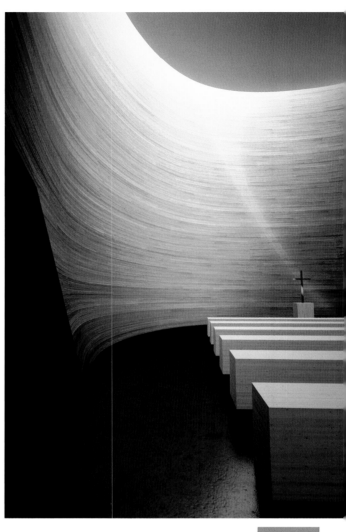

Simonkappeli, Helsinki, Finland, 2008–. With its simple wooden profile, this ecumenical chapel in the center of Helsinki acts as a beacon of tranquility in one of the city's busiest commercial districts. A thin opening at the top of the chapel allows a stream of light to enter the space, creating a sacred atmosphere.

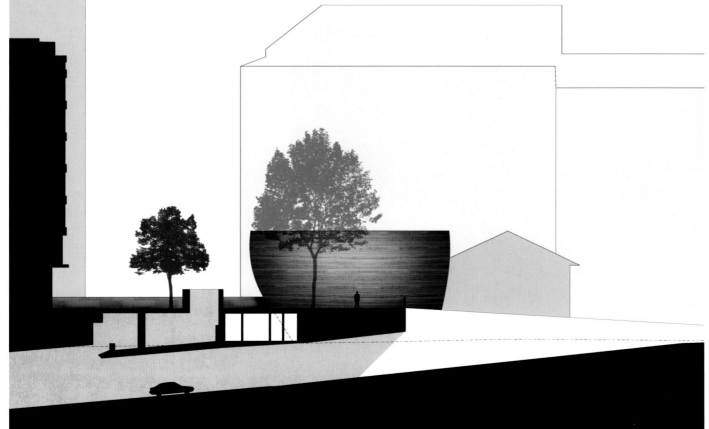

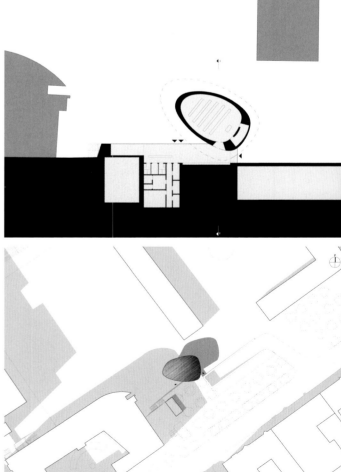

ENTER Sipoo Upper Secondary School, Sipoo, Finland, 2004–7. ENTER is a technology college close to Helsinki. The L-shaped building forms the last corner of an existing school campus. The urban setting is dominated by two curved yards: a larger one toward the campus garden and a smaller courtyard connected to the main road. A concrete stair cast on site forms the core of the building and is crowned by a large conical top light.

The young team of the Finnish architecture firm K2S—Kimmo Lintula, Niko Sirola, and Mikko Summanen—attracted considerable attention with their roof for the Helsinki Olympic Stadium, a modernist landmark built in 1938. The underside surface of the new roof is clad in pine wood strips, providing a warm contrast to the roof's exterior, with its clear but elegantly curved form emphasizing the contemporaneity of the addition. A similar approach is evident in Villa Sarvilahti, a clear white cube with a wooden interior that stands on a hill in a small wood of birch trees next to a lake—things could hardly be more Finnish. Here the sense of natural warmth is provided most directly by the side buildings—a sauna, a summer house, and a guest house—which are made of solid wood beams that show their good carpentry.

Yet the firm can also create solutions that would not necessarily be expected of traditional Finnish architects. The IT college in Sipoo, with two arching sections cut out of its boxlike plan, has a playful and yet clearly formal layout that catches the eye. Summannen studied one year in Tokyo and for a time worked for the architect Toyo Ito, which may contribute to the international feel of K2S's work. Yet, the firm points out, "We also like the idea that our architecture has its roots in the Finnish building tradition. The sensitivity to material and light as well as a certain modest approach are all qualities that can exist as well in contemporary architecture." The school, with its scale-like glass facades that contrast with the warm wooden tone of the perimeter walls, is a marvelous piece. Its thoughtful design extends from the outdoor areas through to the interior materials, such as the green curtains, the bright wooden paneling, and the curved in-situ concrete stairs. The search for an overall form has been stronger here than just differentiated detailing, which is refreshing in a country famous for its classical designs. Another stunning example is the architects' design for a chapel in downtown Helsinki, which proposes a large, clear egg shape that appears to be made of solid wood. The more angular side-rooms are located in an annex, which covers the underground carpark tunnel, to ensure that they do not disturb the spectacular appearance of the egg. // Peter Cachola Schmal

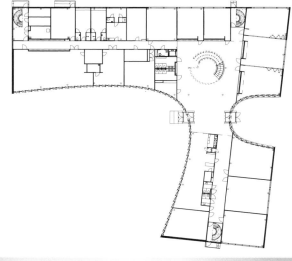

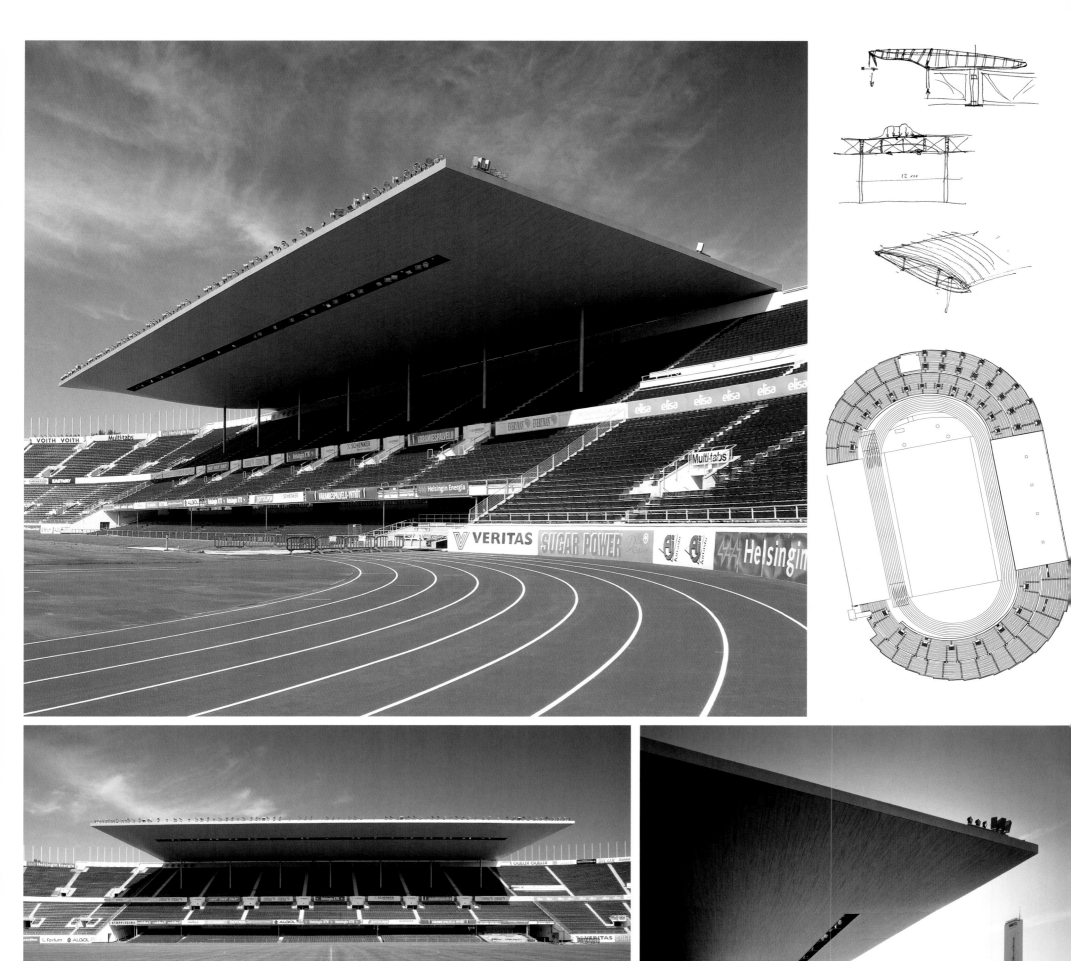

New Roof for the Olympic Stadium, Helsinki, Finland, 2003–5.
The new roof covers roughly one quarter of the stadium on
its east side. It is almost invisible from the exterior, respecting
the pure functionalist architecture of the stadium, yet has a
strong contemporary presence in the stadium interior. It also
mirrors the existing roof on the west side in size and position
but remains distinct through its form and materials.

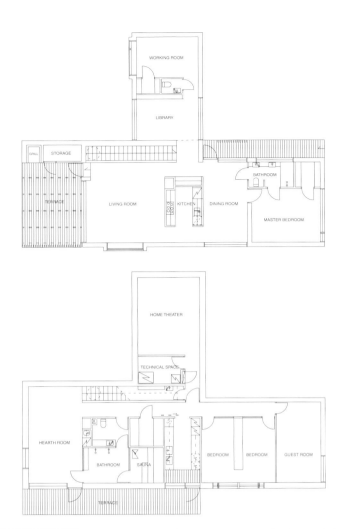

Villa Sarvilahti, Luumäki, Finland, 2004–8. Villa Sarvilahti is a summer retreat built for a pharmacist. The white plastered building is located on the hilly shore of a lake in southeast Finland, featuring views of the wooded landscape typical of the region in various directions. Small auxiliary wooden buildings are also located on the site, accommodating two kinds of saunas and additional bedrooms for visitors.

K2S Architects

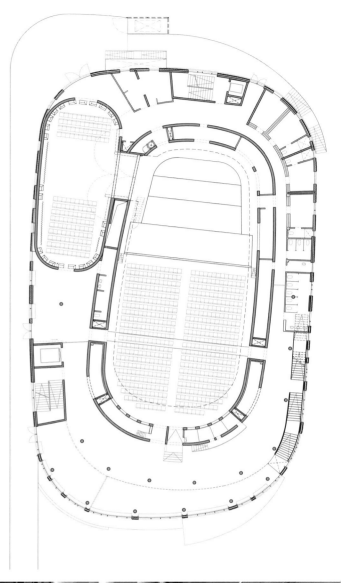

Concert Hall, Pärnu, Estonia, 2001–2. Circulation inside this concert hall moves clockwise with the sun. In the mornings, the eastern section containing the music school and administrative offices is more active, while in the evenings the public spaces come to life. The rhythm inside the building is reflected on the outside through the changing density of the facade—thicker on the northeast side and more open on the southwest side.

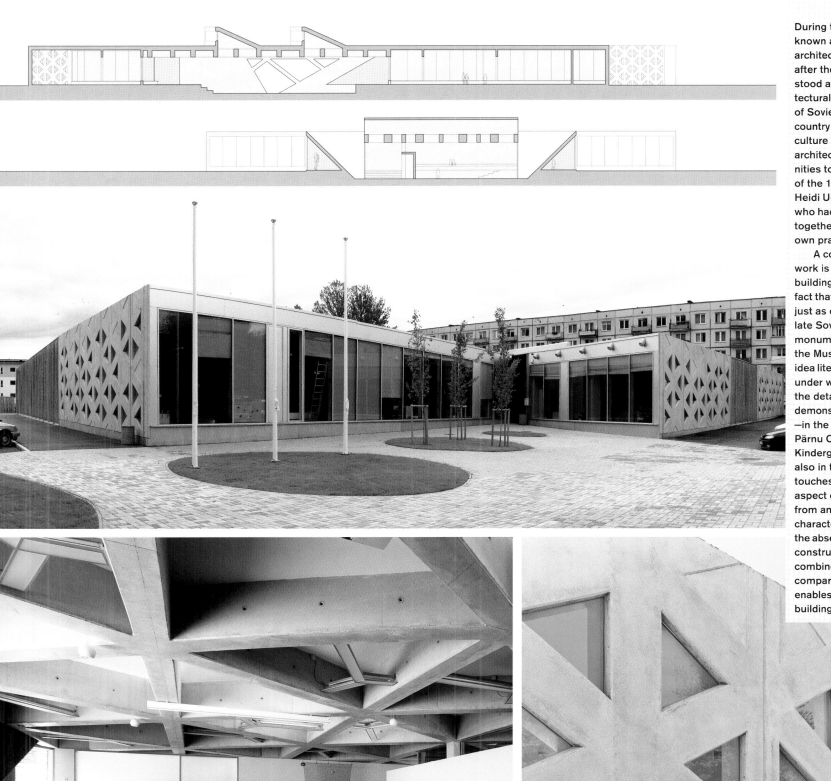

During the Soviet era, Estonia was already known as the republic with the most advanced architecture. Of course, this did not mean that after the revolution of 1991 Estonia immediately stood at the forefront of the international architectural scene—local architects were still products of Soviet schools. However, in recent years the country has developed an impressive architectural culture with outstanding buildings by young architects who took advantage of new opportunities to study abroad after the political changes of the 1990s. In 2002, Katrin Koov, Kaire Nõmm, Heidi Urb, and Siiri Vallner, four female architects who had studied abroad, and had already worked together in various constellations, started their own practice, called Kavakava.

A common denominator among Kavakava's work is the desire to make non-monumental buildings. It is tempting to attribute this to the fact that the architects are women, but one might just as easily see in it an impulse to oppose late Soviet architecture, with its heaviness and monumentality. This is certainly the case with the Museum of Occupations. It conveys the idea literally by lifting up one corner of the building under which visitors can enter the museum, and the detailing is delicate and light. Other projects demonstrate a similar rejection of monumentalism —in the ovals that form the floor plan of the Pärnu Concert Hall, or the triangles of the Tartu Kindergarten, used not only in the floor plan but also in the windows and the construction. This touches upon what may be the most interesting aspect of contemporary Estonian architecture from an international perspective: the specific character of how things are made. It is probably the absence of a sophisticated and fully developed construction industry with standard detailing, combined with a labor force that is cheap in comparison with the costs of materials, that enables the use of custom details for a low-budget building such as a kindergarten. // Bart Goldhoorn

Kindergarten, Tartu, Estonia, 2006–8. This building for a kindergarten is intended to act as a point of focus in a scattered suburban environment. The concrete walls with small colored glass windows and the bamboo fence function as a filter between the kindergarten and the outside world. There are no corridors— the wings of the building wind around a central core, which is devoted to play.

Lasnamäe Track and Field Center, Tallinn, Estonia, 2000–2003. The facade of this athletic facility will eventually be covered with ivy, changing its appearance over time to symbolize the slow and constant process of physical training.

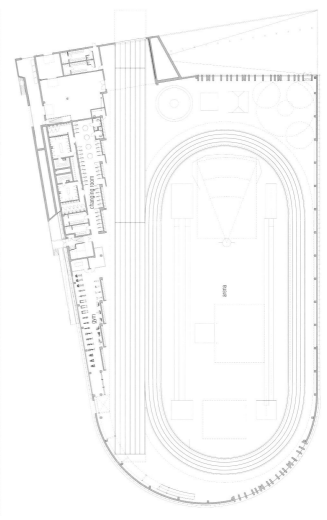

Museum of Occupations, Tallinn, Estonia, 2001–3. The entrance to this museum, dedicated to the German and Soviet occupations of Estonia between 1940 and 1991, is located in a small courtyard with a memorial composed of a birch grove. The trees bring the varying rhythms of nature into the museum. The building's lightness is intended to contrast with the more conventional monumentality of traditional historical memorials.

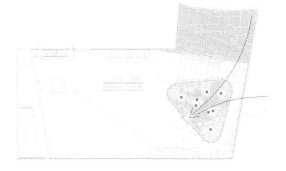

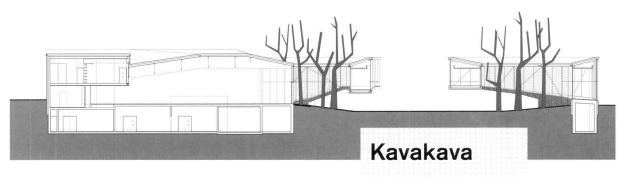

Kavakava

Diébédo Francis Kéré   Berlin D / Ouagadougou BF

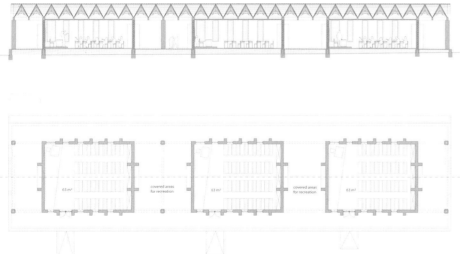

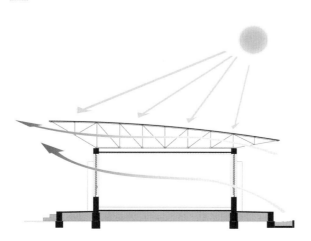

Primary School, Gando, Burkina Faso, 2000–2001. The recipient of the Aga Khan Award for Architecture in 2004, this project, designed while the architect was still a student, emphasizes climate control paired with low-cost construction, using local materials and handcraft techniques.

The young architect Diébédo Francis Kéré, born in Burkina Faso and based in Berlin and Ouagadougou, came to international attention in 2004 when he won an Aga Khan Award for the design of a primary school in his native village of Gando. This project brought together the technical sophistication of his training in Germany—evident in the elegant space frame of the roof—and a keen awareness of local materials and climate—as expressed by the earthen walls, which provide physical protection and thermal insulation. After the success of the Gando School, Kéré had the opportunity to build another school in Burkina Faso, this time in Dano, where his ideas about sustainable construction, inexpensive, easily available materials, and the tapping of the local labor force were again put to use. In undertaking projects such as facilities for adult education, women, and health care, the architect has joined the technical skills of a builder with the organizing drive of a community leader. He has become an advocate of local development in his native country and in Germany, where he teaches a "Habitat Unit" at Berlin's Technical University. He has also been able to use international platforms and events to move audiences with his ethical attitude and warm eloquence.

In 1999, while still a student, Kéré launched the association Schulbausteine für Gando (Bricks for Schools for Gando), a nonprofit organization whose goal is to promote education, health, and development aid in Gando. Since its founding, Kéré has matured professionally, but he has kept intact his sense of purpose, his loyalty to his people, and fertile connection to his roots. These traits inspire not only his buildings but also the extraordinary choreography that brings them to completion. // Luis Fernández-Galiano

Primary School addition, Gando, Burkina Faso, 2007–8. The Gando primary school was straining its capacity after nearly seven years, making an expansion necessary. The new building is based on the same construction, climate control, and sustainability principles, but uses a new architectural expression.

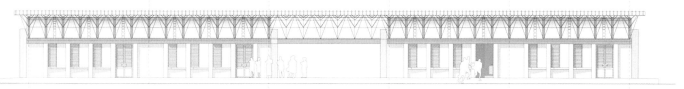

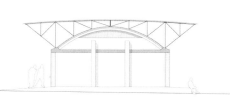

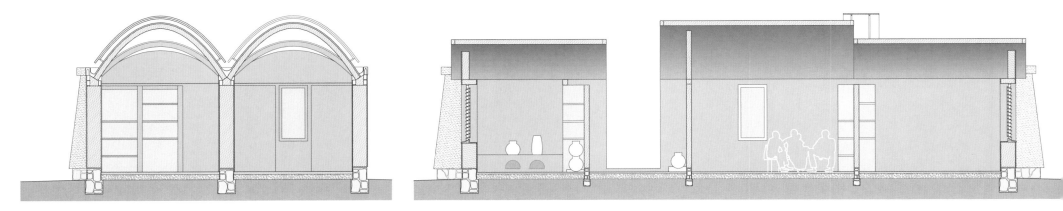

Teachers' Housing, Gando, Burkina Faso, 2004–5. In addition to the original primary school, a pilot project for staff accommodations was initiated. Modules the size of a traditional round hut, that can be added to form a complex, were designed and developed with local materials and simple construction methods that can be easily adapted.

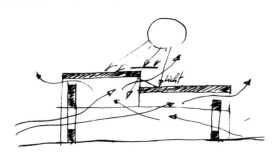

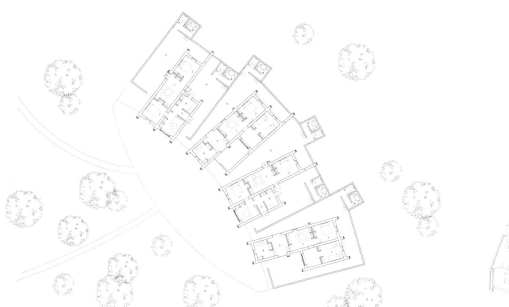

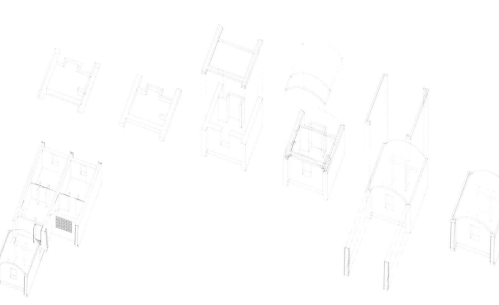

School addition, Dano, Burkina Faso, 2006–7. This addition to an existing high school consists of three classrooms, a roofed, shaded seating area, an office space, and a computer room. The project stressed the innovative use of local materials applied to imported construction techniques combined with natural climate control methods and sustainable low-cost design.

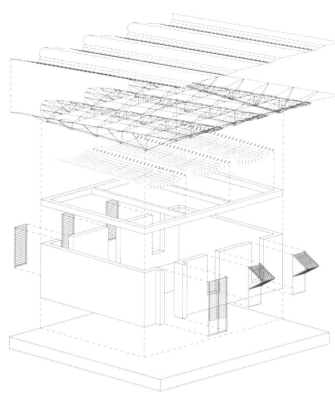

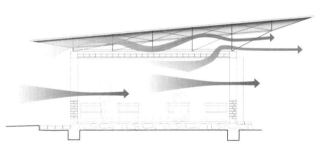

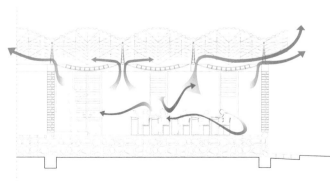

Diébédo Francis Kéré

Klein Dytham architecture (KDa) describes itself as a Tokyo practice, not a Japanese practice. This is not a pedantic distinction, but registers the architects' attachment to the chaotic flux of the city in which they work, in contrast to the stillness that the world has come to associate with Japanese architecture. After graduating from London's Royal College of Art, Astrid Klein and Mark Dytham went to work in Toyo Ito's office, then founded KDa in 1991.

From the moment they opened their doors, they seized every opportunity to practice, working with tight budgets (Heidi House), tight sites (Billboard Building), and short lifespans (i-fly Virgin Atlantic Airways campaign, Tokyo, 2000). There is a fearlessness in their work, embracing the visual and the performative, the disposable and the eternal, technology and horticulture, decadence and discount. What holds it all together is the clarity of decision making evident in each project.

A good example is the Leaf Chapel in Kobuchizawa, a wedding chapel conceived as two leaves. One is glass and stationary; the other, perforated white steel that lifts as the groom lifts his bride's veil. It is simple and seductively lyrical. The design also, incidentally, allows one group of wedding guests to exit stage left as the white leaf descends while the next wedding group enters. Here is beauty and efficiency. Minimizing construction costs presents another opportunity to keep it simple. Heidi House consists of a timber-frame structure, clad on the interior in sheet plywood for lateral strength, with a skin of glass wrapped around the whole. A repeated Tyrolean motif cut into the plywood allows light to enter while providing privacy. No complicated finishing or fussy detailing is needed.

The architects readily admit that the audacity of their approach comes in part from the freedom of being outsiders in Japan—forever *gaijin*. Yet the work, if not the architects, is unambiguously of this city, consistent with Tokyo's "pet architecture" (a term coined by their colleagues at Tokyo's Atelier Bow-Wow): niche projects that exploit serendipitous opportunities in this sprawling, spontaneous conurbation. As their practice develops they are being rewarded with larger projects; no longer niche architects, KDa is not only attuned to the cultural contingency of the vigorous Tokyo architecture scene, they are at its heart.
// Andrew Mackenzie

Billboard Building, Tokyo, Japan, 2004–5. Since the building appeared to be almost entirely facade, the architects gave it the characteristics of a billboard. They used a strong, simple image of a bamboo grove stenciled in white onto the glass facade, and painted the back wall bright green. By day, the graphic becomes a striking and simple form of sun-shading; by night, green light dapples over the intersection—a luminous bamboo plantation in the heart of the metropolis.

Leaf Chapel, Kobuchizawa, Yamanashi Prefecture, Japan, 2001–4. This wedding chapel sits within the grounds of the Risonare Hotel Resort in Kobuchizawa, a green setting with beautiful views of the mountains. It is formed by two leaves, one glass and one steel. The white steel leaf, perforated with 4,700 holes, opens when the groom lifts the bride's veil, revealing the pond and nature beyond.

TBWA\Hakuhodo, Tokyo, Japan, 2006–7. For the headquarters of a new advertising agency, the architects converted an old bowling alley in a large eight-story amusement complex. After the removal of the suspended ceiling, a double-height space with downstand beams 6 ft. (2 m) thick was revealed. A "park" runs through the middle of the space, and a series of shelter-like meeting rooms and offices generates a small townscape, where the raised areas on top of the shelters create pleasant spots for breaks.

Heidi House, Tokyo, Japan, 2004–5. Located in a residential area of Tokyo, Heidi House is a low-cost studio and office space. The simple, playful wood-framed structure is lined on the interior with plywood for lateral strength, but the exterior is covered with glass. Unlike many Japanese houses, which are made of wood but are covered with metal, plastic siding, or even imitation bricks, the house transparently reveals its construction and materials.

Klein Dytham architecture

Totan Kuzembaev Architectural Workshop | Moskva RUS

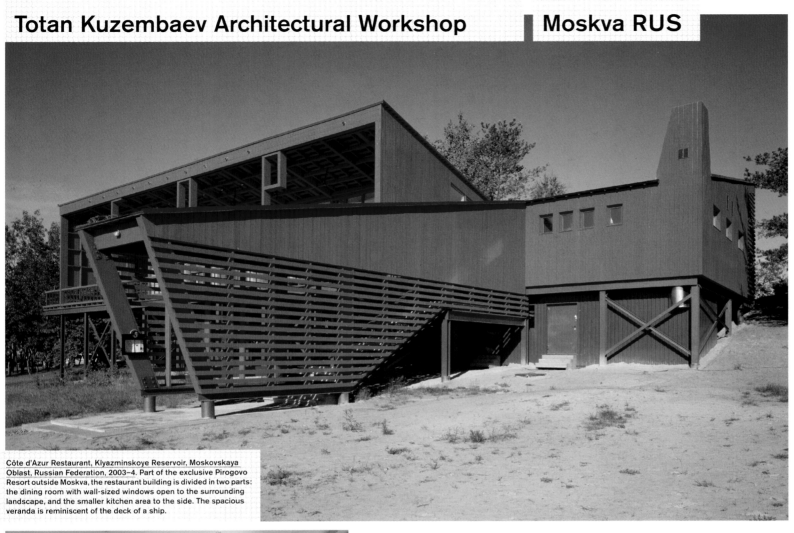

Côte d'Azur Restaurant, Klyazminskoye Reservoir, Moskovskaya Oblast, Russian Federation, 2003–4. Part of the exclusive Pirogovo Resort outside Moskva, the restaurant building is divided in two parts: the dining room with wall-sized windows open to the surrounding landscape, and the smaller kitchen area to the side. The spacious veranda is reminiscent of the deck of a ship.

Klyazminskoye Reservoir is one of a group of artificial lakes just north of Moskva that has become a holiday destination for wealthy Russians from the capital. This lake, surrounded by woods that are slowly making way for the red brick villas of the nouveaux riches, is the site of a former Soviet-era resort. It was bought in 2002 by entrepeneur Alexander Yezhkov—who soon became one of the most important patrons of Russian architecture—and gradually the area is being redesigned as a luxury resort, but in a manner that one would not necessarily expect from the "New Russians." The aesthetic of the exclusive Pirogovo Resort refers more to the Russian wooden hut or *dacha* than to marble neoclassical villas.

The first building was Alexander Brodsky's Restaurant 95 Degrees (see p. 68). After that, the resort developed quickly and now includes a yacht club, a golf course, another restaurant, and numerous houses—the apartment blocks have since been demolished. Though a considerable number of Moskva architects are involved in the project, Totan Kuzembaev is the most prolific. In fact, all he has ever built is in this resort.

The origins of Kuzembaev's work lie in the Russian "paper architecture" movement of the 1980s. In the 1990s, he had a marginal design practice, but his association with Yezhkov has finally allowed him to open a proper office. All of Kuzembaev's buildings are made of wood, but, unlike many other Russian architects, he avoids creating variations on the prototypical log cabin. His first works on the site, the Guest Houses, are a clear allusion to Constructivism: the small summer dwellings are nearly exact reproductions of the units for OSA (Union of Contemporary Architects) Group's linear city of the 1930s. In more recent buildings, such as the Golf Club and Yacht Club, Kuzembaev experiments with the possiblities of wood for making screenlike structures and large constructions, which are often reminiscent of the work of Japanese architects such as Kengo Kuma. He seems to be constantly exploring, and pushing, the possibilities of wooden architecture further.

In that sense, the resort is like a laboratory of experiments. It is questionable whether these kinds of buildings could ever survive outside of this protected area. They are like models made of cardboard—Kuzembaev has never stopped being a paper architect. // Bart Goldhoorn

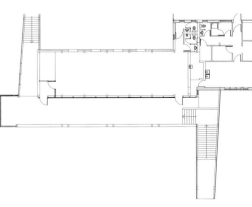

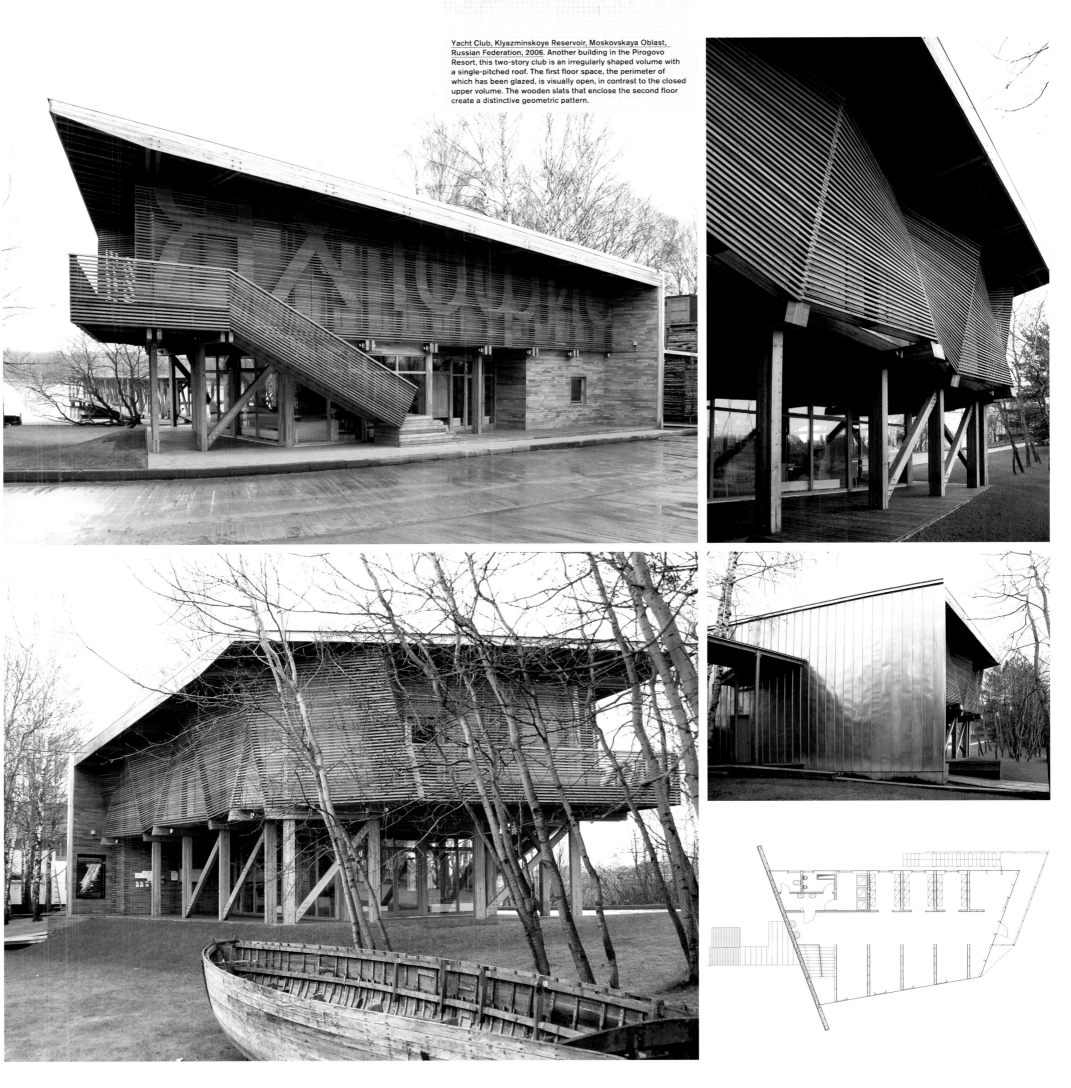

Yacht Club, Klyazminskoye Reservoir, Moskovskaya Oblast, Russian Federation, 2006. Another building in the Pirogovo Resort, this two-story club is an irregularly shaped volume with a single-pitched roof. The first floor space, the perimeter of which has been glazed, is visually open, in contrast to the closed upper volume. The wooden slats that enclose the second floor create a distinctive geometric pattern.

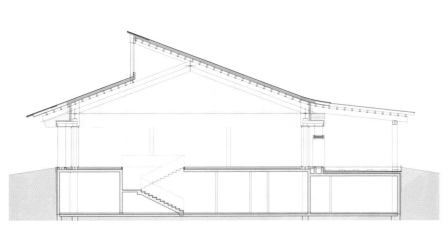

Golf Club, Klyazminskoye Reservoir, Moskovskaya Oblast, Russian Federation. 2005–7. The one-story Golf Club is at the center of all the buildings comprising the Pirogovo Resort complex. The structural grid of bearing pillars forms the basis of the spatial arrangement. The terrace, elevated on pylons, gives the club the appearance of floating above the ground, as a ship gliding through water.

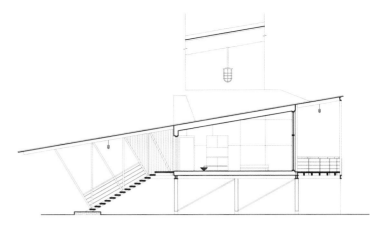

Guest Houses, Klyazminskoye Reservoir, Moskovskaya Oblast, Russian Federation, 2003–4. Totan Kuzembaev's Guest Houses in the Pirogovo Resort are devised as three small, indepedent, red structures. The interior spaces are allocated in a functional way and open to the surrounding landscape. A fully glazed wall and semicircular balcony opens each room to views of the lake.

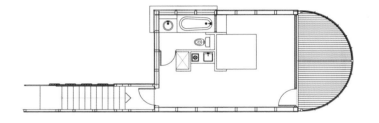

Totan Kuzembaev Architectural Workshop

Master Plan for Polanco, México D.F., Mexico, 2007–10. The plan for this northern district of México D.F. is one of the largest urban development projects in progress in the country, on a site of 592,000 sq. ft. (55,000 sq. m), fifty percent of which is devoted to green space. It will include the headquarters of major international companies such as Grupo Carso and Telcel, as well as housing, restaurants, theaters, and the largest indoor parking area in México D.F.

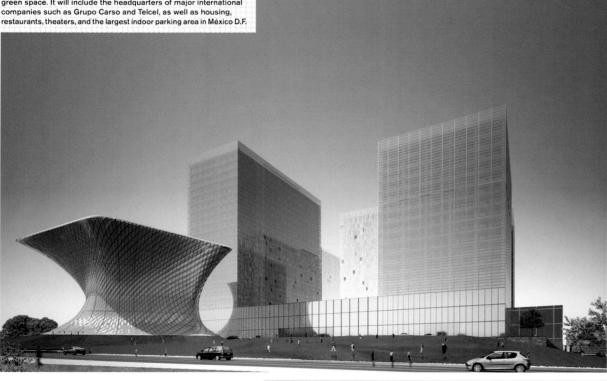

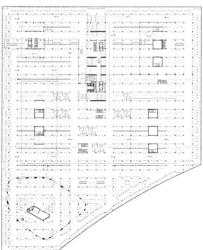

Translation, the title of one of Fernando Romero's recent books, is also a key to understanding the way the architect works. After graduating from the Ibero-American University in México D.F. in 1995, he collaborated with Enric Miralles, Jean Nouvel, and finally the Office for Metropolitan Architecture (OMA) from 1997 to 2000. The influence of Rem Koolhaas appears in Romero's cosmopolitan and multidisciplinary vision of architecture and his approach to design culture as a system of knowledge. In 1999, Romero founded LCM (Laboratorio de la Ciudad de México) in México D.F., with the aim of "translating" the needs of contemporary society into architecture. Seen in these terms, the role of each project is to find a connection between experimental research and construction by revising the modernist parameters. With this objective in mind, in 2005 Romero created LAR (Laboratory of Architecture), headquartered in Los Angeles. The firm works internationally in widely different fields (design, architecture, urban planning, multimedia, cultural events, and publications), all of which nurture one another.

While many of his projects reveal his interest in the formal study of new geometries and organic volumes, Romero's declared purpose is to discover new spaces by "translating traditions." Bridging Tea House, one of the pavilions built in the Jinhua Architecture Park conceived by Ai Weiwei in Zhejiang Province, China, combines two traditional elements of the Chinese garden: the bridge and the teahouse. A structural frame of colored concrete spans the pond. The interior is laid out as numerous "cells," which expand the ancient contemplative experience of the tea ceremony. Similarly, while the cantilevered design for Villa S is determined by a biomorphic analogy, the small windows and the circulation route through the building—as a succession of interiors—resemble the arrangement of the typical Mexican home, with the family living room as its core.

After completing an in-depth analysis of the urban transformations taking place in the urban area known as the Metropolitan Zone of the Valley of Mexico in his book *ZMVM: Zona Metropolitana del Valle de México* (2000), in 2006 the architect received a commission to draft a master plan for the Polanco neighborhood in the northern part of the city. The project includes the Soumaya Art Museum, which will house one of the most important private art collections in Mexico, and embodies the architect's design philosophy for a multipurpose public building. Its sinuous lines are modeled by an elegant torsion, with a curving skin made of frosted glass to diffuse sunlight in the interior. As with all of Romero's works, it is global in outlook, yet an outgrowth of the place in which it is created. // Mercedes Daguerre

Soumaya Art Museum, México D.F., Mexico, 2007–10. This new museum, part of the Polanco master plan, will house a significant private collection of twentieth-century art, as well as an auditorium, a library, offices, a restaurant, and a lounge. The ceiling height varies on each level between 13 and 32 ft. (4 and 10 m). A large subterranean structure will include four levels of underground parking and two levels of storage and restoration labs.

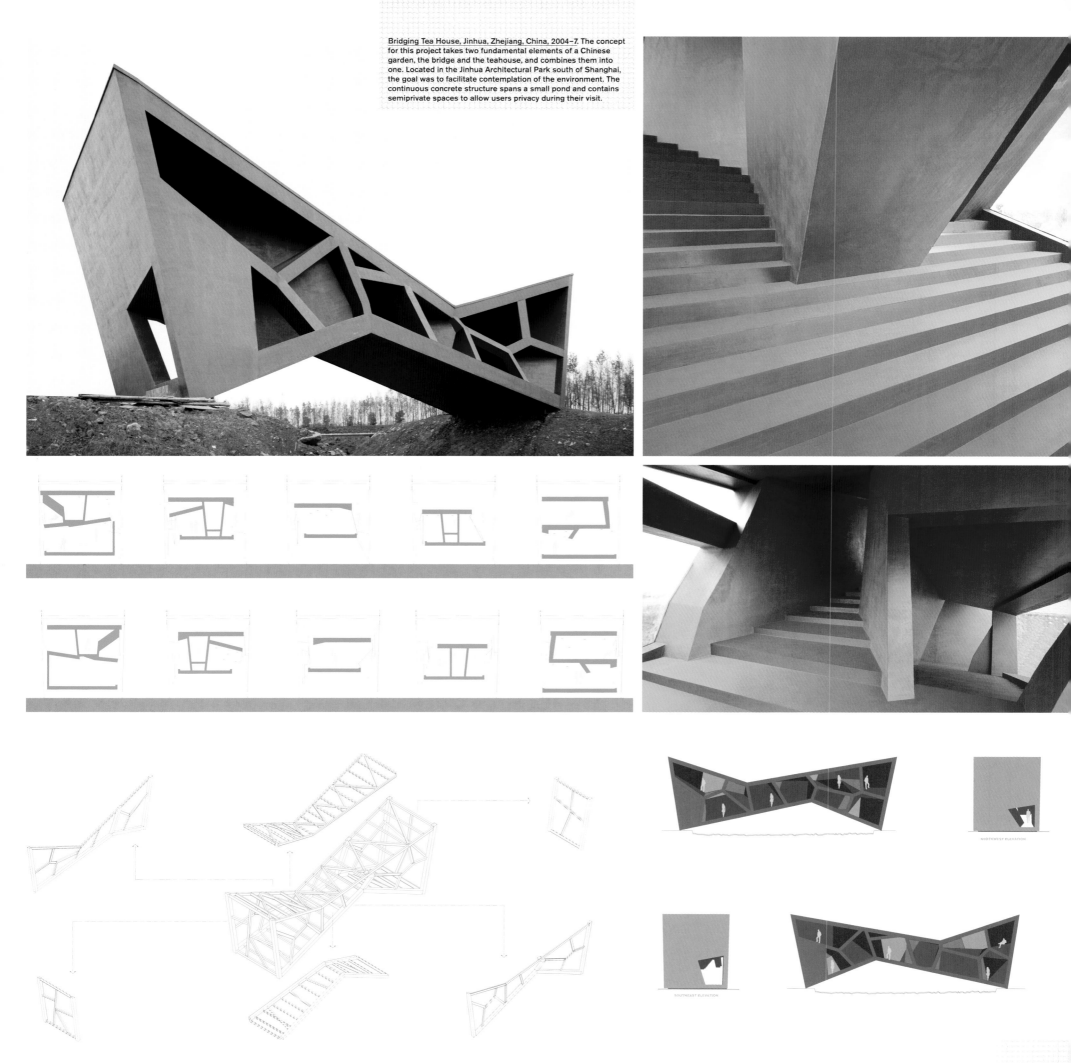

Bridging Tea House, Jinhua, Zhejiang, China, 2004–7. The concept for this project takes two fundamental elements of a Chinese garden, the bridge and the teahouse, and combines them into one. Located in the Jinhua Architectural Park south of Shanghai, the goal was to facilitate contemplation of the environment. The continuous concrete structure spans a small pond and contains semiprivate spaces to allow users privacy during their visit.

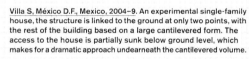

Villa S, México D.F., Mexico, 2004–9. An experimental single-family house, the structure is linked to the ground at only two points, with the rest of the building based on a large cantilevered form. The access to the house is partially sunk below ground level, which makes for a dramatic approach undearneath the cantilevered volume.

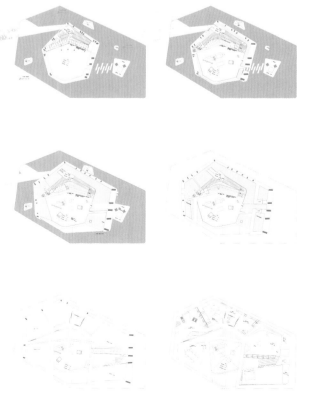

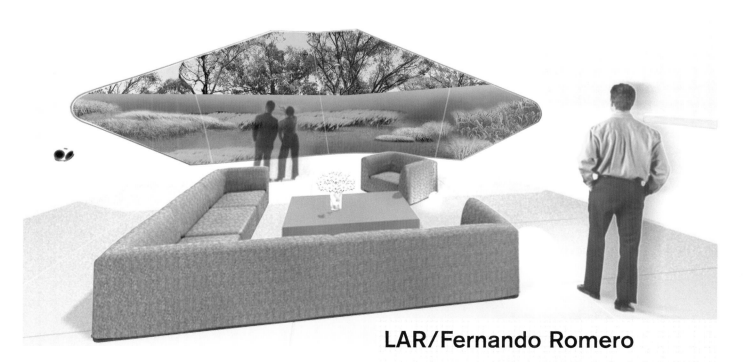

LAR/Fernando Romero

Brisbane Girls Grammar School (BGGS) Creative Learning Center, Brisbane, Queensland, Australia, 2003–6. This six-story building brings together the art, music, drama, and technology facilities of a prominent inner-city school into a single structure. The center also accommodates significant new social spaces, performance and exhibition rooms, and a refectory.

Queensland University of Technology (QUT) Human Movement Pavilion, Brisbane, Queensland, Australia, 2003–5. This project provides the low-cost provision of a teaching space, stores, and a covered outdoor space on a site adjacent to an existing green metal shed. Rather than disregard the shed, the architects engaged it, embedding its recognizable iconic form and inexpensive construction techniques in the new pavilion.

To date, the work of the Australian architecture firm m3architecture has been almost exclusively located within Queensland, and, at the risk of indulging locality, there are qualities in the work that make particular sense in this subtropical northern region of the country, starting with solar protection. Rather than resorting to the default application of acres of timber slats, the sine qua non of Queensland "lifestyle" architecture, m3architecture plays with a variety of solutions for blocking the harsh sun, including deep setback apertures, sensible orientation, and perforated deck shading.

m3architecture's facades and screens are often deployed to engage the language of contemporary architecture. A stunning example is the western facade of the Brisbane Girls Grammar School (BGGS), where a double screen—one made of bronze anodized aluminum vertical slats, the other an inner white wall with black vertical stripes—creates a dynamic moiré effect. This is not just decoration. Thresholds matter to m3architecture. This solution renders connectivity, balancing the intimate and the social within the building, while on the exterior the facade demarcates a territory and enhances the civic life of the street.

In distinguishing history from heritage, m3architecture has little interest in romanticizing Queensland colonial architecture, yet embraces "the ordinary, familiar, and everyday" of the urban fabric. When given the task of designing a building alongside a standard industrial grade shed, as with the Queensland University of Technology (QUT) Human Movement Pavilion, instead of jazzing it up or hiding it, m3architecture designed a respectful addition that embraces the budget commodity and simple tectonic order of the existing shed. Meanwhile, at the University of Queensland (UQ) Micro Health Laboratory, the firm rediscovered the material richness of red brick. The laboratory's exterior walls are composed of alternating brick bonds, alongside layers of highly textured brick. By roughly chipping the ends off hundreds of bricks, the architects created patches of rough materiality not unlike rusticated stonework.

m3architecture transforms commonplace materials and conventional construction methods to imposing effect, a strategy that is shared with other Queensland architects enured to tough conditions and low budgets—Donovan Hill's tilt-slab concrete or Gabriel Poole's industrial bracing come to mind. In this, as in all of its work, m3architecture is a firm of adaptable experimenters, curious researchers, and lateral thinkers. For as much as it is well anchored within its location, more importantly m3architecture's work is embedded within a play of ideas, fostered by a cross-disciplinary and collaborative approach to each new project. // Andrew Mackenzie

Kinloch Residence, Brisbane, Queensland, Australia, 2001. This house was designed for a young family on a hilltop site in Hamilton, Brisbane. The L-shaped plan is designed around a northeastern yard, maximizing views to the south across the river and to the city. The inner edge of the L is used for circulation, which culminates in the garden. The house is planned over three levels, with various large and playful two-story volumes as well as visual connections and views through the house.

University of Queensland (UQ) Micro Health Laboratory, Gatton, Queensland, Australia, 2000–2002. The concept for this building reflects on the two polar elements of human study and investigation: science and the creative arts. On the one hand, science is represented by precision and quantifiable processes, with the interior of the laboratory derived from strict codes and formulas that impose a necessary order and logic. On the other hand, the external brick skin represents artistic theory and creative processes as an exploration into the unknown and imprecise.

m3architecture

Denmark Pavilion, København, Denmark, 2006–. The Denmark Pavilion, conceived as a 2,900-sq.-ft. (269-sq.-m) traveling exhibition piece, represents the first *made in China* house available on the European continent. This particular export differs from low-priced, low-quality products made in China, however. Its formal point of origin is an imagined, yet-to-evolve lifeform.

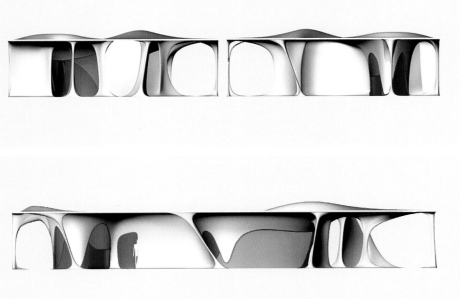

The extraordinary economic growth of China, which has changed the geopolitical balance of the world, has also hatched a new generation of Chinese artists and architects. Often trained in the West, they are transforming the cultural landscape of this immense, ancient country. While Chinese artists have been quick to establish their identity on the international scene, Chinese architects have until now been overshadowed by the many foreign stars imported to design the iconic buildings of the 2008 Beijing Olympic Games. But the situation is changing with the emergence of studios like MAD Office. Though it has completed little other than a small lakeside pavilion, the Hong Luo Clubhouse, with an exquisitely detailed, waving thick slab that hovers weightlessly over the gathering spaces of a social club in a residential district of Beijing, MAD Office already has commissions in Canada, Dubai, and several Chinese cities.

The firm was started in Beijing in 2004 by Yansong Ma, a Beijing-born graduate of Yale University who worked with Peter Eisenman and Zaha Hadid; Yosuke Hayano from Nagoya, Japan, with a master's degree from London's Architectural Association, who also worked in Hadid's office; and Qun Dang, originally from Shanghai but who spent most of her career in the United States. MAD Office, whose architectural language reveals its debt to Eisenman and Hadid, established itself with lightning speed. It won the competition for the Absolute Towers in Mississauga, Ontario, as well as the New York Architectural League's Young Architects Forum Award in 2006. The Absolute Towers, two residential high rises with an oval, rotating plan, present themselves as an immediate architectural icon of "frozen movement."

The firm's exhibition *MAD in China* opened at the 2006 Architecture Biennale in Venezia, and was shown as a floating city at the Danish Architecture Centre in København. It included an intriguing proposal for a pavilion manufactured in China. The low-energy, single-family house, shaped with warped surfaces that give it the appearance of a futuristic cave of dazzling white interiors and immaterial glass walls, will finally be placed in København after being exhibited in Barcelona and Berlin. // Luis Fernández-Galiano

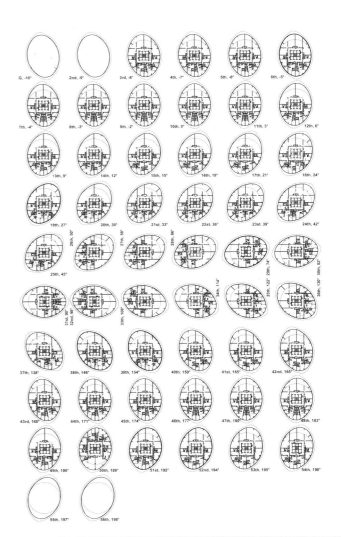

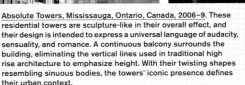

Absolute Towers, Mississauga, Ontario, Canada, 2006–9. These residential towers are sculpture-like in their overall effect, and their design is intended to express a universal language of audacity, sensuality, and romance. A continuous balcony surrounds the building, eliminating the vertical lines used in traditional high rise architecture to emphasize height. With their twisting shapes resembling sinuous bodies, the towers' iconic presence defines their urban context.

Hong Luo Clubhouse, Beijing, China, 2006. Situated along the shore of Hong Luo Lake, in a suburban area north of Beijing, this shared leisure and entertainment facility appears as a continuous, reflective surface, becoming first the roof and then the walls of the house. A single open space houses a bar, kitchen, and dining area, enveloped in glass. A sunken garden, 4 ft. (1.2 m) below the lake's surface, leaves visitors feeling as if they are walking through water to access the building.

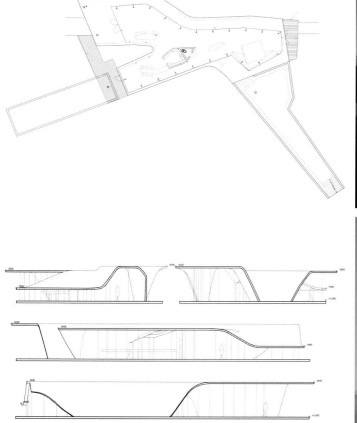

Sinosteel International Plaza, Tianjin, China, 2006–12. The design for this business center includes two towers: a 311-ft. (95-m) hotel, and a 1,175-ft. (358-m) office tower. Six-sided windows, adopted from traditional Chinese architecture, not only provide views but also comprise the main structural system, eliminating the need for internal columns, except at the building's core. There are five different sizes of windows, positioned for energy efficiency to regulate heat loss in winter and excess heat in summer.

MAD Office

Francisco Mangado | Pamplona E

Francisco Mangado was born in 1957 in Estella, Spain, a small town southwest of Pamplona. In 1983, just two years after finishing his studies, he began to teach at his alma mater, the University of Navarre, in Pamplona, and embarked on a prolific professional and teaching career, at such American universities as Yale, Harvard, and the University of Texas. In recent years the architect has won a string of important competitions in Spain, where he established his office, and abroad.

Three recent Spanish works demonstrate the architect's deft, lucid, and virtuoso hand at work. The Football Stadium in Palencia is a compelling work, with a facade of perforated aluminum panels and four gigantic lights at each of its chamfered corners. What impresses most about this luminous stadium is its material lightness and supple economy. It is a building content with the elegance of legibility, a discreet container for the boundless passions of soccer to take center stage.

The Spanish Pavilion at Expo Zaragoza 2008 is a work of exquisite execution and beguiling beauty. Built as a forest of customized columns of differing diameters that delineate and encase the pavilion, the building delights with its musical counterpoint and constructive rigor. It transcends the often-miscast vanities of typical fair structures, contributing instead a timely and timeless work to the annals of architecture. After the Expo's fireworks and lights are extinguished, Mangado's pavilion will continue to have a versatile life in future exhibitions and as a cinema.

The Congress Center and Hotel in Palma de Mallorca (in progess), a gargantuan commission won through an invited international competition, is one of Mangado's largest projects to date. It is also the culmination of the architect's dexterity in designing this building type, exhibiting a finesse that had its debut in the eloquent Congress Center and Auditorium of Navarra (Baluarte), in Pamplona. Following other such centers designed for the cities of Ávila and Alicante (both in progress), the congress center in Mallorca consolidates Mangado's young master status. With its expansive porosity and dramatic vistas to the sea echoed by cross breezes, it becomes an essential and mesmerizing construction along the seashore. // Carlos Jimenez

Football Stadium, Palencia, Spain, 2005–6. The stadium's perimeter is perforated aluminum cladding; the four light towers at each corner provide illumination and establish a dialogue in the landscape with Palencia's cathedral. The stadium's interior is a large void in which, in addition to football games, a variety of public spectacles can be viewed. To make use of the stadium year-round, perimeter offices and other public spaces were included; they are located on the ground floor, with direct access from the street.

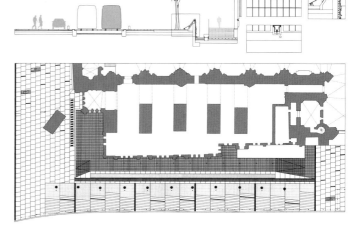

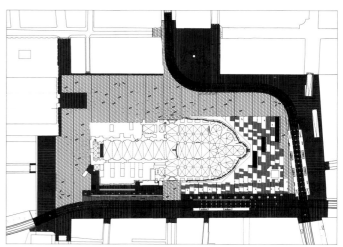

Pey-Berland Square, Bordeaux, France, 1998–2003. The approximately 323,000-sq.-ft. (30,000-sq.-m) square, which includes the cathedral and the city hall, is the most important public space in Bordeaux. The scheme removed most traffic from the square (except the low-impact streetcar) and created a clearing: a continuous, paved pedestrian area marked by bench slabs and custom lighting.

Spanish Pavilion, Expo Zaragoza, Spain, 2005–8. The pavilion evokes a bamboo forest, created with the goal of energy efficiency and environmental awareness. The vertical elements, a metallic core clad in terra cotta, absorb water and generate air currents that act as cooling microclimates. The 10-ft. (3-m) wide roof is clad in panels of recycled wood shavings.

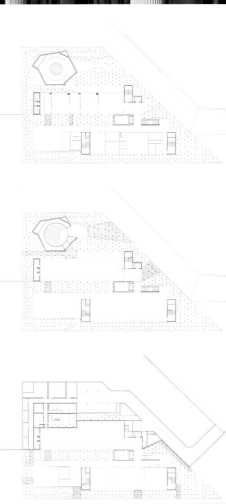

Congress Center and Auditorium of Navarra (Baluarte), Pamplona, Spain, 1999–2003. This project, the largest architectural undertaking in Navarra in recent history, includes multiple halls—one each for 1,600 and 600 people, and four for 300 people—a 54,000-sq.-ft. (5,000-sq.-m) exhibition area, and facilities for catering, storage, and offices. The building employs a variety of materials: the facades are clad mostly in black quartzite, while light-toned beechwood and dark ipe paneling bring contrast inside.

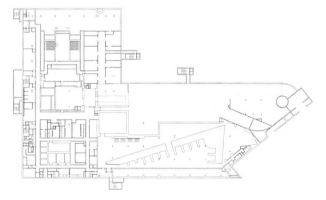
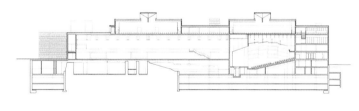

Francisco Mangado

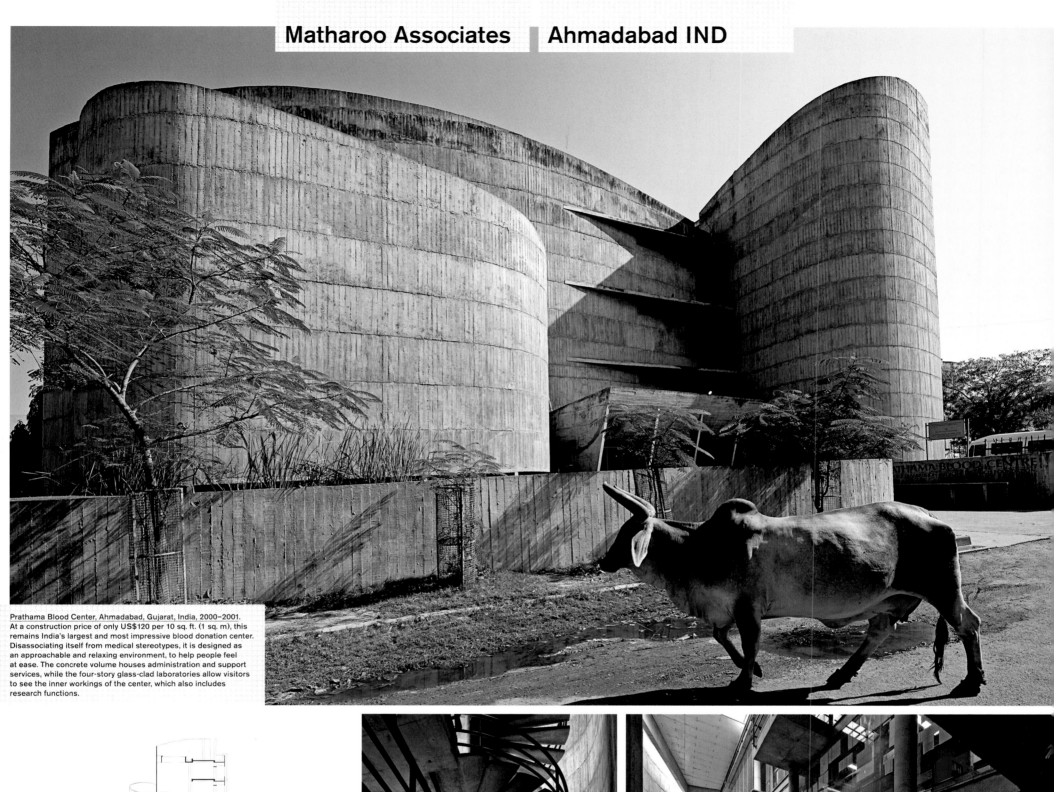

Prathama Blood Center, Ahmadabad, Gujarat, India, 2000–2001.
At a construction price of only US$120 per 10 sq. ft. (1 sq. m), this remains India's largest and most impressive blood donation center. Disassociating itself from medical stereotypes, it is designed as an approachable and relaxing environment, to help people feel at ease. The concrete volume houses administration and support services, while the four-story glass-clad laboratories allow visitors to see the inner workings of the center, which also includes research functions.

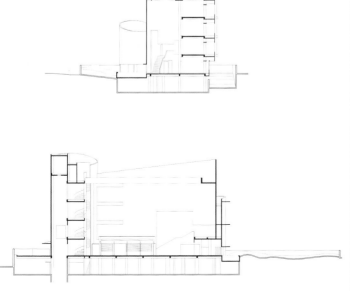

Cattiva Mobile Blood Van, 2005. A mobile extension of the Prathama Blood Center, the van takes blood donation out into the community. Cattiva is equipped with four automatic donor chairs, a medical examination cubicle, a refreshment area, and a lounge.

Matharoo Associates, founded by Gurjit Singh Matharoo, and located in Ahmadabad, India, is involved with industrial, product, and structural design, in addition to architecture. The architectural projects range from single family residences to crematoriums and blood donation centers. While the works resonate with the scale and material qualities of early Modernism, they retain a distinctly Indian flavor in their rudimentary palette of materials.

The Prathama Blood Center, with its large curving concrete forms, has a monumentality that recurs in Matharoo's architecture. With scale, texture, and basic materials, he stamps his character onto the building and instills an aroma of India into the design. He is able to answer direct social needs with his powerful forms. For the Cattiva Mobile Blood Van, Matharoo designed a project that breaks out of the confines of architecture. The van serves as an extension of the Prathama Blood Center, attracting donors to the four reclining chairs within the vehicle.

A tale from the Ordos 100 project—where 100 architects from around the world were commissioned to each design a villa in Nei Mongol, China—helps convey Matharoo's singular nature: As the members of the different architectural studios arrived in the desert to present their proposals, they all seemed a bit lost, but Matharoo stood out because of the way he rose above his particular plight. All of his proposal documents and models had been lost on the plane ride from India to China. Where some might have been frantic, he sat, silently, in apparent relaxation. He told his unfortunate story to those who pried, not as an excuse or a plea for sympathy, but as a factual condition. The most stranded of all the displaced architects, Matharoo was nonetheless able to present his proposal and intrigue the jury through the sheer force of his character and ideas. Like an expression of his strange sensitivities, awkward awareness, and alertness, his unconventional shapes display a unique, non-commercial style. // Ai Weiwei

House for a Fish Breeder, Ahmadabad, Gujarat, India, 2004. With four large glass tanks running the length of the living space, this weekend house, designed for a fish breeder, uses harvested rain water, biogas (gas produced from the breakdown of organic matter), and earth tube heat exchange technology.

Parag Shah Residence, Surat, Gujarat, India, 2005–6. Located in the fast growing industrial city of Surat, the house shuts itself off from the hubbub and heat outside. Designed for a family with a large art collection, it creates an insulated cocoon, centered on a courtyard. Double-height living and dining rooms and a travertine-clad drawing room with an outdoor pavilion make it suitable for entertaining as well.

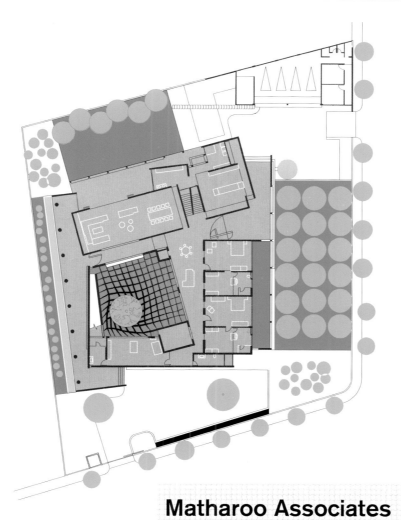

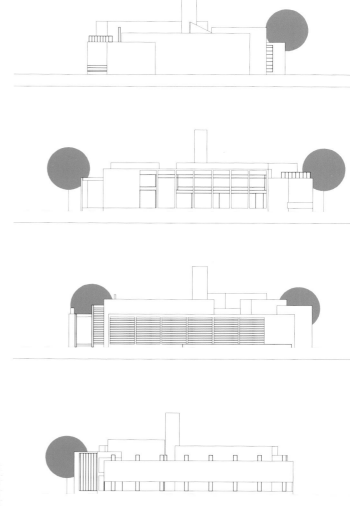

Matharoo Associates

McBride Charles Ryan | Melbourne AUS

Klein Bottle House, Rye, Victoria, Australia, 2006–8. Located on sand dunes among tea trees, the concept for this vacation house began as a sea-shell-like form and developed into a more complex spiral inspired by the Klein bottle. The final building is an angular "origami" version of the topological shape.

220/221

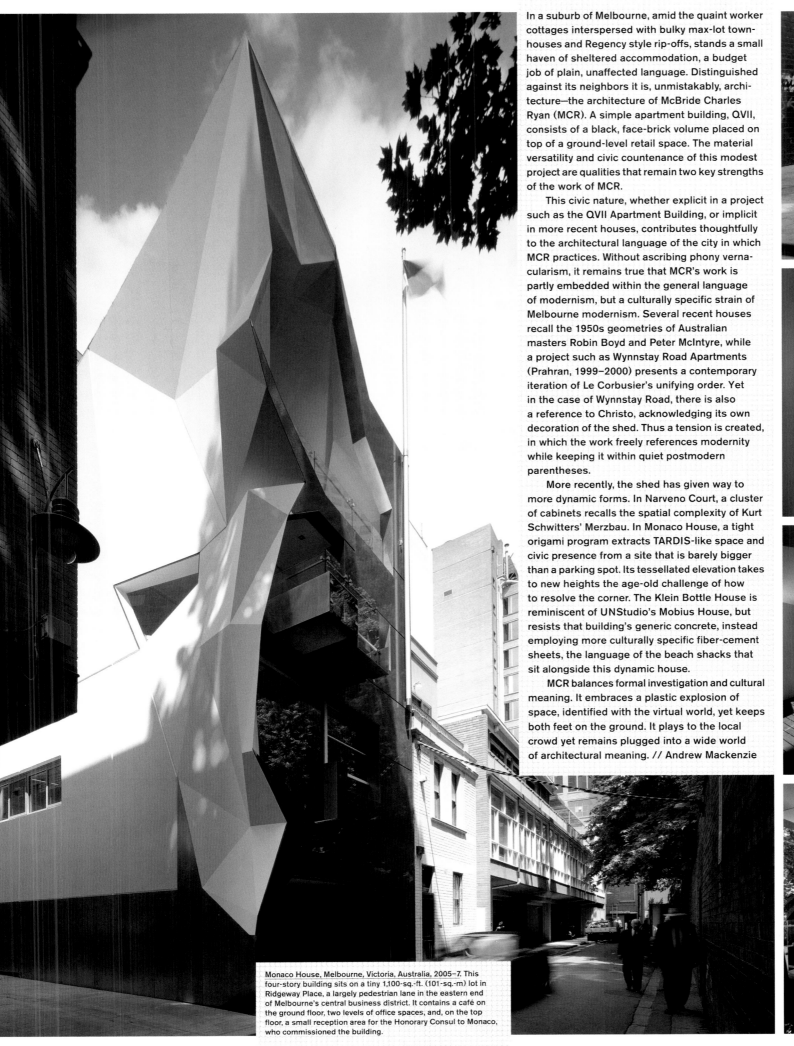

In a suburb of Melbourne, amid the quaint worker cottages interspersed with bulky max-lot townhouses and Regency style rip-offs, stands a small haven of sheltered accommodation, a budget job of plain, unaffected language. Distinguished against its neighbors it is, unmistakably, architecture—the architecture of McBride Charles Ryan (MCR). A simple apartment building, QVII, consists of a black, face-brick volume placed on top of a ground-level retail space. The material versatility and civic countenance of this modest project are qualities that remain two key strengths of the work of MCR.

This civic nature, whether explicit in a project such as the QVII Apartment Building, or implicit in more recent houses, contributes thoughtfully to the architectural language of the city in which MCR practices. Without ascribing phony vernacularism, it remains true that MCR's work is partly embedded within the general language of modernism, but a culturally specific strain of Melbourne modernism. Several recent houses recall the 1950s geometries of Australian masters Robin Boyd and Peter McIntyre, while a project such as Wynnstay Road Apartments (Prahran, 1999–2000) presents a contemporary iteration of Le Corbusier's unifying order. Yet in the case of Wynnstay Road, there is also a reference to Christo, acknowledging its own decoration of the shed. Thus a tension is created, in which the work freely references modernity while keeping it within quiet postmodern parentheses.

More recently, the shed has given way to more dynamic forms. In Narveno Court, a cluster of cabinets recalls the spatial complexity of Kurt Schwitters' Merzbau. In Monaco House, a tight origami program extracts TARDIS-like space and civic presence from a site that is barely bigger than a parking spot. Its tessellated elevation takes to new heights the age-old challenge of how to resolve the corner. The Klein Bottle House is reminiscent of UNStudio's Mobius House, but resists that building's generic concrete, instead employing more culturally specific fiber-cement sheets, the language of the beach shacks that sit alongside this dynamic house.

MCR balances formal investigation and cultural meaning. It embraces a plastic explosion of space, identified with the virtual world, yet keeps both feet on the ground. It plays to the local crowd yet remains plugged into a wide world of architectural meaning. // Andrew Mackenzie

Monaco House, Melbourne, Victoria, Australia, 2005–7. This four-story building sits on a tiny 1,100-sq.-ft. (101-sq.-m) lot in Ridgeway Place, a largely pedestrian lane in the eastern end of Melbourne's central business district. It contains a café on the ground floor, two levels of office spaces, and, on the top floor, a small reception area for the Honorary Consul to Monaco, who commissioned the building.

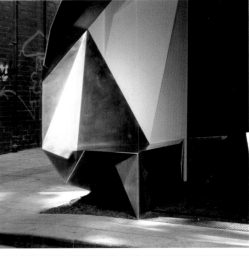

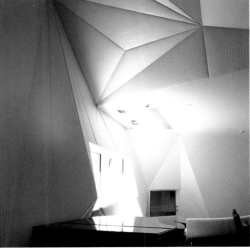

Narveno Court, Hawthorn, Victoria, Australia, 2001–4. The house was designed to be able to accommodate, at varying moments, a family, a single person, or a single person with a large visiting family. The concept is a sphere that has been eroded in part to bring the garden into the house. The various materials—including wood, stone, and brick—are used in the excavated copper dome to create a richly textured exterior space.

QVII Apartment Building, Melbourne, Victoria, Australia, 2000–2004. The eight-story apartment building stands above a three-story retail space by another firm; its sinuous shape unlocks views and contrasts with the base below. The building comprises seventeen unique apartments on each floor, the majority of which are compact one-bedroom units, available in four color schemes.

McBride Charles Ryan

Meixner Schlüter Wendt Architekten | Frankfurt am Main D

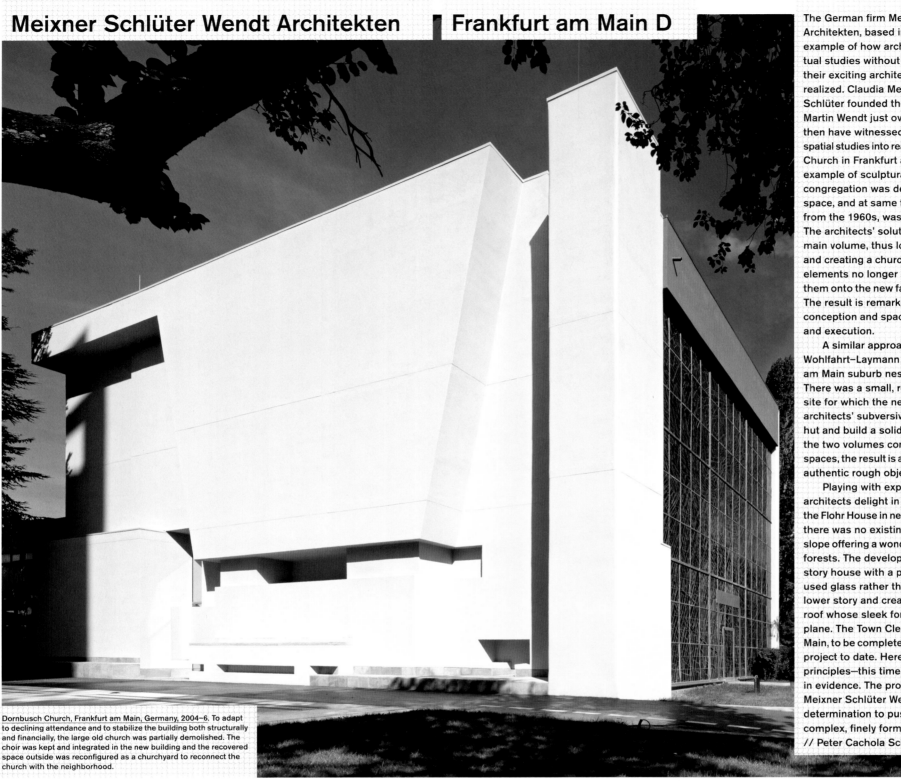

The German firm Meixner Schlüter Wendt Architekten, based in Frankfurt am Main, is an example of how architects who produce conceptual studies without a client can one day see their exciting architectural proposals finally realized. Claudia Meixner and husband Florian Schlüter founded their studio together with Martin Wendt just over ten years ago, and since then have witnessed the transformation of their spatial studies into realized projects. The Dornbusch Church in Frankfurt am Main is an extreme example of sculptural rationality. The parish's congregation was declining and required less space, and at same time the church, which dated from the 1960s, was also in need of renovation. The architects' solution was to scale down the main volume, thus lowering renovation costs and creating a churchyard. They took the stylistic elements no longer needed and transposed them onto the new facade of the reduced volume. The result is remarkably innovative in terms of conception and space, with outstanding planning and execution.

A similar approach is evident in the Wohlfahrt–Laymann House in a leafy Frankfurt am Main suburb nestled in the Taunus hills. There was a small, romantic wooden hut on the site for which the new owner had no use. The architects' subversive concept was to retain the hut and build a solid, neutral box over it. With the two volumes connected via the interstitial spaces, the result is a fascinating contrast between authentic rough object and white cube.

Playing with expectations is a device these architects delight in employing. In the case of the Flohr House in neighboring Kronberg im Taunus there was no existing architecture, just a clear slope offering a wonderful view of the surrounding forests. The development plan specified a two-story house with a pitched roof. The architects used glass rather than solid material for the lower story and created a sculptural, inhabitable roof whose sleek form is evocative of a fighter plane. The Town Clerk's Office in Frankfurt am Main, to be completed in 2009, is the firm's largest project to date. Here again strong sculptural principles—this time stacking and layering—are in evidence. The project demonstrates again Meixner Schlüter Wendt Architekten's unflagging determination to push the limits of their highly complex, finely formulated architecture.
// Peter Cachola Schmal

Dornbusch Church, Frankfurt am Main, Germany, 2004–6. To adapt to declining attendance and to stabilize the building both structurally and financially, the large old church was partially demolished. The choir was kept and integrated in the new building and the recovered space outside was reconfigured as a churchyard to reconnect the church with the neighborhood.

Town Clerk's Office, Frankfurt am Main, Germany, 2005–9. The design reflects an intermediation of nearby buildings and the curves of neighboring railway lines. The spiral band structure permits a combination of urban densification and openness with high-quality light exposure. The usual distinction between front and back, and street and courtyard facades, is eliminated.

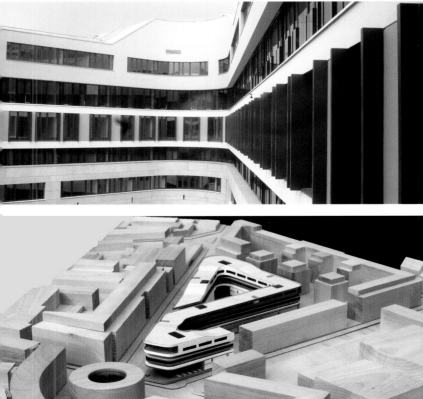

Flohr House, Kronberg im Taunus, Germany, 2005–7. Due to local regulations a pitched roof was the starting point for this house, and it became its defining feature. The ostensibly pitched roof, which contains the top floor, hovers above the glazed ground floor embedded in the slope. The effect is that of a dynamic, levitating object accentuating the openness underneath.

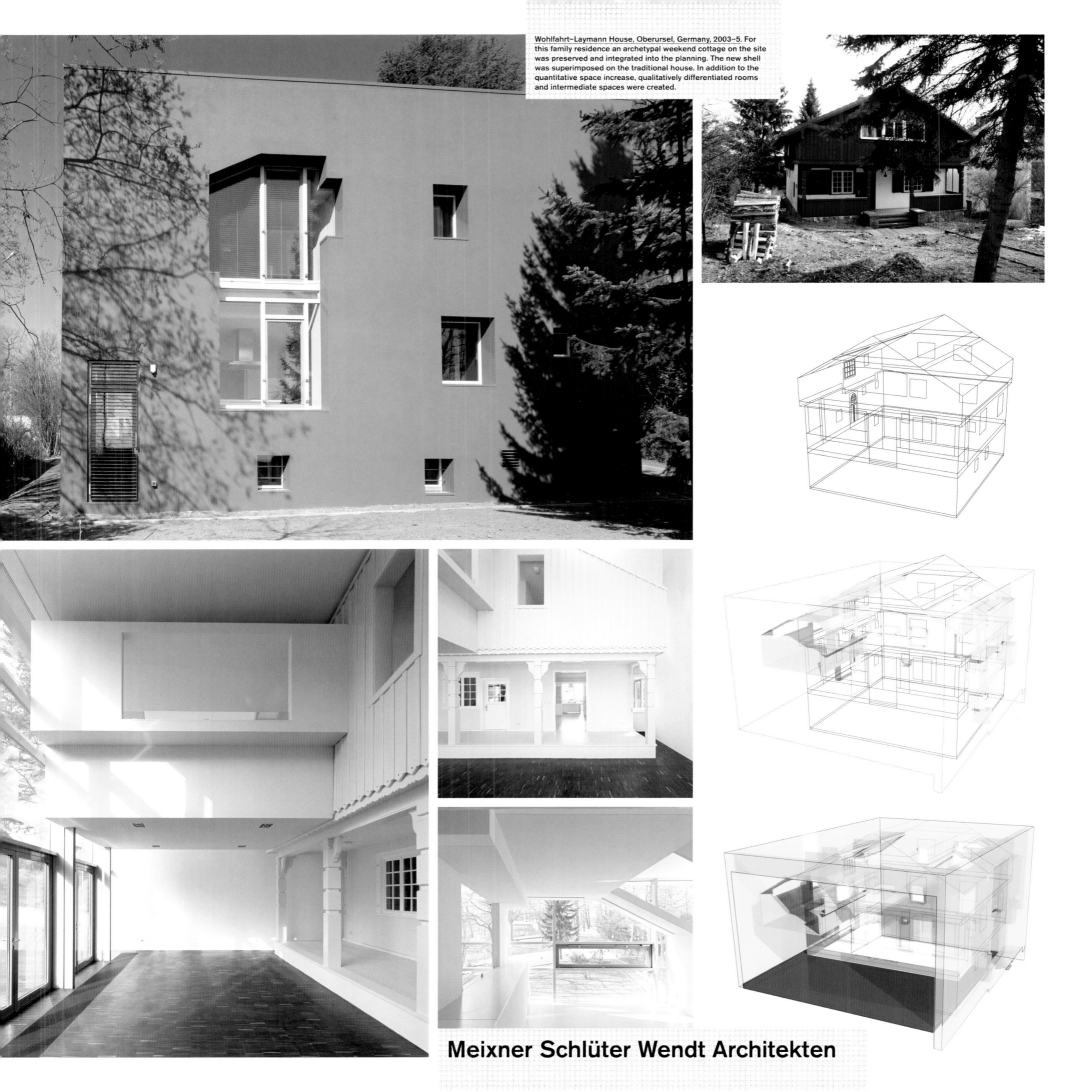

Wohlfahrt–Laymann House, Oberursel, Germany, 2003–5. For this family residence an archetypal weekend cottage on the site was preserved and integrated into the planning. The new shell was superimposed on the traditional house. In addition to the quantitative space increase, qualitatively differentiated rooms and intermediate spaces were created.

Meixner Schlüter Wendt Architekten

Miller & Maranta   Basel CH

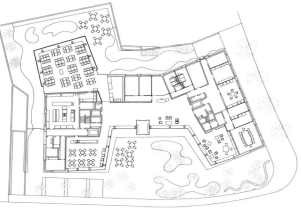

Quintus Miller and Paola Maranta have been active professionally in Basel since 1994. Like a number of young Swiss architects, they trained in Fabio Reinhart's office, joining in his effort to reinterpret the teachings of Aldo Rossi, and taking it in new directions. Miller & Maranta has devised its own tactile and expressive approach to architecture through a process of formal clarification, seeking to grasp the "spirit of place." The comparison between different impressions, feelings, and memories—translated into proportion, height, depth, thickness, and texture—leads to the formulation of a new material reality. The result is a series of buildings that are spare and discreet yet embody recognizable signs of everyday life.

In Basel's Schwarzpark Residences the nearby greenery prompted an analogy with a tree branch, starting from an approach that insisted on a restrained and natural way of fitting the complex into the context. The polygonal plan has sloping sides articulated according to the views they offer. The facades feature subtle rhythmic variations in the grid and a monochromatic brown color scheme, with glass paneling that reflects the ever-changing sky and vegetation. The building's base is splayed and the idea of the root can be traced in the structural system.

In the Residence for Senior Citizens, in the Altstetten neighborhood of Zürich, the appearance of the building seeks to affirm its institutional identity, while evoking significant features of buildings from the 1950s, so as to fit into the context of the neighborhood. The plan's irregular geometry allows the facade to open onto loggias or gardens, with diverse urban views. The refined study of the materials is evident in the grainy texture and coloring of the exterior concrete. The use of wood in the common areas, and the varied shades of color on interior surfaces, illuminated from above, evokes domesticity.

The Spa in Samedan expresses respect for the urban fabric of the village, evident in the smooth, continuous volumes of the building and the imagery evoking Roman baths in the decorations of the different rooms, linked by labyrinthine flights of steps. Moreover, the conception of design as a way to arouse a tactile and visual response to the materiality of the project appears in the colorful vistas of the interiors, with the arrangement of the skylights producing pools of shadow and a play of light. As with much of Miller & Maranta's work, by framing views on the natural setting, their (hyper-) realism paradoxically produces a metaphorical vocabulary that endows the architecture with an altogether distinctive character.
// Mercedes Daguerre

Residence for Senior Citizens, Zürich, Switzerland, 2004–6.
The building recalls 1950s designs, which define the surrounding
neighborhood of Altstetten. The ground floor contains open areas
with a restaurant and living room organized around a garden
courtyard. On the upper floors, apartments and rooms are
connected by spacious halls and corridors that form collective
spaces with views through the wide windows.

Schwarzpark Residences, Basel, Switzerland, 2001–4. The apartment building was designed as a conversation with the old trees in Basel's Schwarzpark. The dyed concrete structure recalls trunks and branches; the large glass windows create a transparent volume while also reflecting the surrounding trees. The house unites the experiences of living in nature with the advantages of a modern apartment building.

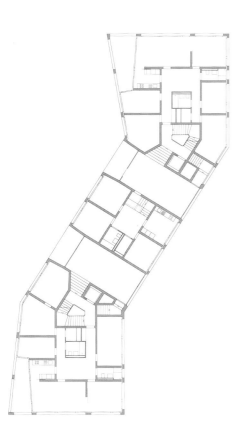

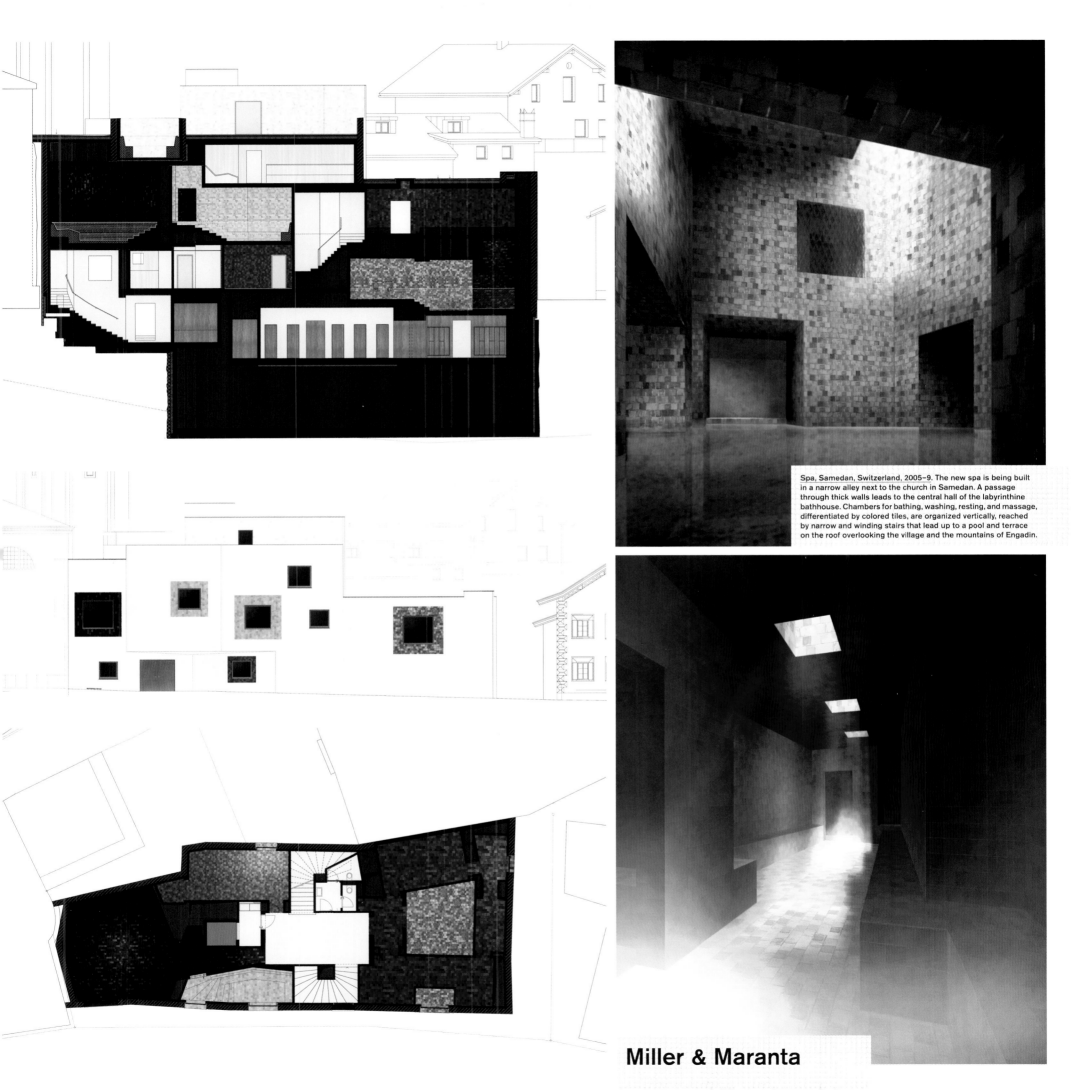

Spa, Samedan, Switzerland, 2005–9. The new spa is being built in a narrow alley next to the church in Samedan. A passage through thick walls leads to the central hall of the labyrinthine bathhouse. Chambers for bathing, washing, resting, and massage, differentiated by colored tiles, are organized vertically, reached by narrow and winding stairs that lead up to a pool and terrace on the roof overlooking the village and the mountains of Engadin.

Miller & Maranta

Minsuk Cho/Mass Studies   Seoul ROK

Ring Dome, New York, New York, USA, 2006–7. The Ring Dome was conceived as a temporary structure for New York's Storefront for Art and Architecture's 25th anniversary and has since been installed at various locations around the world. Composed of approximately 1,000 plastic hula hoops and 10,000 zip ties, it was designed to be easily assembled by nonprofessionals, then dismantled so the materials could be reused.

"I think there is a struggle going on in the minds of the younger generation," Minsuk Cho observed in a recent interview, speaking of the challenges facing architects in his native Republic of Korea. "[W]hat is 'Korean-ness' at this moment in time? What is our relationship to tradition, to the architectural identity of this culture?" As an alumnus of Columbia University in New York, and having worked at the Office for Metropolitan Architecture (OMA) in Rotterdam, Cho found himself compelled to address many of these questions when, in 2001, he returned to Seoul and established what has become one of the city's most successful young practices, Mass Studies. As the effects of the Asian economic boom manifest themselves through the birth of glitzy new neighborhoods and increasingly jagged skylines, architects fortunate enough to be riding the wave are forced to make quick decisions. What makes Korean architecture *Korean*: a set of stylistic gestures, or an entirely new approach to materiality, form, and the very concept of urbanism?

There can be little doubt that Minsuk Cho has opted for the latter. In terms of pure imagination and enthusiasm for the latent potential in high-density urbanism, it is difficult to rival his schemes for the future possibilities of the South Korean capital. Seoul Commune 2026, an unrealized vertical waterfront redevelopment project sited in what is already one of the most densely populated places on Earth, supposes a congregation of bulbous, beehive-like towers that integrate living units and parks into what is, in effect, an entire vertical city. It would be easy to discount such a proposal as empty utopian rhetoric if Mass Studies had not already implemented many of these strategies in existing works: in Boutique Monaco, a luxury condominium in the center of Seoul, small open-air green spaces with trees and lawns are scattered across its twenty-seven stories, and a complex reinforced-concrete webbing, not dissimilar to that imagined for Seoul Commune 2026, supports the building's lowest four floors. A much smaller project, a boutique in Seoul for Belgian fashion designer Ann Demeulemeester, is a study in vegetative architecture: the entire facade is alive, clad in a luscious coat of moss.

"I think my generation has answered the question of identity by saying: let's just forget about that for a minute," notes Cho. "That is not to say that we should blindly follow Western architecture—what I mean is that we need to develop a new form of Korean-ness, more spontaneous and more responsive to today's hyper-dense, media-saturated reality." // Joseph Grima

Boutique Monaco, Seoul, Republic of Korea, 2004–8. This tower features commercial, cultural, and public spaces on the lower levels, and apartments (*office-tels*) on floors five through twenty-seven. The fifteen empty spaces carved out of the building were introduced to reduce mass and increase exterior surfaces for more natural light and better views.

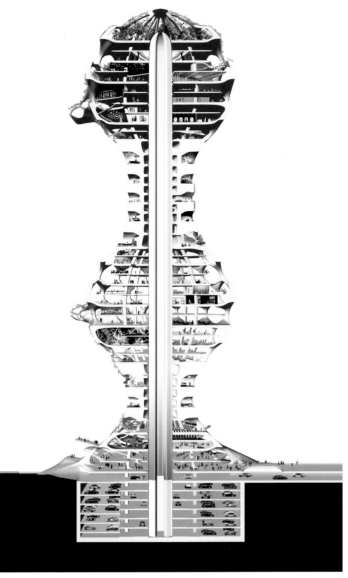

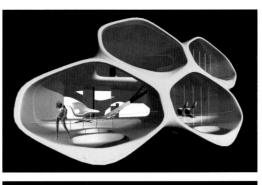

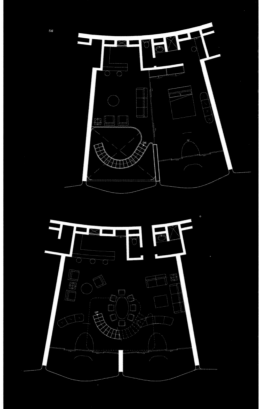

Program Composition

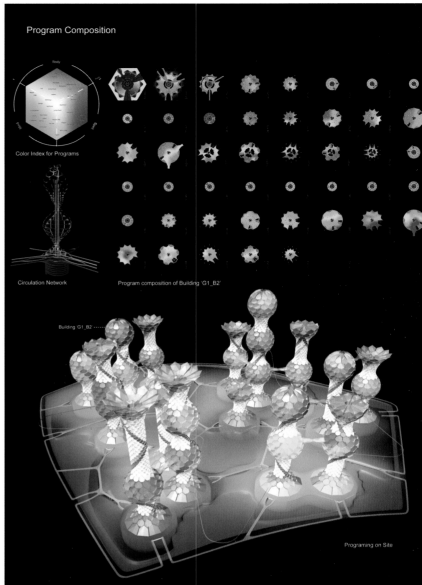

Color Index for Programs

Circulation Network

Program composition of Building 'G1_B2'

Building 'G1_B2'

Programing on Site

Seoul Commune 2026. Seoul, Republic of Korea, 2005. This unrealized project investigates the viability of an alternative and sustainable community structure in the overpopulated metropolises of the near future. The imagined community is a concrete architectural and urban proposal that reconfigures the existing "towers in the park" form, creating a complex network of private, semipublic, and public spaces.

Ann Demeulemeester Store, Seoul, Republic of Korea, 2007.
This proposal, a store for the high-end fashion designer Ann
Demeulemeester, is an attempt to incorporate as much nature
as possible within the constraints of a high-density urban
environment building of 4,070 sq. ft. (378 sq. m). Containing
the Ann Demeulemeester Store on the first floor, a restaurant
on the top floor, and a multi-store in the basement, the building
is an amalgamation between natural and artificial, and interior
and exterior.

Minsuk Cho/Mass Studies

Miró Rivera Architects | Austin USA

The work seemed atypical for a young American practice: the careful attention to detail, the conceptual use of materials, the contextual approach. Juan Miró, born in Barcelona, studied in Madrid and completed his post-graduate degree at Yale University in the United States. Miguel Rivera was born and raised in Puerto Rico where he graduated from the University of Puerto Rico School of Architecture before receiving a post-graduate degree at Columbia University in New York. In 2000 they joined forces to found an architecture studio in Austin, Texas.

One of the first buildings of the émigré architects is without doubt also one of their strongest. For the boat dock on Lake Austin the architects arrived at an original spatial solution in a simple and very convincing way: with its reduced vocabulary and delicate expression, the longitudinal box for two boats clad with tubular steel elements boasts a sail-like tent structure to provide welcome shade on the wooden patio.

A smaller project further refined the light touch the architects achieved with the boat dock: a pedestrian bridge on a large private property outside Austin, intended to provide a link between the main building and a guest house. The architects used five round steel tubes to span the 82 feet (25 meters), creating an arched structure which they then outfitted with reinforcing rods that resemble the local reeds, protruding in part upward, in part downward. The bridge's material is intended to oxidize to better complement the surrounding natural landscape.

The Stonehenge House, also in Austin, was in fact the conversion of a house that had just been expanded—something of a design emergency job. Yet the result, which makes careful use of materials—copper, wood, aluminum, travertine, and white plastered walls—is spacious and pleasant, touching and beautiful.

One of the latest jobs realized by Miró Rivera is the most modest so far: the Trail Restroom for a public park. Even with a small budget, the architects demonstrated with great sensitivity that effort and resourcefulness pay off in design, and a new place can be created that enhances day-to-day life. // Peter Cachola Schmal

Pedestrian Bridge, Austin, Texas, USA, 2002–5. With a design inspired by the reeds that cover the lake, this pedestrian bridge is a light structure integrated in its setting. The bars/reeds intertwine at the abutments and "grow" over the bridge, camouflaging and turning it into a symbiotic, almost invisible link. To further integrate the bridge into its setting the steel is left unfinished, as are the rope handrail and the stone ramps.

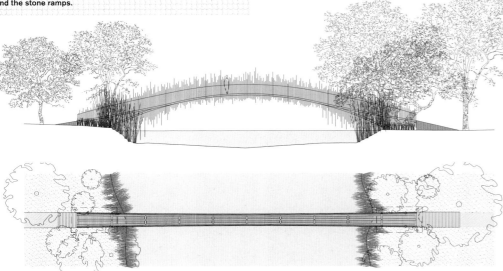

Lake Austin Boat Dock, Austin, Texas, USA, 2001–2. The boat dock is located at the base of a heavily wooded bluff on Lake Austin. The design is light and dynamic—a structure that appears to float, belonging with the boats in the lake. The box consists of a structural steel frame. The canopy is a tensile structure providing shade to the upper deck; its white stretched fabric, mast, tensioning cables, and stainless steel gear are inspired by sailboats.

Stonehenge House, Austin, Texas, USA, 2001–5. The architects were asked to make adjustments to a house that had just recently been renovated. The ground-floor entertaining room was greatly expanded by eliminating the screened porch and second floor above, creating a double-height space, including a tall copper-clad fireplace. A terrace and trellis were designed to better unify the house and garden, and the dining room was appropriated to create a foyer with a large door clad in copper tubing.

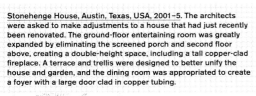

Trail Restroom, Austin, Texas, USA, 2004–8. The Lady Bird Lake Hike and Bike Trail is a linear park with scenic trails along the banks of the Colorado River in downtown Austin. The restroom was conceived as a sculpture, a dynamic object along the trail. It consists of forty-nine vertical Corten steel plates 0.75-in. (19-mm) thick, whose width and height vary significantly. The panels are arranged into a spine that coils at one end to form the restroom walls.

Miró Rivera Architects

Mount Fuji Architects Studio | Tokyo J

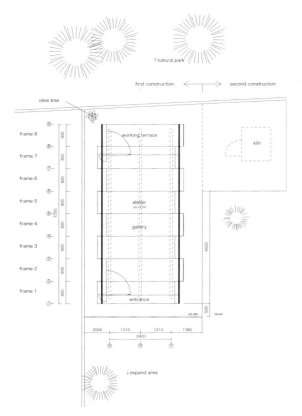

↑ natural park

first construction ←→ second construction

olive tree

frame 8 — working terrace
frame 7
frame 6
frame 5 — atelier
frame 4 — gallery
frame 3
frame 2
frame 1 — entrance

kiln

↓ expand area

XXXX House, Yaizu, Shizuoka Prefecture, Japan, 2003. The budget for this studio-gallery—1.5 million Japanese yen, or approximately US$16,000—was initially intended to purchase a car. The client decided instead to build a ceramics studio. Built in three days, the open-air gallery is made entirely of plywood sheets, glued together to create the structural frame and finished surface. A shifted truss system creates the X-like profile.

Danish architect Jørn Utzon's father was a shipbuilder who built yachts and helped his son with the model for the Sydney Opera House. Several buildings by the Japanese firm Mount Fuji Architects Studio—founded by Masahiro Harada, whose father also designed ships, and Mao Harada—move beyond Utzon and far beyond the conventions of current construction.

This can be seen acutely, for example, in the XXXX House. This small project was not created in an architect's office or by a builder. Instead, it was constructed by a woodworker from Odawara named Kagawa, a craftsman who creates high-quality but affordable wood furniture. Accordingly, this piece of architecture (if indeed that is what it can be called) achieves a grace and humor that are missing from the techniques employed in architecture today. While the hand-crafted household furnishings by Mr. Kagawa are known to designers in Japan, it was astonishing to discover that his skills could be used to build an entire house.

There have been numerous architects interested in creating buildings that look like furniture, but that notion went no further than their own thoughts. Again and again their attempts lacked the grace of household furnishings. In contrast, XXXX House could only have been accomplished in collaboration with a fine furniture maker. It achieves a unique texture and weightlessness that is absent from current architecture.

In the future, who will create buildings and how will they be built? There is a potential for major changes in architectural design. Today, the twentieth-century methods of design execution—with their primary emphasis on concrete, steel, and glass—feel heavy and old in comparison to the many new techniques that surround us. Mount Fuji Architects Studio offers a glimpse of this potential with XXXX House. Their most important challenge will be to continue to match this accomplishment in future projects.
// Kengo Kuma

M3/KG, Tokyo, Japan, 2004–6. The site for this private residence is located at one end of a quiet residential area dating back to the beginning of the Showa period, within the center of the city. The two-story house, 1,900 sq. ft. (177 sq. m), is clad in rough concrete, double-height glazing, and laminated veneer lumber; together with the Indian sandstone floor, the materials place the house's emphasis on texture.

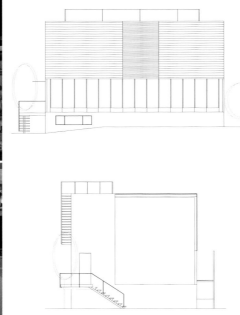

Sakura House, Tokyo, Japan, 2005–6. This house was designed for a couple's living and working space on a corner lot in a residential neighborhood. Two ribbon walls partially wrap around the building to enclose a small patio area and stairwell at the house's entrance. The walls of the facade are made of steel sheets, perforated to depict cherry blossoms, or *sakura*; the walls lining the entrance and patio space are floor-to-ceiling glass panels that maximize natural light.

Art Site, México D.F., Mexico, 2008–. The construction process used to create this proposed contemporary art museum is "earth mold architecture": digging holes at the site, pouring in concrete, then lifting the solidified concrete walls in place. The dug holes are intended to be left as exhibition spaces.

Mount Fuji Architects Studio

Nendo   Tokyo J

Book House, Shikine-jima, Tokyo Municipality, Japan, 2004–5.
By using bookshelves to clad the exterior walls, this combination
house and library protects the privacy of its inhabitants' living
space while inviting visitors to peruse the books. Semitransparent
reinforced plastic fiberglass divides the interior and exterior
spaces, allowing soft light to filter through between the bookshelves during the day and letting the light out at night.

Nendo is a cross-disciplinary creative practice powered by the versatile imagination of its founder, Oki Sato. As mercurial as it is pragmatic, Nendo moves seamlessly between design, architecture, and product design, all coalesced into a portfolio of work that tells stories, transforms the banal into the unexpected, and celebrates small moments of magic in the everyday. The studio name, Nendo, means "clay" in Japanese—the ultimate free-form material that fittingly conjures a creative attitude without preconceptions. Unconcerned by signature styles or a formal architectural language, Nendo defines its architecture through lived experience and the interplay of the transitory and the permanent.

For example the Fireworks House, designed to provide an elderly client with a wheelchair-friendly house, features an entire second floor dedicated to an annual social gathering to witness the fireworks of Chichibu, Japan, and to strengthen bonds between family and friends. Meanwhile, an office situated alongside the Meguro River takes a different, though similarly user-defined, approach to the socialization of space, employing a whimsical series of space dividers. A looping, sagging panel system strikes a balance between necessary privacy and the collective buzz of shared working. Both the Book House and the Drawer House are driven by the spatial needs and living habits of the client. In the case of the Book House, the iconic ceremonial function of the tea-house is replaced by the ceremony of reading, with the whole small building designed around a defined performative function.

In all this work one can observe a comfortable acceptance of Japan's two most celebrated cultural modes: that of Shinto austerity (now morphed into classic high modernism), and the vulgarity of the baroque pop visible any day in Tokyo's Harajuku neighborhood. Avoiding either extreme, Sato's work is conceptually disciplined and unafraid of lean, spartan interiors while also being eclectic, playful, and unwilling to take itself too seriously.

Architect Arata Isozaki, in his erudite and compelling book *Japan-ness in Architecture*, included a chapter entitled "Western Structure Versus Japanese Space." Here he makes a case for the distinction between a Western tradition of imposing one's will on reality, as opposed to what he defines as the more Japanese tradition of letting a thing "become," whereby architecture comes to life when it is used, not simply built. This surely is the quality that makes Nendo's architecture (as well as its whole oeuvre of creative design) so poignant; it becomes through occupation. It is architecture that is not just built but performed. // Andrew Mackenzie

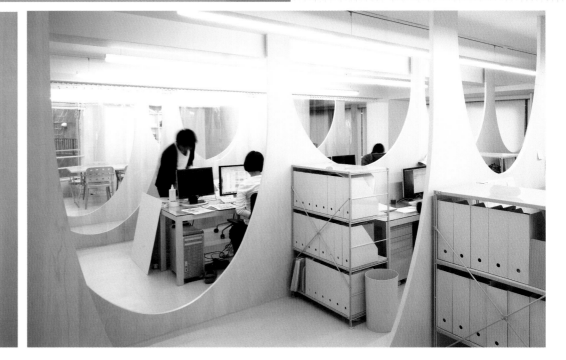

Meguro Office, Tokyo, Japan, 2007–8. Here the usual spaces and functions of an office—meeting space, management, work space, and storage—remain separate while maintaining a connection. The space is divided with walls that seem to sag and flop like a piece of cloth held up between two hands, enclosing the various spaces more than usual office partitions but less than actual walls. Spaces that need more sound-proofing are closed-in with plastic curtains that leave them quiet without being isolated.

Fireworks House, Chichibu, Saitama Prefecture, Japan, 2004–5.
To satisfy the client's wish that her elderly mother be able to
watch the fireworks of an annual festival, Nendo designed the
roof with glass panels for easy viewing from the second floor.
Plumbing and other utilities are concentrated in the center of
the first floor, surrounded by living space in a wheelchair-acces-
sible open plan. The traditional wooden framework is clad with
gray galvanized steel.

Drawer House, Tokyo, Japan, 2002–3. The residential functions of this compact house are condensed into one side of the wall and can be pulled out when necessary, like drawers. It is a simple mechanism that makes this adaptive and flexible space highly effective for the constrained housing conditions in Tokyo.

Nendo

Neville Mars/Dynamic City Foundation

Amsterdam NL / Beijing CN

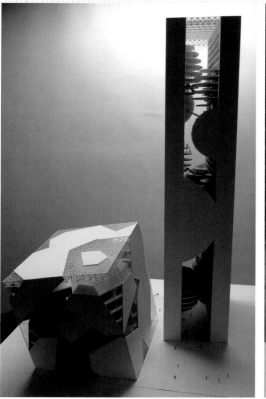

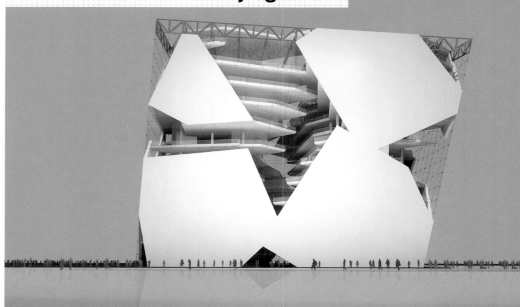

Tianjin Planning Museum and Office Tower, Tianjin, China, 2008–. The combined commission of a museum and government building allowed the architects to blur the borders between public and private spaces so that exhibitions crawl up into the tower atrium and the offices seep down into the museum. Designed as a single integrated sustainable project, the complex's buildings are connected underground; the tower works as a naturally ventilating chimney, pulling air up through the voids of the museum.

Virtually all who witnessed the opening of the 2008 Beijing Olympic Games marvelled at the breathtaking panache of the performances and the ways in which China projected its history into global theater. But the pyrotechnics also clearly dramatized a redrawing of the geopolitical map in a profound way, with China promoting a return to its former glory. Architect Neville Mars moved from Amsterdam to China in 2004 with a small group of colleagues to observe firsthand China's unequalled urban ambition to realize 400 new cities by 2020. Though the cities' names would not be recognized by those in the West, their populations will rival those of New York or London. These "cities from zero" are the urban equivalent of the brilliant fireworks on display at the opening ceremony of the Beijing Olympic Games.

Mars and his firm Dynamic City Foundation (DCF) subsequently produced a tome entitled *The Chinese Dream: A Society under Construction*, which collates vital statistics and lived experiences around the rapid urbanization process. Calling upon economists, historians, journalists, and political scientists, *The Chinese Dream* is an important research document that attempts to grapple with a twenty-first-century city we do not yet know. The concluding pages of the book are illustrated with speculative projects by Mars and DCF. The common thread in the work is the idea that there should be no division between architecture, infrastructure, and city. Artificial landscape can hide parking. A neighborhood can be a city. Ring roads can be a permanent moving walkway for mass pedestrian traffic. These projects often appear like huge declarative one-liners. But behind the graphic wit and bold playfulness lies a tradition going back to the radical Italian architecture firm Superstudio. Mars believes the Chinese to be pragmatists—and from there he goes on to speculate what happens when a nation of pragmatists dreams up a Utopia. DCF's proposals have to be seen in this light: pragmatic Utopias driven by radical actuality rather than nostalgic romanticism.
// Shumon Basar

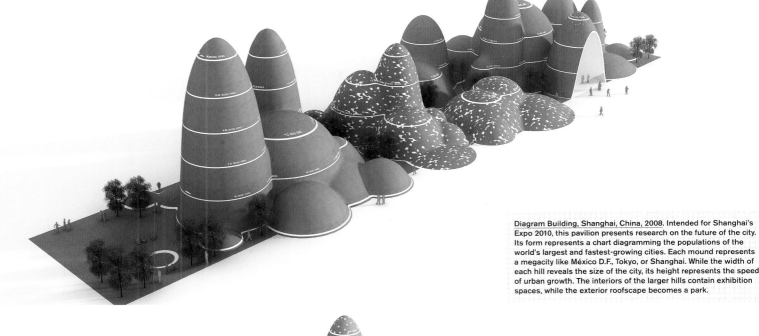

Diagram Building, Shanghai, China, 2008. Intended for Shanghai's Expo 2010, this pavilion presents research on the future of the city. Its form represents a chart diagramming the populations of the world's largest and fastest-growing cities. Each mound represents a megacity like México D.F., Tokyo, or Shanghai. While the width of each hill reveals the size of the city, its height represents the speed of urban growth. The interiors of the larger hills contain exhibition spaces, while the exterior roofscape becomes a park.

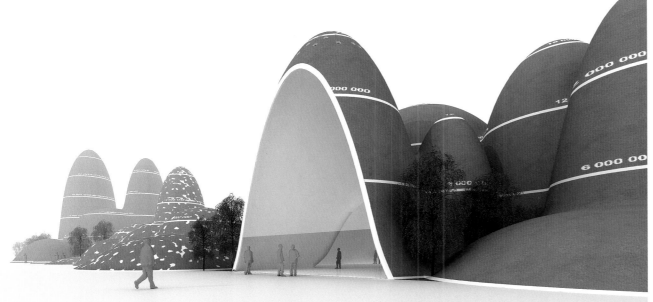

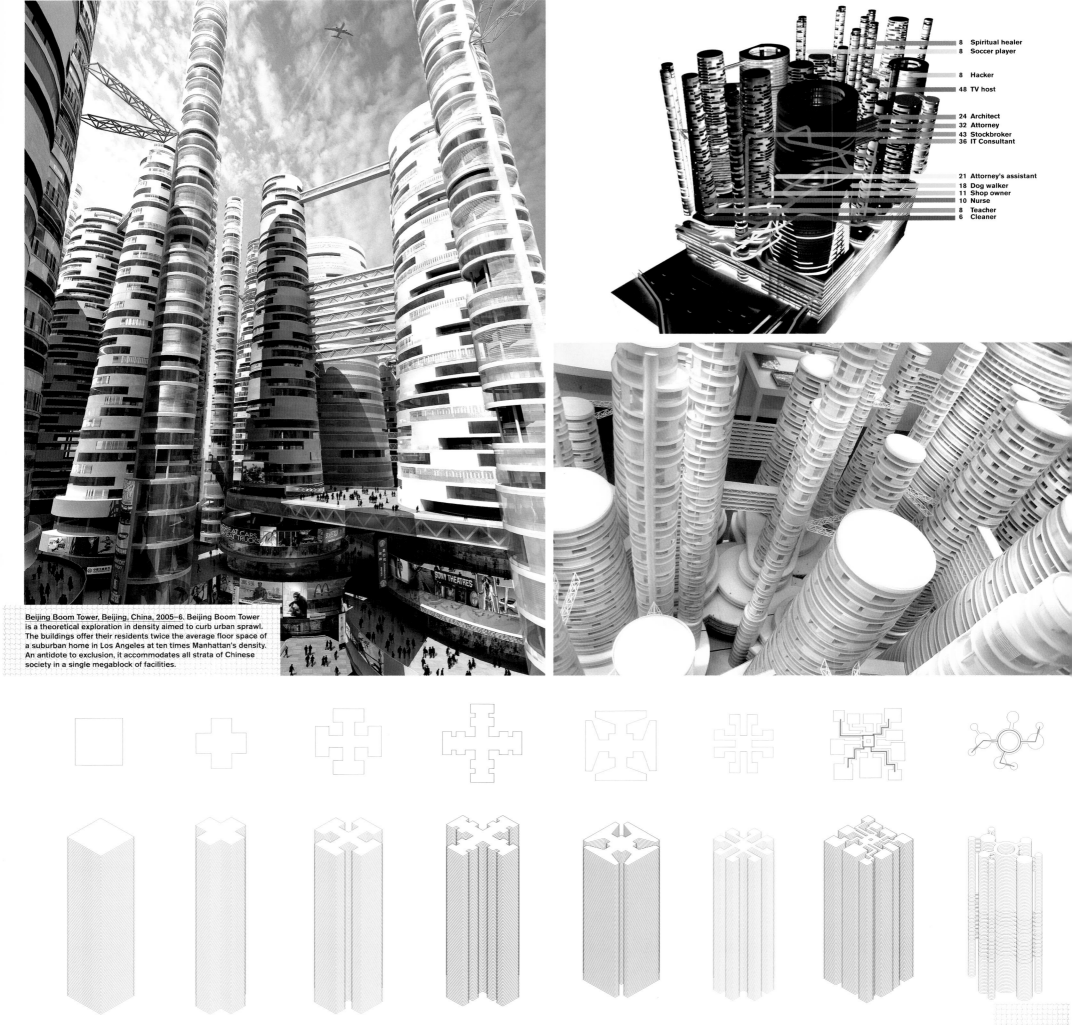

8 Spiritual healer
8 Soccer player

8 Hacker
48 TV host

24 Architect
32 Attorney
43 Stockbroker
36 IT Consultant

21 Attorney's assistant
18 Dog walker
11 Shop owner
10 Nurse
8 Teacher
6 Cleaner

Beijing Boom Tower, Beijing, China, 2005–6. Beijing Boom Tower
is a theoretical exploration in density aimed to curb urban sprawl.
The buildings offer their residents twice the average floor space of
a suburban home in Los Angeles at ten times Manhattan's density.
An antidote to exclusion, it accommodates all strata of Chinese
society in a single megablock of facilities.

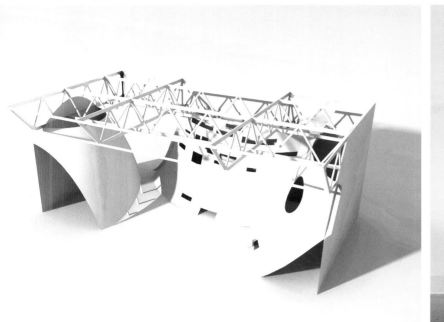

Tanggu Exhibition Hall, Tianjin, China, 2008–. This exhibition hall presents proposals for new architecture in the Yujia Pu District of Tianjin. A mirrored projection system creates images of the proposals that appear to float in front of the tilted facade on their intended sites. In order to minimize the energy used to dispose of the excavated dirt from the construction sites, the soil will be used to bolster the sides of the exhibition hall, making the hills grow as the projects advance.

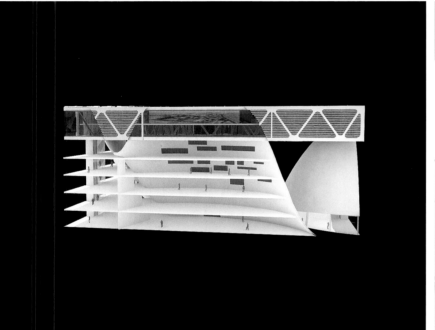

Neville Mars/Dynamic City Foundation

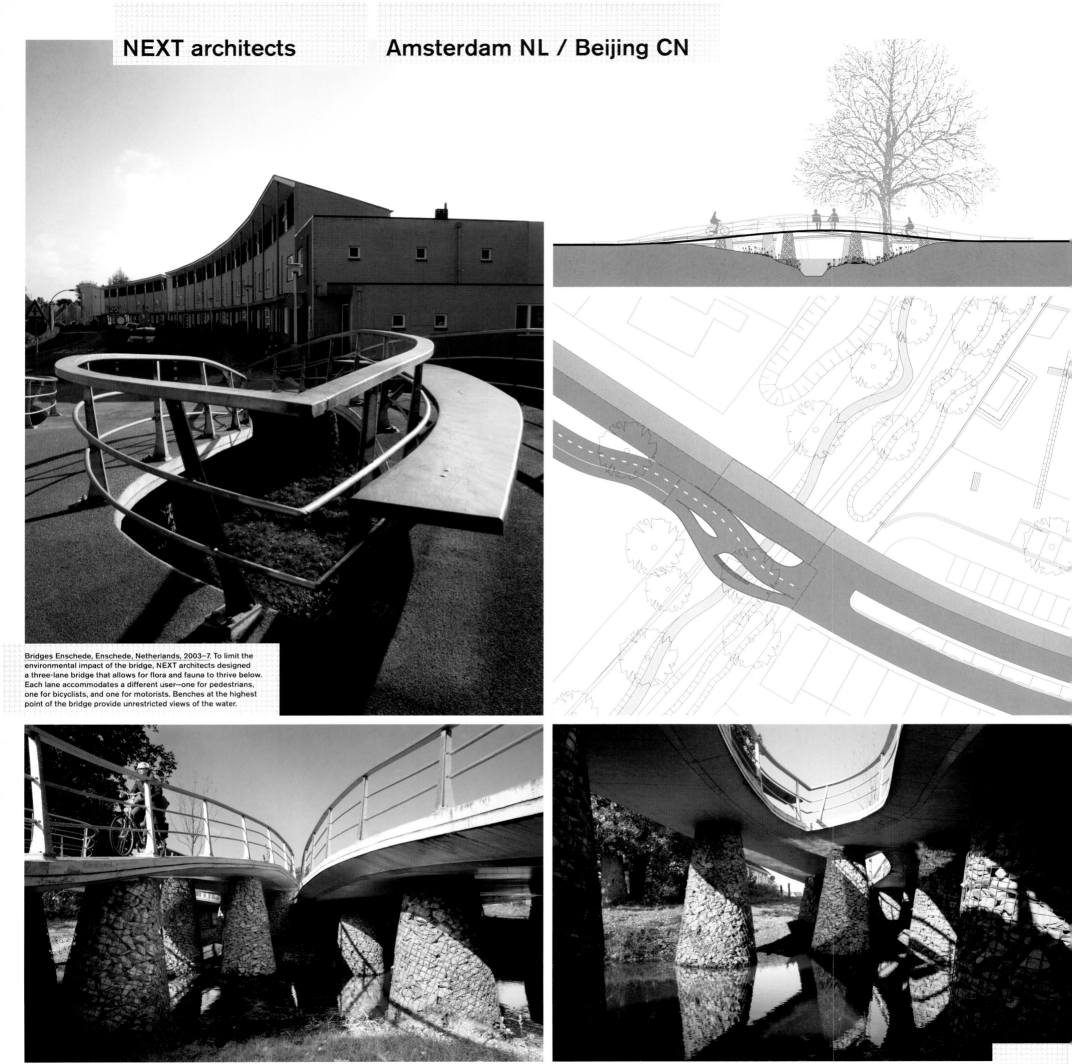

Bridges Enschede, Enschede, Netherlands, 2003–7. To limit the environmental impact of the bridge, NEXT architects designed a three-lane bridge that allows for flora and fauna to thrive below. Each lane accommodates a different user—one for pedestrians, one for bicyclists, and one for motorists. Benches at the highest point of the bridge provide unrestricted views of the water.

Immediately after NEXT architects was founded in 1999, its members (who had just graduated from Delft University of Technology in The Netherlands) received two equally interesting commissions. They were asked to make a study for the Delta Metropolis, which encompasses the whole region of western Holland, and they were invited by the well-known Dutch design firm Droog to develop an object for an exhibition in Milan. This broad range has become typical of the studio's work, which spans diverse scales, disciplines, and geographies. NEXT architects designs products and urban developments, is involved in scientific research and art projects, and has offices in Amsterdam and Beijing. With this broadness of scope, NEXT architects represents a new generation for whom the development of digital communications technology has made borders between countries and disciplines obsolete.

Spreading out its activities over such a large field affects the extent of the small firm's involvement in each project. In China, where NEXT architects' work includes a number of realized buildings of considerable size, the firm collaborates with a much larger architectural studio that is responsible for the construction. The clarity and intelligence of the concepts by NEXT architects assure that the realized buildings sustain a high level of quality despite the inevitable adaptations during construction.

The quality of NEXT architects' concepts is also visible in its work in the Netherlands. Consider, for instance, the Villa Overgooi in Almere or the interior renovation of the Wieden + Kennedy offices in Amsterdam: both projects are based on the precise adjustment of basic three-dimensional matrices reminiscent of the architects' research into density at the Delft University of Technology. Once these schemes are fixed and everything has found its place, the architecture evolves almost automatically. If the basic concept works, the rest will follow. And since NEXT architects are masters at all scales, they can even design the furniture for the project. This fluidity allows the work to be laconic, free of *Sturm und Drang*, and ultimately very charming. // Bart Goldhoorn

House M&M, Amsterdam, Netherlands, 2008. The only things inside the House M&M, renovated in collaboration with Claudia Linders, are white cubes. Each of the four cubes serves as a large furnishing that determines the function of the area around it. The first contains a toilet, bath, and shower; the second, a wash basin and wardrobe; the third cube envelops a double bed and a bookcase; and the fourth contains two single beds and a workplace.

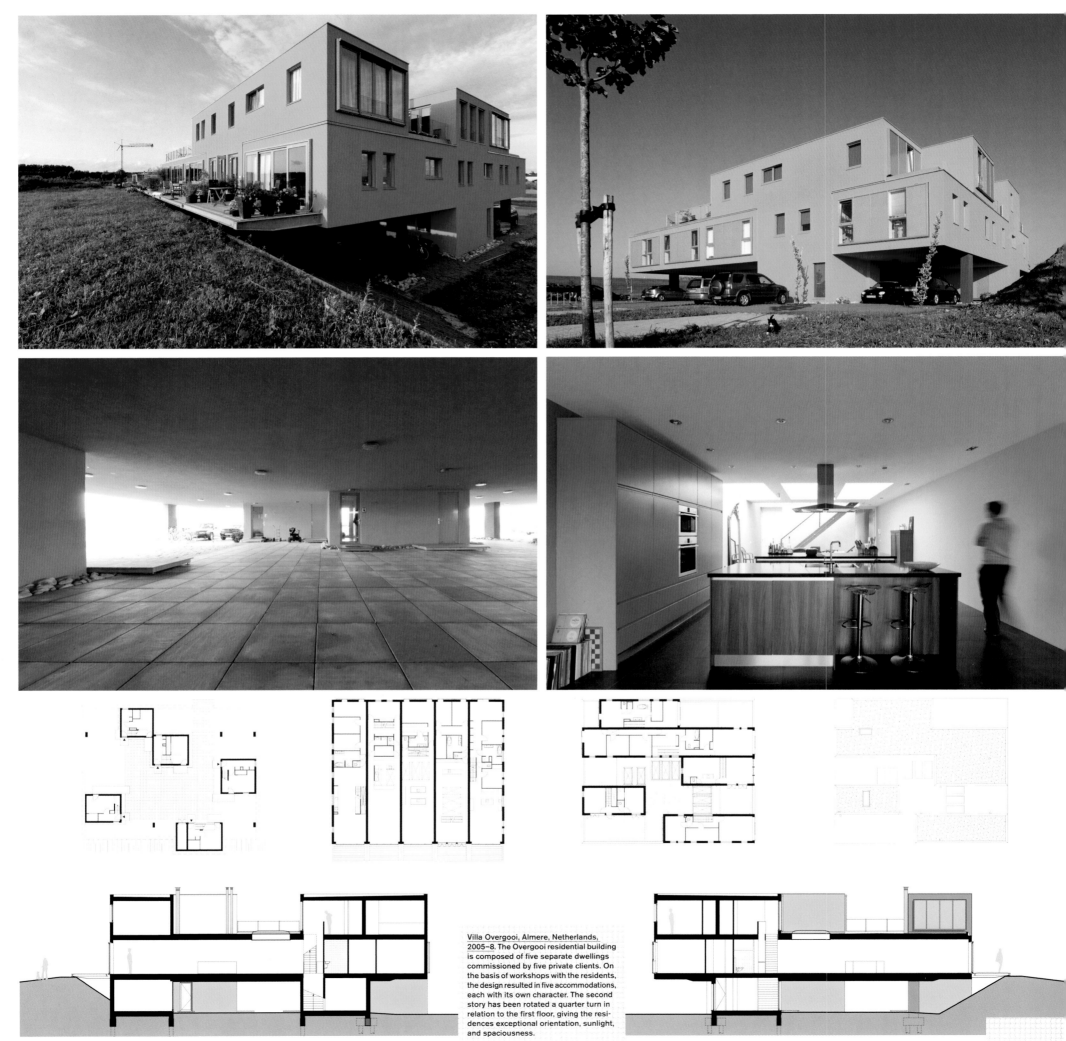

Villa Overgooi, Almere, Netherlands, 2005–8. The Overgooi residential building is composed of five separate dwellings commissioned by five private clients. On the basis of workshops with the residents, the design resulted in five accommodations, each with its own character. The second story has been rotated a quarter turn in relation to the first floor, giving the residences exceptional orientation, sunlight, and spaciousness.

Wieden + Kennedy, Amsterdam, Netherlands, 2006–8. The new offices of the Wieden + Kennedy advertising agency, on a canal in Amsterdam, are housed in what were two separate properties fused by centuries of additions and renovations. The architects inserted three glass shafts of double-high spaces, used as presentation and meeting rooms, that cut through all six floors, creating diagonal sight lines among the floors. Shop floors are left rough and unfinished, while surfaces in the presentation rooms are polished and smooth.

NEXT architects

Spanish architects Fuensanta Nieto and Enrique Sobejano are partners in life and in work. They both graduated with architecture degrees from the Superior Technical School of Architecture of Madrid (ETSAM) and Columbia University in New York. They established an office—initially dividing their time between various publishing and teaching commitments—that soon became one of the most influential in Spain. Ever since winnning the EUROPAN–IV award in 1996 (a competition for architects under forty that is a launching pad for young talent), and building the social housing project in Sevilla for which they won the prize, their career has been a dazzling sequence of winning competitions for museums, cultural and sports centers, congress halls, auditoria, town halls, university buildings, department stores, and, indeed, housing.

In all of their projects, the Madrid couple shows its extraordinary formal inventiveness, conceptual clarity, and professional discipline: the stark sculptural statement of the freestanding and almost metaphysical Mérida Auditorium and Conference Center (1999–2004); the self-effacing yet exquisite grid of subterranean patios of the Madinat al-Zahra Museum in Córdoba (2002–9); the jagged, eloquent profile of the Zaragoza Expo Auditorium and Congress Center (2005–8); the traces of Islamic geometrical patterns in the proposal for the Córdoba Center for Contemporary Art. The first commission abroad came in 2005 with the extension to the Moritzburg Contemporary Art Museum in Halle, Germany, a very delicate work in an existing fortress where they could draw on their previous experience designing museums inside historical buildings in Las Palmas and Valladolid, Spain. This commission was followed by two competitions won in the Austrian city of Graz, for an extension of the Kastner & Öhler department store and an extension of the Joanneum Museum (2006–11), which, in turn, led to the opening of an office in Berlin and to Sobejano's appointment to a chair at Berlin's University of the Arts (UdK), all of which establish the office firmly on the international stage.
// Luis Fernández-Galiano

National Sculpture Museum Extension, Valladolid, Spain, 2001–7. The old schoolyard and cloisters of the former San Gregorio College, dating from the fifteenth century, have been preserved within their original structure, with the most valuable architectural features restored. A new pavilion conceived as an independent unit, contemporary in its form and materials, establishes a dialogue in scale and materials with the existing historic architecture.

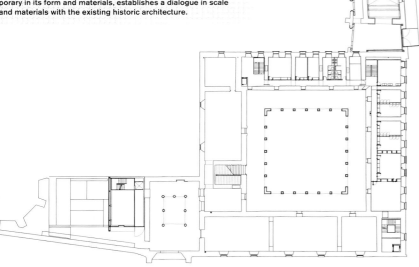

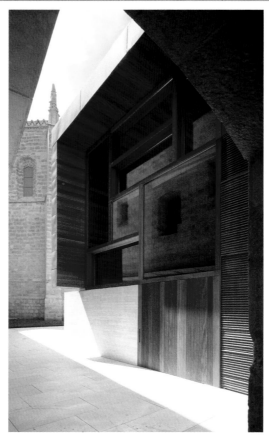

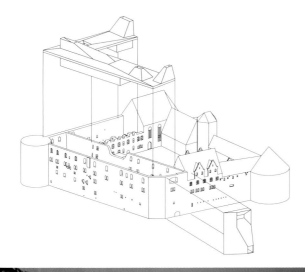

Moritzburg Contemporary Art Museum Extension, Halle, Germany, 2005–8. The extension of the ancient castle of Moritzburg is conceived as a new roof: a large folded platform that rises and opens to allow natural light to enter, and from which the new exhibition rooms are suspended. The angular geometry of the new roof landscape creates a dialogue with the existing irregular shapes of the building, continuing the process of transformation over time that characterized the castle.

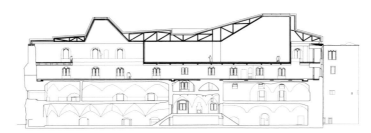

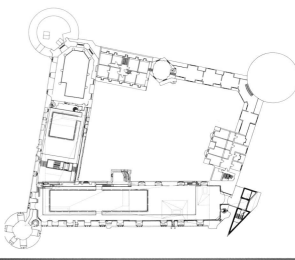

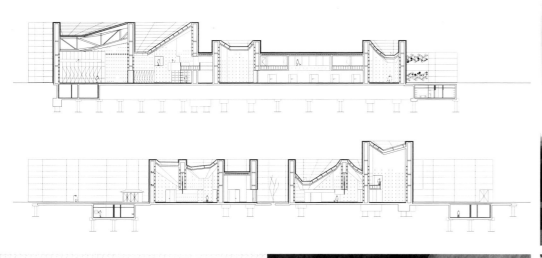

Córdoba Center for Contemporary Art, Córdoba, Spain, 2006–10. Like a literary structure composed of a story within a story, this project is conceived as a self-similar geometric pattern originating in a hexagonal shape. The permutations of three types of polygonal rooms generate sequences of different spaces that define a non-centralized "organism" for the production, research, and exhibition of new media in contemporary arts. The eastern media facade, developed in collaboration with Realities United, will showcase video installations designed specifically for the location.

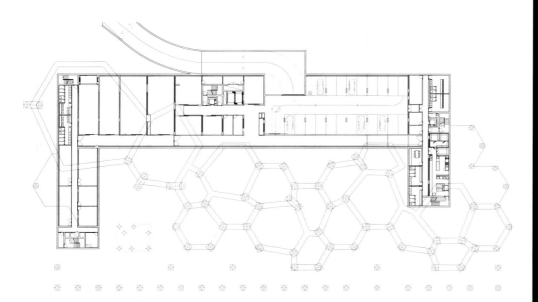

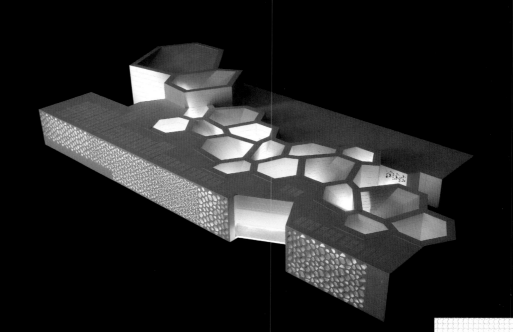

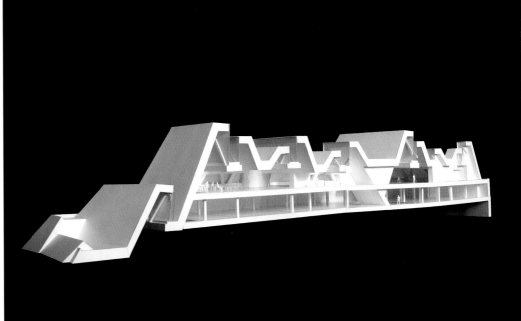

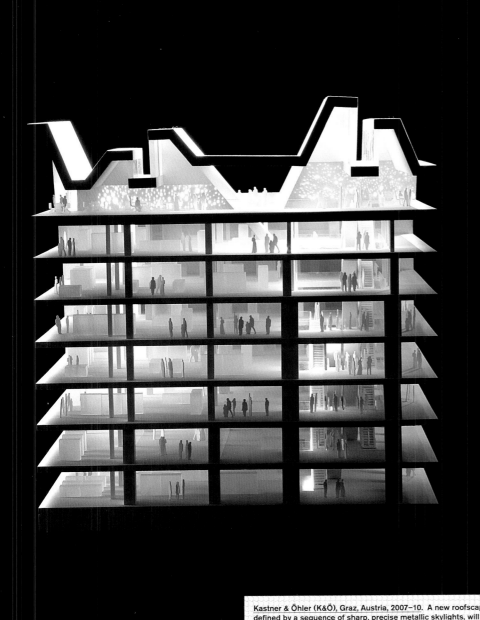

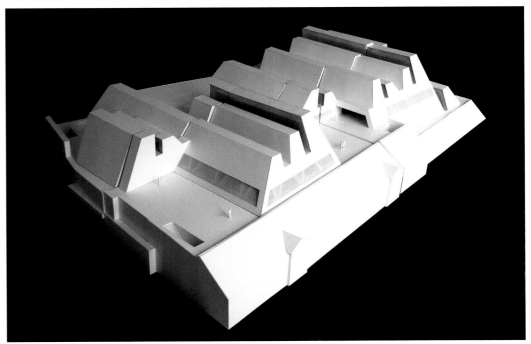

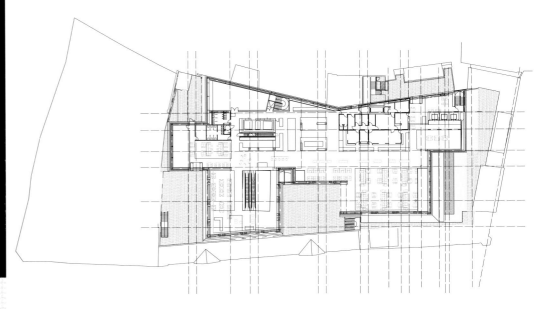

<u>Kastner & Öhler (K&Ö), Graz, Austria, 2007–10.</u> A new roofscape, defined by a sequence of sharp, precise metallic skylights, will extend the existing Kastner & Öhler department store, and include restaurants, cafés, and terraces. The geometric system of the new roof will blend into the skyline of expressive medieval roofs that make up the historic center of Graz.

Nieto Sobejano Arquitectos

Whole Earth Project, Tokyo, Japan, 2005–6. This combination residence and office is located in the Shimokitazawa neighborhood of Tokyo. It consists entirely of a structural system of reinforced concrete masonry using more than 7,000 blocks that function as the formwork, the structure, and the interior and exterior finishing.

After Tadao Ando's Row House, completed in 1976 in Sumiyoshi, Japan, took the closed-off style of architecture to an extreme, Japanese residential design gradually moved toward openness and transparency. Today, Ken Niizeki is revisiting the closed style, prompted by an interest in the possibility of designing self-contained residences for urban areas. By focusing on two aspects of building design—materials and environmental sustainability—Niizeki has pushed open a door that seemed to close in 1976.

Niizeki's first successful decision was to experiment with new materials. Ando, by limiting his material to concrete, a symbol of the twentieth century, succeeded in building a monument to the twentieth century. Architectural materials, however, have always been full of variety, adaptable to many regions, and rich in individuality. Niizeki shuns concrete and pursues the possibilities of diverse materials. In doing so, he has created buildings that belong to the twenty-first century.

From the standpoint of sustainability, there have been numerous problems with architecture and building methods that use unfaced concrete. Niizeki's second achievement was to link building materials to sustainability. At first glance, Niizeki's buildings may appear very abstract and seem to deny many possibilities. In fact, they are friendly to both the environment and people.

Niizeki has taught us anew that there is still a profusion of possibilities in the closed style of architecture. Closed buildings can have a claustrophobic effect. When one looks at Niizeki's creations, however, closed in as they may be, there is no feeling of confinement. Closed does not mean denial. Niizeki shows us that buildings can be closed in style but still possess softness. They can be closed but still be warm and welcoming.
// Kengo Kuma

Residence in Atami, Shizuoka Prefecture, Japan, 2000–2001. This private house is located on a mountaintop where it commands a view of the Pacific Ocean and valley below. The house, which rests on a grassy mound, features a mostly subterranean basement that protrudes out of the mountainside. The ground-floor level is covered over with turf mound, continuing the dynamic landscape, while the upper floor consists of a black box that juts out over the steep slope.

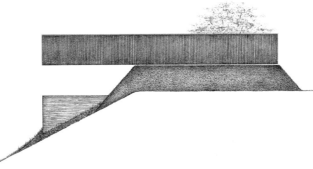

Residence in Kamogawa, Chiba Prefecture, Japan, 2000–2005. Surrounded by a lake and forest, this residence was planned as a weekend house for a family working in downtown Tokyo. Three separate boxlike structures made of wood open to various landscapes on the ground level. The upper floor, surrounded by greenery, seems to float between the boxes. The bath is located on the rooftop.

Residence in Yachimata, Chiba Prefecture, Japan, 2001–2.
Located in a Tokyo suburb, this private residence and hair salon
operated by the house's owner takes the form of wood-frame
boxes, their exteriors covered with black cedar panels. While
the monolithic appearance is reinforced by the seeming absence
of openings, the interior is filled with sunlight from windows
hidden behind the facade.

Kenichiro Niizeki/Niizeki Studio

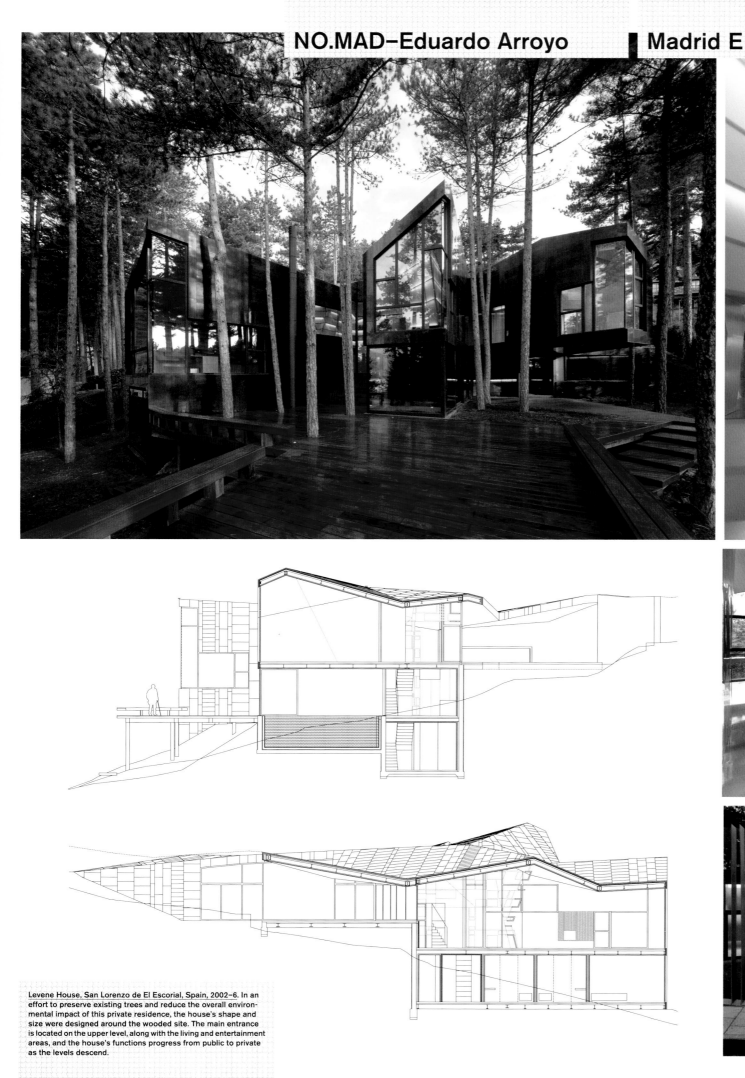

Levene House, San Lorenzo de El Escorial, Spain, 2002–6. In an effort to preserve existing trees and reduce the overall environmental impact of this private residence, the house's shape and size were designed around the wooded site. The main entrance is located on the upper level, along with the living and entertainment areas, and the house's functions progress from public to private as the levels descend.

Born in the Basque region of Spain, but educated and based in Madrid, Eduardo Arroyo is a true *wunderkind* of his generation, a sparkling personality who has led a rather restless, peripatetic life, in keeping with the name of his practice, NO.MAD. After graduating with an architecture degree from the Superior Technical School of Architecture of Madrid (ETSAM) in 1988 and working with Rem Koolhaas at the Office for Metropolitan Architecture (OMA) in Rotterdam, Arroyo spent a few years in Paris and in his native Bilbao, finally choosing Madrid as his base of operations in 1996.

That year marked his first independent project, the design of a nursery school in Sondika, near Bilbao. Completed in 1997 to great critical acclaim, it demonstrated—beyond the inevitable debt to Koolhaas—an unexpected maturity for an *opera prima*. Shortly after, the architect undertook two public commissions—Desert Square and the Lasesarre Football Stadium—both in the Basque city of Barakaldo, whose realization established Arroyo as one of the most promising designers of contemporary Spanish architecture. The randomly checkered pattern of the square creates a varied yet orderly grid of landscape inventions, playful and provocative in its palette of textures, colors, and warped surfaces. The soccer stadium, on the other hand, seamlessly combines material sophistication, geometric order, and chromatic appeal, taking a cue from OMA in the haphazard color scheme used for seating.

Since then Arroyo has entered various architectural competitions, and has realized private projects including the Levene House for the editor of an architecture magazine. Located on a wooded site in an upscale neighborhood outside Madrid near El Escorial—the seat of the famous Renaissance monastery built by Philip II— the house is a rather organic, romantic language of folded glass that dissolves the volume of the residence among the pine trees. Each new project presents a bold new formal language adapted to its specific program, demonstrating that the talent of this young architect will continue to shine. // Luis Fernández-Galiano

Desert Square, Barakaldo, Spain, 1999–2002. This 130,000-sq.-ft. (12,000-sq.-m) public plaza was designed as a subtle tribute to the steelworkers, boatbuilders, and land tillers of this industrial port city north of Bilbao. The layout is deliberately non-prescriptive so that, over time, residents can help decide how to use the benches, ponds, and undulating topography.

Lasesarre Football Stadium, Barakaldo, Spain, 1999–2003.
This soccer stadium is a series of independent buildings organized
around the playing field so that local organizations can utilize the
smaller segments when games are not being played. To ensure
that spectators are never too far from the field, seating is arranged
as one, rather than multiple tiers. The roof is cantilevered over
the stadium, its polycarbonate panels jutting out at right angles.
The colored seating gives the impression of a full stadium even
when it is empty.

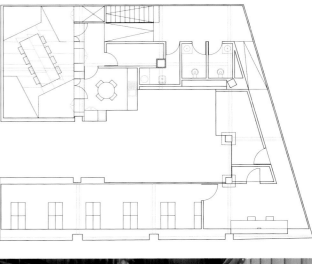

Banco Arquia, Bilbao, Spain, 2007–8. Sensual, transparent glass tubes form a wall that sharply separates the public space of this bank from the more private working area, erasing the concept of the "office landscape" and imposing distance between the client and the banking services.

NO.MAD–Eduardo Arroyo

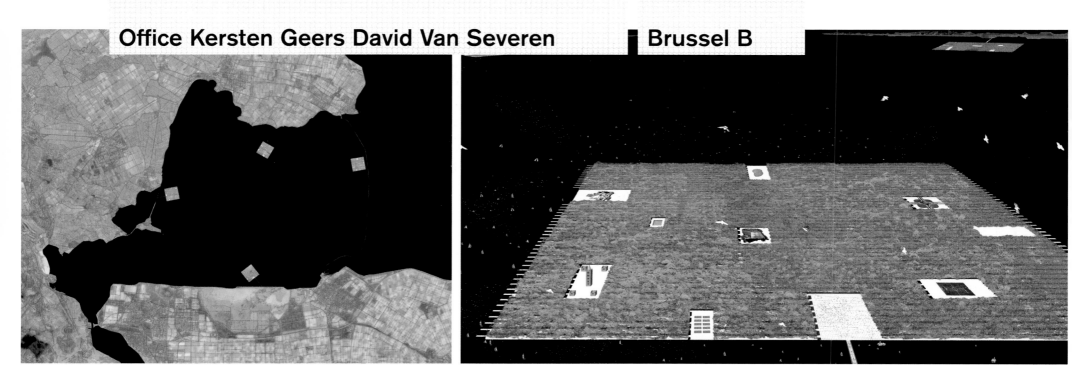

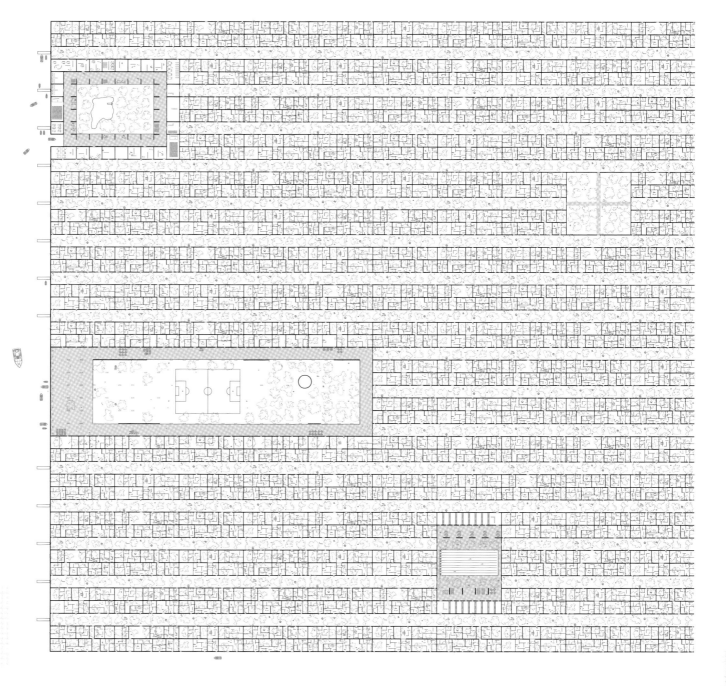

A Green Archipelago (Care City), Markermeer, Netherlands, 2007.
Care City investigates how to organize health care spatially in a
series of man-made islands. Projecting a future of constant curing,
caring, and attention to wellness, the idea of the city seems to
increasingly coincide with that of a hospital. In a grid of trees,
patio-villas alternating with long corridors form the base structure,
while large cut-outs define the collective spaces.

Hundreds and thousands of brightly colored confetti were strewn across the floor, a carpet of delicately disorganized paper detritus. A few black chairs were scattered about. The rest of the pavilion seemed empty, almost abandoned, bereft of the usual feverish desire to explain, show off, divulge, or disclose. Confetti extended outside, into the garden, too. The title of this mise-en-scène, conceived by Belgian architects Kersten Geers and David Van Severen, was *After the Party*, and it was one of the most striking installations at the 2008 Architecture Biennale in Venezia. Geers and Van Severen's canny move—or anti-move—was to highlight the peculiarity of national pavilions in Venezia's strange celebratory microcosm. From the outside, the historic Belgian pavilion was no longer visible but wrapped in a huge, 23-foot (7-meter) high galvanized-steel wall. The title, *After the Party*, carries multiple inferences: Was the party the twentieth century? Modernism? Communism? Or, in light of the economic crisis that began in 2008, was the party global capitalism?

This poignant installation piece fits within the careful and quietly critical body of work that Office Kersten Geers David Van Severen has built up over the past seven years. Reconversion of Grain Silos in Leuven, Belgium, calls to mind Le Corbusier's fascination with these purist pieces of industrial architecture he so lovingly wrote about in *Vers une architecture* (1923). Nature is captured in a raised floor level, contrasting the inorganic forms of the building with organic life. The perforated tubes seem to update the old functionalist aesthetic with something altogether more hi-tech and yet equally functionalist. The firm's forthcoming Villa in Ordos, 25 Rooms, is a relatively restrained proposal compared to some of the other designs for this high-concept masterplan in Nei Mongol, China. But, on close inspection, one discovers a subtle contrariety literally embedded in its plan. The bottom two floors are sunk into the ground and open onto an enclosed garden patio, hidden from the most prying of eyes. Like a refrain through this practice's work, nature acts as an infill for tranquil reflection: hard versus soft, tame versus wild.

At first glance, one might assume these works to be good examples of well behaved late minimalism, but then more ambitious references become apparent, such as the Italian design studio Archizoom, or the late German architect O.M. Ungers. Here, apparently rational forms do not necessarily emerge from strictly rationalist thought. // Shumon Basar

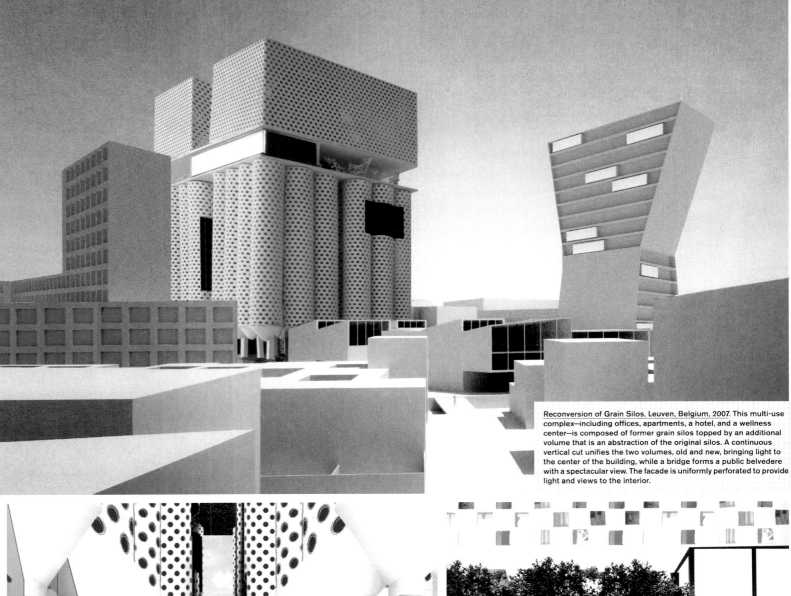

Reconversion of Grain Silos, Leuven, Belgium, 2007. This multi-use complex—including offices, apartments, a hotel, and a wellness center—is composed of former grain silos topped by an additional volume that is an abstraction of the original silos. A continuous vertical cut unifies the two volumes, old and new, bringing light to the center of the building, while a bridge forms a public belvedere with a spectacular view. The facade is uniformly perforated to provide light and views to the interior.

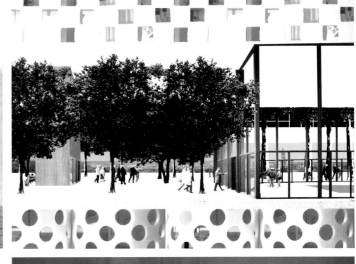

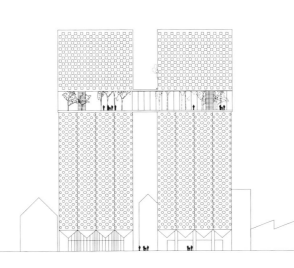

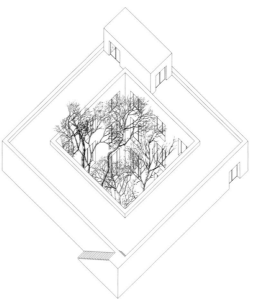

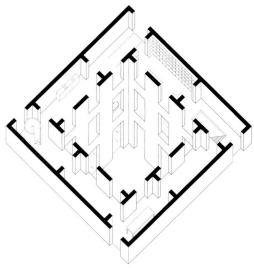

25 Rooms (Villa in Ordos), Ordos, Nei Mongol, China, 2008–.
Two of the villa's three stories are submerged underground
and organized around a hidden garden in the deep central patio.
The patio-void, surrounded by a sequence of twenty-four identical
rooms, organizes the entire house. The servant's quarters make
an enigmatic twenty-fifth room, the only one to exist outside
of the introverted scheme, appearing as a watchtower above
a thick wall.

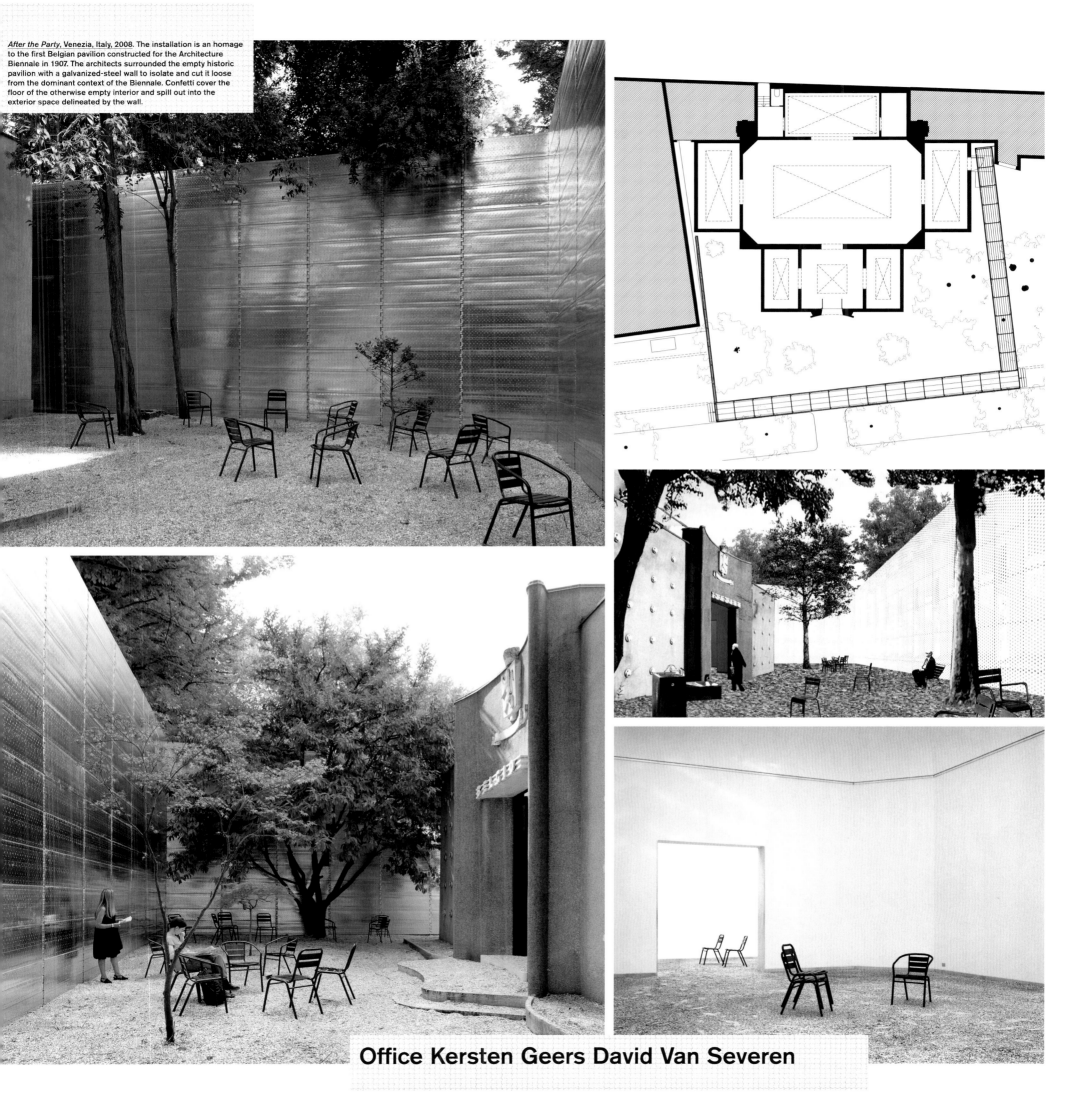

After the Party, Venezia, Italy, 2008. The installation is an homage to the first Belgian pavilion constructed for the Architecture Biennale in 1907. The architects surrounded the empty historic pavilion with a galvanized-steel wall to isolate and cut it loose from the dominant context of the Biennale. Confetti cover the floor of the otherwise empty interior and spill out into the exterior space delineated by the wall.

Office Kersten Geers David Van Severen

Satoshi Okada architects | Tokyo J

House in Wakabadai, Kawasaki, Kanagawa Prefecture, Japan, 2005–6. This house, with a building area of less than 710 sq. ft. (66 sq. m), is raised on large *pilotis* to accommodate the owner's request for sheltered parking space and to offer better views. Exterior walls are covered with rustproof steel sheets, placed 1/5 in. (5 mm) from the base steel plates to create a heat-insulating air buffer in between. The house's lightweight, wooden construction treads lightly on the site's weak ground.

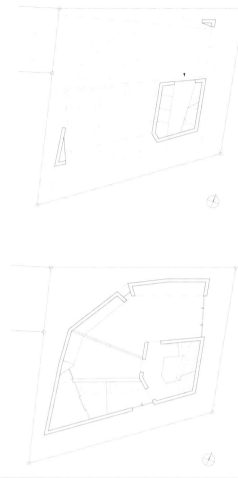

Trained in Japan and the United States, Satoshi Okada opened his practice in Tokyo in 1995 and has taught at the Graduate School of Architecture of Chiba University since 2002. His work is notable for the invention of an original construction system, the Container Structure System (CSS), which he developed, together with the engineer Hirokazu Toki, for the Gallery in Kiyosato. The technology is based on a system of ship-shaped structures that contain the functional spaces of the house—the kitchen and bathroom, for example—which Okada calls "secondary spaces." These prefabricated, ship-shaped secondary spaces act as load-bearing walls, positioned freely around the primary space of the house.

The high-density urban setting defines the compositional elements of Okada's House in Ogikubo in the Suginami area of Tokyo. The program for this two-family house is a response to the contemporary Tokyo phenomenon of younger families living with their parents due to the high cost of urban housing. On the small trapezoidal site, Okada articulated the plan in three irregular elements linked as a single building but providing independent spaces for the two families. The House in Wakabadai emphasizes the evolution of Okada's research, based mainly on the definition of the volume and experiments with building methods. The single-family house is a new opportunity to explore the potential of his CSS, now perfected to offer protection against earthquakes. Its signature ship-shaped load-bearing components are positioned to shape an unusual morphology with a strongly expressionist character.

The Agri-Community Center responds to the request for a building that would intrigue and attract visitors. The CSS elements adapt easily to functionally diversified interiors (collective spaces, cooking areas, areas for displaying and selling the local products, and guest rooms), achieving a flexibility particularly well-suited for its public functions. As with his work in general, Okada's expressive vocabulary is the result of figurative ideas attuned to the environment and innovative construction methods, based on the reinterpretation of traditional practices. His achievements to date confirm him as one of the most original of young contemporary architects. // Mercedes Daguerre

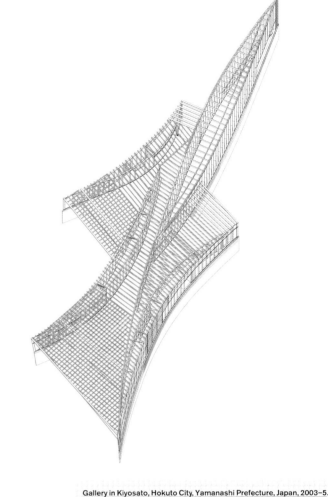

Gallery in Kiyosato, Hokuto City, Yamanashi Prefecture, Japan, 2003–5. This building, located in a densely wooded site, is a guesthouse and an art gallery. It features Satoshi Okada's newly invented Container Structure System (CSS), a wood construction method that promotes flexibility in composition and plan. The primary space, loosely articulated, is an open space for living; ship-shaped construction volumes make up the secondary spaces that include the kitchen, restroom, stairs, chimney, and closet. The soaring facade acknowledges the verticality of the surrounding trees.

House in Ogikubo, Tokyo, Japan, 2004–5.
This private residence, located in Ogikubo, one of Tokyo's most dense residential districts, houses two generations of one family that wished to live on the same site, but in separate houses. The wall separating the two homes tilts toward the elder's dwelling. The home of the younger family contains a double height space while the other one is more compressed and dimly lit.

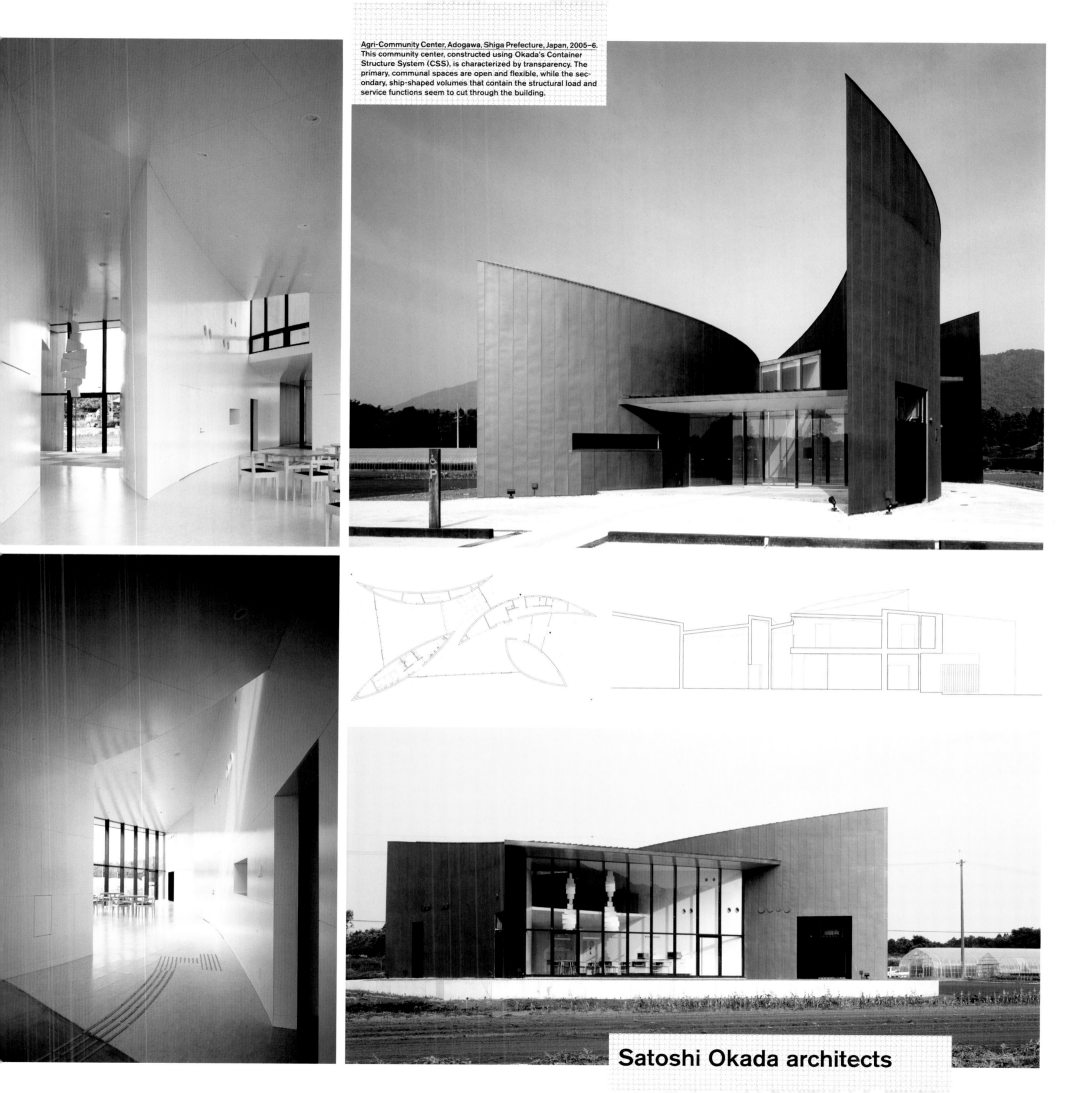

Agri-Community Center, Adogawa, Shiga Prefecture, Japan, 2005–6.
This community center, constructed using Okada's Container
Structure System (CSS), is characterized by transparency. The
primary, communal spaces are open and flexible, while the secondary, ship-shaped volumes that contain the structural load and
service functions seem to cut through the building.

Satoshi Okada architects

Onix   Groningen NL / Helsingborg S

Ecological Farm, Haren, Netherlands, 2001–3. The program for this biological farm consists of several specific farming functions combined with a few recreational facilities such as a teahouse, a shop, an educational space, and a children's farm. The designers chose to bring all the facilities under one continuous roof, providing a literal translation of the program. The wooden roof is the connecting element under which all parts of the program take place.

When I was studying architecture at Delft University of Technology in the Netherlands, one of the recurrent discussions involved architects who complained that the general public didn't understand anything about modern architecture. This was a bad thing, they argued, because modern architecture was good for people. As an example of the public's illiteracy, someone cited the fact that most people wanted to live in a house with a pitched roof. Most participants did not see anything strange in this statement or question this assumption. Pitched roofs were not considered progressive, along with red brick walls, symmetry, and any construction based on pressure instead of tension. At that time in the early 1980s, these notions were still politically and morally charged, and stating otherwise would have immediately led to one's isolation as a conservative pariah in a palace of enlightenment. These days, the political connotations have disappeared, but the moral judgment still exists, though good and bad is replaced by interesting and not interesting, meaning fashionable and not fashionable.

Within this context, Onix is suspect. First of all, the architects of this firm do not work in the Randstad (the western region in Holland that includes the big cities of Amsterdam, Den Haag, Rotterdam, and Utrecht), but in Groningen in the north of Holland. Second, they design buildings with pitched roofs. Of course, these two factors are interdependent. In contrast to the west, in the northeast of Holland many building sites are at the fringes of urban settlements in areas composed of low-rise, low-density housing, and the relationship with the existing landscape is a major concern. Moreover, this landscape is dotted with traditional farms offering a rich palette of articulated typologies (each region has its own). Over the years, playing with the typology of the traditional Dutch house has become the main theme in the work of Onix. This concerns not only the aforementioned pitched or sloping roof, which is transformed into a zigzag, a ramp, or a folded plane, but also the relationship of the house with its surroundings. The traditional Dutch practice of giving each dwelling a fenced-in garden is abandoned and replaced by a new layout where the houses stand surrounded by a common garden or open space. // Bart Goldhoorn

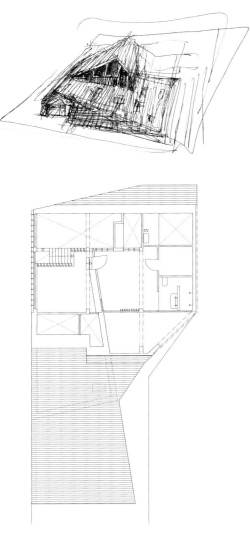

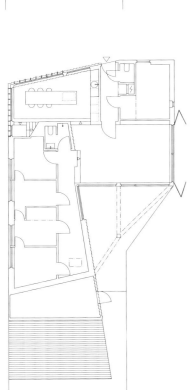

Villa Maarsingh, Leeuwarden, Netherlands, 2004–5. The client—a family of psychologists and experts who advocate Zen meditation—wanted a home where they could experience the Japanese concept of Yugen, or a sense of the infinite. The result is a house that is intimate but at the same time open and welcoming, where the garden and house blend as a continuous space yet offer opportunity for personal isolation.

Verandah Houses, Almere, Netherlands, 2003–6. Ten villas comprising a total of thirty-six dwellings were built in a clearing in a poplar wood. Ten artificial mounds similar to the levees built by the Dutch in medieval times were built to accommodate them. Each of the villas, all of which are detached, contains three or five homes. Factors such as privacy, sunlight, and access determined the positions of the buildings within the clearing.

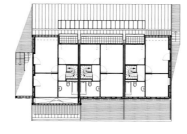

SECOND FLOOR

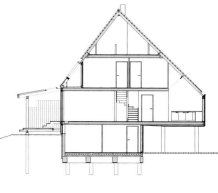

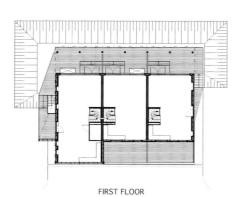

FIRST FLOOR

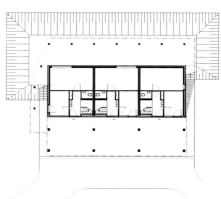

GROUND FLOOR

Searching House, Lemmer, Netherlands, 2005–7. This project was a request to convert a traditional Frisian farmstead into a modern dwelling. In order to keep the elements with special aesthetic qualities such as the trusses and the large monumental roof, the architects translated the assignment into an architectonic exploration of a house within a roof. The project gets its name in part from the process of seeking new locations for living, eating, working, and relaxing.

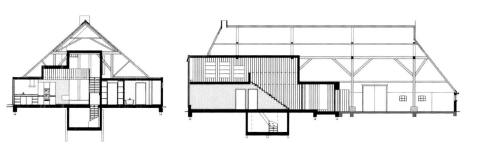

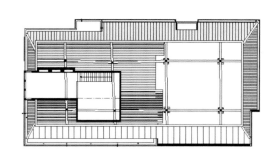

Onix

John and Patricia Patkau, both from Winnipeg, Manitoba, Canada, received their professional degrees from the University of Manitoba. The couple originally established their firm in Edmonton, Alberta, in 1978, relocating to Vancouver in 1984. As if to mark the propitious move to Canada's third-largest city, the Patkaus built their own house in a sloping and densely wooded site in the city, demonstrating at once their keen sense for integrating site and formal concerns as complementary expressions. A series of schools and houses built in the 1990s throughout British Columbia cemented the architects' reputation, the bravado of their tectonic inventiveness, and their painstaking dedication to craft. A building that best encapsulates these emblematic qualities is the Barnes House in Nanaimo, British Columbia (1991–3), a marvelous work of observant subtlety, comfort, and invention.

Since 2000, two projects in particular have expanded the architects' explorations to a much larger rural and urban scale. The Agosta House, built across the border on San Juan Island in Washington State, is a work totally at ease with its astonishing site: a setting of undulating grassy meadows, profuse Douglas fir forests, and commanding views of the Gulf islands along the southern coast of British Columbia. The house is an elongated volume intent on maximizing these views from multiple vantage points. Interior and exterior combine to create a rich and warm variety of spaces, rooms, and terraces, each of them revealing a distinct view of the near and distant landscape.

The Central Library of Québec in Montréal, selected in 2000 as the winning entry in an international design competition and completed in 2005, is the architects' largest work to date. It successfully consolidates multiple urban and cultural requirements, among them the various collections from other libraries of the region. As the province's main public library, the vast facility is a vital resource and center of information, archival materials, and diverse learning activities. The six-level structure occupies the entirety of its site, yet it manages to promote an active street life along its glass and copper-clad facades. Equally bustling activity unfolds the moment one enters the impressive ground level. A luminous promenade guides the dynamic itinerary of the library and its multifaceted program. Floating stairs and surprising ramps and pathways conspire to create a truly public thoroughfare at all levels of the library. It is a place that inspires not only through the diversity of its program but also, especially, through the pedagogical generosity of its architecture.
// Carlos Jimenez

Central Library of Québec, Montréal, Québec, Canada, 2000–2005. Designed in collaboration with Croft Pelletier and Menkès Shooner Dagenais, the Central Library houses two major collections for Québec, the *Collection québécoise* and the *Collection universelle*. These collections are housed within large wooden containers, accessed from an architectural promenade that rises upward from the entrance of the library through a series of reading rooms. A glass and copper exterior, opaque in some places, diaphanous in others, offers enticing glimpses of the library from the outside.

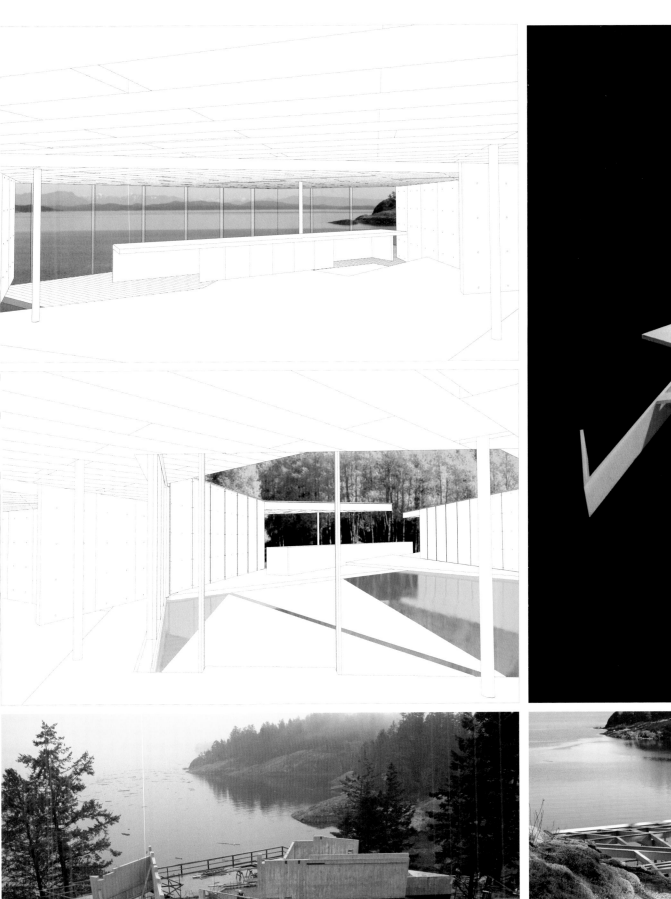

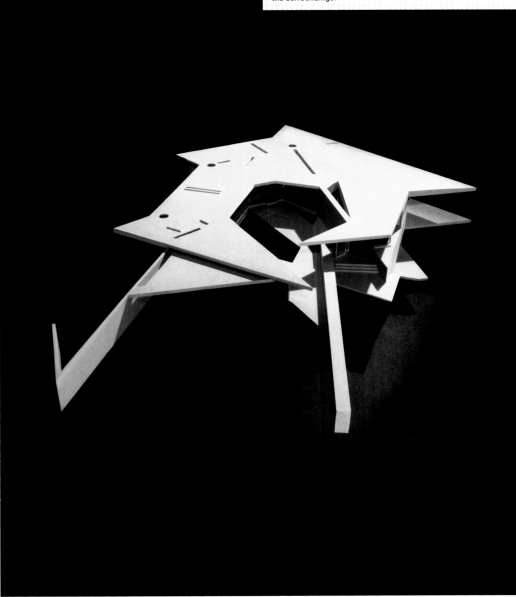

Peterson/Munck House, Quadra Island, British Columbia, Canada, 2006–9. The Peterson/Munck house is located on a remote island, at the edge of a cliff 44 ft. (13 m) above the Pacific Ocean. The geometric and spatial order of the house reflects the irregularity of the site's rock ledges, forest, and beach. A loose arrangement of concrete walls, clad in black fiber-cement panels, defines the house's plan, while the roof, planted in moss, will blend in with the surroundings.

Winnipeg Centennial Library Addition, Winnipeg, Manitoba, Canada, 2002–5. The 1970s Winnipeg Centennial Library was transformed by the addition of a new terraced reading room and fourth floor. The reading room forms a grand stair that interconnects all of the library floors; fully glazed, it fills the library with natural light, and offers generous views to the adjacent park.

Agosta House, San Juan Island, Washington, USA, 1996–2000. The Agosta House sits in a meadow enclosed by forest on three sides; the fourth side opens to a spectacular view to the northwest. The house spans the ridge of the meadow, forming a "spatial dam" that divides the site. The exterior is clad mostly in Zactique metal to protect it against wild fires, while the structure consists of exposed heavy-timber fir framing and stud framing clad with gypsum board, founded on a simple concrete slab-on-grade.

Patkau Architects

Paul Morgan Architects | Melbourne AUS

Cape Schanck House, Cape Schanck, Victoria, Australia, 2003–6. The analysis of dynamic forces—wind energy, turbulence, and phototropism—informed the modeling of the building's envelope. In the living room the ceiling wraps down to form an internal "bulb" water tank. The tank cools the ambient air of the room during the summer, and structurally carries the roof load. In an era of climate change, the bulb tank becomes the symbolic locus of the house, replacing the fireplace, television, or computer.

Sustainable architecture in Australia is often conflated with a lyrical bush tradition that attempts to mimic natural processes in building design. This approach does render some sublime moments, but, in the process, largely turns its back on the city and its historical corollary, technology. For much of the world it has come to embody what architecture in Australia does well. The architect Paul Morgan, however, assumes a radically different position. Consciously resisting the romanticism of this pastoral tradition, Morgan prefers to explore more analytic territory, embracing technology to explore a new dialogue with nature. It is in this spirit that the architect's recent projects demonstrate a critical approach to site, technology, language, and culture. Together they are evidence of an uncanny capacity to appear at once alien and autonomous, yet adapted to a place and time.

Cape Schanck House is his most richly layered completed work to date. Other projects currently under construction promise to build on the strengths of this project, but this compact weekender, an hour's drive south of Melbourne, is pivotal. It is a house that has been designed and engineered using local wind analysis to optimize the building's form and orientation, and collects rainwater within a sensuously bulbous water tank for passive climate control. It is a finely tuned environmental home, owing nothing to the rhetorical expression of "sustainability" and rather a lot to the aesthetic of a 1960s science fiction movie. This investigative design process also owes a debt to the fertile vision of Buckminster Fuller and the plastic futurism of John Lautner. Whereas this weekender type is often associated with the routine formulas of indoor-outdoor planning (the beach as extended living room), Cape Schanck House quotes Fuller's architecture-as-life-support: shielding and protecting here, opening in a controlled fashion there.

An even more autonomous object exists in the form of the sound studios for the Royal Melbourne Institute of Technology's (RMIT) Spatial Information Architecture Laboratory. Given the task of designing a highly specialized acoustic environment, Morgan was asked to create a solution for a research zone of perfect dead silence, while harnessing the cinematic language of science and technology to create a compressed synthesis of cultural meaning. This and other examples of his recent machine aesthetic allow for fresh synthesis, responsive to native conditions yet plugged into an aesthetic as universal as the one that was once commonly imagined for the future. // Andrew Mackenzie

Building Barn, Box Hill, Victoria, Australia, 2005–6. The simple steel-framed structure, built within a limited budget, houses a vocational education program for carpentry and plumbing apprentices. The design of the building envelope responds to wind effect, solar movement, site easements, and acoustic demands. A large elliptical opening on the street elevation acts as a contemporary proscenium exposing the mechanisms of the learning programs to public view.

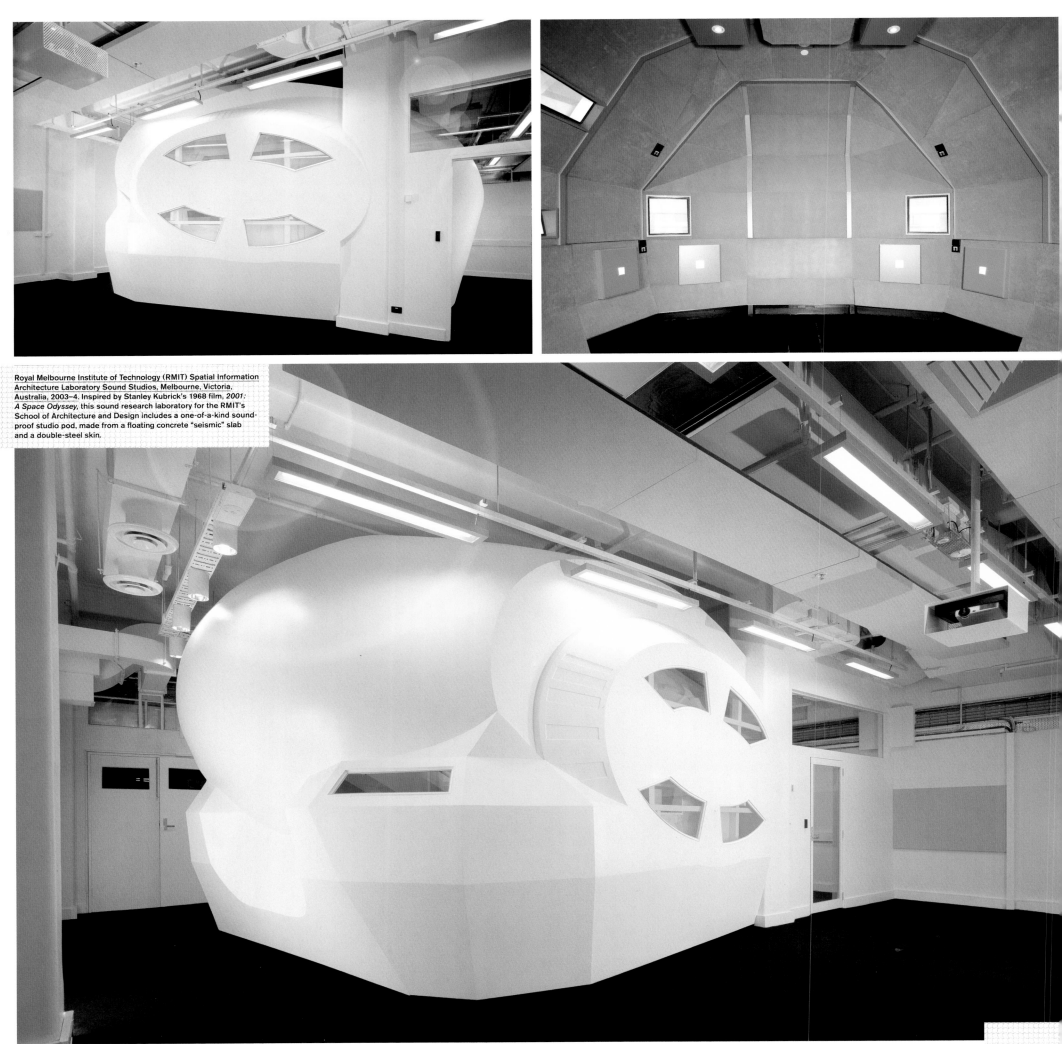

Royal Melbourne Institute of Technology (RMIT) Spatial Information Architecture Laboratory Sound Studios, Melbourne, Victoria, Australia, 2003–4. Inspired by Stanley Kubrick's 1968 film, *2001: A Space Odyssey*, this sound research laboratory for the RMIT's School of Architecture and Design includes a one-of-a-kind sound-proof studio pod, made from a floating concrete "seismic" slab and a double-steel skin.

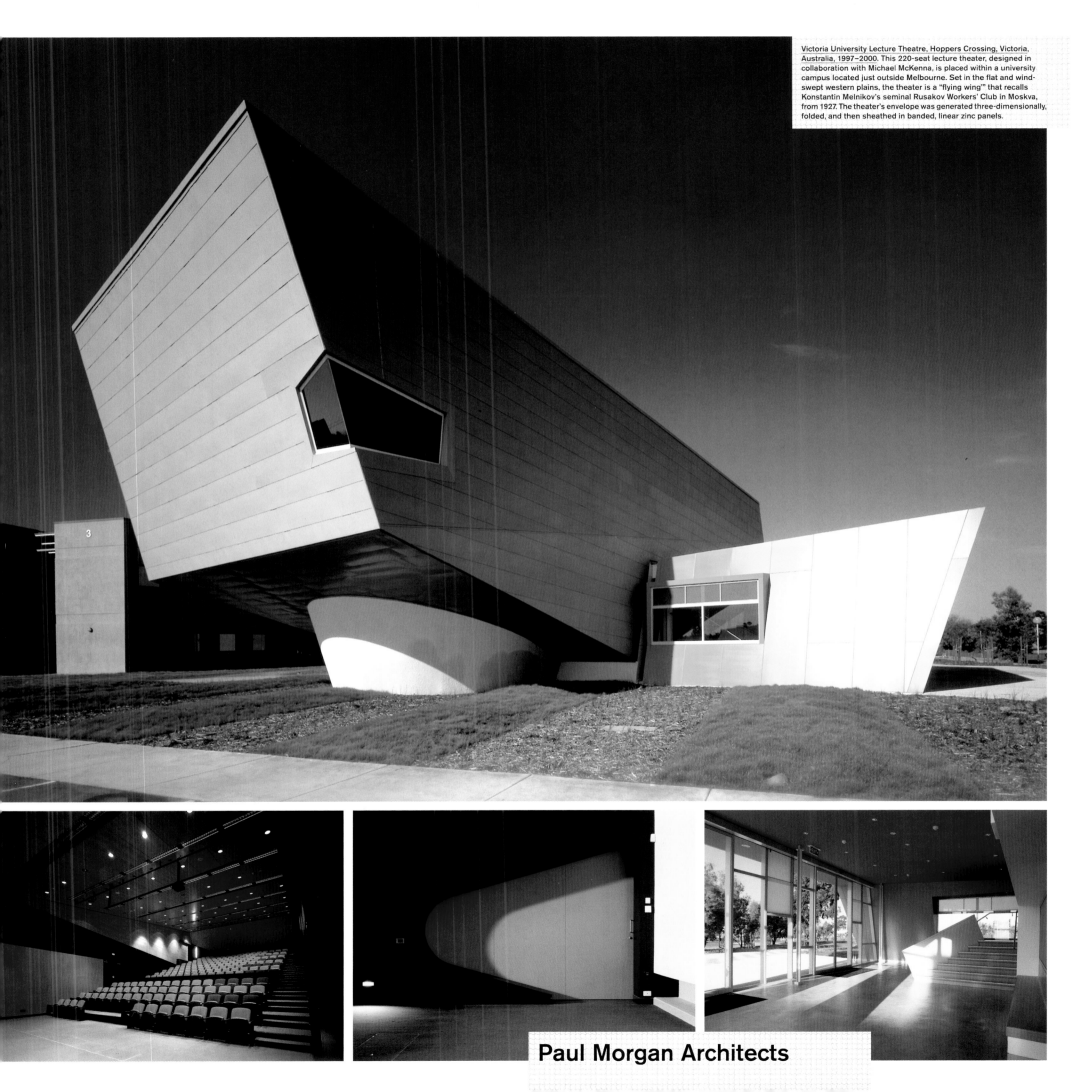

Victoria University Lecture Theatre, Hoppers Crossing, Victoria, Australia, 1997–2000. This 220-seat lecture theater, designed in collaboration with Michael McKenna, is placed within a university campus located just outside Melbourne. Set in the flat and wind-swept western plains, the theater is a "flying wing'" that recalls Konstantin Melnikov's seminal Rusakov Workers' Club in Moskva, from 1927. The theater's envelope was generated three-dimensionally, folded, and then sheathed in banded, linear zinc panels.

Paul Morgan Architects

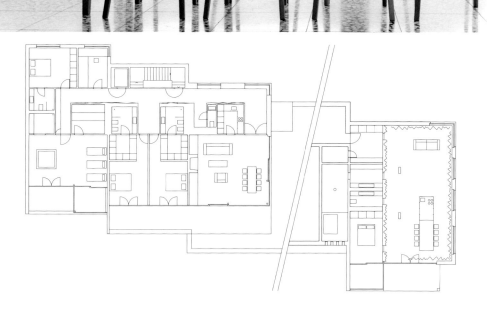

Davos Residence, Davos, Switzerland, 2005–6. Two existing apartments in a multi-family house were gut renovated and turned into two independent leisure residences. The architects eschewed the traditional mountain ski chalet style in favor of open space, maximum natural light, and unconventional patterning on the floors and walls.

Pedrocchi Meier Architects was founded in 2005 in Basel, Switzerland, by the duo Reto Pedrocchi and Beat Meier. The pair displays fine attention to detail in their designs primarily for the residential sector, from interior renovations to ground-up constructions. The interior renovations are a testament to the architects' competence and show off their abilities in interior design. For example, different rooms might express individuality through their varying colors, materials, and details; in one project, the unique qualities of the finishes and materials resonate with 1960s style and sensitivity.

Approaching a project such as the Ordos Villa in Nei Mongol, China, is like approaching a cave in the desert. Pedrocchi Meier Architects designed the project with a simple, massive concrete structure and skin. Conscious of lighting, they created an interesting environment that at times seems to evoke a parking garage rather than a villa. The Ordos Villa is an excellent example of the firm's ability to distill the building's functions into clear geometries and divide them in a way that organizes the spaces effectively. Influenced by the idea that "my home is my castle," the villa is divided into sections so that the upper floor is an open plan containing the master's domain, while the lower level is subdivided for functions catering to other inhabitants and guests. The division of the ground-floor plan is expressed in the ceiling and roof lines of the second level.

Another demonstration of Pedrocchi Meier Architects' ability to organize space for residential applications is the apartment house they designed in Riehen, outside Basel. The simple central core, with a mirrored and reversed distribution of space, is another example of the pair's ability to extract simple geometry from the program, meeting the project's functional needs while offering an inventive spatial quality. // Ai Weiwei

Ordos Villa, Ordos, Nei Mongol, China. 2008–9. The large, east-west orientated upper floor is an open plan that unites all functions of stately contemporary living. Regular volumes, arranged to offset each other, form staggered ceiling joists and divide the empty space above the large living room. By creating zones in the ceiling, the room remains perceptible as a whole but also freely divisible into use areas.

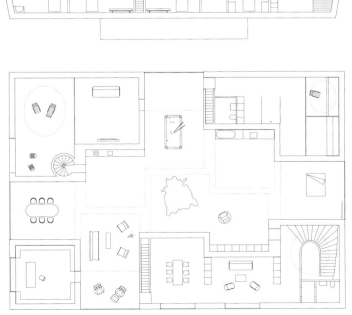

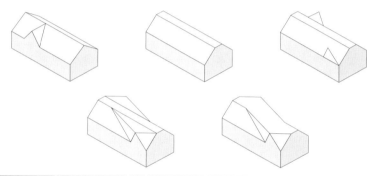

Apartment House, Riehen, Switzerland, 2006–9. This apartment house, situated next to an old public park, is a plain volume with an ordinary footprint, but marked by a distinctive roof, inspired by classical roof shapes and turrets.

St. Johanns Park Pavilion, Basel, Switzerland, 2008. The concept for this unrealized pavilion, adjacent to an existing villa in the park, was to help create a new identity for the neighborhood, park, and Rhine River waterfront.

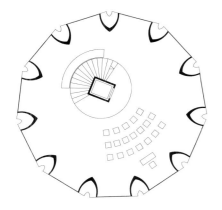

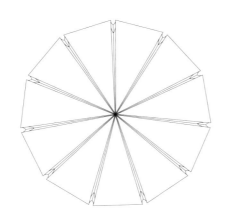

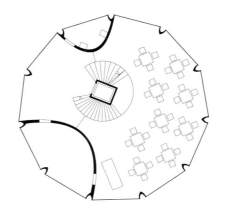

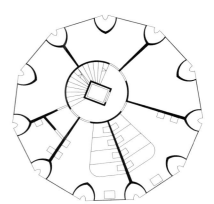

Pedrocchi Meier Architects

Parr House, Chiguayante, Chile, 2006–8. This single-story house was built on the site of the client's childhood home. Composed of twelve rooms and nine outdoor courtyards, the 5,300-sq.-ft. (500-sq.-m) building has a series of roofs that taper away from the courtyards to allow for maximum sunlight. The facade's aluminum-zinc tiles match the clay tiles of the original house.

The architects Mauricio Pezo and Sofia von Ellrichshausen established a joint practice in Buenos Aires in 2001. The couple soon left Argentina and settled in Concepción, in southern Chile, where Pezo had grown up. The practice rapidly flourished with commissions for private houses and artworks. (Pezo, who is the director of the *Movimiento Artista del Sur*—MAS—considers himself foremost a visual artist.) However, it is the houses—often in extraordinary, dramatic locations—that have captured the attention of the architectural community, garnering early recognition in the form of biennials, prizes, and publications in Latin America and Europe.

The Rivo house was the first building by the firm to attract attention, but it was the Poli House that brought the architects widespread acclaim. A work of bold sculptural quality, the Poli House is a punctured concrete cube that sits on a very steep site overlooking the Pacific Ocean, intended to function as both a residence and an art center. All service areas—kitchens, bathrooms, storage, and stairs—are located inside a wide buffer wall that forms the perimeter of the volume. A similar strategy of placing secondary spaces in a perimeter wall had been used in the Rivo House, located on a densely wooded site, which is made of wood tinted with oil and tar. However at the Poli house this composition, reminiscent of house plans by Kazuyo Sejima, is interpreted with even greater aplomb and appeal. The Poli House has laid the foundations of an extraordinarily promising future for Pezo von Ellrichshausen Architects, which has also yielded such accomplishments as the Wolf House and Parr House.
// Luis Fernández-Galiano

Poli House, Coliumo, Chile, 2002–5. The house, which functions as a summer home and cultural center, is located in a rural setting sparsely populated by farmers, fishermen, and summer tourists. The compact building gives the impression of a podium surrounded by vastness. The service functions are arranged around the perimeter, freeing the interior for multiple activities.

Wolf House, San Pedro, Chile, 2005–7. Unlike the adjacent houses, Wolf House has a flat roof, enabling full use of the third story. The structural frame of this private family residence is made up of eight steel beams supported by two concrete slabs; the windows, frameless and flush with the outside walls, offer tailored views of the surroundings. Textured metal siding clads the facade.

Pezo von Ellrichshausen Architects

Bill Price   Houston USA

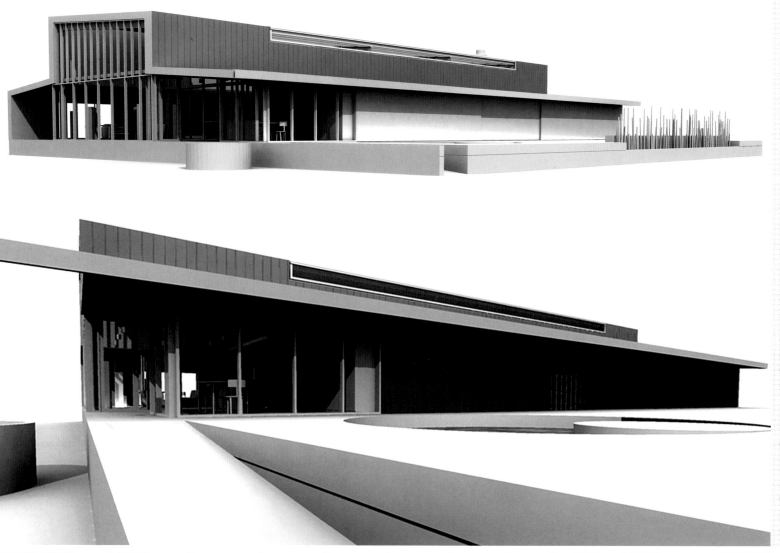

Bill Price, who founded his office in 2001 in Houston, Texas, consistently demonstrates a clear approach toward object making. Price is an architect who is driven by his desire to develop materials and to apply them in unexpected ways. Both his reserved approach to design and his passion for materials are demonstrated in his sculptural formulation of buildings. Evidence of this approach can be discovered in the Perez/Landmeier House. The design is essentially a container of corrugated steel sitting atop a western red cedar–planked fence that spirals from the exterior boundary into the building's substructure. The duality of the two materials, coupled with the juxtaposition of the two forms, creates an elegant sculptural object.

To understand Price's general approach toward design, one must examine the methodologies apparent in his work. His projects, carefully and sculpturally formed, address the process of object making. Always attentive to the effect of layering, Price repeatedly explores the stacking of forms. By stacking dissimilar objects atop each other, he reveals his clear foundations in postmodernism, in which unfamiliar objects are often juxtaposed to create a tension or composition. Balancing forms compositionally, Price uses openings and materials to attune the objects' overall aesthetic. Dealing with texture and shapes, his restrained and fragile style has an almost choreographic resonance.

In terms of Price's material explorations, his experimental work is exemplified by his contributions to the development of translucent concrete since 1999. The concrete panels in his research project Pool House_Translucent Concrete Pavilion 2 (2008), a partially enclosed swimming pool pavilion, allow light to pass through the thousands of translucent points incorporated into the naturally opaque concrete. // Ai Weiwei

House in a Forest, Magnolia, Texas, USA, 2004–. On a large wooded lot northwest of Houston, this private residence, organized around a large conservatory for ferns and other plants, is conceived as a plate that is folded in response to the program's height limits. The ground floor, elevated on a concrete socle to escape potential flooding from a nearby stream, is enclosed with insulated glass, cellular polycarbonate panels, and perforated metal screens to allow for maximum views into the conservatory and the surrounding landscape.

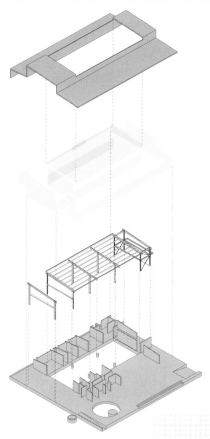

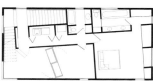

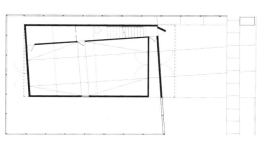

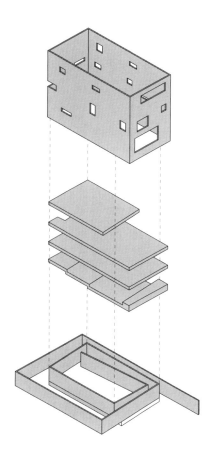

Perez/Landmeier House, Houston, Texas, USA. 2002–4. The house provides living space for a family of three and studio space for a graphic designer. The formal organization is conceived as a tubular container of corrugated metal placed on top of a continuous spiraling line clad in western red cedar planking, which functions as both socle and fence. To maximize usable space and to respond to city setback requirements, the container is cantilevered toward the street and used to cover the entryway.

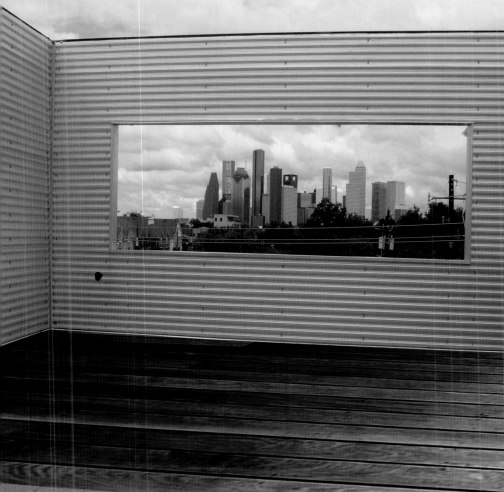

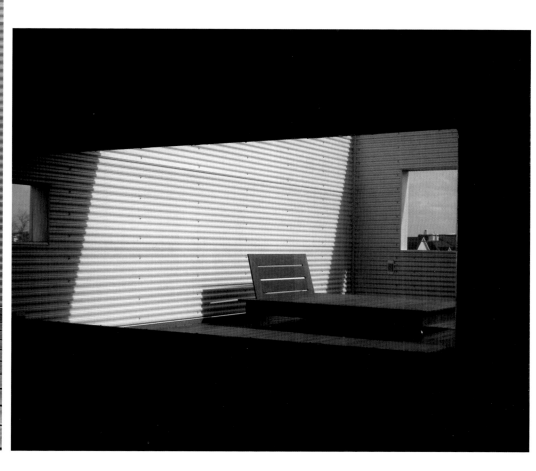

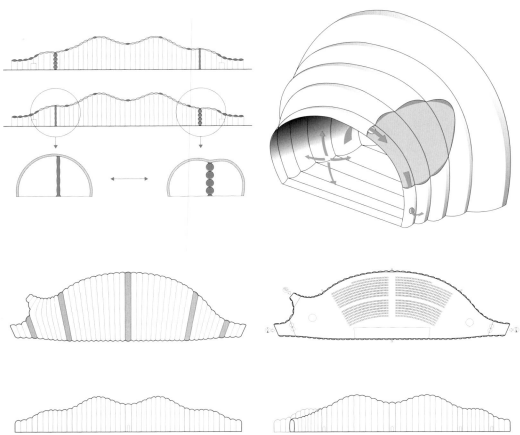

Inflatable Air Dome, Seoul, Republic of Korea, 2008. A direct commission from the Seoul Metropolitan Government, the project called for a design to house 1,200 people and stages for receptions within Seoul's Jamsil Olympic Stadium. Using an inflatable structure with a radial plan, the seats are organized so that the audience has direct sight lines to the stage. The two primary entrances to the inflatable dome are longitudinally aligned with the plan of the track, thus allowing its circuit to remain intact.

Translucent Concrete, 1999–present. For the past ten years, Bill Price has conducted research on translucent concrete. He has perforated traditional cement-based concrete to allow light to pass through the otherwise nontransparent material. He has also developed a material that replaces traditional concrete components with a crushed-glass aggregate and plastic binder. The Mue Store in Seoul (above), designed with Mass Studies, features dividing walls made up of translucent concrete bricks using the latter technique.

Bill Price

Productora

México D.F. MEX

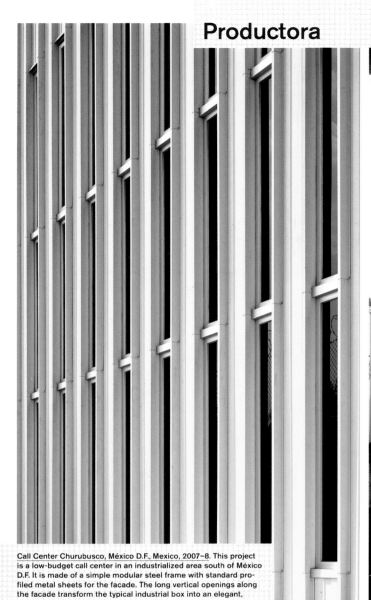

Call Center Churubusco, México D.F., Mexico, 2007–8. This project is a low-budget call center in an industrialized area south of México D.F. It is made of a simple modular steel frame with standard profiled metal sheets for the facade. The long vertical openings along the facade transform the typical industrial box into an elegant, translucent curtain.

Productora was founded in México D.F. in 2006 by partners Abel Perles, Carlos Bedoya, Victor Jaime, and Wonne Ickx. Employing methodologies that generate daring forms, the office is completing international projects that range from single-family residences to corporate headquarters. If design is the elimination of options, then Productora excels in choosing the right options to eliminate, leaving them with bold forms based on solid ideas.

The Villa in Ordos, designed for the Ordos 100 project in Nei Mongol, China, demonstrates the strength of Productora's high aesthetics and classical proportions. Beginning with a single, 10,000-square-foot (1,000-square-meter) cube, they subsequently sliced the cube diagonally, creating a negative-positive relationship while simultaneously subdividing the building's functions. Depending on one's vantage point, the villa can be perceived as a solid brick mass, a series of barlike volumes, or a sequence of glazed surfaces.

Another beautiful volume that plays with solid and void is the Call Center Churubusco. This project exemplifies Productora's ability to design compelling buildings despite a tight budget and utilitarian program. Responding with simple construction methods and materials, they use profiled metal sheets and modular steel framing to create a seductive, syncopated facade.

Productora's work shows high aesthetic ambition. There is an underlying attention to geometry and to the classical rules of mathematical proportion in their hard-edged designs. Integrated with their boldness and rationality is a sensitivity to form and use, which completes the architecture. Strongly defining their ideas without compromising their forms, Productora makes architecture with the vivid severity of the pyramids. // Ai Weiwei

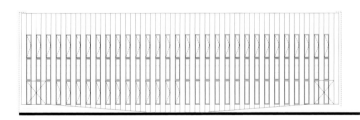

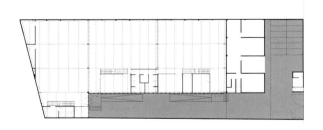

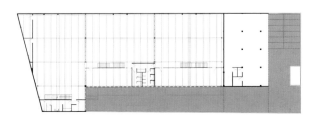

CAF Headquarters, Caracas, Venezuela, 2008–. This competition
for the new headquarters of the CAF (Andean Development
Corporation) required a building with a very small footprint to
generate as much public space as possible. The tower, developed
in collaboration with Lucio Muniain et al., has a transparent and
open grid at its base. On top of this seemingly fragile structure,
a monolithic white volume seems suspended over the plaza.

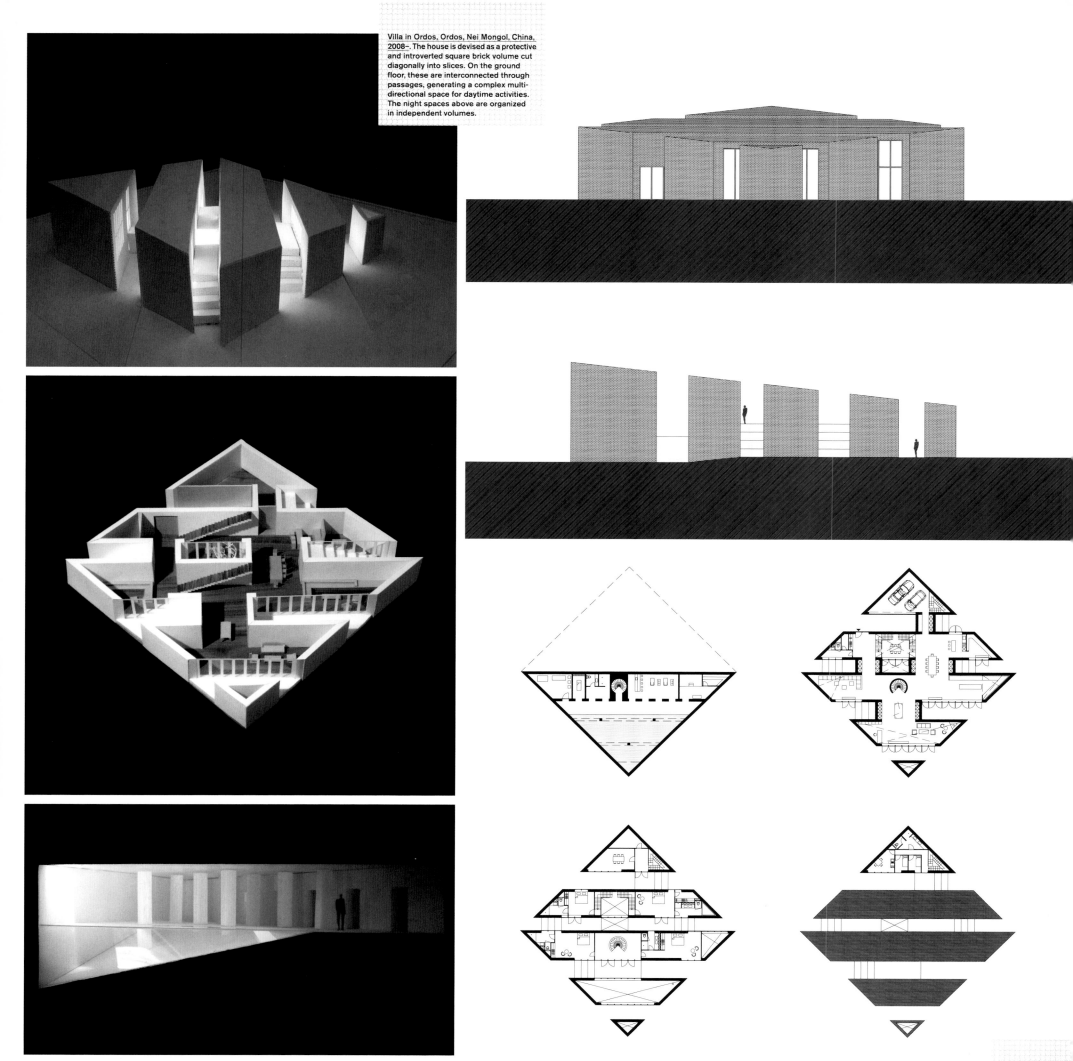

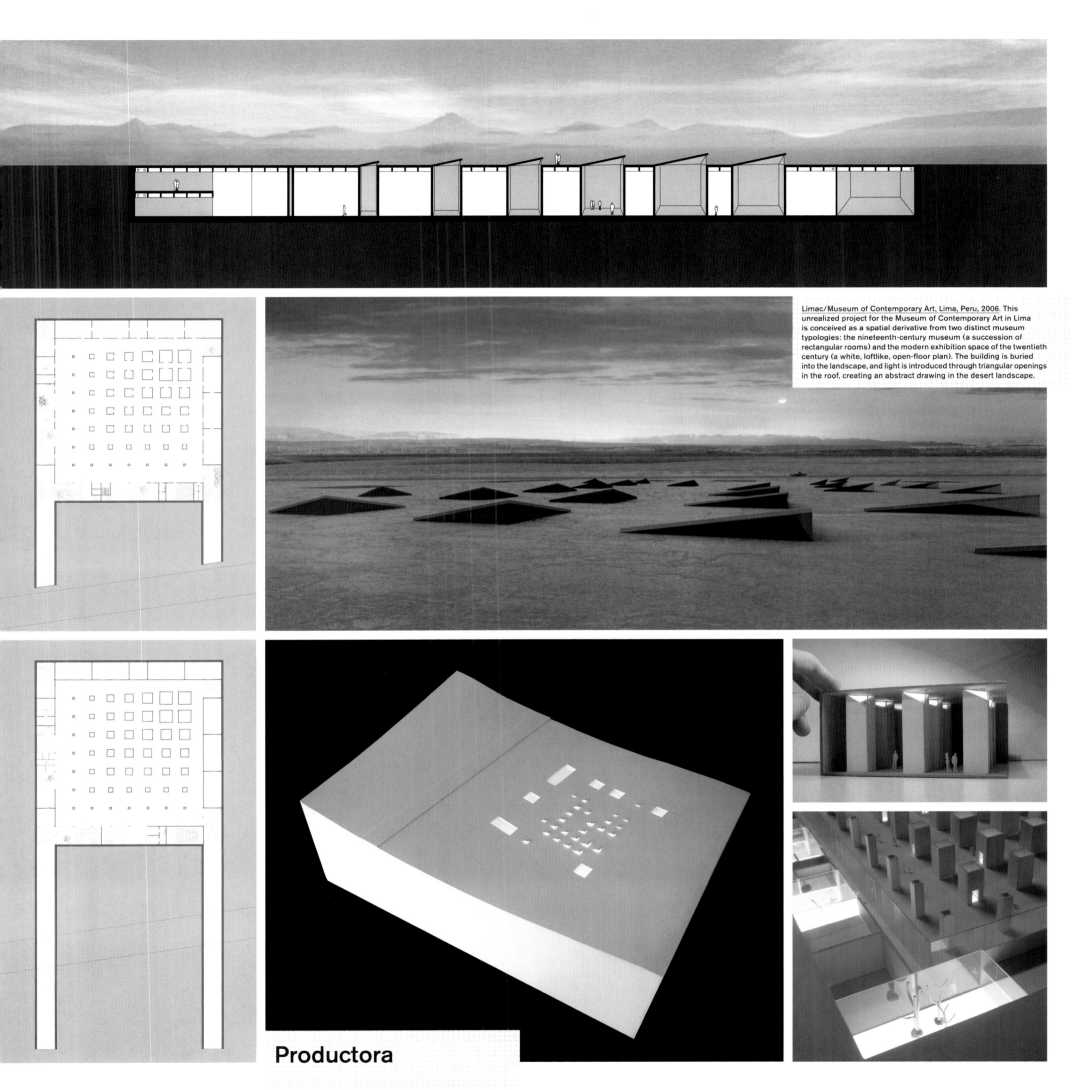

Limac/Museum of Contemporary Art, Lima, Peru, 2006. This unrealized project for the Museum of Contemporary Art in Lima is conceived as a spatial derivative from two distinct museum typologies: the nineteenth-century museum (a succession of rectangular rooms) and the modern exhibition space of the twentieth century (a white, loftlike, open-floor plan). The building is buried into the landscape, and light is introduced through triangular openings in the roof, creating an abstract drawing in the desert landscape.

Productora

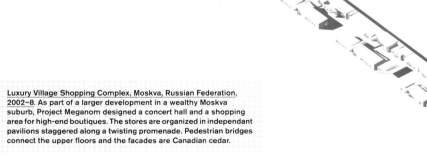

Luxury Village Shopping Complex, Moskva, Russian Federation, 2002–8. As part of a larger development in a wealthy Moskva suburb, Project Meganom designed a concert hall and a shopping area for high-end boutiques. The stores are organized in independant pavilions staggered along a twisting promenade. Pedestrian bridges connect the upper floors and the facades are Canadian cedar.

In a rating of the most expensive apartments in Moskva by the Russian newspaper *Kommersant* a few years ago, two of the three highest ranking complexes were designed by Project Meganom, a young Moskva firm that, in just a few years, had managed to become the most promising architectural office in the Russian Federation. Though its connection with expensive real estate might be more chance than conscious pursuit, its position in this segment allows Project Meganom to bypass many problems other Russian architects are struggling to overcome, and, in so doing, develop an impressive body of work. The office is able to produce state of the art architecture as a rule rather than an exception.

New Russian wealth is offering the opportunity to produce remarkable works of architecture. This is particularly true in the private field. While there is a willingness to splurge for luxurious apartment interiors and private villas, clients are less prodigal and their taste is more conservative when it comes to business developments. The radicality of Project Meganom's works is therefore as much a result of the unusual context in which they operate as it is of the firm's talent to take advantage of it. The Villa Ostozhenka, for instance, a private home with blind walls in the middle of a building block, could only exist here because of the strange rules—or absence of rules—governing the development of the area as a whole.

Russian profligacy is not limited to private residences, however. Luxury Village Shopping Complex, a shopping mall with only the world's most expensive brands, combined with a theater, in an area with upscale dachas outside Moskva, is another example of the country's current extragavance. And the towers in the Yalta Hotel and Residential Complex in the Ukraine, though far from Moskva, seem to mock the ideas of economy and functionality that govern projects in other parts of the world. // Bart Goldhoorn

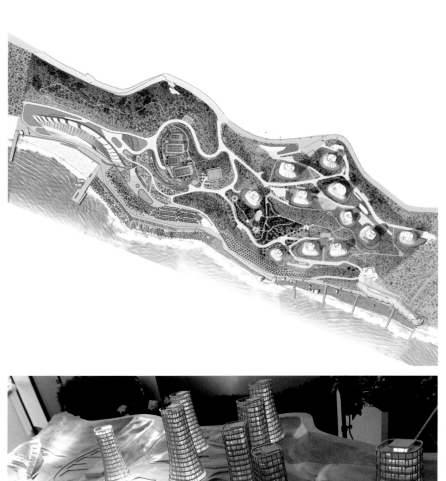

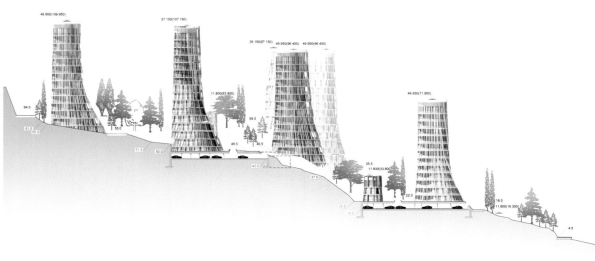

Yalta Hotel and Residential Complex, Yalta, Ukraine, 2006–.
This project is situated in a park on the southern coast of Crimea,
composed of eleven towers ranging from six to fifteen stories,
and a five-star hotel of 100 rooms.

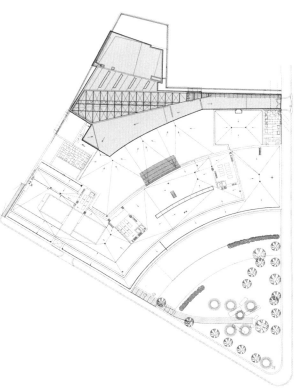

Villa Ostozhenka, Moskva, Russian Federation, 2001–3. This private house in the center of Moskva, an imposing 15,000 sq. ft. (1,400 sq. m), is surrounded by multi-story apartment buildings. The house's entrance is a winter garden with an illuminated wedge-shaped glass roof, but otherwise the residence is largely sealed off from public view. The house, which includes several levels including an underground space completely isolated from the outside, contains a pool, a sauna, and a library.

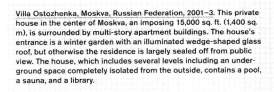

Project Meganom

Smiljan Radic | Santiago RCH

Copper House 2, Talca, Chile, 2004–5. In this house, the modulated structure of the crimped electrolytic copper imitates certain aspects of its surroundings. The design is a reference to the simple geometries of local structures deformed by successive extensions and collapses.

Smiljan Radic is a young Chilean architect of startling maturity. Scattered across the varied geographies that make up his long and narrow country, Radic's astonishing structures assert their intuitive power as if extracted from some telluric realm of place and imagination. Three recent works clearly demonstrate Radic's deft yet lyrical sensibility. CR House, the architect's own home, is a radical transformation of a nondescript house in a typical residential neighborhood of Santiago. The house's mansard roof of cement tiles was removed in its entirety to make room for a top floor living space. Radic's plan to replace the heavy roof with a light, inflatable, and translucent membrane prompted his neighbors to organize countless protests against the new structure. The architect persevered and was able to build his luminous tent anchored by the house's ground floor where a new kitchen, dining room, and bedroom are located. The living space is amplified by its seeming ethereality and by a compelling display of whispering shadows from the surrounding trees.

The Pite House, located in the small coastal town of Papudo, about two hours south of Santiago, is a work that simultaneously conforms to and defies its exuberant and rugged landscape. A remarkable work of architecture, even though it is camouflaged as a work of infrastructure, the Pite House appears at times to be a platform from which to view the wide open sea, an elongated pathway to the seashore, or a seamless merger of sea and sky. The house's program has been dispersed throughout the site while remaining a fully integrated composition echoing the overwhelming beauty of the surroundings.

Further south in the agricultural region outside Talca the architect recently completed Copper House 2. This house, like most of Radic's work, surprises with its beguiling simplicity. On closer inspection, though, a complex geometry emerges outlining an unseen yet familiar object, this time wrapped in copper and tiptoeing on short *pilotis* over its tilled site. // Carlos Jimenez

Pite House, Papudo, Chile, 2003–5. This coastal weekend house is made up of three indepedent levels: the uppermost level contains the main rooms of the complex, including the living area, kitchen, master bedroom, and bathrooms, as well as the terrace and swimming pool. An external passageway along the edge of the cliff leads to the guest bedrooms. The third level is located 59 ft. (18 m) further down and contains the children's villa. The complex will continue settling into its site as the native vegetation reclaims it by growing into the interstices and grooves of the pavement.

Civic District, Concepción, Chile, 2000–2007. This project, designed in collaboration with architects Eduardo Castillo and Ricardo Serpell, will be built in stages, two of which have been partially completed: the conversion of the train station into the headquarters of the regional government, and the construction of pavilions for the new offices of the Ministry of Public Works.

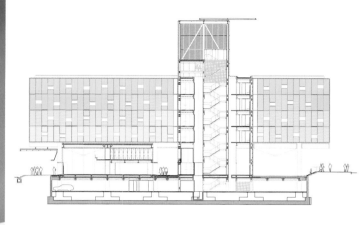

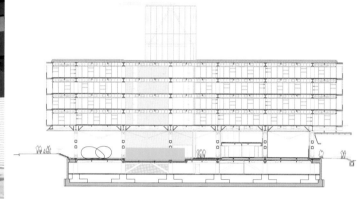

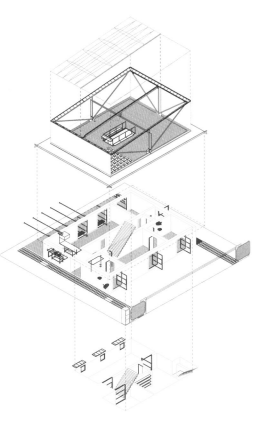

CR House, Santiago, Chile, 2002–3. For his own home, the architect tore away the upper floor of the original house, a heavy mansard of cement tiles, and redistributed the ground floor. The upper floor was reconstructed around two "floaters" of inflated membrane connected to a small 100-watt compressor that regulates the air pressure. This system makes the roof self-supporting, which allowed the elimination of secondary structures.

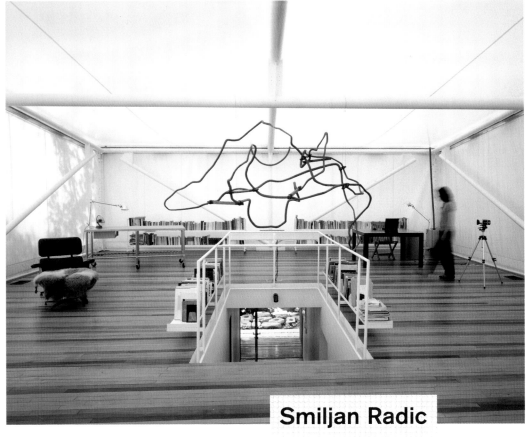

Smiljan Radic

Philippe Rahm Architectes

Paris F / Lausanne CH

One way of seeing modernism in the twentieth century is as a progression toward dematerialization and disappearance. It happened in music, in literature, in theater. And, one could say, it also occurred in architecture. Philippe Rahm's architecture is dematerialization for the twenty-first century. He does not follow the purist purging of Mies van der Rohe or Gerrit Rietveld, where emptiness began to stand in for fullness. Rahm's designs cannot really be captured on the page in all their sensory fullness. He manipulates invisibilities. Things like temperature, humidity, dryness, luminosity. Things that in a funny way are not actually things at all but processes, fluxes, determinants of ambience.

This work has its roots in earlier collaborations with Jean-Gilles Décosterd, when the duo produced some of the most provocative architectural innovations seen in decades. Décosterd and Rahm became infamous for a nearly clinical understanding of how space affects the human body, making it comfortable, anxious, or unsettled. Rahm's work since parting with Décosterd has operated in two realms: a series of beautiful gallery installations that test specific technical experiments, and a number of built proposals, such as the house for French artist Dominique Gonzalez-Foerster. Surfaces, such as floors and walls, are heated to different temperatures that are determined by different domestic activities.

In all of Rahm's work, architectural hardware, such as partition walls, is minimized, but without sacrificing the comforts of interior intimacy. Sometimes his visions evoke past Utopias, as in his beautiful, 1960s-inflected installation at the 2008 Architecture Biennale in Venezia, which felt like a missing scene from a long-lost movie by the Italian architecture collective Superstudio. At other times, Rahm's eulogy of the technology that makes modern life possible (electricity, air conditioning) is flavored with a real taste of apocalypse. We wired the modern world, and now the same wiring might well destroy us. Never has the significance of our fragile ecology been so prominent in political discourses. Rahm's projects highlight the difficult ambiguities of wanting to protect the earth from our addiction to architecture. // Shumon Basar

Meteorological Museum, Wroclaw, Poland, 2008. In this unrealized design for a museum, two poles—hot and cold—exist along a diagonal. The temperature difference generates a thermodynamic imbalance that moves air masses to draw an atmospheric landscape. Using climatic software, Rahm modeled spaces according to air warmth. Plans and sections were designed taking into account the ideal temperature for each space, for example, storage at 61°F (16°C), and exhibition rooms at 64°F (18°C).

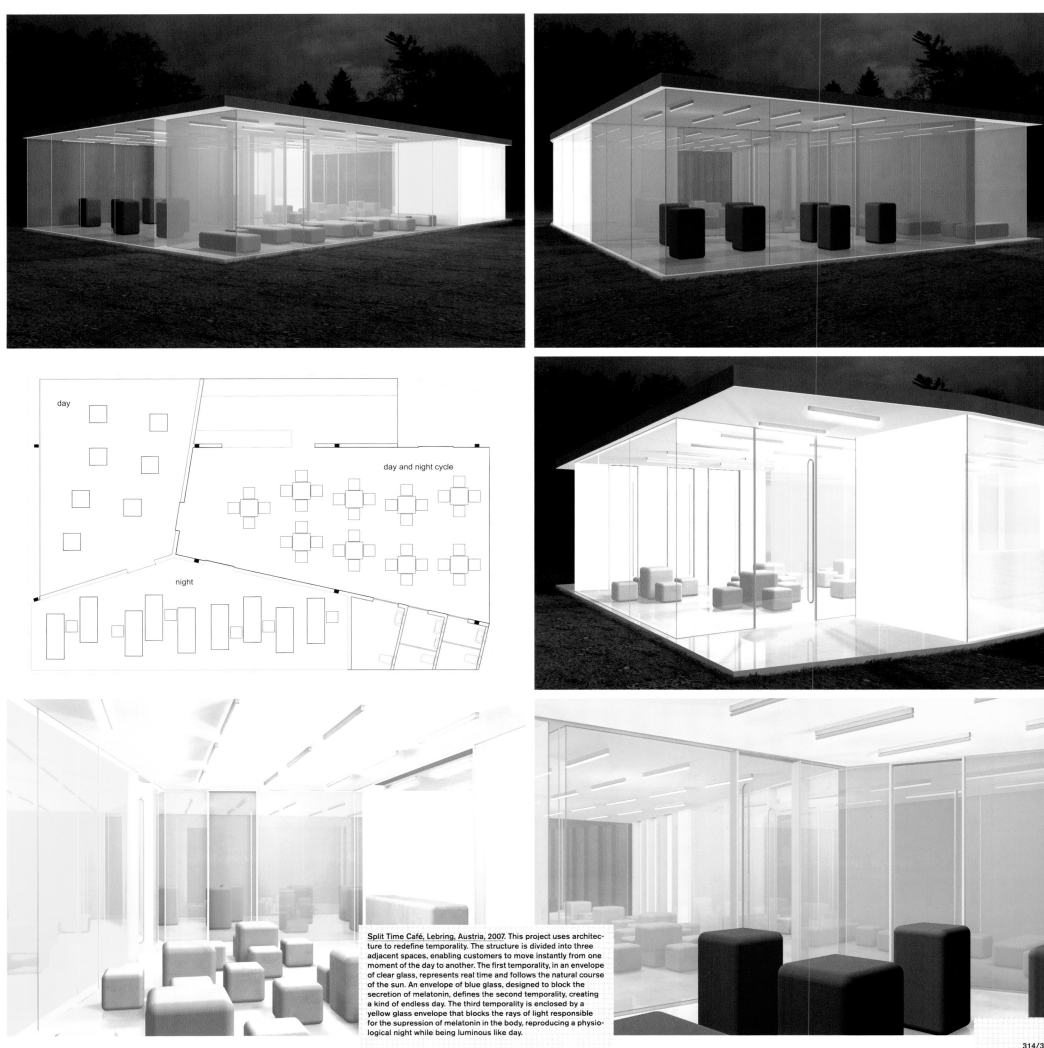

Split Time Café, Lebring, Austria, 2007. This project uses architecture to redefine temporality. The structure is divided into three adjacent spaces, enabling customers to move instantly from one moment of the day to another. The first temporality, in an envelope of clear glass, represents real time and follows the natural course of the sun. An envelope of blue glass, designed to block the secretion of melatonin, defines the second temporality, creating a kind of endless day. The third temporality is enclosed by a yellow glass envelope that blocks the rays of light responsible for the supression of melatonin in the body, reproducing a physiological night while being luminous like day.

kitchen

living room

bathroom

toilet

bedroom

bedroom

19 °C   20 °C   22 °C

16 °C   17 °C   18 °C

19 °C   20 °C   22 °C

16 °C   17 °C   18 °C

Gonzalez-Foerster House, Paris, France, 2008–. Instead of warming all rooms at a uniform temperature, two sources of heat create thermodynamic tension throughout this house. The colder pole, at 59°F (15°C), is situated in the upper levels of the house. The opposite pole, at 72°F (22°C), is situated in the lower levels. Using convection, the poles create a constant thermal flow, like a miniature Gulf Stream.

Philippe Rahm Architectes

Randić-Turato   Rijeka HR

Zagrad Center, Rijeka, Croatia, 2003–7. This mixed-use complex is divided into six separate office buildings, each with a different facade. Overlaying the office buildings is a continuous, unifying structure of apartments designed as individual two-story residences accessed from the terrace with gardens on the roof.

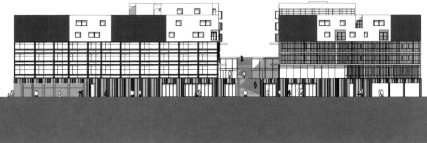

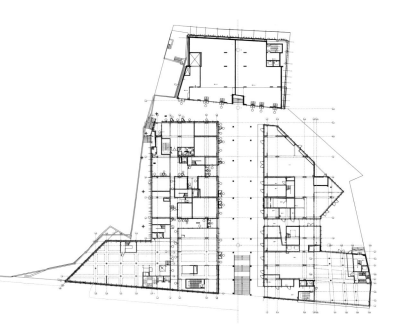

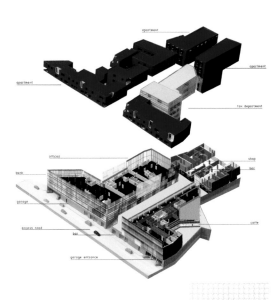

Even by the tumultuous standards of Eastern European territorial politics, Croatia has over the past two decades been the site of an unparalleled series of transformations that will—if current agreements hold—culminate in European Union membership in 2010. For better or worse, architects found themselves on the front line of an ongoing battle for urban regeneration in a context of latent instability.

Croatia's coastal transformations are of particular interest to one of the most dynamic practices to have emerged from the region in recent years, Randić-Turato. Saša Randić and Idis Turato established their partnership in 1993, at a moment when the country began to face up to the challenges posed by crumbling Soviet-era infrastructure and rampant disregard of construction codes. In the years that followed, Randić-Turato spearheaded the emergence of a particularly fertile generation of young designers intent on rebuilding post-socialist Croatia.

Randić-Turato's Fran Krsto Frankopan Elementary School demonstrates their "soft-touch" approach to interventions in historic urban sites. Situated just inside the walls of the medieval city of Krk, the dimensions and proportions of the project are determined by the surrounding buildings and the existing urban axes. The morphology of the building follows the form of the terrain and boundaries of the site, as well as the inclination of the ancient medieval wall that flanks the site.

Pope John Paul II Hall in Rijeka was commissioned to provide space for catechism classes on a site that had been the destination of pilgrimages for many years. A stone wall separates the building from the adjacent road; the main body of the hall straddles the wall and a colonnade reminiscent of a traditional cloister. The slender but deep pillars of the colonnade allow priests to use the narrow spaces between them to hear confessions. The hall itself is a prismatic red brick structure; in the place of windows, bricks have been subtracted from the walls and roof, allowing dappled daylight to penetrate into the interior. At night, the interior glows like a lantern, painting the facade with an illuminated pattern. // Joseph Grima

Fran Krsto Frankopan Elementary School, Krk, Croatia, 2003–5. Conceived as part of the medieval town, this elementary school erases the borders between the public space and school areas by integrating the building with the city. The floor plan is largely defined by the old city wall that borders the school; the main entrance, library, and cafeteria are all visible from the street through continuous ground-floor glazing.

Pastoral Center Pope John Paul II Hall, Rijeka, Croatia, 2003–8.
Built in honor of Pope John Paul II's visit to the Church of Our Lady
of Trsat in 2003, this building consists of two elements: the defining
volume of the hall clad in terra cotta bricks, and a columned portico
that creates a new public court within the church complex.

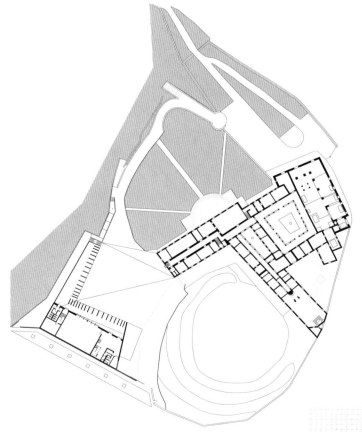

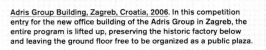
Adris Group Building, Zagreb, Croatia, 2006. In this competition entry for the new office building of the Adris Group in Zagreb, the entire program is lifted up, preserving the historic factory below and leaving the ground floor free to be organized as a public plaza.

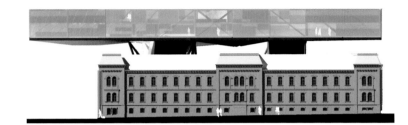

Randić-Turato

raumlaborberlin | Berlin D

The members of raumlaborberlin began working on issues of contemporary architecture and urbanism in 1999, at a moment when their own city, Berlin, was in the grips of a seemingly never-ending post-unification economic hangover. For raumlaborberlin, the German capital, with all of its seemingly unsurmountable challenges, was the perfect testbed for an extensive series of urban experiments, architectural projects that probe the possibilities offered by the contemporary metropolis. It is an almost obsessive interest in architecture as a language through which to create instant communities, reclaim public space, and challenge the preexistent notions of order that makes their work unique today.

One of raumlaborberlin's best-known projects, the Kitchen Monument (or *Küchenmonument*), questions the role and the potential of the monument in contemporary urbanism: How can a monument generate vibrant social space? How can it come to reflect the communities and identities of various neighborhoods? For raumlaborberlin, the answer is a radical departure from the conventional notion of the monument: it should be a generator of temporary communities, a Trojan horse capable of generating urban identity, transporting identity into the public sphere, and recapturing public space. The Kitchen Monument is a mobile structure that consists of two separate elements, a box and an inflatable polyurethane bubble. The box houses the fan that maintains the pressure inside the bubble, but also serves as an entrance and as a mobile container for transporting the Kitchen Monument. Striking as the bubble is, the architecture is only a pretext and starting point for the events that happen inside. An integral part of the project are the dinners that take place in the Kitchen Monument; these are usually hosted—and cooked—by raumlaborberlin themselves, the guests being members of the local community. Other events include children's workshops, dancing sessions with local tango groups, lectures, and screenings.

The Mountain and Hotel Bergkristall (2005), two raumlaborberlin projects situated at Berlin's Palast der Republik building, adopted a similar strategy, albeit less mobile and on a larger scale. Their aim was to highlight the overlooked potential of a public monument slated for demolition, transforming it from a disused relic into a generator of urban collectivity. While The Mountain, a temporary large-scale sculpture inside the Palast's hollowed-out shell, encouraged visitors to explore the monolithic building, Hotel Bergkristall offered the possibility of reappropriating the space by inhabiting it temporarily. // Joseph Grima

Kitchen Monument, various locations, 2005–6. Developed in collaboration with Plastique Fantastique, this mobile sculpture is composed of two elements: a zinc sheet–clad box outfitted with a fan capable of inflating a large polyurethane bubble that transforms into a temporary public space. Its broad spectrum of functions includes banquet hall, conference room, cinema, concert hall, ballroom, dormitory, boxing arena, and steam bath. It first appeared in Germany in Duisburg and has traveled to Berlin, Liverpool, Warsaw, Hamburg, and other locations.

The Orbit, Freiburg, Germany, 2006. The Orbit is a mobile, extendable spatial module that can adapt to its environment. As a satellite of the Freiburg Theater, it drifts around the city, uncovering new urban places and subjects for the theater's work.

Moderato Cantabile, Graz, Austria, 2008. This project was a design for the Steirischer Herbst Festival Center in Graz. The center is located in an empty baroque museum building where the architects designed a café, ticket office, and exhibition space, as well as a pavilion in the form of an "explosion" on the building's exterior. The extrusion is a metal construction built around various trash, including chairs and laundry drying machines.

The Mountain, Berlin, Germany, 2005. Shortly before the controversial demolition of Palast der Republik in Berlin, the architects, in collaboration with Sophiensaele and Club Real, built a huge mountain formation in, on, and in front of the building. Built from fiberglass textile and scaffolding, The Mountain creates a unique public space that raises the question of the role and meaning of a city's historic center.

raumlaborberlin

The work of Joshua Prince-Ramus and his firm, REX, cannot be separated from that of Rem Koolhaas and the Office for Metropolitan Architecture (OMA). Prince-Ramus was a founding partner of OMA's New York office in 2001, and in 2006 he left to establish REX with architect Erez Ella, also formerly of OMA. In contrast to other architects like Winy Maas or Alejandro Zaera who cut their teeth at the Dutch OMA office to later follow independent careers, Prince-Ramus, as a partner in the US office, negotiated an agreement that guaranteed him credit for works completed at OMA like the Guggenheim Las Vegas or the Seattle Central Library, and received some in-house commissions such as the Wyly Theater in Dallas and Museum Plaza in Louisville, Kentucky.

The Pop imagery of the Guggenheim Las Vegas has clear references to Koolhaas's interest in Venturi, and the stealth aesthetic of the Seattle Central Library cannot be understood in isolation from OMA's Casa da Música or House Y2K. But despite the evident references to OMA, the sense of purpose and leadership strength of the office, which believes in collaborative work, contractual accountability, and performance-oriented design processes, signal that REX is distinguishing itself as a significant firm. This is already apparent in its pragmatic handling of its first independent commission, the Vakko Headquarters in Istanbul, where REX manages to extend OMA's hardcore realism in a business-oriented environment. Prince-Ramus is building up his profile, orchestrating the work of REX with his individual (re)presentation. Even though the firm still lacks a group of completed works that establishes an unmistakable identity, the charisma and drive of Prince-Ramus promise a prominent practice in the near future. // Luis Fernández-Galiano

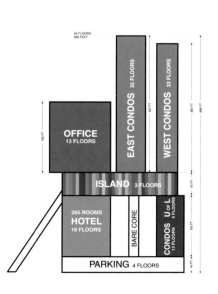

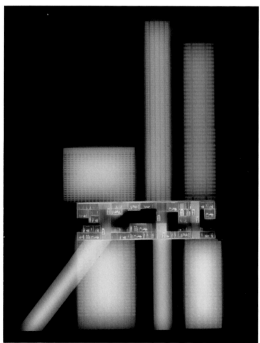

Museum Plaza, Louisville, Kentucky, USA, 2005–11. This 62-story skyscraper on the banks of the Ohio River contains a contemporary art institute, the University of Louisville's Master of Fine Arts program, a 250-room hotel, 98 luxury condominiums, 117 lofts, office space, restaurants, shops, parking for 800 cars, and a sculpture garden. An "island" that bridges the two towers twenty-four stories above ground level contains the public art institute, with the other programs distributed above and below.

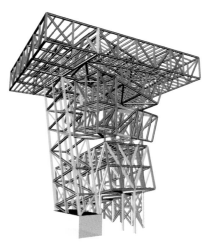

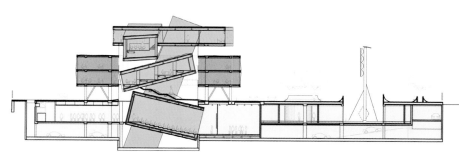

Dee and Charles Wyly Theater, Dallas Center for the Performing Arts, Dallas, Texas, USA, 2004–9. The Wyly Theater repositions traditional front-of-house and back-of-house functions below-house and above-house and, in the process, redefines the traditional theater. Exposed on all sides, the perimeter of the theater's chamber can directly engage the city around it. No longer shielded by transitional and technical zones—lobbies, ticket counters, and backstage facilities—theater and reality can mix when and where desired.

REX

Nestlé Chocolate Museum, Toluca, Mexico, 2007. The concept for this visitor center/museum and observation walkway for a chocolate factory is a playful folding shape, evocative of an origami bird or a spaceship. The foundation and supporting columns are made of concrete, while the structure is corrugated steel that changes direction constantly, reflected in the interior as winding tunnels. The tempered glass facade opens onto the highway.

foundations
reinforced concrete columns

grill
14" I steel beams
peripheral 18" steel beam with epoxic primer

slab
lightened concrete on metal deck
with 6mm epoxic resin finish

main structure
12" I steel frames with epoxic primer

sub-structure
4" HSS steel section with epoxic primer

inner skin
plaster panel with vinyl coating
over WR tcast panel

The work of Michel Rojkind and his practice, Rojkind Arquitectos, is emblematic of a new generation that, over the past decade, has seen México D.F. burst with great vitality onto the international scene. Rojkind Arquitectos is one of at least a half dozen practices in the Mexican capital garnering attention on the international stage for its idiosyncratic and highly energetic production. It operates in a city of contrasts, where exceptional wealth rubs shoulders on a day-to-day basis with extreme poverty, and leafy, well-heeled neighborhoods are intertwined with sprawling slums marked by decaying infrastructure. Sustained economic growth over the past fifteen years has fostered dialogue, research, and experimentation among the post–Enrique Norten generation, a fact that has not gone unnoticed abroad. Both the Vitra Design Museum in Germany and the Art Center College of Design in Pasadena, California, have recently exhibited Rojkind's work, and he and his peers have become a fixture on the short lists of international design competitions and conferences around the world.

Rojkind founded his practice in 2004, and a number of small and medium-size projects completed in swift succession have demonstrated the firm's ability to successfully translate a digitally derived aesthetic into a compelling and vibrant built form. An example of this can be seen in a recently completed commission, a chocolate museum attached to the Nestlé factory in Toluca, near México D.F., where the entire process of design and construction lasted a mere two and a half months. Situated along a main highway, the building has become an instant landmark in the neighborhood because of its angular shape and bright color. Its main purpose is to allow visitors access to the factory and to offer them a first-hand experience of the chocolate production process. The interior of the lightweight faceted structure is composed of a child-friendly lobby, a museum shop, and a theater.

In another, earlier design, a small private house on a thickly settled hillside, Rojkind's sinuous forms were inspired by the occupant's profession as a ballet dancer. The project, called Pr 34 House, is perched on the roof of an existing house, of which it is effectively an extension, making intelligent use of it as a garden terrace. The new house appears as a bright red winding ribbon that wraps around the living spaces and frames a view over the valley below. The exterior shell, made from rolled steel panels, is finished with automotive paint to give the building a smooth, rendering-like sheen. // Joseph Grima

outer skin
hunter douglas colordeck 408 panel red ferrari

window
6" x 3" HSS steel framing with black epoxy small
9mm tempered glass

reception
78 square meters

sanitaries
24 square meters

auditorium
88 square meters

museum shop
81 square meters

Pr 34 House, México D.F., Mexico, 2002–3. Located in the suburban area of Tecamachalco, outside México D.F., the house is a rooftop extension of an existing building, a private apartment for the client's daughter. The looping ribbon of red steel forms a continuous surface, enveloping two volumes at different levels. The higher one contains the kitchen and the living and dining rooms, while the lower volume includes the bedroom and TV room. The glass walls are set at varying distances into the volumes, creating balconies of different depths.

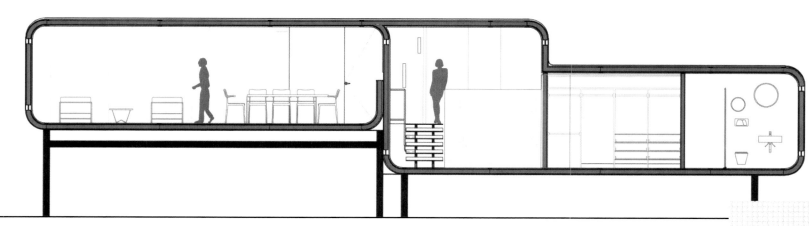

Falcón Headquarters, San Angel, Mexico, 2004. The new head-quarters for Corporativo Falcón was conceived as a crystal box floating in a garden. While the translucent skin serves as filter between the building's interior and exterior, the perforations allow employees to observe the outdoors as if they were looking through the branches of a tree.

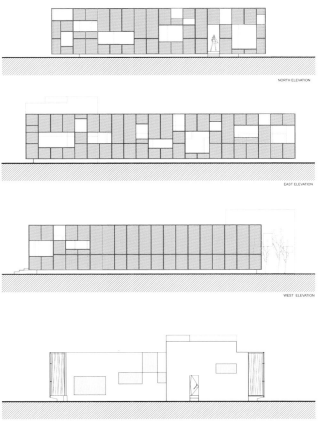

NORTH ELEVATION

EAST ELEVATION

WEST ELEVATION

SOUTH ELEVATION

Rojkind Arquitectos

savioz meyer fabrizzi architectes   Sion CH

Roduit House, Chamoson, Switzerland, 2004–5. The original building, constructed in stages since 1814, is made up of three adjacent volumes on different levels. The old stone construction echoes the rocky mountainside, and the renovation project sought to maintain and reinforce this character, while using concrete for the interior renovation. The exterior volume was not changed; the stone facades were preserved and lined with an insulating layer of concrete based on foamed recycled glass (Misapor).

Hôtel de la Poste renovation, Sierre, Switzerland, 2005–7. This project called for the renovation of an existing hotel from the mid-eighteenth century. The architects created fifteen individualized guest rooms and a new glazed, clover-shaped pavilion to house the restaurant, located in the back garden.

It can be extremely unsettling to look at the Roduit House in Chamoson, Switzerland, by savioz meyer fabrizzi architectes. This is despite the fact that the house is very relaxed, with nothing at all offensive about it. The renovation even appears rather conservative at first glance, and all the details have been carried out perfectly. The unease comes from the fact that the existing house and the new addition are treated with complete parity.

Conventional renovations do not give equal weight to the original structure and the additions. Normally, there are only two ways in which previous structures and new additions can relate: deference or denial. These two positions are polar opposites. One yields the appearance of diametrical opposition, and the other results in close resemblance. For both methods, it is important to show what has been done—that is, to make clear whether deference or denial has prevailed. Accordingly, there is not much concern for the newly completed whole. Such renovation projects are "political" renovations, in the sense that the most important thing for politicians is always to make their stance clear. Is one going along or criticizing? It is crucial that everyone declare a strong opinion right away.

But architects are well aware that, in the final analysis, design is not a question of deference or denial. This is because design is a complex enterprise with aspects of both. Deference and denial are not just part of renovation, they are applicable to all acts of design. Even the construction of a new building involves a pre-existing lot as well as adjacent land and houses. So, all design is renovation.

The more one looks at the house in Chamoson, the harder it is to see whether the stone was already there and the concrete was added, or whether the concrete was there first and the stone was added. It is not a question of deference or denial; this is a world in which we cannot know this with precision. It is a world where everything is already in place. // Kengo Kuma

450 517 574 1611 1942 2009

Rubble Protection for the Archaeological Ruins of Saint-Maurice
Monastery, Saint-Maurice, Switzerland, 2004–9. Created in
collaboration with the engineering firm Alpatec, the covering
protects the remnants of seven abbeys, built successively on
the site since the sixth century, from the impact of weather and
the fall of rubble. The ten tons of stones suspended above the
site are a reference to the historical impact of the rubble, which
has caused tremendous damage over the building's history.

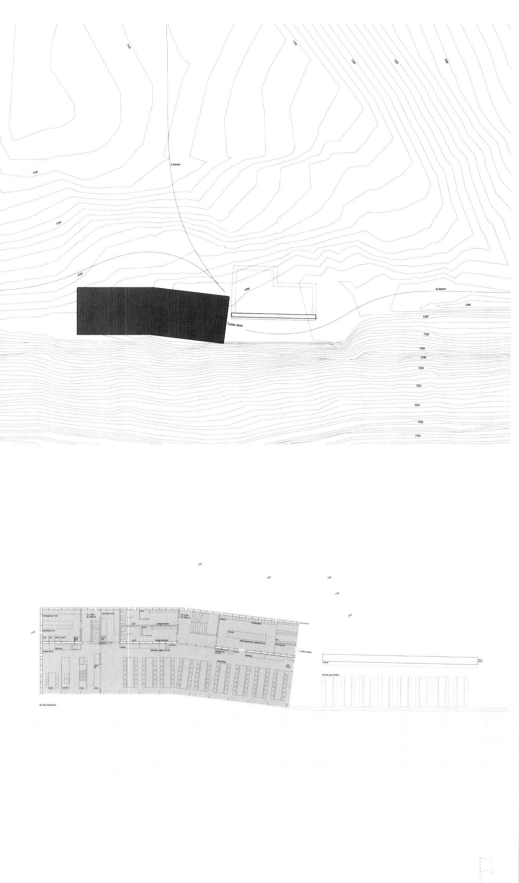

savioz meyer fabrizzi architectes

Tracuit Hut, Zinal, Switzerland, 2008–10. This alpine hut, a way station for skiers and mountain climbers, sits on a ridge at an altitude of 10,500 ft. (3,200 m). The south facade is glazed to benefit from passive solar energy and provides sweeping views of the mountainscape. Prefabricated, lightweight wood panels, a material easily transported by helicopter, is used for the construction; the siding consists of panels of synthetic fibers whose sheen evokes the surrounding snow.

SeARCH   Amsterdam NL

Wolzak House, Zutphen, Netherlands, 2002–4. This farmhouse renovation and extension situates the living accommodations in the existing building; the adjoining part of the extension houses a large open kitchen and the entrance, which connects the old and new spaces; the guest accommodations, workroom, and garden shed are all located in the remainder of the new volume, separated from the living spaces by a large conservatory.

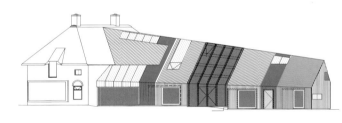

When SeARCH was first established in 2002, the work of its founding partner Bjarne Mastenbroek was quite well-known in the Netherlands because of his collaboration with Dick van Gameren for the Architectengroep. This experience has given SeARCH the virtuosity and maturity one would expect from a much more experienced firm. In fact, due to the favorable architectural climate in the Netherlands, many young architects tend to develop these qualities much earlier than in other countries. In the case of SeARCH, however, this maturity has not led to a loss in the eagerness that is usually associated with younger offices. Each work is innovative, fresh, and unexpected. In each design the office looks for a specific solution evoked by its context in a broad sense—the commission, the client, the location. With this approach the name of the office fits the content of its work very well; it is always searching for new answers.

Still, in its originality, SeARCH does not stray far from traditional architectural means, stressing spatiality and fine detailing. It does not look for confrontation or seek to become radical by being too blunt or rough. Looking at Mastenbroek's own history, this makes sense. During his studies at the Delft University of Technology, he mounted an exhibition on Le Corbusier and Adolf Loos that traveled around the world, and then worked for the firm Mecanoo and Enric Miralles. The result of this training is expressed most overtly in his masterly control of the construction process, where daring concepts are paired with detailing that would seem impossible to achieve in the context of generally limited construction budgets.

SeARCH continually creates stunning buildings, but the firm's work is difficult to categorize. The projects do not fit into a definite style or concept. Perhaps young architecture firms should not continuously search for answers, but rather put one answer forward and stick to it, especially if they want to establish themselves as a viable "brands." The result would certainly be highly marketable, but also highly predictable—inevitably, less tailored to the needs of the task, the site, and the user. // Bart Goldhoorn

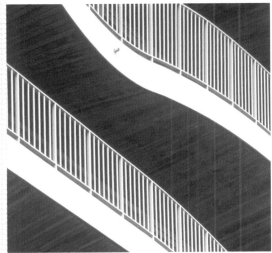

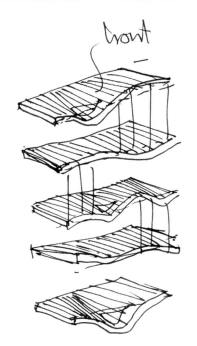

Soft-edge, Lelystad, Netherlands, 2002–7. This office and apartment building, built on the smallest and last remaining parcel of a new development, is owned by the same client as the neighboring parcel, which offered the possibility of combining certain services. By annexing the elevator and stairs of the adjacent building, the architects liberated precious living space. The crimped form of the balconies suggests that the building is being squeezed by its larger neighbors.

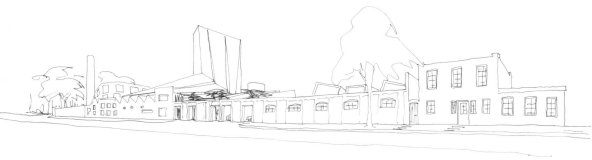

Roombeek Culture Cluster, Enschede, Netherlands, 2003–8. This project involves the restoration, renovation, and extension of a nineteenth-century textile factory and its direct surroundings into a "Culture Cluster" housing a museum of local history and culture, a café, a study center, a center for modern art, and artists' studios. The new tower, housing the museum's nonpublic functions, is connected to the old warehouse via a pedestrian bridge and an underground tunnel.

Junior College, Den Helder, Netherlands, 2004–8. The challenge for this project was to design a highly flexible secondary school building in a neighborhood without a master plan. The architects connected all the classrooms and support spaces along a spiraling hallway that surrounds a covered atrium—filled with bamboo plants—that can be used year-round for multiple purposes. The balloon-like roof, with a span of 46 ft. (14 m), is formed from three inflatable transparent membranes.

SeARCH

Spanish architects José Selgas and Lucía Cano's first significant project arrived in 1999 with their winning submission in the competition for the Conference Center and Auditorium in Badajoz. The project, which adheres to the competition brief for a pentagonal site defined by the city walls, is an innovative structure inscribed within the circular outline of the ancient *plaza de toros*. The area formerly occupied by the spectators in the bullring becomes the circulation corridor running around the structure's perimeter. The arrangement is visible from outside as a central illuminated cylinder encircled by a translucent outer ring. The result is an evanescent structure that renews the site's ties with its urban context.

This considerable achievement led to new developments in the firm's subsequent projects, including the Conference Center and Auditorium in Plasencia. The aim there was to mark the boundary between town and country while respecting the surrounding topography. It is the section of the complex that defines its form, while anthropomorphic analogies determine the choice of the materials used ("skin and bones" signify the contrast between light/elastic and massive/rigid).

selgascano takes building with greenery as their principal challenge. "Artifice with naturalness" was the self-imposed brief for the architects' own home, Silicon House, which they treated as a laboratory for structural experimentation. The interior spaces, excavated below grade and placed under two sinuous platforms, occupy the interstitial spaces between the mature trees on the site. Rich in scientific and ecological ideas, the architects' interest in plants as a compositional resource takes an even more radical form in their most recent residential project, 20 Garden Villas, where a garden grid envelopes the whole neighborhood.

Playful and ironic, selgascano's work reflects at once a disenchanted and poetic outlook. The architects are attracted to paradox and improvisation, and they draw inspiration sensitively from widely different sources, from art to literature and movies, botany and design (with a preference for the organic forms of the 1960s), but also from personal memories, feelings, and sensations. // Mercedes Daguerre

Conference Center and Auditorium, Badajoz, Spain, 1999–2006. This conference center is located inside a pentagonal-shaped fortress that is part of the seventeenth-century city wall. The project uses the excavated footprint of an old bullring as its starting point, with the main hall occupying the former arena space. It is enveloped in a semitransparent skin made from fiberglass rings that re-create the outer volume of the stands. The cylindrical enclosure of the main hall is surrounded by translucent methacrylate pipes, turning it into a luminous volume at night.

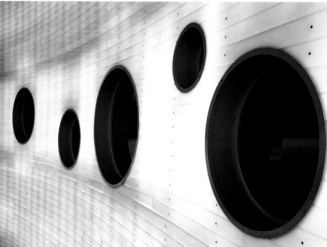

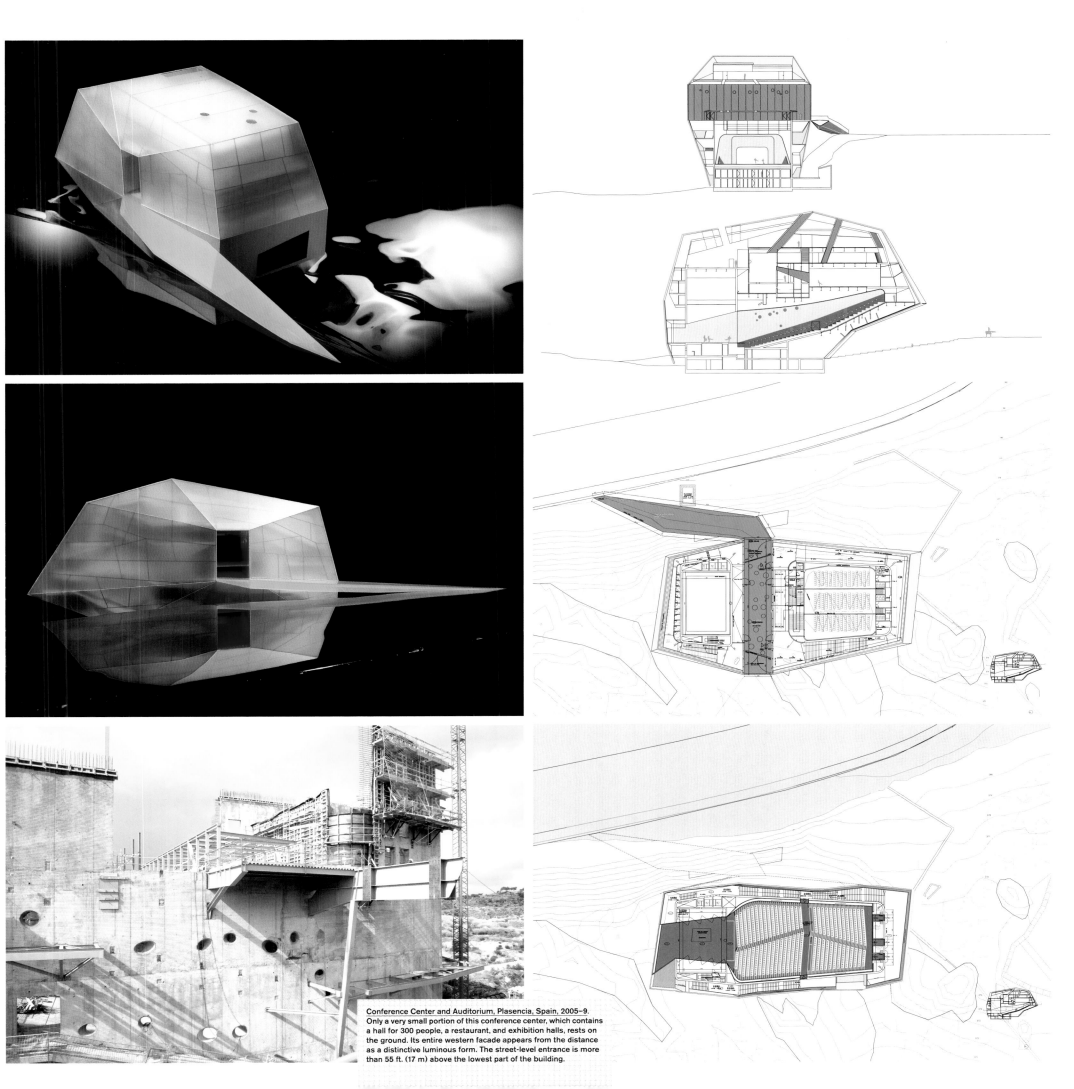

Conference Center and Auditorium, Plasencia, Spain, 2005–9.
Only a very small portion of this conference center, which contains
a hall for 300 people, a restaurant, and exhibition halls, rests on
the ground. Its entire western facade appears from the distance
as a distinctive luminous form. The street-level entrance is more
than 55 ft. (17 m) above the lowest part of the building.

20 Garden Villas, Madrid, 2006–8. Ampelopsis, honeysuckle, jasmine, ivy, Virginia creepers, and passion fruit form the basis for the nonarchitecture of this residential project. Other non-plant materials are kept to a minimum: metal mesh to hold the plants and help them cling and climb, prefabricated concrete panels for the structure and partitions between the dwellings, glass frontage in the dwellings (to maximize natural light and views of the greenery), and continuous rubber flooring.

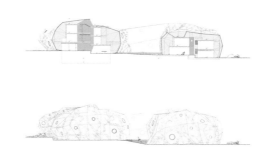

Silicon House, Madrid, Spain, 2002–6. The house, designed for the architects themselves on the outskirts of Madrid, is surrounded by a forest of oak, elm, ash, acacia, prune, and plane trees. It is set beneath two platforms that direct views above the natural setting toward the eastern sky, while views from within the house open out to the site at ground level. The two plane roofs, each a different color and set at a different height, are layered in soft pavement to accommodate outdoor living.

selgascano

Shim+Sutcliffe Architects   Toronto CDN

Brigitte Shim and Howard Sutcliffe, born in Kingston, Jamaica, and Yorkshire, England, respectively, worked for some of Canada's most accomplished architects, such as Arthur Erickson, Ron Thom, and Barton Myers, before officially founding their firm, Shim+Sutcliffe Architects, in 1994. Throughout these formative work experiences, the couple maintained an active collaboration by executing small works of architecture and landscaping, as well as furniture designs. Shim and Sutcliffe see architecture, landscape, and furniture as an integrated enterprise, as well as an opportunity for hands-on fabrication of their designs, and these early interests became the foundation for their practice when they settled in Toronto, Canada's largest city and a culturally vibrant metropolis. The city's rich diversity has proved a fertile setting for the collaborative husband and wife studio, enabling them to find supportive clients and similarly enthusiastic craftsmen.

Since the completion of the Garden Pavilion and Reflecting Pool in Don Mills, Toronto (1992), the architects have remained steadfast in their probing exploration of all of the particulars of site. In this serene but powerful work, landscape and furniture establish an architecture that blends with its site as much as it transcends it with soothing and reflective interludes of water. The architects apply their meticulous and sophisticated sensibility to all of their works regardless of scale, budget, or locality, be it a small house in a dense urban site or a large structure along a remote shoreline.

Two recent projects in particular further reveal the architects' commitment to achieving exquisitely detailed works. The Craven Road Studio, an addition to their previously completed Craven Road House of 1996, is a work of discreet materiality yet executed with the architects' customary intensity and luxury of detail. The result is an uplifting sanctuary for the owner's collection of architectural books and posters. Integral House is Shim+Sutcliffe Architects' largest residential work to date, a work of unfolding complexity and ambition, an "integral" environment for living and working along a Toronto ravine. Built for a mathematician, this layered and sinuous flow of spaces and volumes occupies its compelling site with authority. Working with an ideal client, the architects did not spare any detail in the design. The result is a meaningful work that demonstrates the high potential of inspired patronage. If the Craven Road Studio is a haiku, then Integral House is a novel, an absorbing celebration of architecture. // Carlos Jimenez

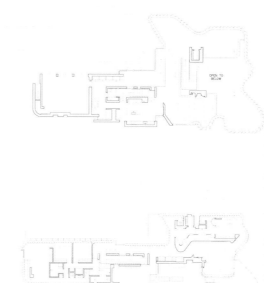

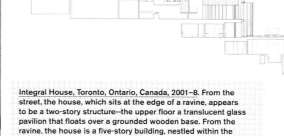

Integral House, Toronto, Ontario, Canada, 2001–8. From the street, the house, which sits at the edge of a ravine, appears to be a two-story structure—the upper floor a translucent glass pavilion that floats over a grounded wooden base. From the ravine, the house is a five-story building, nestled within the surrounding forest. The heart of the home is the living room, a double-height performance space. With its undulating perimeter of wooden fins, the view to the ravine is revealed or concealed depending on one's perspective and movement through the house.

Craven Road Studio, Toronto, Ontario, Canada, 2005–6. This project is part of a series of building and landscape interventions on the site of the Craven Road House completed ten years earlier for the same client. Designed for study, display, and storage, this urban studio receives indirect illumination through a system of narrow light coffers around the building's perimeter.

House on Hurricane Lake, Haliburton, Ontario, Canada, 2001–5.
A 23-ft. (7-m) high covered exterior space—an outdoor living room—
is framed on either side by two volumes and a connecting glazed
bridge. One volume contains the public functions of this private
lake house, while the other contains a master bedroom suite. The
upper portions of the volumes appear to sit atop a steel wall that
extends outward, anchoring the building firmly into the landscape.
On the bottom of each volume, behind the steel wall, are guest
accommodations and service rooms.

Ravine Guesthouse, Toronto, Ontario, Canada, 2001–4. The structure stands amid a lush landscape abutting a Toronto ravine. This small glowing lantern, a quiet retreat and a pool house, blurs the distinction between inside and outside: a large fireplace is central to both interior and exterior living areas, wood flooring continues seamlessly from the inside to the outside terrace, and large glass and wood doors open fully to the outdoors. A steel structure suspends the continuous clerestory that connects the interior and exterior living spaces beneath it.

Shim+Sutcliffe Architects

Srdjan Jovanovic Weiss/NAO

Philadelphia USA

Crematorium, Novi Sad, Republic of Serbia, 2003–6. The objective for this 16,000-sq.-ft. (1,500-sq.-m) structure, designed with the architect's father, Miodrag Jovanovic, was to preserve a generic appearance. Very few details are left visible on the surface other than the brickwork and window pattern. The sequence inside is a simple succession of rooms to be used during ceremonies. One restrained skylight marks the place of gathering and a point of farewell.

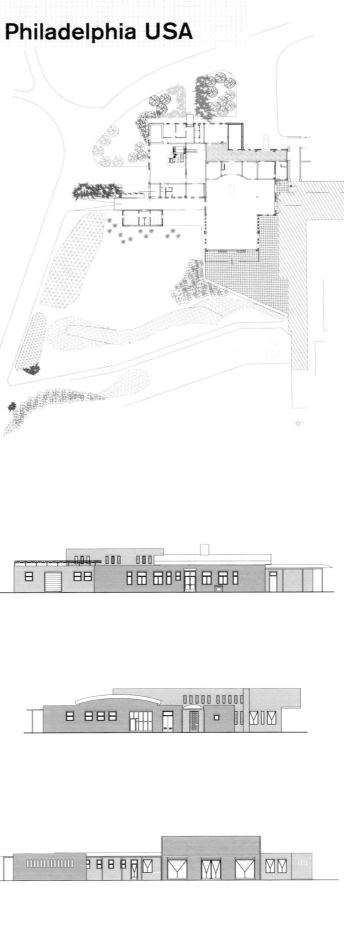

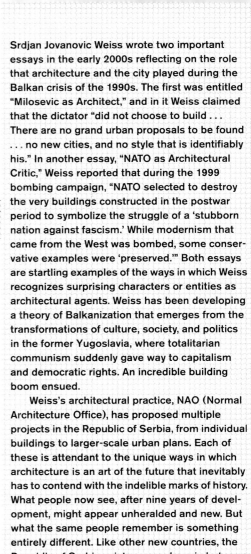

Srdjan Jovanovic Weiss wrote two important essays in the early 2000s reflecting on the role that architecture and the city played during the Balkan crisis of the 1990s. The first was entitled "Milosevic as Architect," and in it Weiss claimed that the dictator "did not choose to build . . . There are no grand urban proposals to be found . . . no new cities, and no style that is identifiably his." In another essay, "NATO as Architectural Critic," Weiss reported that during the 1999 bombing campaign, "NATO selected to destroy the very buildings constructed in the postwar period to symbolize the struggle of a 'stubborn nation against fascism.' While modernism that came from the West was bombed, some conservative examples were 'preserved.'" Both essays are startling examples of the ways in which Weiss recognizes surprising characters or entities as architectural agents. Weiss has been developing a theory of Balkanization that emerges from the transformations of culture, society, and politics in the former Yugoslavia, where totalitarian communism suddenly gave way to capitalism and democratic rights. An incredible building boom ensued.

Weiss's architectural practice, NAO (Normal Architecture Office), has proposed multiple projects in the Republic of Serbia, from individual buildings to larger-scale urban plans. Each of these is attendant to the unique ways in which architecture is an art of the future that inevitably has to contend with the indelible marks of history. What people now see, after nine years of development, might appear unheralded and new. But what the same people remember is something entirely different. Like other new countries, the Republic of Serbia exists somewhere in between these two images.

Having spent time studying with Rem Koolhaas at Harvard University and collaborating with Herzog & de Meuron in Basel, Weiss has established himself professionally in the United States, where he teaches at the University of Pennsylvania in Philadelphia. From this vantage point, NAO represents a contemporary worldview that undermines the conventions of East and West in a manner wholly congruent with the strange condition of twenty-first-century globalization. // Shumon Basar

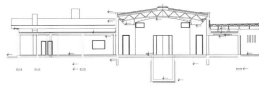

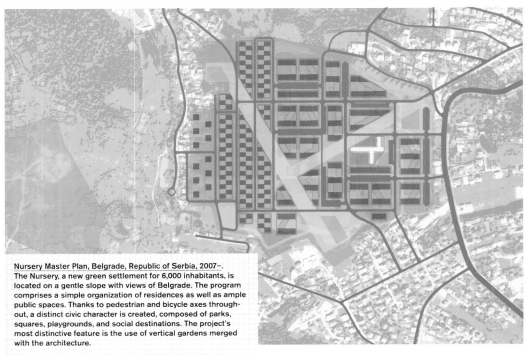

Nursery Master Plan, Belgrade, Republic of Serbia, 2007–.
The Nursery, a new green settlement for 6,000 inhabitants, is located on a gentle slope with views of Belgrade. The program comprises a simple organization of residences as well as ample public spaces. Thanks to pedestrian and bicycle axes throughout, a distinct civic character is created, composed of parks, squares, playgrounds, and social destinations. The project's most distinctive feature is the use of vertical gardens merged with the architecture.

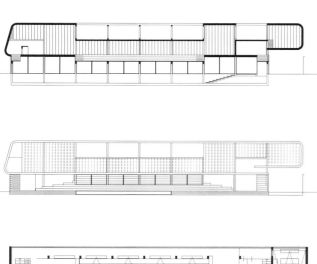

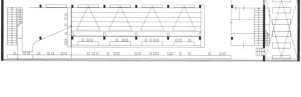

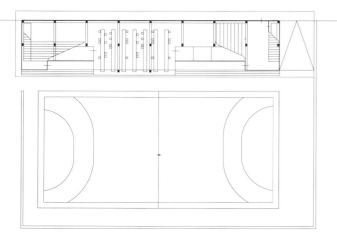

Stadium, Center for Recreation and New Media, Novi Sad, Republic of Serbia, 2005–. The decade of crisis in Serbia during the 1990s resulted in the total neglect of both official and unofficial institutions for youth. Stadium is an ongoing project to preserve an abandoned handball court and renovate and expand it into new youth center.

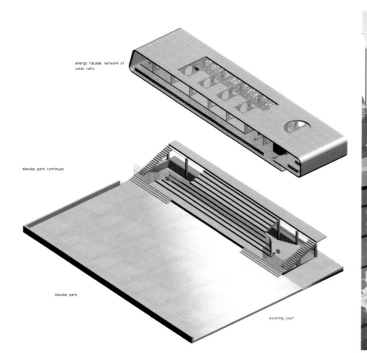

Ordos Villa 62, Ordos, Nei Mongol, China, 2007–. Villa 62, part of the Ordos 100 project, is designed to "collect" the desert. The exterior skin, which can best be described as a continuous shelving system, is designed to retain various weather and plant elements on the facade—snow, sand, rain, moss—changing with the seasons.

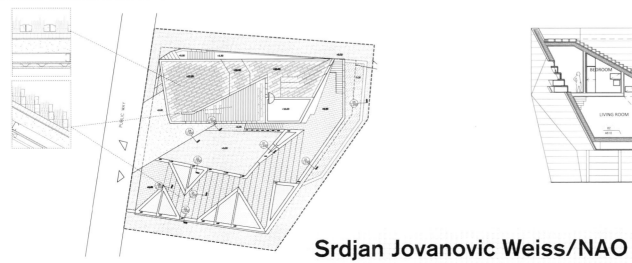

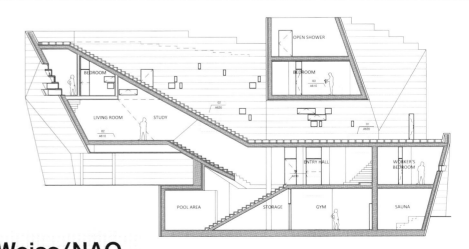

Srdjan Jovanovic Weiss/NAO

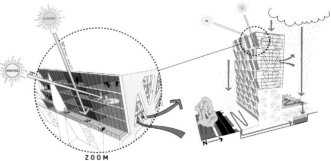

Solstice on the Park, Chicago, Illinois, USA, 2006–10. This 26-story residential tower is literally shaped for optimum solar exposure. The surface is oriented at precisely at 71 degrees, the optimum angle (for Chicago's latitude) to allow sunlight to enter the apartments during winter for passive solar warming, and to keep it out during the summer to reduce the need for air-conditioning.

The commission for the Bengt Sjostrom Starlight Theater, in 1997, proved to be an auspicious work for Studio Gang Architects, established earlier that year. Not only did it launch its founding principal, Jeanne Gang, into the appreciative network of the Chicago architectural community, but the building's intriguing kinetic roof became an instant success on the quiet campus of Rock Valley College. It also introduced Gang's intrepidness and courage as a designer, characteristics that have greatly contributed to the growth of her collegial and research-driven studio. An all-inclusive reach of practice and teaching nurtures this research, as it does Gang's interest in how materials behave and expand potentials for architecture.

The Aqua Tower, presently under construction in Chicago, is one of Gang's most recent and significant works. Situated a few blocks away from Lake Michigan and overlooking Millennium Park, the 82-story hotel and residential high-rise, with retail and commercial space at its base, is an impressive and iconic presence on this prized urban peninsula. The predominantly glass tower is softened as it is shaded by a myriad undulating concrete balconies or terraces, extending out to 12 feet (3.6 meters) in certain areas. The effect gives the building a multitude of available views while adding a svelte and rippling profile to the fabled Chicago skyline.

Solstice on the Park is another residential building near the University of Chicago, overlooking Hyde Park. Its facade is angled precisely to maximize sunlight in the winter and shade in the summer. The result is a 26-story building whose syncopated and cascading elevation enlivens the whole and each individual unit alike.

The Ford Calumet Environmental Center, located on the South Side of Chicago in the vicinity of a Ford automobile plant, is an exemplary environmental work whose core mission is to raise ecological awareness in the Chicago area. The design incorporates salvageable material from the surrounding industrial area. Foremost among these rescued materials is a mesh of recycled steel that encircles and camouflages the building, resulting in the appearance of a nest-like construction—an appropriate counterpoint for this center, which will look out to a beautiful and active wilderness preserve.
// Carlos Jimenez

Aqua Tower, Chicago, Illinois, USA, 2004–9. The mixed-use 82-story tower includes a hotel, apartments, offices, and parking, totaling more than 1.75 million sq. ft. (162,575 sq. m). Aqua Tower is designed to capture otherwise-unattainable views through a series of outdoor terraces that extend away from the facade. Each floor slab is unique, changing slightly over the height of the building. The result is an undulating form when viewed close-up, which transforms into a slim rectangle from farther away.

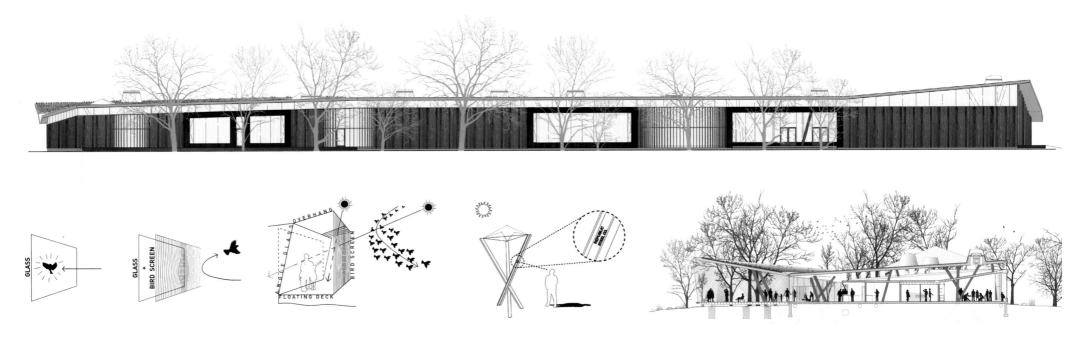

Ford Calumet Environmental Center, Chicago, Illinois, USA, 2004–9.
Like for a nest, materials for the building will be collected from that
which is abundant, nearby, and discarded, such as slag and steel.
The south-facing porch is enclosed with a basketlike mesh of salvaged
steel to protect migrating birds from colliding with the glass.

Bengt Sjostrom Starlight Theater, Rockford, Illinois, USA, 1999–2003. The theater's kinetic roof enables open-air performances without the threat of rain cancellations. The folded origami-like structure and lawn seating create an intimate social setting that is a porous boundary to the landscape. In fair weather, the roof forms an unexpected vertical axis to the sky.

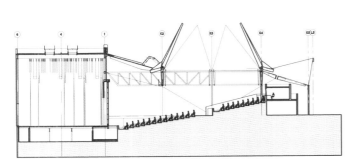

Studio Gang Architects

studio mk27   São Paulo BR

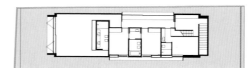
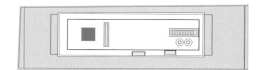

Corten House, São Paulo, Brazil, 2006–8. The front facade is made of Corten weathering steel, creating a dialogue among textures—the rusty steel on the outside and the stone, wood, white mortar, and glass on the inside—that defines the space. On the ground floor, the main living space features a ceiling height of 17 ft. (5.2 m) and four folding doors that open out to the deck and an external fireplace. A freestanding wooden volume within the main living space houses the kitchen and other service areas.

Born in 1952 in São Paulo, Marcio Kogan graduated from the school of architecture at Mackenzie University, one of the city's oldest and most prestigious institutions of higher education. In 1977 the architect's graduation thesis was published in a noted Brazilian cultural journal, the first among a series of distinctions and awards that have earned Kogan a prominent place in Brazil's architectural community. Throughout his career, the architect has concurrently maintained a strong interest in film, completing several short movies and designing sets for film as well as theater productions. Kogan's passionate interest in cinematic devices such as framing and editing have not only influenced but also honed his compositional and spatial skills as an architect. His best works are in fact carefully constructed stages for living, as well as precise settings for either condensing or amplifying the exotic natural beauty for which Brazil is renowned.

In recent years, the output of studio mk27, Kogan's architectural practice, has gathered momentum as well as considerable international attention. Two works of this period, the cosmopolitan Fasano Hotel in São Paulo, completed in 2003, and the exuberant Du Plessis House in Paraty, clearly manifest Kogan's unique and vibrant sensibility as a designer. The Du Plessis House, located in a residential community about 150 miles (240 km) southwest of Rio de Janeiro, is a work that reconciles the polarities of tradition and modernity, a common pursuit that can be found throughout the architect's body of work. At first glance, the Du Plessis House's concise geometry, massing, and detailing suggest the profile of a classically modernist house, albeit one clad in an elegant native stone. Yet, on closer inspection, the house reveals layered spaces, carefully edited views, and a celebration of local materials that are fully immersed in the structure's unique setting of coastal prairies and lush forests, like a mediation between the flowing yet contrasting landscapes. The Panama House, a recently completed residence in Brasília, reinforces not only Kogan's masterful combination of elemental compositions—almost Miesian in their planar economy—but also his instinct for integrating expressive local materials. His works are at once aligned with global sensibilities and intimate with Brazilian culture. // Carlos Jimenez

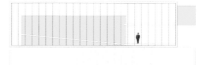

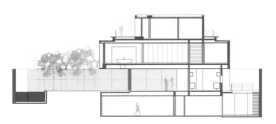

Panama House, São Paulo, Brazil, 2006–8. This house is organized on three floors with a central hall distributing the program: living spaces, library, utility spaces, and vertical circulation. The library overlooks a Maria Martins sculpture reposing over a reflecting pool in front of an exterior stone wall. The vast span of the living room opens entirely to the garden.

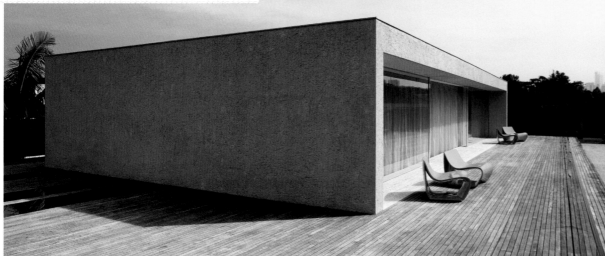

Du Plessis House, Paraty, Brazil, 2001–3. The concept for this house is a "double face," modern on the outside and traditional inside. From the exterior, the house is simply a big box with a facade of stone from the Brazilian state of Minas Gerais. From the central patio where four jabuticaba trees emerge from the swirled pebbled pavement, the house, with its ceramic tiled roof, appears perfectly conventional.

studio mk27

Palmyra House, Nandgaon, Maharashtra, India, 2005–7. Air and light filter through the two louvered boxes set on stone plinths within a coconut plantation. Views of the sea, sky, and landscape are taken in while moving through the spaces of the private home. A network of stone aqueducts, inhabited by moss, lichen, and ferns, irrigates the plantation, drawing water from artesian wells, as has been the practice for generations.

The beauty of the work by Studio Mumbai lies not just in their delicate screens made of wood, stone, and other natural materials. It is possible to convey the screens' beauty through a picture. The essence of their work lies instead in the relationship between land and architecture.

This is a relationship that is impossible to convey with just a picture. Only when one goes to the locations and experiences these spaces in person can this relationship between land and architecture be understood. Because of this, I can speak only from my imagination. By closing my eyes, concentrating, and envisioning the site, I am able to appreciate how much effort they devote to the relationship between the land and their design.

I once surveyed settlements throughout the world and studied the placement of buildings. In desert villages there are distinctive rules for the positioning of structures in dry areas; similarly there are rules for moisture-laden villages in wet areas such as Japan. Indian villages differ from both these scenarios, and to my eyes they looked utterly random and disorderly. The rules were hard to discover, but as my studies continued I became aware that there is an extremely intelligent strategy for handling nature in the layout of Indian villages.

Studio Mumbai's layouts are similar. At first they look jumbled, but if one closes one's eyes and imagines oneself standing in the spaces between structures, one experiences a richness and complexity that does not exist in villages located in the desert or in humid regions. The layout of Palmyra House, for instance, best reflects these characteristics. At first glance, the location of the guest house, situated at a slight angle from the main house and separated from it by a narrow pool, appears to be determined by modernist geometric principles. Upon closer inspection, however, one realizes the location has been determined by the distance of the guest house from the surrounding palm trees, enriching the visitor's spatial experience. This plan should be called the "strategy of space." And not just for buildings in the countryside—Studio Mumbai's plans display the firm's splendid effects in dense cities as well. // Kengo Kuma

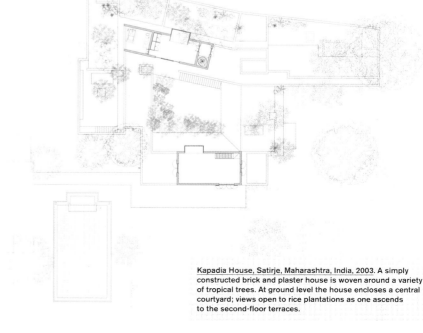

Kapadia House, Satirje, Maharashtra, India, 2003. A simply constructed brick and plaster house is woven around a variety of tropical trees. At ground level the house encloses a central courtyard; views open to rice plantations as one ascends to the second-floor terraces.

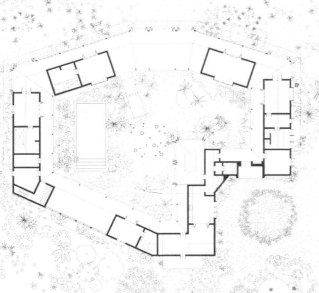

Tara House, Kashid, Maharashtra, India, 2004–6. The house, shared by a multi-generational family, is configured around a garden filled with Plumeria, ferns, grasses, bamboo, and jasmine. Beneath the garden, a room fills with water from a subterranean aquifer, providing water for the house and gardens throughout the year.

Leti 360 Resort, Uttaranchal, India, 2006–7. Leti 360 Resort was built by hand in the winter of 2007 in the Indian Himalayas. The site, a three-acre ridge, is accessible via a narrow footpath 5.5 miles (9 km) from the nearest navigable road. The five small structures are set into natural terraces and surrounded by fields tended and worked throughout the year. The project had to be built in such a way that it could be disassembled and removed from the site easily, returning the land to the farmers from whom it is leased.

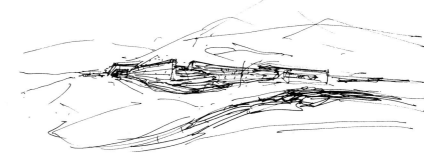

Studio Mumbai

SYSTEMarchitects is determined to rethink its role within the larger picture of how new architecture is created. As the name implies, the firm is interested in broadening the scope of architectural responsibilities and embracing the language of construction efficiencies, packaging and delivery, brand awareness, and scalability. Borrowing from the competencies of manufacturing and product and industrial design, SYSTEMarchitects incorporates a range of skills and concerns that are normally considered outside of, if not anathema to, the proper concerns of the architect.

With BURST*003, principals and co-founders Jeremy Edmiston and Douglas Gauthier (Gauthier left to start his own firm in 2007) wanted to see how far they could go in employing industrial design techniques to respond to the challenges of making architecture. This involved the digital cutting of over 1,100 non-identical timber elements using powerful digital design tools. The structure was designed to employ not only simple materials but also—since in most cases labor outstrips the cost of materials—construction techniques that did not require specialized, expensive installation. (Construction of the house was undertaken largely by a team of Newcastle University architecture students.) It was also a project that employed software developed for the fashion industry to help "nest" the 1,100 unique parts, indicating that this kind of customized prefabrication has definite scalability.

Other projects such as kosovoKIT and wellFLEET similarly attempt to challenge the craft tradition of architecture, without sacrificing the need to innovate in form, space, and process. The kosovoKIT project is a response to the recent war in and around Kosovo. What distinguishes this project from the many other failed attempts at architecture-as-welfare is SYSTEMarchitects's capacity to understand the vital roles of construction and delivery. Looking at recent precedents, efficiencies in construction have proven to be the determining factor in the success of projects, such as Shigeru Ban's refugee shelter. Obviously prefabrication, a subject of perennial fascination, is not new to architecture, but this work by SYSTEMarchitects makes a unique contribution to its development while overcoming the elitism and privilege of much contemporary architecture. // Andrew Mackenzie

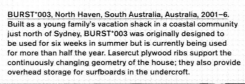

BURST*003, North Haven, South Australia, Australia, 2001–6. Built as a young family's vacation shack in a coastal community just north of Sydney, BURST*003 was originally designed to be used for six weeks in summer but is currently being used for more than half the year. Lasercut plywood ribs support the continuously changing geometry of the house; they also provide overhead storage for surfboards in the undercroft.

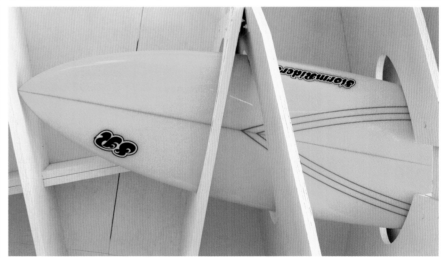

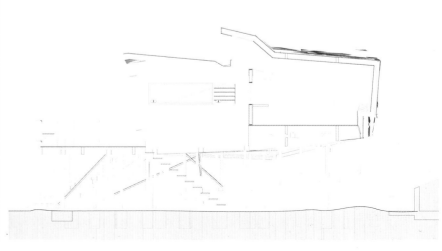

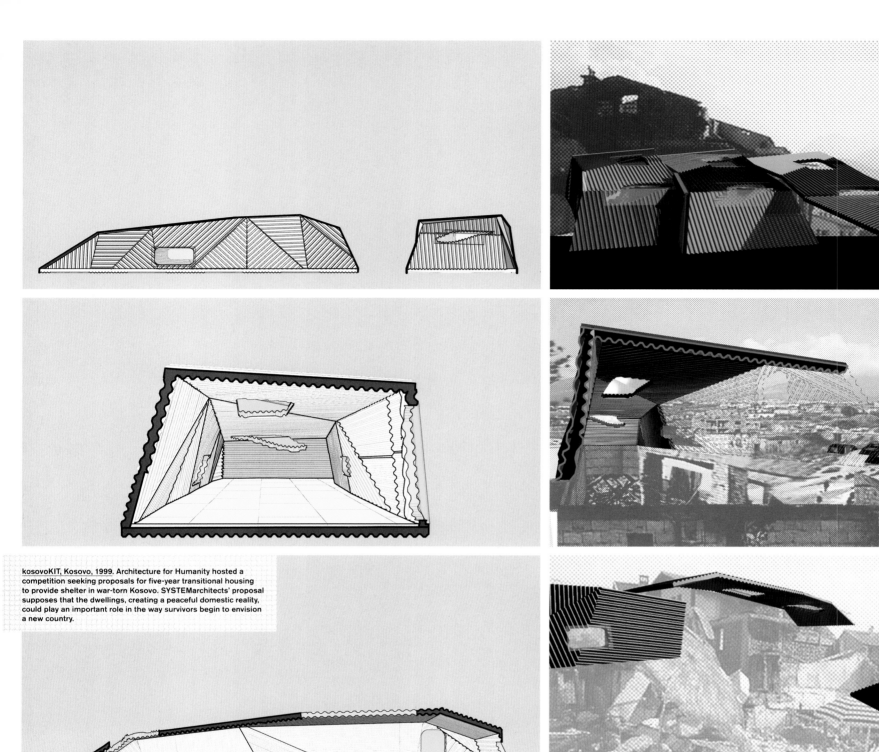

kosovoKIT, Kosovo, 1999. Architecture for Humanity hosted a competition seeking proposals for five-year transitional housing to provide shelter in war-torn Kosovo. SYSTEMarchitects' proposal supposes that the dwellings, creating a peaceful domestic reality, could play an important role in the way survivors begin to envision a new country.

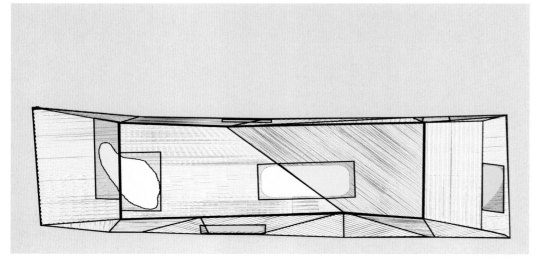

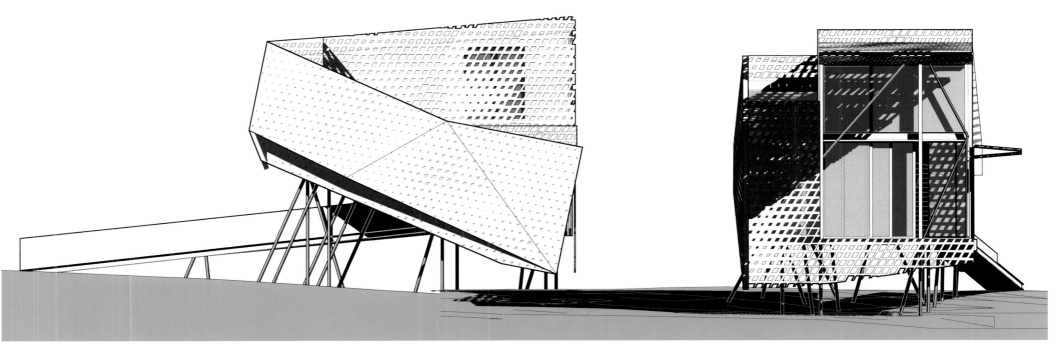

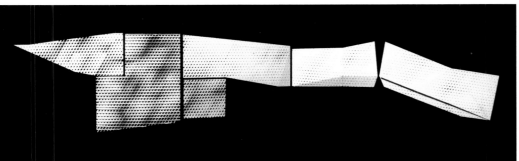

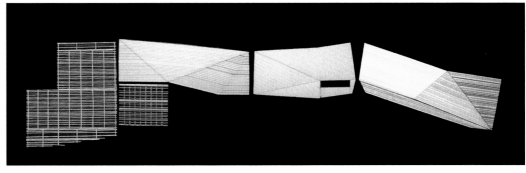

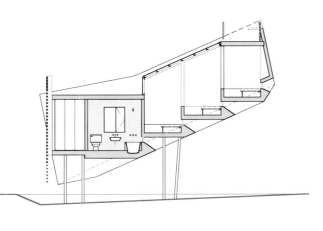

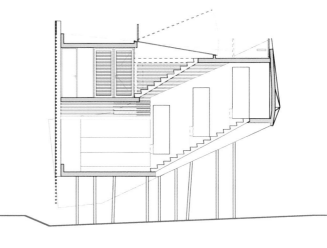

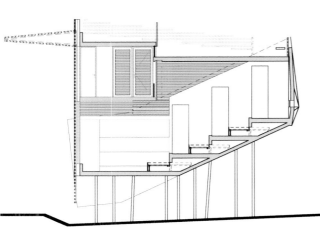

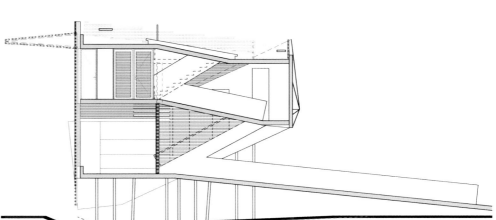

wellFLEET, Wellfleet, Massachusetts, USA, 2002–5. The wellFLEET project is a guest house on Cape Cod, Massachusetts. Nestled in a national forest, the house was limited to a 600-sq.-ft. (56-sq.-m) plan with a height limit at the tree line. Raised off the ground to minimize the impact on the forest, it uses a series of ramps and stairs to access a cocktail terrace on the roof with views of the Atlantic Ocean. In winter, movable exterior screens protect the glazing.

SYSTEMarchitects

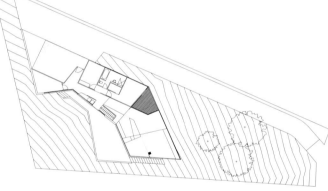

Tolmans Hills House, Hobart, Tasmania, Australia, 2002–4. The visual noise of the adjacent suburban houses prompted this "house as shadow": the simplest formal response and color palette possible. The house moves along the contours of the site, offering little resistance to the natural landform, and at the rear cradles a group of mature eucalyptus trees that anchor the building. The front is clad in slate gray metal "sticks" that recall the thin trunks of adjacent trees.

Terroir was established a decade ago by three Tasmanian architects commuting between offices in Tasmania and Sydney and, in the space of ten years, has produced a wide portfolio of projects across varying scales and building types. The architects' work moves fluidly between research and education, publishing and criticism, and encompasses collaboration between architecture, design, art, and philosophy.

As one might expect from the name of the practice, taken from the notoriously complex French viticultural term, Terroir's work demonstrates a charged engagement with site and context, defined as including—but not limited to—the immediate landscape, orientation, and topography of a given project. Peppermint Bay, a restaurant, tourist destination, and observation point located in rural Tasmania, represents a key expression of Terroir's architectural ambition to negotiate the dichotomies of native and imported, natural and man-made, monumental and intimate, journey and destination. A long, low undulating roof plane galvanizes the building's many elements, creating one flowing contiguous form. In counterpoint, in plan, a line unfurls, delineating a journey born of the existing contours of the land and suggesting a labyrinth or ceremonial progression. Combined, these elements create a range of interactions between enclosure and the surrounding expansive landscape—a constructed wilderness.

Commonwealth Place Kiosks is a modest, recent project in Canberra, set within the giant empty spaces of mandated civic pride, surrounded by processional axes and bunkered monumental institutions. Amid the fabricated pastoral order of sloping grassy banks, placid lakes, and avenues of trees, two awkward, unnatural forms stand out, unwilling to accept or engage the invented landscape that surrounds them. The kiosks, by not blending in, insist on their own artificiality, thereby exposing the artificiality of the parklands, and indeed, of pastoral Australia.

Terroir's work makes a case, project by project, for a complex and challenging reading of place; one that is open to the contemporary discourses of a global future, yet mindful of the colonial imprint of northern Europe on Australia's cities, architecture, and landscape. By refusing to "belong," the architecture echoes the historic exclusions that underpin Australia's colonial legacy. // Andrew Mackenzie

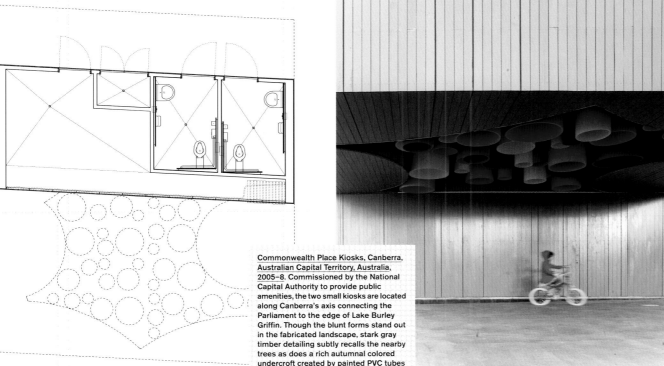

Commonwealth Place Kiosks, Canberra, Australian Capital Territory, Australia, 2005–8. Commissioned by the National Capital Authority to provide public amenities, the two small kiosks are located along Canberra's axis connecting the Parliament to the edge of Lake Burley Griffin. Though the blunt forms stand out in the fabricated landscape, stark gray timber detailing subtly recalls the nearby trees as does a rich autumnal colored undercroft created by painted PVC tubes that filter and disperse light.

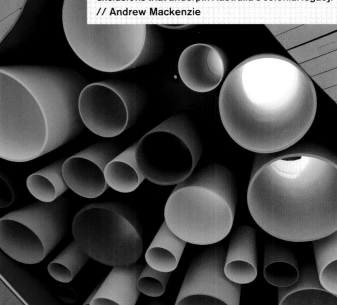

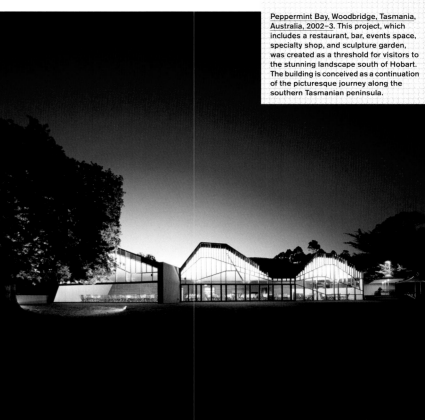

Liverpool Crescent House, Hobart, Tasmania, Australia, 2004–5. The house is a blunt cube on the exterior, with a contrastingly intimate interior. This play on contradiction is repeated in the spatial concept. Interiors are given the qualities of an exterior, for example by using zinc-coated sheet steel as ceiling linings and applying exterior render finish to interior walls. Floor-to-ceiling glazing also creates a vertiginous relation to the exterior.

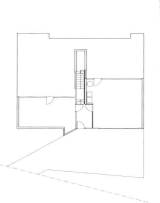

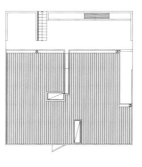

Terroir

Thomas Heatherwick/Heatherwick Studio   London GB

It is commonly thought that Thomas Heatherwick's work is closer to art than to architecture. To some it seems as if he is cut off from ordinary reality and wants to create a dream world of his own. Upon close observation, however, Heatherwick emerges as an extremely realistic architect who thoroughly studies the world around him. He arrives at such unique solutions to clients' programs precisely because of his accurate observations and his understanding of reality, avoiding rigid classifications and preconceived solutions.

His reality is by no means boring or predictable. For example, Heatherwick's proposed British Pavilion for the 2010 Shanghai World Expo (2007) reveals the distinctive opportunities provided by expositions and their unique sites, and in so doing, exposes the collective ignorance of previous pavilion design. Heatherwick's Rolling Bridge inspires a similar awareness that many structures are built without rigorously identifying the demands or particularities of the location. This sort of negligence and lack of study are all too common; architects who disregard the present reality—of a site, a program—in favor of past conditions produce dull results and miss opportunities for the kind of innovation that creates compelling architecture.

Heatherwick charges his fellow architects with each and every one of these acts of negligence, without being a scold. Instead, with a magician's flourish, he unexpectedly scatters a set of unique truths throughout the world in forms so fresh and vivid that no one has ever seen anything like them. To do this, he surely must have the openness and wonder of a child, the concentration and stamina of youth, and the experience and knowledge of age. // Kengo Kuma

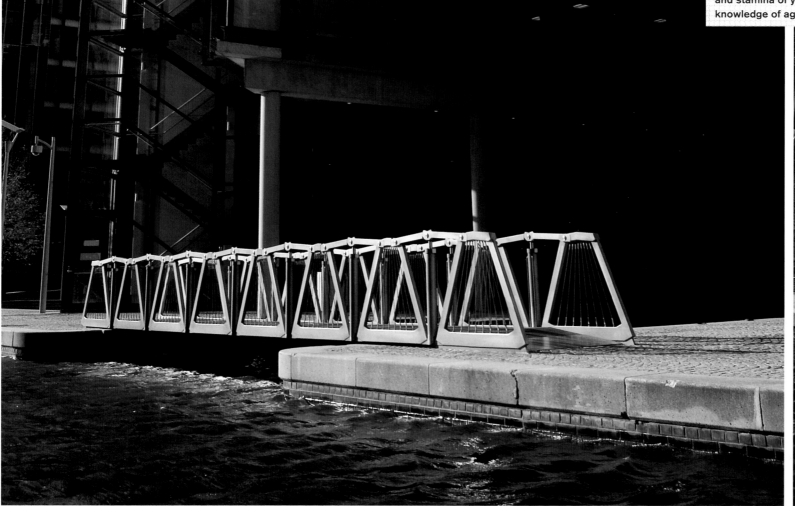

Rolling Bridge, London, England, UK, 2004. Rather than being composed of a single rigid element that lifts to allow the passage of river traffic, the Rolling Bridge opens by curling smoothly until it transforms from a conventional pedestrian platform into a circular sculpture. The bridge—40-ft. (12-m) long in its horizontal position—is made of eight steel and timber sections; hydraulic rams set into the handrail between each section are used to curl the bridge up.

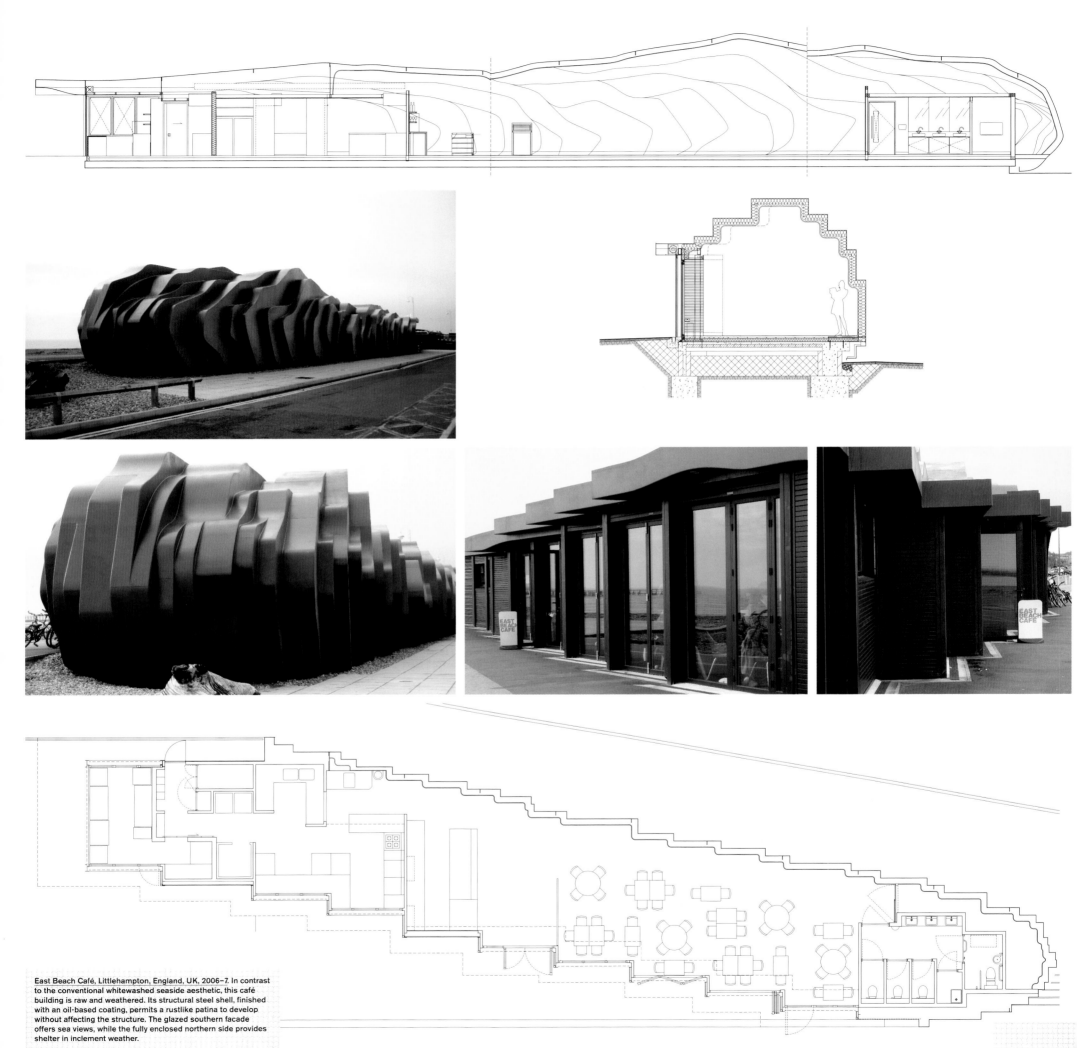

East Beach Café, Littlehampton, England, UK, 2006–7. In contrast to the conventional whitewashed seaside aesthetic, this café building is raw and weathered. Its structural steel shell, finished with an oil-based coating, permits a rustlike patina to develop without affecting the structure. The glazed southern facade offers sea views, while the fully enclosed northern side provides shelter in inclement weather.

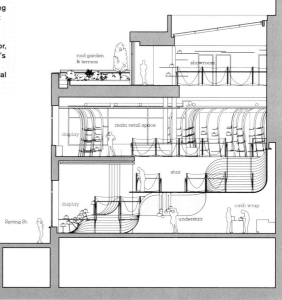

La Maison Unique (Longchamp Store), New York, New York, USA, 2006. The Longchamp store in New York's SoHo neighborhood is composed of cascading ribbonlike forms of hot-rolled steel that create a topography of walkways and landings. Weighing 60 tons, the stair landscape connects the store's first floor, situated above street level, to the store's main, second floor. A large glazed core cuts through the building, allowing natural light to draw people up the landscape.

Thomas Heatherwick/Heatherwick Studio

Thomas Phifer and Partners   New York USA

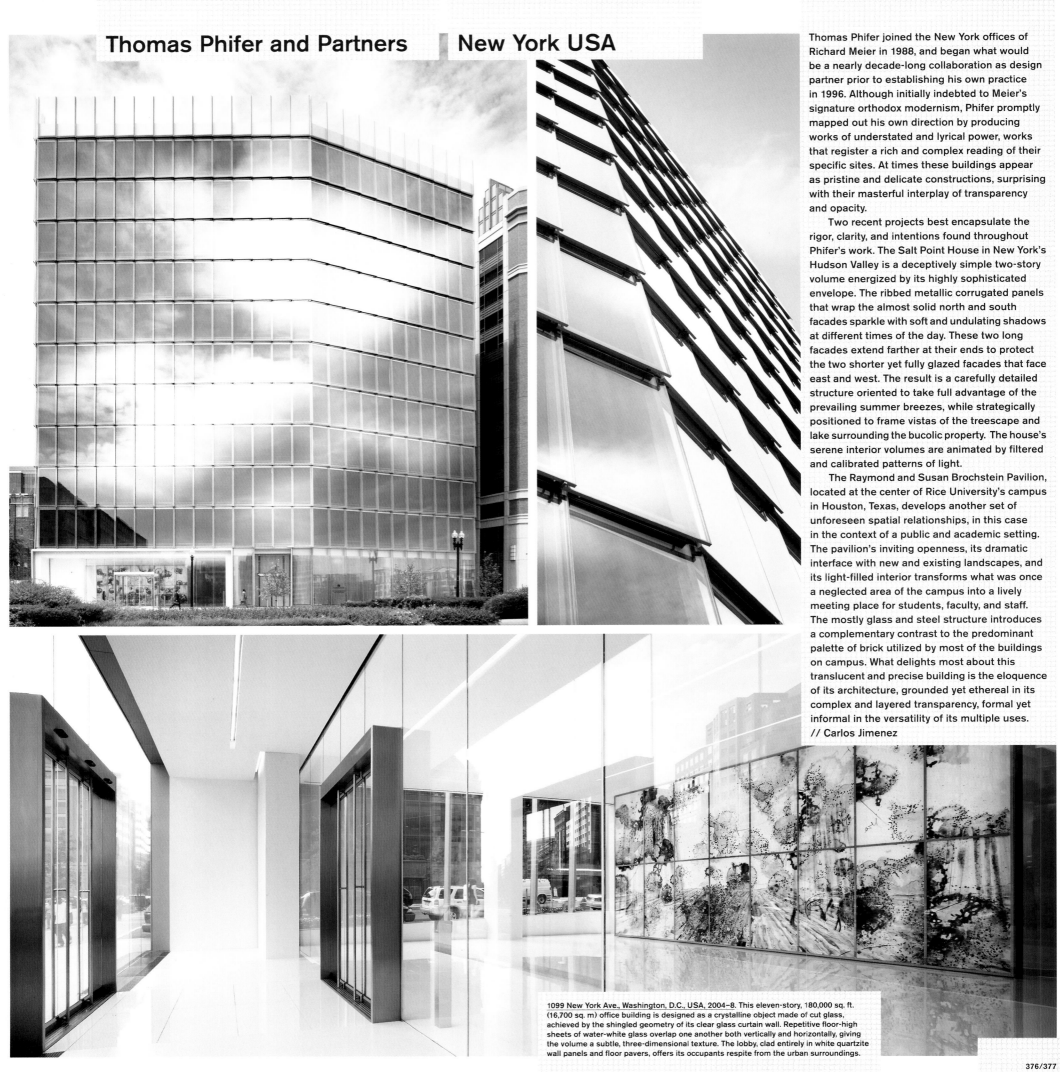

Thomas Phifer joined the New York offices of Richard Meier in 1988, and began what would be a nearly decade-long collaboration as design partner prior to establishing his own practice in 1996. Although initially indebted to Meier's signature orthodox modernism, Phifer promptly mapped out his own direction by producing works of understated and lyrical power, works that register a rich and complex reading of their specific sites. At times these buildings appear as pristine and delicate constructions, surprising with their masterful interplay of transparency and opacity.

Two recent projects best encapsulate the rigor, clarity, and intentions found throughout Phifer's work. The Salt Point House in New York's Hudson Valley is a deceptively simple two-story volume energized by its highly sophisticated envelope. The ribbed metallic corrugated panels that wrap the almost solid north and south facades sparkle with soft and undulating shadows at different times of the day. These two long facades extend farther at their ends to protect the two shorter yet fully glazed facades that face east and west. The result is a carefully detailed structure oriented to take full advantage of the prevailing summer breezes, while strategically positioned to frame vistas of the treescape and lake surrounding the bucolic property. The house's serene interior volumes are animated by filtered and calibrated patterns of light.

The Raymond and Susan Brochstein Pavilion, located at the center of Rice University's campus in Houston, Texas, develops another set of unforeseen spatial relationships, in this case in the context of a public and academic setting. The pavilion's inviting openness, its dramatic interface with new and existing landscapes, and its light-filled interior transforms what was once a neglected area of the campus into a lively meeting place for students, faculty, and staff. The mostly glass and steel structure introduces a complementary contrast to the predominant palette of brick utilized by most of the buildings on campus. What delights most about this translucent and precise building is the eloquence of its architecture, grounded yet ethereal in its complex and layered transparency, formal yet informal in the versatility of its multiple uses. // Carlos Jimenez

1099 New York Ave., Washington, D.C., USA, 2004–8. This eleven-story, 180,000 sq. ft. (16,700 sq. m) office building is designed as a crystalline object made of cut glass, achieved by the shingled geometry of its clear glass curtain wall. Repetitive floor-high sheets of water-white glass overlap one another both vertically and horizontally, giving the volume a subtle, three-dimensional texture. The lobby, clad entirely in white quartzite wall panels and floor pavers, offers its occupants respite from the urban surroundings.

Raymond and Susan Brochstein Pavilion and Central Quadrangle, Rice University, Houston, Texas, USA, 2006–8. The pavilion was conceived as a destination for Rice University students and faculty to interact in a relaxed environment. The project includes a 6,000-sq.-ft. (557 sq.-m) coffeehouse, a large shaded terrace with seating, and the landscape design for the Central Quadrangle in which the pavilion is located. The building is capped by a steel and aluminum trellis structure, which extends in all directions and protects the building and terrace from the harsh Texas sun.

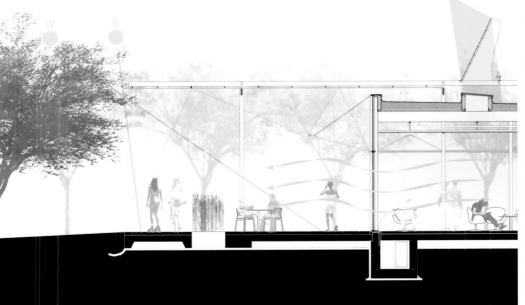

Spencertown House, Spencertown, New York, USA, 1998–2001.
This private house is situated on a rolling meadow, commanding
dramatic views of an agricultural valley and the distant Catskill
Mountains. The primary organizational element is a 6-ft. (1.8-m)
high concrete wall, which retains the earth on the uphill side
and defines a large entry court in the middle. All of the entry and
living spaces are arranged linearly along the downhill side of the
wall under a gently vaulted, wing-like roof, and open directly to
the meadow below and valley views beyond.

Salt Point House, Salt Point, New York, USA, 2004–6. Constructed of elegantly efficient and economical materials, this private house is situated on a meadow with views to a small lake. Strategically placed operable windows and ventilating skylights allow air to flow through the building. The natural ventilation in the interior, in combination with the shading effect of the exterior sunscreens, work together to keep the house comfortable, without air-conditioning, throughout the warm summer months.

Thomas Phifer and Partners

TNA Takei Nabeshima Architects | Tokyo J

A photograph of the Ring House, a weekend house in the hills around the popular resort town Karuizawa, shows a small tower in a misty wood on a slope, taken against the light. It is a very atmospheric, even mysterious photograph, taken by Daici Ano. It is hard to gauge the size of the Ring House. It is minimalist, the stairs are thin, with hardly any railing—clearly Japanese. The slender vertical supports might form the load-bearing structure; the horizontal glass panels might brace the house. It is hard to tell from the photograph. For such a modestly scaled structure—four stories totaling 1,076 square feet (100 square meters)—the house has attracted a great deal of attention for TNA Takei Nabeshima Architects. Founded in 2005 by Makoto Takei and Chie Nabeshima, who met while working in the studio of Takaharu and Yui Tezuka, the masters of the small refined house, the young firm has already realized more than ten unique private residences.

While the view into and through the Ring House is perfect and undisturbed, the slightly angled, sculptural Mosaic House has almost no openings in its white concrete facades, but it is filled with natural illumination from a generous skylight. By contrast, the nocturnal photos of the Plaster House, another weekend home, are highly reminiscent of Julius Shulman's famous photograph of Pierre Koenig's Case Study House above the lights of Los Angeles, only here Mount Fuji is in the background. One of their latest buildings, the Passage House, looks like a dark, ring-shaped UFO that has been rammed into a very steep slope. The concrete ring, painted black, with horizontal end-to-end glazing, is home to the usual array rooms—but here they are placed one behind the other and divided by transparent glass walls. The color scheme is, as with many buildings by TNA Takei Nabeshima Architects, dark on the outside, pale wood on the inside; the ceiling is painted white, and all the furniture, including the stove, are TNA designs. Only the entrance is not readily apparent: a kind of trapdoor in the ground, it is accessed from below by a slender staircase. It is a characteristically delightful detail. // Peter Cachola Schmal

Mosaic House, Tokyo, Japan, 2006–7. The small house sits on a narrow, trapezoid-shaped plot with a taller, four-story building to the south and the threat of high-rise developments to the east. In an effort to open the house to sunlight, the entire roof is a sky-light. The house bends to one side, leaving a sliver of space for parking underneath the curvature of the structure.

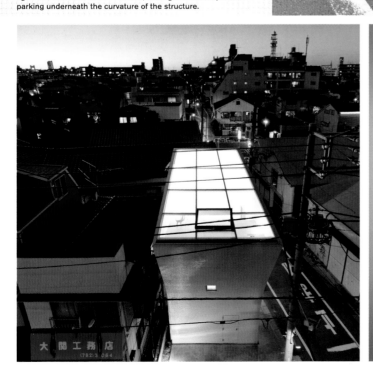

Passage House, Miyota, Nagano Prefecture, Japan, 2006–7. The house juts out from its site high on the ridgeline of a mountain; the point at which the building and slope touch was made as small as possible, maximizing the dramatic effect of the cantilever. The architects used curved glass to create panoramic views from the dramatic mountainside site.

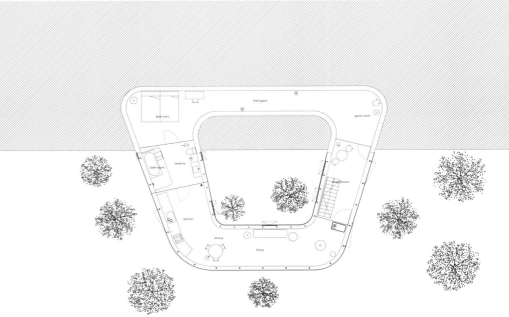

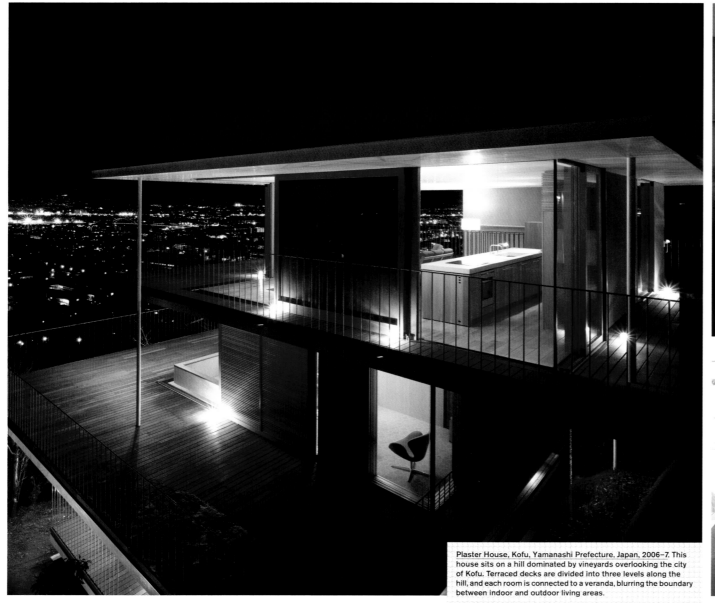

Plaster House, Kofu, Yamanashi Prefecture, Japan, 2006–7. This house sits on a hill dominated by vineyards overlooking the city of Kofu. Terraced decks are divided into three levels along the hill, and each room is connected to a veranda, blurring the boundary between indoor and outdoor living areas.

Ring House, Karuizawa, Nagano Prefecture, Japan, 2005–6. This weekend cottage is situated in the woods of Karuizawa. Continuous bands of glass and wood form the exterior walls, allowing for 360-degree views of the surrounding forest from multiple heights. Nothing obstructs views into or out of the house because all horizontal surfaces—floor slabs, landings, kitchen counters, etc.—are in line with one of the solid bands.

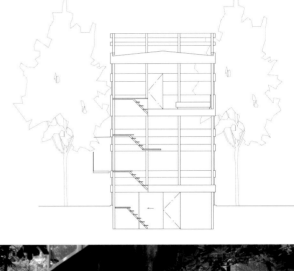

TNA Takei Nabeshima Architects

Werner Tscholl | Morter I

Since opening his office in Morter, Italy, in 1983, Werner Tscholl has worked mainly in the mountainous northern Italian region of Alto Adige. It is in this setting that he has gradually defined the distinctive features of his work. Tscholl seeks to achieve a clear contrast between ancient and modern, rejecting any mimetic interpretation of the local building tradition. This is combined with precise geometries, permeable volumes, and a restrained use of materials (glass, steel, wood), together with a concern to identify sustainable building techniques.

The distinctive stamp of Tscholl's architecture emerges above all when viewed against the medieval ruins studding the mountainous landscape of the region, as in the architect's restoration of Castel Firmiano. In addition to strengthening the city wall and the existing buildings, his project introduced new spaces to house the Messner Mountain Museum. Tscholl inserted the new structures into the cylindrical cavities of the towers (carefully detached from the walls so that the work can be reversed if required). The respect shown for the existing structures—with a sensitive interpretation of the morphology, materials, and textures of the ancient fragments—does not prevent the project from asserting itself through contrasting elements that clearly distinguish its parts.

The recent Mondadori Office Complex in Milan was a singular challenge for Tscholl, and not just because he had to work outside his usual regional context. The project involved reorganizing and extending an old farmhouse, with the constraint of a rigidly predefined plan. He designed two glass buildings covered by a continuous metal strip that marks the perimeter of the original courtyard and forms a sunshade that defines the entrance portico. It carefully focuses the views, while a deck made of sheets of perforated galvanized steel supports the volumes, which seem to float above the ground. This artifice, like the footbridge that provides access, is not alien to the architect's traditional vocabulary, though here it presents itself in a new form. These features also allude to the building's illustrious neighbor: the 1968 Mondadori Headquarters by Oscar Niemeyer, an icon of twentieth-century architecture. While cherishing the lesson of the Brazilian master and tactfully presenting his own project, Tscholl emerges strengthened from the inevitable comparison. His solutions are never based on predetermined formal choices, but take the form of effective and concrete responses to complex situations. // Mercedes Daguerre

Castel Firmiano Renovation, Bolzano, Italy, 2002–6. This project involved the restoration of the historic tenth-century castle and city wall, and the creation of the fourth location of the Messner Mountain Museum, within the castle. On the interior, the inserted black steel structures absorb the light to the point where they seem to vanish, emphasizing the irregular pattern of the existing walls and museum exhibitions. On the exterior, the newly constructed volumes and walkways were allowed to rust naturally to harmonize with the color of the stone.

Tramin Winery, Tramin, Italy, 2008–9. The design for the renovation and extension of the winery, a new symbol for the village of Tramin, is based on the concept of a vine growing out of the courtyard, wrapping around and shaping the new building. The old winery, built in the 1970s, becomes the heart of the new complex; the two new wings extend from it to welcome visitors with "open arms."

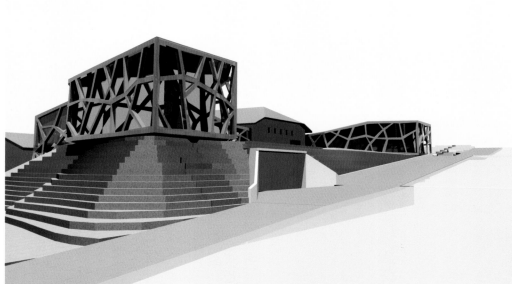

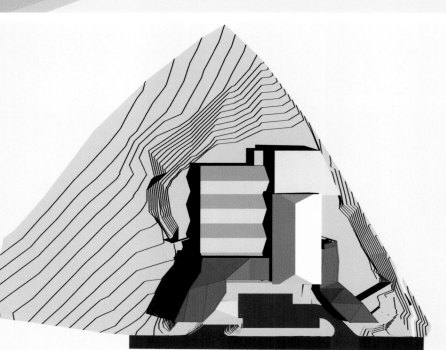

Mondadori Office Complex, Tregarezzo, Italy, 2004–7. A seemingly endless steel deck is conceived so that the building—containing two new wings added to an existing building, an old farmhouse—appears to hover above the ground. A metal overhang, which forms the focal point and entrance to the complex, is conceived as a protective mantle for the two glass blocks containing the new offices.

Werner Tscholl

UnSangDong Architects Cooperation | Seoul ROK

UnSangDong Architects Cooperation was founded in 2001 by Yoon Gyoo Jang and the somewhat younger Chang Hoon Shin. Their work is deeply influenced by Conceptual art (in fact, Jang runs an art gallery in Seoul that exhibits conceptual work), but at the same time is solidly grounded in their professional architectural experience at various South Korean firms. With a group of projects and completed buildings characterized by their experimental nature, sculptural boldness, and sophistication, UnSangDong has established itself at the forefront of the country's architecture, which has received heightened attention since the 1988 Olympic Games in Seoul.

Completed in 2006, the eight-story building for the private Gallery Yeh is a good example of UnSangDong's work, and indeed of the vitality of Korean architecture. It sits as a freestanding sculpture in the urban landscape of Seoul, with folded concrete vertical slabs that illuminate, through slits and cracks, the rooms of the sculpture collection. A similar sculptural use of folded slabs is evident in the KTNG Culture Complex, while a more topographical approach—tiered slabs, ramps, and staircases shaping floors into artificial landscapes—can be seen in the Life & Power Press, in the Gwangju Design Center (2004), and in the Design Center of Hongik University (2006), as well as in the brilliant hammock-like civic building proposed for the Asian Culture Complex in Gwangju (2005). A recently completed building, the Kring: Kumho Culture Complex, features a stepped interior profile reminiscent of Carlo Scarpo, and an extraordinary facade punctured by oculi of different diameters. Spectacularly enlarged, the apertures become an urban symbol of the prosperity of contemporary South Korea, whose architects have now entered the world stage with the same energy as its filmmakers and artists in the previous decade.
// Luis Fernández-Galiano

Life & Power Press, Paju, Republic of Korea, 2007. This office and exhibition space for a publishing company is located an hour from Seoul in Paju's Book City, a large development dedicated to the creation and production of books. Here, the architects have created an unconventional building topography, with an undulating facade of red cedar panels that extend to the interiors.

Gallery Yeh, Seoul, Republic of Korea, 2005. This eight-story art gallery is made of a bending exposed concrete skin that becomes a blank urban canvas. The folds in the facade's five vertical bands expose glazing to allow for natural light in the galleries. The interior's epoxy-coated panels and exposed concrete form the backdrop for a private sculpture collection.

Kring: Kumho Culture Complex, Seoul, Republic of Korea, 2008. This four-story building is used to exhibit model luxury apartments for the real estate developer Kumho Engineering and Construction, as well as host art exhibitions, design competitions, and dance performances. The stainless steel facade is punctuated with circular apertures of varying diameters; the interior contains a soaring three-story atrium.

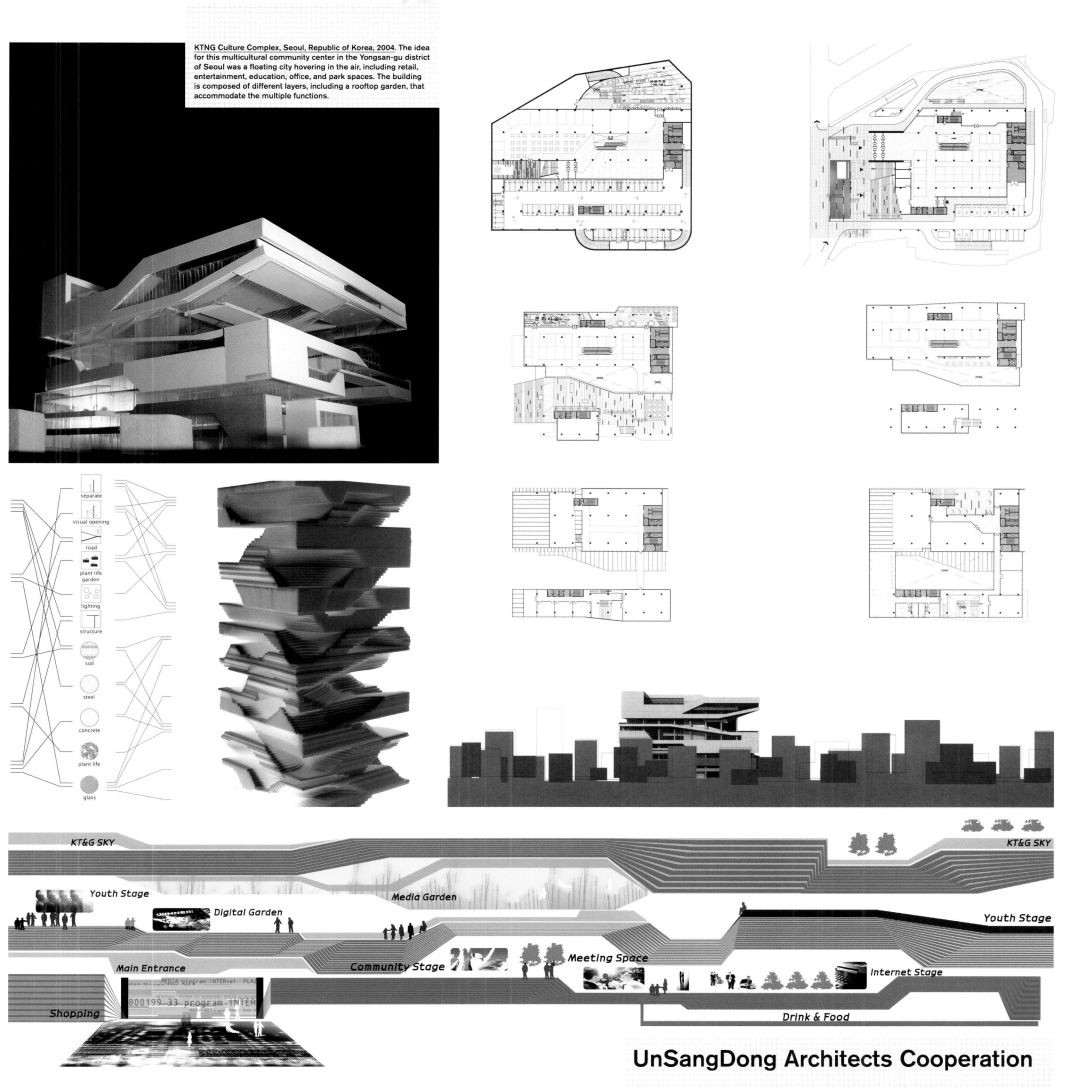

KTNG Culture Complex, Seoul, Republic of Korea, 2004. The idea for this multicultural community center in the Yongsan-gu district of Seoul was a floating city hovering in the air, including retail, entertainment, education, office, and park spaces. The building is composed of different layers, including a rooftop garden, that accommodate the multiple functions.

separate
visual opening
road
plant life garden
lighting
structure
soil
steel
concrete
plant life
glass

KT&G SKY

Youth Stage

Digital Garden

Media Garden

KT&G SKY

Youth Stage

Main Entrance

Community Stage

Meeting Space

Internet Stage

Shopping

Drink & Food

UnSangDong Architects Cooperation

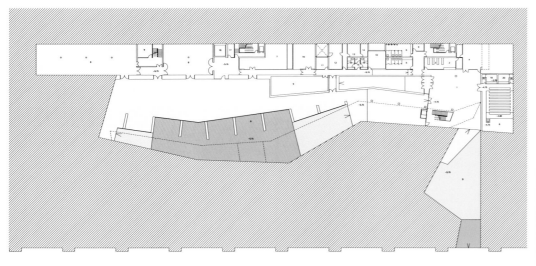

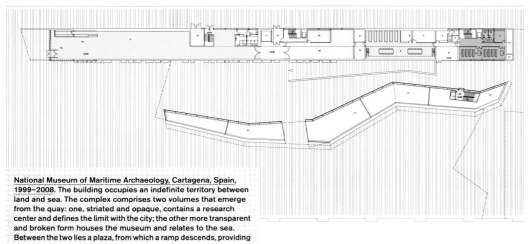

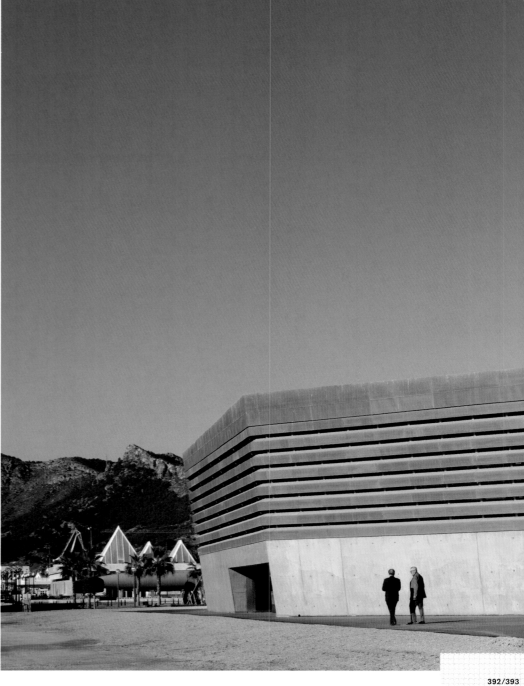

National Museum of Maritime Archaeology, Cartagena, Spain, 1999–2008. The building occupies an indefinite territory between land and sea. The complex comprises two volumes that emerge from the quay: one, striated and opaque, contains a research center and defines the limit with the city; the other more transparent and broken form houses the museum and relates to the sea. Between the two lies a plaza, from which a ramp descends, providing visitors with an entry to the museum.

The work of the Sevilla-based architect Guillermo Vázquez Consuegra can best be summed up by an expression often used to describe intense yet emotive works: "poetic rationalism." This theme has been a constant in the Spanish architect's work, from the striking Rolando House (1980-83), a courtyard house in which the typological rigor and lyrical undercurrent of the Andalusian vernacular are visible, to the seminal Rámon y Cajal Public Housing (1983–87), in which the urban growth of Sevilla found stewardship and a new paradigm. An urbanist at heart, Vázquez Consuegra has benefited from his keen understanding of architecture as an indispensable enterprise whose goal is, to borrow a phrase from Aldo Rossi, the "construction of the city."

In fact, one of the architect's most comprehensive and insightful works is a daunting urban project: the reconfiguration of the waterfront in the seaside city of Vigo. The difficult task of reimagining a neglected strip of industrial fabric between the city and the sea was masterfully resolved by Vázquez Consuegra's intrepid yet patient sensibility. The exactitude and cadence characteristic of the architect's language wove the intricacies of landscape, infrastructure, architecture, and sea as if they formed an inevitable destination. The architect managed what few modern architects have achieved at this scale: a work of distinct authorship, yet one that lyrically dissolves within the history of the city, its civic ambitions, and the multiple mirrors of the sea, to the point where it is difficult to know where one or the other begins or ends. The work makes seamless gestures between past and present; the future is experienced as the ongoing narrative of a sea-facing promenade, for it is here that many stories are told, and many more await to unfold.

Another recent work, the Castilla–La Mancha Regional Archive, is a compact citadel-like structure, whose material duality is brilliantly expressed by its colorful exterior and glazed interior void. The result is a building whose heavy appearance is lightened by the alternating strata of ceramic tile bands that make up the facades. In contrast, the building's interior is a calm and luminous volume, unifying the various floors and blurring their hierarchical levels. This building illustrates not only Vázquez Consuegra's versatile mastery in the handling of materials and spaces, but also the architect's core belief that architecture must ennoble and enrich its surroundings.
// Carlos Jimenez

Vigo Waterfront, Vigo, Spain, 1994–2004. The aim of the project, to open the city of Vigo to the sea, is achieved through the construction of a paved floor—a unifying base from which the city can contemplate the ocean. Within this extensive excavated floor, large cut blocks of granite and carved stone form stairs and seating. The architecture is designed to be invisible to best serve its civic program.

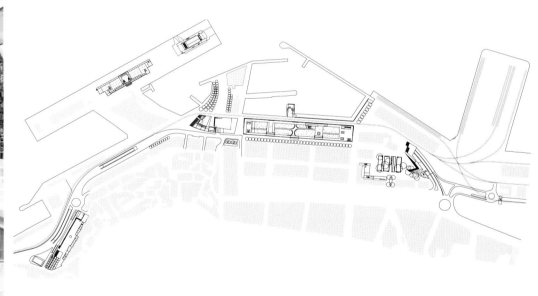

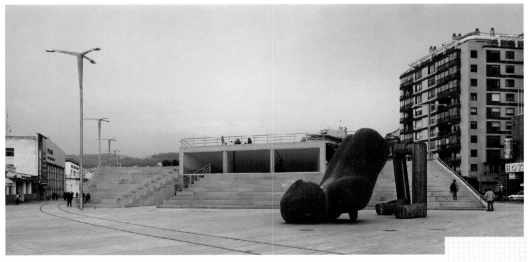

Castilla–La Mancha Regional Archive, Toledo, Spain, 1998–2005. Essentially a large vault, the building is a closed, introverted compact volume that establishes a sense of place through its formal autonomy. Inside, the solid block is transformed into a grand void with abundant natural light, an unusal feature for buildings of this type.

Guillermo Vázquez Consuegra

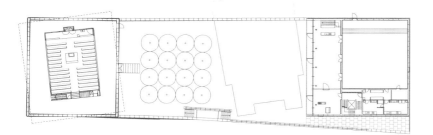

New Synagogue, Dresden, Germany, 1997–2001. Exploring the implications of stability and fragility, the architecture of the synagogue is characterized by a material dualism: a monolithic structure of precast concrete stones and an interior structure of metallic textile. The twisting stone structure of the synagogue follows the geometry of the site and the requirement of an orientation toward the east.

Three friends from the Technical University in Darmstadt, Germany—Andrea Wandel, her husband, Wolfgang Lorch, and Nikolaus Hirsch—won their first competition, for the Judengasse Monument in Frankfurt am Main, during one of their last years of study. (Rena Wandel Hoefer, Andrea's sister and the fourth founding member of the firm Wandel Hoefer Lorch + Hirsch [WHL+H], had graduated a few years earlier.) In 2001 they completed the New Synagogue on an impressive site along the bank of the Elbe River in Dresden, which brought international recognition. The slightly twisted, monolithic building has a persuasively powerful and striking sculptural form with fine detailing such as the staggered layers of sandstone on the facade and the metal woven curtain inside that creates a strong religious mood. The Jewish Center in München, recently completed, is more complex. Here, the architects employ materials in an exemplary manner while at the same time introducing design innovations. A broad range of travertine was employed: rustic for the synagogue's facades, polished for the center's museum, and stacked and sawn slabs for the courtyards of the community building.

In the work of WHL+H, the urban context always plays an important role: in München, the three different volumes of the Jewish Center structure the surrounding neighborhood, creating new plazas and pathways. By contrast, the context of the Museum and Document Center in Hinzert called for quite a different approach. A picturesque landscape concealed the site's brutal past as a concentration camp. With their singular sculpture made of Corten steel, the architects disrupt the expectations of visitors and locals alike—the 141-foot (43-meter) long monolith does not exude reconciliation but crouches recalcitrantly on the green field. Distinguished by its innovative use of an inverted ship's hull with a warm, wooden interior, the triangular structure of self-supporting steel panels, with its consistent application to all elements of the interior, is a masterful achievement.

Their latest edifice is no less distinctive. The ten-story Hybrid High-rise Pixel 34 building in Tbilisi, Georgia, is truly worthy of its name: repetitive boxed window elements, recessed or protruding, structure the distinctive cube, which is home not only to retail outlets, a food court, and supermarkets, but also to the city's most exclusive office premises. // Peter Cachola Schmal

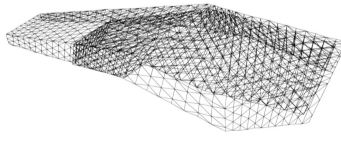

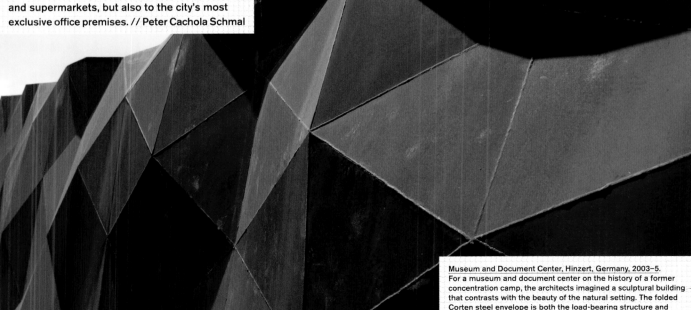

Museum and Document Center, Hinzert, Germany, 2003–5.
For a museum and document center on the history of a former concentration camp, the architects imagined a sculptural building that contrasts with the beauty of the natural setting. The folded Corten steel envelope is both the load-bearing structure and exterior facade. The steel triangles are welded together, creating a vaulted, irregular space inside the museum.

Hybrid High-rise Pixel 34, Tbilisi, Georgia, 2006–9. This mixed-use high-rise is distinguished by its sustainable facade, which combines new technology with traditional casement windows. Approximately 3,000 glass pixel elements modulate the volume, creating a stunning new landmark for the Georgian capital.

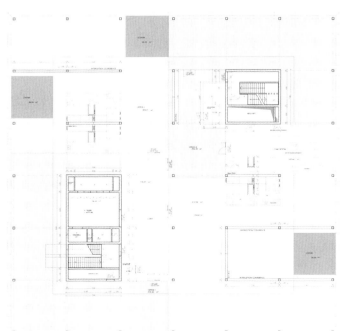

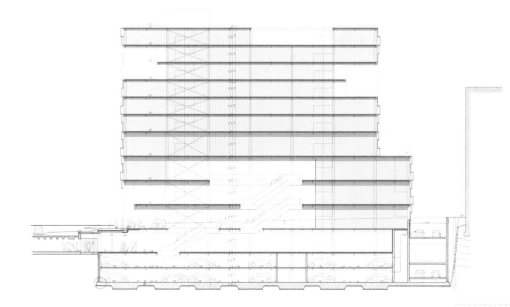

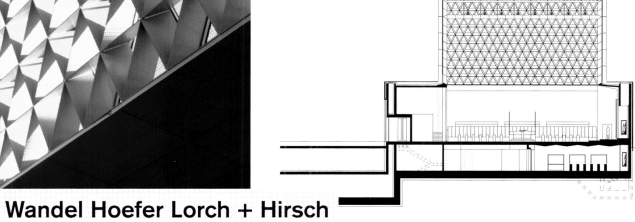

Wandel Hoefer Lorch + Hirsch

Jewish Center, München, Germany, 2001–7.
This community center, synagogue, and
Jewish museum form a balanced ensemble,
designed as autonomous structures that
carefully correlate. The synagogue is a
transparent glass and steel cube emerging
from a rough stone base, while the museum
has a glazed ground floor and an opaque
cube for exhibition spaces above. The
community center, containing elements
of both, sits against the edge of the site.
A succession of squares and passageways
merge into the surrounding neighborhood.

Territories, multiple locations, 2003–4. *Territories* is a series of exhibitions and installations that investigate the strategic use of architecture and urban planning in times of political conflict. Based largely on the research of Eyal Weizman, Anselm Franke, and Rafi Segal, the exhibition has traveled to Berlin, New York, Rotterdam, and Malmö, Sweden. Photographs, videos, maps, and models raise questions about how war can be constructed and sustained by the creation and/or destruction of housing, the physical landscape, and urban infrastructure.

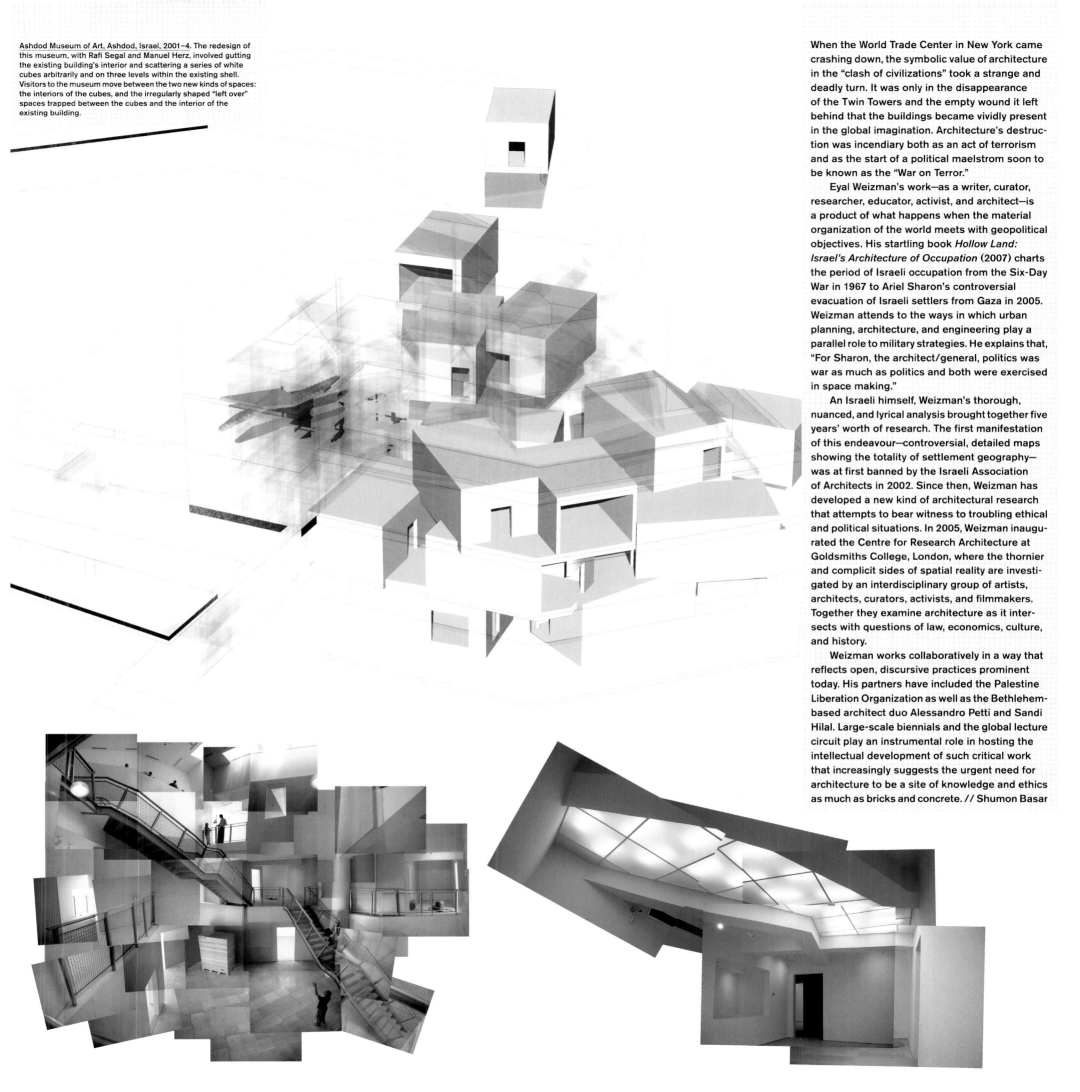

Ashdod Museum of Art, Ashdod, Israel, 2001–4. The redesign of this museum, with Rafi Segal and Manuel Herz, involved gutting the existing building's interior and scattering a series of white cubes arbitrarily and on three levels within the existing shell. Visitors to the museum move between the two new kinds of spaces: the interiors of the cubes, and the irregularly shaped "left over" spaces trapped between the cubes and the interior of the existing building.

When the World Trade Center in New York came crashing down, the symbolic value of architecture in the "clash of civilizations" took a strange and deadly turn. It was only in the disappearance of the Twin Towers and the empty wound it left behind that the buildings became vividly present in the global imagination. Architecture's destruction was incendiary both as an act of terrorism and as the start of a political maelstrom soon to be known as the "War on Terror."

Eyal Weizman's work—as a writer, curator, researcher, educator, activist, and architect—is a product of what happens when the material organization of the world meets with geopolitical objectives. His startling book *Hollow Land: Israel's Architecture of Occupation* (2007) charts the period of Israeli occupation from the Six-Day War in 1967 to Ariel Sharon's controversial evacuation of Israeli settlers from Gaza in 2005. Weizman attends to the ways in which urban planning, architecture, and engineering play a parallel role to military strategies. He explains that, "For Sharon, the architect/general, politics was war as much as politics and both were exercised in space making."

An Israeli himself, Weizman's thorough, nuanced, and lyrical analysis brought together five years' worth of research. The first manifestation of this endeavour—controversial, detailed maps showing the totality of settlement geography— was at first banned by the Israeli Association of Architects in 2002. Since then, Weizman has developed a new kind of architectural research that attempts to bear witness to troubling ethical and political situations. In 2005, Weizman inaugurated the Centre for Research Architecture at Goldsmiths College, London, where the thornier and complicit sides of spatial reality are investigated by an interdisciplinary group of artists, architects, curators, activists, and filmmakers. Together they examine architecture as it intersects with questions of law, economics, culture, and history.

Weizman works collaboratively in a way that reflects open, discursive practices prominent today. His partners have included the Palestine Liberation Organization as well as the Bethlehem-based architect duo Alessandro Petti and Sandi Hilal. Large-scale biennials and the global lecture circuit play an instrumental role in hosting the intellectual development of such critical work that increasingly suggests the urgent need for architecture to be a site of knowledge and ethics as much as bricks and concrete. // Shumon Basar

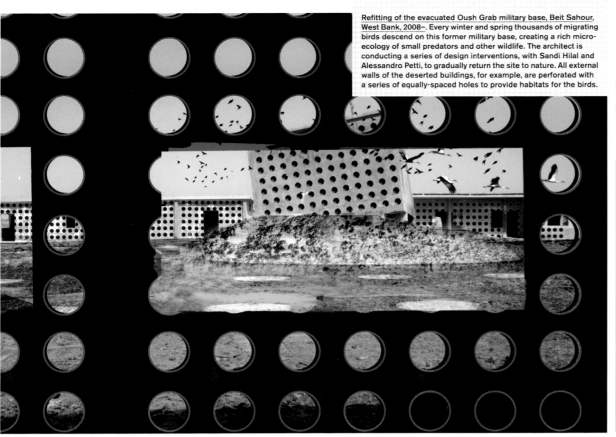

Refitting of the evacuated Oush Grab military base, Beit Sahour, West Bank, 2008–. Every winter and spring thousands of migrating birds descend on this former military base, creating a rich micro-ecology of small predators and other wildlife. The architect is conducting a series of design interventions, with Sandi Hilal and Alessandro Petti, to gradually return the site to nature. All external walls of the deserted buildings, for example, are perforated with a series of equally-spaced holes to provide habitats for the birds.

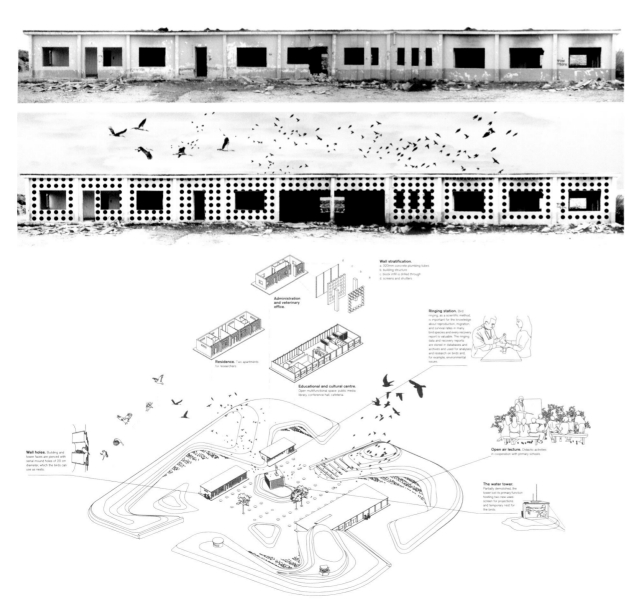

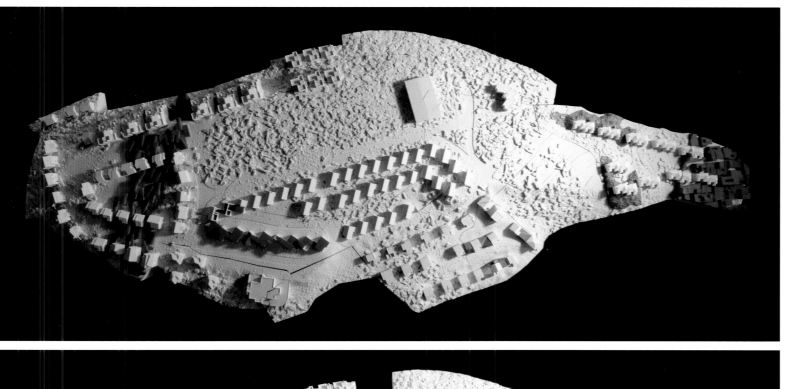

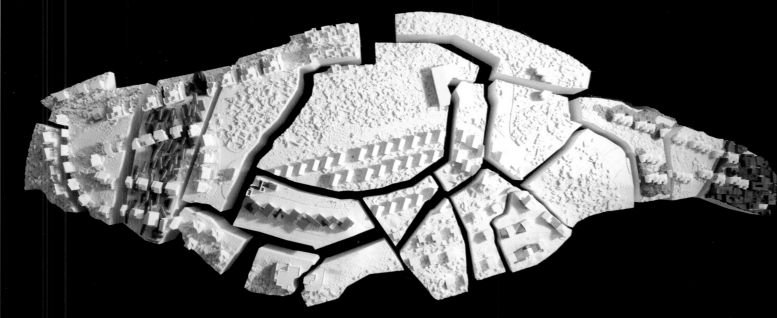

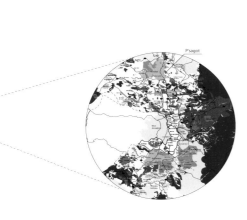

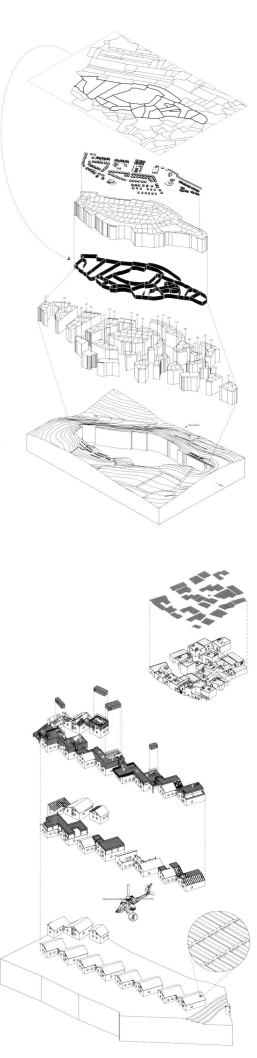

Ungrounding, Psagot Settlement, Ramallah Region, West Bank, 2007–8. This research project, conducted with Sandi Hilal and Alessandro Petti, examines how evacuated Israeli settlements can be appropriated for Palestinian use, utilizing not only the professional language of architecture but also the participation of multiple individuals and organizations from different political perspectives. Because the types of infrastructure are limited—generally similar single or double-family dwellings—the project can be easily adapted for use in other evacuated areas.

Eyal Weizman

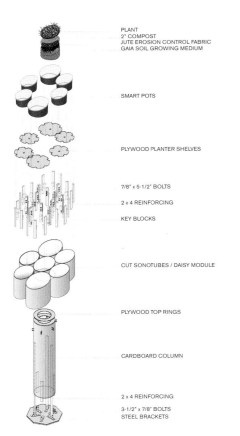

PLANT
2" COMPOST
JUTE EROSION CONTROL FABRIC
GAIA SOIL GROWING MEDIUM

SMART POTS

PLYWOOD PLANTER SHELVES

7/8" x 5-1/2" BOLTS
2 x 4 REINFORCING
KEY BLOCKS

CUT SONOTUBES / DAISY MODULE

PLYWOOD TOP RINGS

CARDBOARD COLUMN

2 x 4 REINFORCING
3-1/2" x 7/8" BOLTS
STEEL BRACKETS

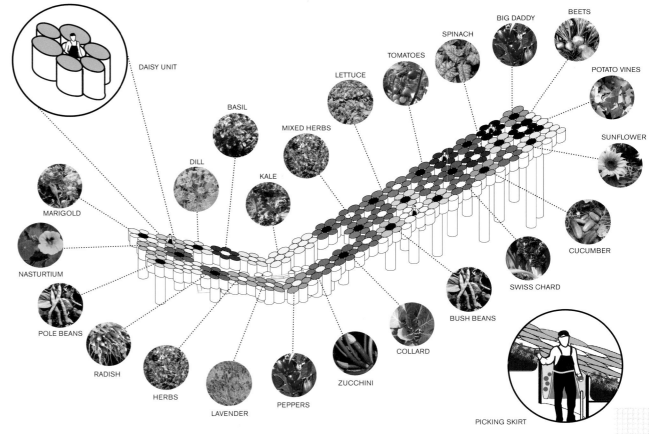

DAISY UNIT

MARIGOLD

NASTURTIUM

POLE BEANS

RADISH

HERBS

LAVENDER

PEPPERS

ZUCCHINI

COLLARD

BUSH BEANS

SWISS CHARD

CUCUMBER

SUNFLOWER

POTATO VINES

BEETS

BIG DADDY

SPINACH

TOMATOES

LETTUCE

MIXED HERBS

KALE

DILL

BASIL

PICKING SKIRT

Public Farm 1 (P.F. 1) Pavilion, P.S. 1 Contemporary Art Center, Long Island City, New York, USA, 2008. The P.F. 1 Pavilion is the winning competition entry for MoMA/P.S. 1's 2008 Young Architects Program. The pavilion consisted of a single folded plane that provided shade, seating, water, and sound and video environments underneath, while supporting a working urban farm above. Built entirely of structural cardboard tubes, the "off grid" installation is solar-powered, utilizing rainwater collection for irrigation. More than fifty varieties of organic vegetables were grown and harvested over the summer.

New York is a notoriously hostile environment for young architects hoping to open their own practice. Competition is ferocious, the cost of living astronomical, and the standard fare for the first years often consists mainly of apartment renovations. It can be a dispiriting challenge, and not one for the faint-hearted. This was not the only challenge Amale Andraos and Dan Wood faced when they founded WORK Architecture Company (WORK AC) on New York's Lower East Side in 2000. They met—as so many of their generation—at the Office for Metropolitan Architecture (OMA), and struggled for some time to shake off the stereotypes often associated with young architects who emerged from the practice in Rotterdam. Their first major opportunity came in the form of a commission to design a new headquarters for the fashion and design company Diane von Furstenberg (DVF) Studio.

Completed in 2007, the DVF Studio Head-quarters consists of a new, six-story structure behind an existing historic facade in New York City's Meatpacking District. The building houses the company's flagship store, a flexible showroom/event space, design and administrative offices for a 120-person staff, an executive suite, and a private penthouse apartment. The ubiquitous bling found in the headquarters is emblematic of WORK AC's ability to cheerfully yet wittily embrace the influences of the client while safeguarding the architectural integrity of the project. The architects' approach is driven less by the aspiration to define a proprietary aesthetic than by a highly developed awareness of the potential and importance of program: architecture's dual obligations as an art form and service to a client are not, in their view, conflictual and can in fact breed new and fertile design strategies.

This approach is especially clear in their most recent realized work, their winning proposal for the 2008 pavilion at the P.S. 1 Contemporary Art Center in Long Island City, New York. One could argue that it is not so much a pavilion as a real-world experiment in one of architecture's hot-button topics of the moment, urban farming. Dubbed "P.F. 1" (for Public Farm 1), WORK AC's pavilion effectively transformed the forecourt of the art center into an elevated field in which vegetables were grown for three months of the summer. An array of cheap cardboard cylinders cut at an angle together formed a tilted plane, a kind of "field in the air" that visitors could walk under and around. There could hardly be a more literal translation of program into architecture. // Joseph Grima

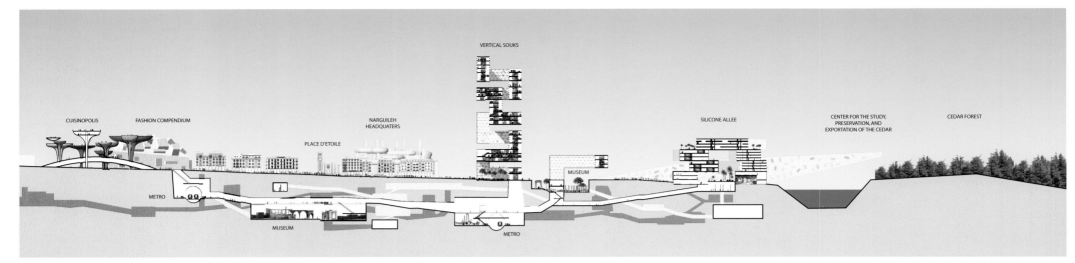

VERTICAL SOUKS

CUISINOPOLIS   FASHION COMPENDIUM   NARGUILEH HEADQUATERS   SILICONE ALLEE   CENTER FOR THE STUDY, PRESERVATION, AND EXPORTATION OF THE CEDAR   CEDAR FOREST

PLACE D'ETOILE   MUSEUM

METRO   MUSEUM   METRO

Cadavre Exquis Lebanese, Beirut, Lebanon, 2007. A theoretical urban project presented at the 2007 International Architecture Biennale in Rotterdam explores possible futures for downtown Beirut. Reacting to the city's status as a seemingly endless site of violence, and questioning the downtown restoration master plan, the project imagines a series of transformative "epochs" for Beirut that celebrate the population's shared culture, channel its humor, and attempt to recreate the layered richness of the city, fusing a vibrant and coherent Lebanese identity.

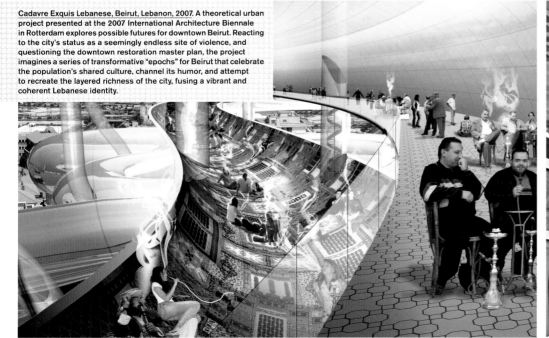

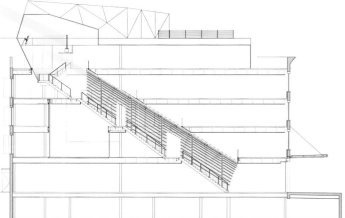

Diane von Furstenberg Studio Headquarters, New York, New York, USA, 2004–7. A six-story structure built behind landmarked facades, the new headquarters unifies its diverse program through a singular iconic gesture: a stairway that collects and distributes natural light throughout the building. A five-story diagonal cut, the "stairdelier," connects a series of double-height multifunctional spaces that culminate in the "diamond"—a faceted glass penthouse holding two heliostat mirrors that track sunlight and reflect it down the stairs.

WORK Architecture Company

10 References

Shumon Basar

Claude Parent

Claude Parent (b. 1923)

By the 1960s, exuberant faith in form alone had disappeared from architecture. Different, more troubled Utopias were dreamt up, distant descendants of Le Corbusier's Plan Voisin of 1924. French architect Claude Parent, born in 1923 in Neuilly-sur-Seine, whose work spans six decades, is an overlooked example of a late modernist who created startling, audacious forms that embodied a radical—sometimes unsettling—view of architecture and of the city. When in the early 1960s artist Yves Klein began to explore a dematerialized architecture of air, he turned to Parent for assistance, knowing that Parent shared his sense of intrigue with an architecture that was there, but also "not there."

A few years later, Parent joined forces with the philosopher and urban chronicler Paul Virilio, and together they launched the landmark magazine *Architecture Principe* in 1966. As well as documenting Virilio's fascination with the mute monolithic forms of military bunkers, *Architecture Principe* published the duo's manifesto, "La Fonction Oblique" (Function of the Oblique), which appeared in the first issue. It posited that history's distinction between the vertical (picture plane, upright man) and the horizontal (ground, reading surface) should be replaced with a system of oblique surfaces on which people would actively choose how to dwell. This principle was eloquently rendered in their Church of Sainte-Bernadette du Banlay in Nevers, as well as in Parent's installation for the French pavilion at the 1970 Architecture Biennale in Venezia. The oblique surface was both historic and ahistoric, primitive and futurist.

Virilio and Parent, the myth goes, went their separate ways in the aftermath of the Paris uprisings of May 1968, unable to reconcile their political differences. Parent's career from this point on is a fascinating split between actualized space-age Brutalist shopping malls and power stations with crazed, visionary drawings of megalithic cities to come. Renowned for a collection of sexy sports cars, and a dandyish mustache to boot, Parent refuses to fit into any predefined category: too opportunistic to be avant-garde, and too eccentric to be mainstream, he has forged his own idiosyncratic and iconoclastic route. Now in his mid-80s, Parent is the paragon of gentlemanly decorum—albeit one that quietly and persistently draws beautiful, impossible, fragmented versions of the near future in graphite on paper. Parent is a reminder of how one should never belong to any school of thought other than one's own and that truth does not converge into a locatable singularity, but spreads in necessarily unexpected and unknowable fluxes. // Shumon Basar

Church of Sainte-Bernadette du Banlay, Nevers, France, 1963–66. This church in central France, designed by Claude Parent and Paul Virilio, is the only built work to come out of the pair's collaboration. Obdurate and unforgiving in its bare concrete exposition, it allows the visitor to enter the architects' enigmatic and revolutionary theory of the oblique: a fault line runs through the plan, causing the space to fissure, and yet, due to its religiosity, there is a calmness and sobriety inside.

Mercedes Daguerre

Eladio Dieste

Eladio Dieste (1917–2000)

The Uruguayan engineer Eladio Dieste was a singular figure in twentieth-century South American architecture. His work is based on rigorous research, sensitive use of form, intellectual breadth, and a deep understanding of local context. Dieste became known for his invention of brick and ceramic tile structures, and a building system capable of roofing large areas inexpensively and quickly. Though he worked far from the principal centers of information, in places then largely unaffected by globalization, his theoretical training, early experiences using reinforced concrete, pragmatic approach, and creativity enabled him to overcome particular local difficulties confronting the practice of architecture.

During Dieste's formative years, Uruguay became a prosperous, open democracy, modern and secular, where he developed in a stimulating cultural milieu, animated by figures such as Julio Vilamajó, Joaquín Torres García, Antoni Bonet,

Rafael Alberti, and Eduardo Diaz Yepes. In this context, Dieste formed the Christian, tolerant, mystical, and avant-garde outlook that guided his work. The Church of Christ the Worker in Atlántida was the first example of his detailed studies of reinforced masonry in the second half of the twentieth century. The all-brick structure is a large double-curved shell, anchored to the ground by pile foundations. The use of embedded rebars and special mortars makes the brickwork structurally active. The design focuses on technical-structural factors but also explores the relationship between expressive modeling and structure. This concern also occupied Dieste in the construction of the house at Punta Gorda in 1963. There he considered the vault the best way to combine traditional craftsmanship with a modern vocabulary.

Antoni Gaudí, Le Corbusier, and Eduardo Torroja are some of the names frequently invoked by critics to suggest Dieste's close ties with the academic world and the international architectural debate. But his churches, such as Christ the

Worker and San Pedro in Durazno, built in 1971, were exceptions in a career largely spent building utilitarian structures. In these he would typically cover large spans using his innovative building system, gradually perfected by the invention of ingenious tools and machinery. Examples are his Gaussian vaults (Caputto Fruit-packing Plant, Montevideo, 1975–77), self-supporting vaults (Massaro Agroindustries, Juanicó, 1980), or sharply pitched vaults with a constant degree of undulation (Silo, Young, 1978).

Religious buildings enabled Dieste to explore the potential of architecture to express symbolic needs while reflecting his innovative conception of the Catholic liturgy. He chose simple materials such as brick, reflecting the lack of specialized skills among the local labor force and limited technical know-how in the local construction industry. Yet he used brick in unconventional ways, from the structure of the building to the play of light across the texture of brickwork, creating an atmosphere conducive to the community spirit that he sought.

Dieste was an anomalous architect in his day. He approached building with the solid background of an engineer, but he fully embraced the formal innovations driving debate in Uruguay in the postwar years. Always interested in exploring the potential of materials, sensitive to proportions and spatial qualities, fascinated by the ideal of the unity of the arts and by the ties between tradition and modernity, Dieste believed the production process was decisive in generating the aesthetic qualities of buildings. It is this aspect of his aesthetic that still provides intrigue, precisely because it is unfashionable. // Mercedes Daguerre

Church of Christ the Worker, Atlántida, Uruguay, 1955–60. This church showcases Dieste's painstaking research in masonry and his enthusiasm in experimentation. The projecting corners of the main facade, the sinuous lateral walls tempered by small colored-glass apertures, the movement of the Gaussian vault covering the nave, all reveal his plastic sensibility in shape and surface treatment, where light is reflected to striking effect.

Luis Fernández-Galiano

El Escorial

El Escorial, San Lorenzo de El Escorial, Spain (1562–84) by Juan Bautista de Toledo and Juan de Herrera

The monastery of El Escorial, built in the sixteenth century near Madrid for King Philip II, is a building of contradictions and dualities. A colossal work completed in only twenty-two years (from 1562 to 1584), a massive construction that hides an amazing variety of spaces, and a happy marriage of a classical plan with a picturesque profile, El Escorial is both timeless and topical, generic and specific, Italian and Flemish. Designed by two architects—Juan Bautista de Toledo, who laid the huge grid of the plan, and Juan de Herrera, who completed the building with the characteristic pitched roofs—the monastery seamlessly joins the granite of the facade with the slate of the tops, combining the experience Toledo acquired while working under Michelangelo on the Basilica of St. Peter in Rome and the images captured by Herrera during his trips with the king in Flanders.

El Escorial presents the three qualities defined by Vitruvius in his treatise *De architectura* (Ten Books on Architecture). In terms of *firmitas*, the building offers many achievements: the astonishing expediency of the work on site, made possible by streamlined construction processes to swiftly complete a structure whose size would usually demand centuries of labor; the geometrical skill and craftsmanship of the stonework, apparent in the intricate execution of the leaning and turning stair vaults and in the tour de force of the flat vault of the choir over the basilica entrance; but also the extraordinary ingenuity of services, from the chimneys to the flushing latrines and the snow wells for summer comfort. El Escorial houses a wealth of technical inventiveness and constructive resourcefulness.

In the realm of *utilitas*, the work is again a source of wonder. The stern grid, which recalls the Palace of Diocletian at Split (AD 295–305) but also draws on medieval cross-shaped hospitals and cloistered Benedictine monasteries, looks endlessly repetitive; nonetheless it contains a monastery, school, library, museum, basilica, a public and a private royal palace, and a pantheon for the Spanish monarchs. Its generic appearance, somehow typological with its strict rectangular footprint, sits easily in the sloping sierra terrain, interacting with the village through elongated ceremonial squares on two sides, and blending with the landscape through terraced gardens and orchards on the other two. Its apparent disdain for local climate is proven wrong by the environmental sophistication of window patterns in the different facades, the unexpected superposition of the summer and winter palaces, and the elegant pentimento of the Gallery of Convalescents, which provides sunshine for the sick.

Last but not least, the quality of *venustas* in El Escorial is appropriately dualistic. Joining Italian and Flemish references, the great monument of the Counter Reformation is also a contemporary version of Solomon's Temple, as famously argued by the Jesuits Jerome de Prado and Juan Bautista Villalpando, and eloquently expressed by the statues of David and Solomon in El Escorial's King's Courtyard. Philip II, a learned and bureaucratic king who identified with the wise Solomon, built the monastery as a royal tomb for his father Charles, a warrior king like David. The God of battles—El Escorial commemorated the victory against the French in the battle of Saint Quentin—is indeed at the center of the building, but the same axis that goes through the altar of the basilica crosses the library, symbolically placing knowledge in a dialogue with the revealed truth of religion, and thereby linking wisdom and faith.

El Escorial is a pedagogic work of *arquitectura desornamentada* (unornamented architecture), dear to the moderns for its lack of ornament and to the postmoderns for its classical gravitas. Its access to the architectural canon is granted not through the heavy granite of its walls but through the collection of engravings that Herrera commissioned from Pedro Perret, the renowned Flemish engraver, in 1589. In these exquisite bird's-eye views, the heavy-weight champion floats like a butterfly in the skies of architecture. // Luis Fernández-Galiano

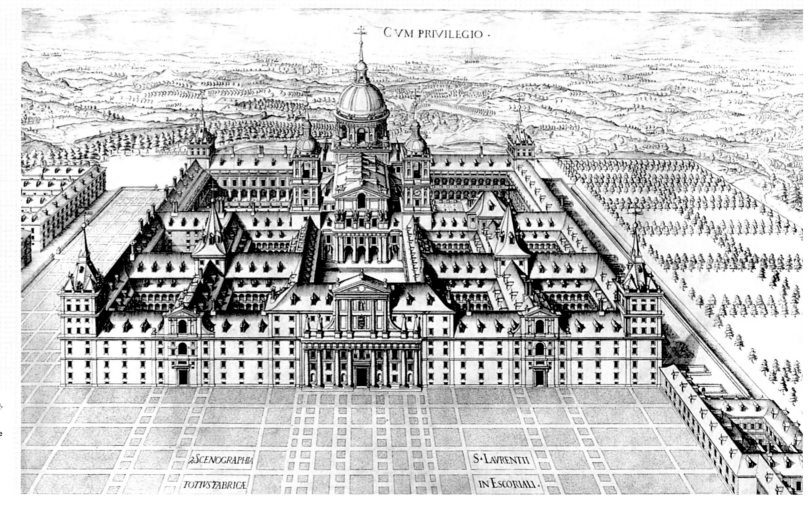

Royal Monastery of El Escorial, San Lorenzo de El Escorial, Spain, 1562–84. This bird's-eye view of El Escorial was one of a series commissioned from the Flemish engraver Pedro Perret by Juan de Herrera, one of the monastery's architects. The complex became known in Europe through these engravings. They circulated widely and expressed masterfully, in perspective, the rationality of the gridded plan, the regular composition of the granite facades, and the characteristic stepped slate roofs, which fuse the Italian and Flemish influences in the design of this seminal work of Spanish architecture.

Bart Goldhoorn

Tokyo Opera House

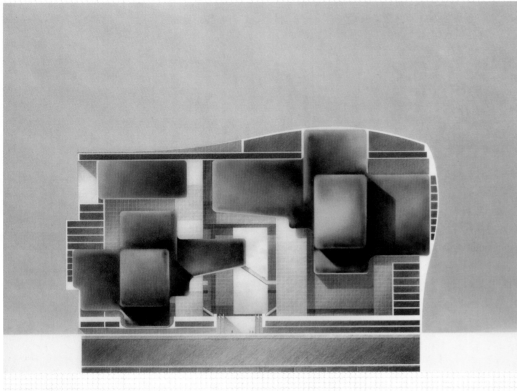

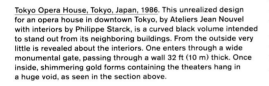
Tokyo Opera House, Tokyo, Japan, 1986. This unrealized design for an opera house in downtown Tokyo, by Ateliers Jean Nouvel with interiors by Philippe Starck, is a curved black volume intended to stand out from its neighboring buildings. From the outside very little is revealed about the interiors. One enters through a wide monumental gate, passing through a wall 32 ft (10 m) thick. Once inside, shimmering gold forms containing the theaters hang in a huge void, as seen in the section above.

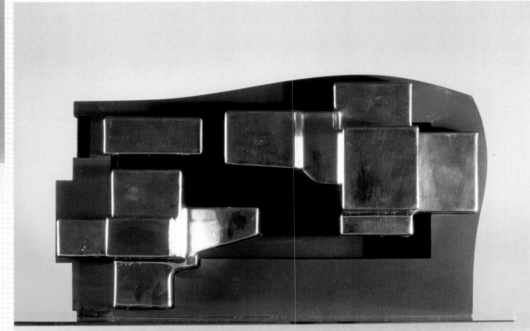

Tokyo Opera House (1986)
by Jean Nouvel and Philippe Starck

In 1987, as a fourth year student of architecture, I studied the work of Jean Nouvel, whose Nemausus social housing project in Nîmes, France (1985-87) and Arab World Institute in Paris (1981–87) were widely published. Although the faculty of Architecture at Delft University of Technology was teaching its typical course of classic modernism flavored with constructivism and Adolf Loos, outside the school a vivid discussion was taking place between deconstructivists and the last believers in postmodernism. While I understood the limitations of a historicist architecture like that featured in Berlin's 1987 International Building Exhibition (IBA), it irritated me that deconstructivists constructed a meta-story to justify their style. In the end, for me the big question was, how can architecture speak, communicate, transfer meaning, and not remain a complete abstraction?

When I came to know the architecture of Nouvel better, I understood that this question is central to his work, and while his architecture between 1978 and 1985 had actually evolved from postmodernism to something more abstract, it nevertheless remained communicative. My interest in Nouvel's work led me to visit Paris in 1988 for an interview with the architect, which was published in the journal *OASE*, of which I was an editor at the time. With the interview we published images of the unbuilt Tokyo Opera House, which Nouvel had designed together with Philippe Starck in 1986.

The design of the Tokyo Opera House consists of a lightly curved polished black box. Vistors enter through a low, wide hall, and from there proceed to a 164-foot (50-meter) high space in which the walls and ceiling are made of black polished granite. In this space three golden volumes—the theaters—protrude from the walls and seem to dangle overhead. Using escalators, visitors move up through the space to arrive at the theaters, which are clad in gold. Their interiors are made of mahogany, like the inside of an instrument, lit by a retractable, luminous column 20 feet (6 meters) high.

For a number of reasons this design made a great impression on me. First was the use of the musical instrument, on a completely different scale, as the reference for an opera house. Then there was the suspense—the way contrast was used to evoke emotion. In addition, the layering of space between the inner and the outer skin of the building was fascinating. This "margin" has become increasingly important: buildings today have double or triple skins, and that is how they differ from modern or classical buildings. I also remember being amazed that it was possible to make such an exciting building with such a simple, symmetrical floor plan; this contradicted what I was being taught at school, where our main task was to produce interesting plans.

There are ideas in Nouvel's work from that time that I think are still extremely relevant for architecture today. Architecture should work like film—rather than show the whole sequence, it should work with suggestion so people can construct the meaning themselves. Architects should not attempt to appeal to common values, but should use contrast: low and high, wide and narrow, hot and cold, dark and light. Architects should work with associations that stick very closely to the basic tactile experience.

Can these qualities be found in the works of the offices that I have chosen for this book? At times. But each work contains its own story about how to make architecture, and that alone is enough to inspire. // Bart Goldhoorn

Joseph Grima

Juliaan Lampens

Juliaan Lampens (b. 1926)

It is often said—and rarely challenged—that the successful architect is equal parts skilled designer and savvy media strategist, preferably erring in favor of the latter. The history of architecture is strewn with the corpses of unknown renegades and unsung revolutionaries, the majority of whom are condemned to eternal anonymity; a lucky few achieve posthumous glory à la Erno Goldfinger. Architecture is a profession that needs and feeds egos, and inventiveness is often driven by the desire for recognition and approval. Yet there are exceptions, and the fact that there are so few makes them all the more interesting. One of these deviants is Juliaan Lampens, a Belgian architect born in 1926.

Other than an exhibition at Antwerp's deSingel Museum in the early 1990s, Lampens's work has never been the object of much critical recognition. The only monograph of his work, to this day, is a rare catalogue for the deSingel exhibition, and it appears that many of his most interesting works have never been published outside Belgium. Yet in the late 1960s and early 1970s, Lampens designed a couple of the most singular and innovative modernist dwellings in Europe.

The bulk of Lampens's work is, by his own admission, relatively humdrum: gabled suburban residences, unremarkable residential conversions, and public architecture of the more mundane variety. "Like everyone else, I needed to pay the bills," he said in a recent interview. "You can't push the envelope on every project. It requires very particular circumstances." On the rare occasions when Lampens was approached by clients whose ambitions surpassed the need to merely place a (pitched) roof above their heads, he was quick to question even the most fundamental and indisputable dogmas of residential architecture.

One such case is House Vandenhoute-Kiebooms, built in 1967 in Huise, outside Gent. It is a low-slung, single-story flat-roof dwelling, commissioned by a couple who had inherited a sliver of land sandwiched between a cornfield and a small country lane. The house, entirely cast in reinforced concrete in true Brutalist tradition, consists of a single open space. The exceptional feature of House Vandenhoute-Kiebooms is the absence of interior walls. (The desire to span the entire breadth of the space without pillars explains the remarkable depth of the roof slab.) As with a small number of his other houses, Lampens's ambition was to create a pillarless open plan in which not even functions such as the shower and bathroom would interrupt the building's spatial continuity. To achieve this the toilet, shower, and other "private" areas are placed inside concrete cylinders, each of which is cut off at eye level, creating an archipelago of semi-enclosed cubicles within a larger open space. For the kitchen, this "island" configuration is inverted: here, the work-space is separated from the rest of the house by a curtain-like wall hanging from the ceiling, cut off at waist height. In a further gesture of spatial integration, the work surface protrudes beyond the kitchen into the living area to become the dining table. Bedrooms, too, are little more than pieces of furniture within the open space of the house.

Despite the similarities between his work and the production of other twentieth-century modernists (particularly those associated with New Brutalism), one could describe Lampens as their antithesis. He never belonged to a movement, never built abroad, and traveled little. He did not fraternize with the stars of the international firmament, with one exception: his work was exhibited once in Brazil with Oscar Niemeyer. Their stories could not be more different, but to this day the two share an ongoing friendship. // Joseph Grima

House Vandenhoute-Kiebooms, Huise, Belgium, 1967. This single family house in the countryside is inhabited today by the same couple who commissioned it in 1967. The house is part of a series of experiments in radical modernism conducted by Juliaan Lampens in the 1960s and 1970s, all of which remain unpublished outside Belgium. These views show the house's exterior and the kitchen, with its concrete hanging half-wall.

Carlos Jimenez

The Menil Collection

The Menil Collection, Houston, Texas (1981–86)
by Renzo Piano

When asked to name a building that has had an impact on my understanding and appreciation of contemporary architecture, The Menil Collection art museum immediately came to mind. Perhaps it is because of the happy coincidence that this poetic and consummate work of architecture is within walking distance of my house and studio. Or perhaps it is because of my deep admiration for a building whose intimate and quiet demeanor speaks volumes about what architecture does in the world. Through the years I have been fortunate to amass countless experiences through visits, events, exhibitions, and lectures in this treasure of a museum.

I have also come to realize how difficult it is to convey the actual experience of being in or near this inimitable work through the approximations of words or photography. The building's patron, Dominique de Menil once commented on the limitations of language when describing artwork by suggesting that "perhaps only silence and love do justice to a great work of art. And yet words can be illuminating." Perhaps the difficulty of describing Renzo Piano's museum is because it embodies not only high artistic achievements but also deep human concerns. That the building encompasses light, faith, humility, bravado, awe, beauty, eloquence, surprise, and generosity is a testament to the aspirations of client and architect alike. The Menil Collection's understated refinement illustrates the auspicious merger of patronage and vision.

In the span of twenty years the building has not only become a critical reference for museums around the world but also an indisputable reminder of what architecture is able to achieve when nurtured by an enlightened patron, a gifted architect, and a supportive community. The building might assert its signature profile of ferro-cement "leaves," yet it echoes the delicate timelessness of the Cycladic figures that complement the museum's collection. I am always amazed by how suddenly the building makes one forget temporarily its compelling architecture, as if its sole intent was to immerse the visitor in the experience of the artworks masterfully framed with light, space, and landscape.

More significantly, perhaps, the Menil building encapsulates the transformative power that a work of architecture provides to a community, even one as dispersed and fragmented as Houston. What impresses me more after each visit is the realization that building, art, and landscape have become an equal and inseparable unity. The building is not an object that landed oblivious to the marvels of place making, or one that relegates works of art to a subservient role, a sharp contrast to the narcissistic indulgences that have afflicted so many art museum buildings of the past twenty-five years. The Menil Collection is a complete sensual landscape intertwined with its neighborhood, treescape, and boundless sky. It is a porous and inviting place where time oscillates in multiple directions as it also stands still. It is a territory for the body and the imagination to meander freely. Sometimes I like to walk around the building's exterior promenade without ever entering the galleries. Sometimes I just cross the museum's internal street to revisit a favorite work from the permanent collection. Or in those special moments when time stands still, I simply linger on a bench and follow the infinite cartography of tree branches gently strumming the gray cypress walls. // Carlos Jimenez

The Menil Collection, Houston, Texas, USA 1981–86. This view of the east elevation of The Menil Collection by Renzo Piano captures the astonishing power of the gray cypress siding and the delicate arcade of ferro-cement "leaves." These same leaves soar through the building's interior, delivering the subtlest light to galleries and other interior spaces. The building awakens in the morning sun yet it glows on its own with an innate light that few museums can claim.

Kengo Kuma

Bruno Taut

Wooden box, c. 1935. German architect Bruno Taut lived in Japan from 1933 to 1936 and designed one house, Hyuga Villa (1935), and a number of products. Many of them were sold at a small craft shop in Tokyo. Kengo Kuma inherited this wooden box from his father, who long treasured it in the family's drawing room. The texture of the wood and the minimalist form, different from both cool modernism and craft, made a striking impression on Kuma.

Bruno Taut (1880–1938)

I was probably about ten years old. One day my father showed me a small round wooden box, and that was the start of my career as an architect. Taking the small box carefully from the back of a shelf, he proudly said, "This was designed by the famous architect Bruno Taut." The small box was unlike anything that I had ever seen. Despite the fact that it was made of wood, its edges were sharp and everything about it was thin and light. Yet despite this sharpness and lightness, the overall impression was different from containers and home furnishings made in the style of so-called modern design. The box was very warm and so simple and graceful that one instinctively wanted to embrace it. I felt its difference vividly, but at that time I had no idea who Taut was or what that difference meant.

The next time I encountered Taut was when I was thirty-five and had just opened my own architectural practice. Fusaichiro Inoue, who operated a construction company in Takasaki, asked me to design a resort hotel in Thailand.

Mr. Inoue was then over ninety years old. I was stunned when he invited me to his home. The rooms were filled with items that had the same aura as the box that had made my father so proud. They were all designed by Taut. In addition to small containers, there were lamp stands made of bamboo as well as chairs and a sofa that were undersized and feminine in appearance but comfortable to sit in. Awestruck, I asked about these items and was told about Mr. Inoue's connection to Taut and what he himself knew of Taut's personality. In 1933 Taut fled the Nazis and came to Japan; it was Mr. Inoue who became his benefactor and supported him during his three-year stay.

My next experience with Taut was a decisive encounter that occurred about five years later. A company in Atami had commissioned a guest house, and as I visited the site a woman came out of the neighboring house. When I introduced myself as an architect, she said that her own home was designed by Taut and asked me to come in and look at it. I knew that Taut had designed one—and only one—small house in Japan, but I had not

known where it was located. I never would have dreamed that it would be next door to a house that I myself would design. I will never forget my feelings when I set foot in Taut's house. I felt as if my own body and the ocean in front of me had merged. The house was built on a steep slope on the coastline, and the sea was some distance below. Nonetheless, it felt as if the sea and I were one.

Taut called this style "the architecture of relationships." He criticized Le Corbusier and Mies van der Rohe as formalists and wrote that the architecture of the future would have to be buildings that were related to their environment. The model for this, he said, was Japanese architecture. In my opinion, no other architect became aware so quickly of the limits of twentieth-century modernism. Taut used his designs of buildings, small objects, and household furnishings to pursue something that existed beyond twentieth-century architecture. That is why I designed the Water and Glass Villa in Atami (1992–95) as an homage to stand beside Taut's own design. // Kengo Kuma

Andrew Mackenzie

Centre Georges Pompidou

Centre Georges Pompidou, Paris (1971–77) by Renzo Piano and Richard Rogers

"Sous les pavés, la plage" [Under the cobblestones, the beach] was a popular slogan in 1968 Paris that represented the radical thinking of many at the time. Although the events of May '68 did not transform the paving stones of Paris into a beach, in the years following this popular uprising there were some truly radical moments of architectural intervention. Most important was the Centre Georges Pompidou (known to locals as the "Beaubourg," after the building's district). Begun in 1971 and completed in 1977, it was a spectacular collaboration for two young architects, Richard Rogers and Renzo Piano, who saw it as a vigorous expression of public, accessible, and culturally inclusive architecture. It was "architecture as a social art," half a century after CIAM coined the term.

There may be other buildings more spatially sublime or dramatic in figural form, but few exist within the public realm. The Beaubourg—which houses the National Museum of Modern Art, a public library, and a center for music and accoustic research—showed the world that contemporary architecture could be formally experimental, socially progressive, creatively engineered, and urbanistically challenging, yet also hugely popular. With over six million visitors still lining up in its western plaza every year to see the latest shows, it remains one of Europe's greatest ambassadors of public architecture.

It was also a political ambassador, representing an unparalleled expression of that period's optimistic internationalism. Alongside the English and Italian architects there was an Anglo-Danish engineering company (Ove Arup) and the Irish structural engineer Peter Rice. Opened to all, both French and tourists alike, it was designed to be a loose-fit, flexible information machine. It replaced architecture's traditional heft with lightweight components and the efficiencies of prefabrication. Its inspiration came unmistakably from the avant-garde architectural group Archigram, and although English architect Cedric Price never did get to build his Fun Palace, the Beaubourg is in many ways it. Architects who currently combine digital technology, new lightweight tectonic possibilities, and the conceptual ideas of the evolutionary city, can thank the Beaubourg for being arguably the only major manifestation of Archigram's urban aspiration, up until, of course, the "Friendly Alien" Kunsthaus of Graz, Austria, by Peter Cook and Colin Fournier.

It gave birth to high-tech in architecture, for which it can be forgiven. While we have all seen the baroque over-engineered sequels, this original resisted high-tech's macho tendencies (thanks perhaps to the lyrical hand of Piano), accommodating the logistics of its utilitarian program, while never forgetting that this is a building for humans, their experiences, and most of all, their delight.

It continues to live and change today, with the curvaceous addition of the Jakob + MacFarlane restaurant on top, and, at plaza level, the city's first open-access wi-fi. The Beaubourg's spirit of popular inclusion continues, with new ways to visit "the beach" while sitting in a city plaza. // Andrew McKenzie

Centre Georges Pompidou, Paris, France, 1971–77. Conceived as a radical departure from typical closed-off museums, the Pompidou possesses a lightness and transparency that open it to the public. This photograph shows the central portion of the building's west elevation, overlooking the Place Beaubourg. Visitors ascend through its transparent tube of escalators to the building's top floor, above the Parisian mansard roofline. With services located on the building's exteriors, floor space is uninterrupted and flexible.

Quinta Monroy Housing, Iquique, Chile, 2003–4. The Chilean government commissioned housing for the families of Quinta Monroy on the site they had occupied for thirty years, in the center of Iquique in the Chilean desert. The site and tight budget, allowing for only about 300 sq. ft. (30 sq. m) per home, led Elemental to work with efficient row houses, rather than isolated residences. They designed and built fifty percent of each dwelling, allowing the residents themselves to build the remaining half. These photo-graphs show the housing before the residents' interventions (above), and after the residents' interventions (left).

Elemental (founded 2004)

Only rarely does something new or revolutionary come along in architecture, which makes the residential projects by Chile's urban design and architecture group Elemental all the more compelling. Elemental, which refers to itself as a "do tank," as opposed to a "think tank," is associated with the Pontificia Universidad Católica (PUC) de Chile in Santiago and supported by the national oil company Copec. Elemental's goal, as outlined by its charismatic executive director, Alejandro Aravena, is to apply intelligent concepts to develop urgently needed affordable and sustainable homes for poor communities, and to do so at the normal, government-subsidized prices of only US$ 7,500 per unit. Elemental builds on land formerly occupied by favelas to create dignified, centrally located, well-networked and dense row housing. Having studied and reinterpreted the basic methods used for social housing projects, the firm determined that it pays off to build in central districts and not on the periphery, so that residents have access to the infrastructure and opportunities available in cities.

Elemental is often quoted as saying that social housing should be seen as an investment and not as an expense. Their trick for keeping costs low: only fifty percent of the final buildings are erected by the architects, in such a way that the kitchens, baths, stairwells, and dividing walls are provided—in other words, the facilities that require technical expertise. They leave space for later expansion by the inhabitants themselves, while providing basic, but key, preconditions, such as spaces that protrude into the garden, and load-bearing ceilings between load-bearing walls that enable further stories to be added. The future size of the residential units is more that of a middle-class home than standard social housing, meaning that inhabitants can, by their own effort, begin to improve their social position, a step toward upward economic mobility. By only partially building the residences, Elemental relinquishes control to the citizens. The resulting opportunities, social cohesion, and formalized neighborhoods are achieved despite being very hard to plan.

The pilot estate, Quinta Monroy, with ninety-three units, has succeeded marvelously. Elemental is developing this innovative approach further in many new projects—two more estates have already been realized, while another five are under construction, and plans now extend to Monterrey, Mexico, where seventy homes are scheduled to be built. Not surprisingly, there is strong international interest in these projects, proving one ought still to be hopeful about architecture's potential for creating innovative, relevant solutions. // Peter Cachola Schmal

Earthquake in Sichuan, China (12 May 2008)

Architecture builds upon its predecessors. To say that one building or one architect is the most significant is to disregard the history of previous designs that have led up to the current achievement.

Architecture is a skill for survival. It is not about the individual but rather about meeting a need. Architecture responds to politics, warfare, poverty, inhuman acts, natural disasters, and all the other things that force us to build new environments. Destruction is the negative, architecture is the positive. When we ask ourselves which architect committed, or what building was, the most significant architectural act of survival, we must first establish the criteria that make architects and buildings significant.

Architecture is never significant unless it is meeting a social need or advancing the use of materials or technology. Whether we look at architecture that resulted from the invention of reinforced concrete or buildings that can scrape the sky because of the use of steel, we are looking at what the advancements in materials have allowed one architect or one building to achieve. In terms of technology, today's primary force is the computer. The computer has become the means by which architects generate complex forms or produce buildings on a grand scale to meet human or commercial needs. Especially in so-called developing countries, like China today, the scale and speed of development depend on the assistance of technology. In the case of architects, an effective response to the demands of the

building boom requires the ability to copy and to mass produce that computer technology provides.

Human need is the second element that stokes the fires of architectural advancement. When disasters like the May 2008 Sichuan earthquake in China rattle our hearts and destroy the built environment, it is human need that looks toward architecture and building technology to create a new environment. Whether designing a shelter, cathedral, skyscraper, or city, architects are meeting both human and commercial needs.

Technological advancements and human need cannot be avoided. But the criteria that more typically earn fame and recognition for architects are style and aesthetics. Yet style and aesthetics do not compare to technology and human need in terms of creating buildings of significance. It is

need, coupled with efficiency, that drives development while providing architects with the opportunity to express themselves and to appeal to human romanticism. Architects do not cause human need; architects merely write the lyrics that make life's song something we want to listen to. And some architects become the candlelight and the sweet whispers that accompany the rape of the environment. // Ai Weiwei

Aftermath of the earthquake, Sichuan, China, 2008. On 12 May 2008, an earthquake devastated Sichuan, China. Though exact figures do not exist, over 90,000 people were estimated dead, with countless more missing, injured, and homeless. Schools—built inadequately due to political corruption and lack of funding—collapsed, killing approximately 20,000 children. In this image, taken on 29 May in Ying Xiu, chemical response workers scour a destroyed town, one that will turn to architecture to rebuild itself.

Architects' Biographies

2012Architecten

www.2012architecten.nl
Jeroen Bergsma born in the Netherlands, 1970; Jan Jongert born in the Netherlands, 1971; Césare Peeren born in Germany, 1968 // Jeroen Bergsma lives and works in Amsterdam and Rotterdam; Jan Jongert and Césare Peeren live and work in Rotterdam // Education Jeroen Bergsma: Architecture diploma, TU Delft, 1996; Jan Jongert: Architecture diploma, TU Delft and Academy of Architecture, Rotterdam, 2003; Césare Peeren: Architecture diploma, TU Delft, 1997 // Recent works 2003: Miele Space Station, multiple locations in the Netherlands and Belgium; 2004: Duchi, Den Haag, Netherlands; 2005: WORM@ VOC, Rotterdam; 2006: Espressobar Sterk, Delft; Robodock, Rotterdam // Recent publications 2006: Daan Bakker, Allard Jolles, et al., *Architecture in the Netherlands Yearbook 2005/06*, NAi Publishers, Netherlands; 2007: Jan Jongert, Césare Peeren, Ed van Hinte, *SuperUse: Constructing New Architecture by Shortcutting Material Flows*, 010 Publishers, Netherlands; Phyllis Richardson, *XS Green: Big Ideas, Small Buildings*, Thames & Hudson, UK and USA; 2009: Robert Klanten and Lukas Feireiss, *Spacecraft 2: Fleeting Architecture and Hideouts*, Die Gestalten Verlag, Germany // Recent exhibitions 2007: *OmBouwen/ReStructure*, Stroom Den Haag, Netherlands; 2008: 11th International Architecture Exhibition, Venezia; 2009: *Shape Our Country*, Netherlands Architecture Institute // Awards 2006–7: Nomination, Best Young Architect, Netherlands Architect Institute

Allmann Sattler Wappner Architekten

www.allmannsattlerwappner.de
Markus Allmann born in Germany, 1959; Amandus Sattler born in Germany, 1957; Ludwig Wappner born in Germany, 1957 // All live and work in München // Education Markus Allmann: Architecture diploma, TU München, 1986; Amandus Sattler: Architecture diploma, TU München, 1985; Ludwig Wappner: Architecture diploma, TU München, 1985 // Affiliations All members of the Chamber of Architects, Germany and France // Recent works 2000: Herz Jesu Church, München; 2001: Südwestmetall, Reutlingen, Germany; 2005: Haus der Gegenwart, München // Recent publications 2008: Noriko Tsukui, "Audi terminal, Munich," *A+U* 459, Japan; Ulrike Schettler, "Office Buildings / Agency, Munich," *AIT*, Germany; Wolfgang Bachmann, "Audi terminal in München," *Baumeister* B8, Germany; Andrea Longhi, *Luoghi di Culto: Architetture 1997–2007*, Libreria Rizzoli, Italy; Chris van Uffelen, *Clear Glass: Creating New Perspectives*, Verlagshaus Braun, Germany // Recent exhibitions 2009: *Bauhaus twenty-21 – An Ongoing Legacy*, German Architecture Museum, Frankfurt; 2008: *Energieeffizientes Bauen und Planen*, München; 2007: International Architecture Biennale São Paulo; 2004–7: Architecture and Religion, Aedes Gallery and Goethe Institut, Berlin, and other locations // Awards 1997: German Architecture Award, Germany; 2001: Lighting Architecture Award, Germany; 2003: German Facade Prize, Germany; 2004: German Steel Design Award, Laudatory recognition, Germany; Leaf Award, UK; 2006: Ecola Award, Germany; Hugo Häring Award, Germany; 2008: Gestaltungspreis der Wüstenrot Stiftung/Energieeffiziente Architektur in Deutschland, Germany

Amateur Architecture Studio

Wang Shu born in China, 1963; Wenyu Lu born in China, 1967 // Both live and work in Hangzhou // Education Wang Shu: M.Arch, Southeast University, Nanjing, 1988; Ph.D. Architecture, Tongji University, Shanghai, 2000; Wenyu Lu: B.Arch, Southeast University, Nanjing, 1989 // Affiliations Wang Shu: Head of Architecture School, China Academy of Art, Hangzhou, 2007; Wenyu Lu: Architecture School, China Academy of Art, Hangzhou, 2003 // Recent works 2005: Museum of Contemporary Art, Ningbo, China; 2006: Vertical Housing, Hangzhou, China; Five Scattered Houses, Ningbo; Ceramic House, Jinhua, China; 2007: New Academy Campus of China Academy of Art, Hangzhou // Recent publications 2007: Wang Shu, "Cultivating a Garden and a Person," *Architect*, China; 2008: Bert de Muynck, "A Small World," *Domus*, Italy; Michael Webb, "Campus Calligraphy," *The Architectural Review* 1337, UK // Recent exhibitions 2003–8: *China International Practical Exhibition of Architecture*, CIPEA, Nanjing; 2006: Chinese Pavilion, 10th International Architecture Exhibition, Venezia; *China Contemporary*, NAI, Rotterdam; 2007: *China Contemporary Architecture*, CITE, Paris // Awards 2007: Nomination, Global Sustainable Architecture Awards, France

Andrade Morettin Architects

www.andrademorettin.com
Vinicius Hernandes De Andrade born in Brazil, 1968; Marcelo Henneberg Morettin born in Brazil, 1969 // Both live and work in São Paulo // Education Vinicius Hernandes De Andrade: B.Arch, University of São Paulo, 1992; Marcelo Henneberg Morettin: B.Arch, University of São Paulo, 1991 // Affiliations Vinicius Hernandes De Andrade: Escola da Cidade, São Paulo, 2005–present, Regional Council of Architects and Engineers of São Paulo, 1992–present; Marcelo Henneberg Morettin: Regional Council of Architects and Engineers of São Paulo, 1991–present // Recent works 2004: Social housing complex, Assembléia Str., São Paulo; 2007: R.R. House, Itamambuca, Brazil; 2008: H.B. House, São Paulo; 2010: Residential complex, Fidalga Str., São Paulo; 2011: Visitors' Center of Comperj, Rio de Janeiro // Recent publications 2007: Various authors, *AV Monografías 127*, Arquitectura Viva, Spain; Michelle Galindo, *Young Architects Americas*, Daab Publishing, USA; 2008: Yoshio Futagawa, ed., *GA Houses 106*, A.D.A. Edita Publishing, Japan; Rashid Taqui, "Tropical Hideaway," *Architecture Plus* 19, United Arab Emirates // Recent exhibitions 2005: 6th International Architecture Biennial, São Paolo; 2006: *Coletivo – Arquitetura Paulista Contemporânea*, Centro Universitário Maria Antônia, São Paolo; *Jovens Arquitetos*, 5th BIAU Ibero-American Biennial of Architecture and Urbanism, Montevideo; 8th Belgrade Triennial of World Architecture, Serbia // Awards 2006: First prize, International competition for sustainable design "Galápagos," Architecture Biennale, Ecuador; 2007: First prize, International competition Living Steel, Belgium; First prize, National competition for the Capes Headquarters, Brazil; 2008: First prize in the National competition for the Visitors' Center of Comperj, Brazil

Antón García-Abril & Ensamble Studio

www.ensamble.info
Antón García-Abril born in Spain, 1969 // Lives and works in Madrid // Education European Doctorate of Architecture, ETSAM, Madrid, 2007 // Affiliations University of Texas at Dallas, 2006; Cornell University, Ithaca, USA, 2008; ETSAM, Madrid, present // Recent works 2002: Music Studies Center, Santiago de Compostela, Spain; 2007: SGAE Headquarters, Santiago de Compostela; 2009: The Museum of America, Salamanca, Spain; 2011: The Reader's House, Madrid; Cervantes Theater, México D.F.; Berklee-SGAE Tower of Music, Valencia, Spain // Recent publications 2007: Philip Jodidio, *Architecture in Spain*, Taschen, Germany; Philip Jodidio, *Architecture Now! 5*, Taschen, Germany; "Piedra al límite," *Arquitectura Viva* 113, Spain; "The Natural House," *AV Monografías 127*, Spain. 2008: Luca Molinari, ed., *Y08 The Skira Yearbook of World Architecture 2007–2008*, Skira, Italy; Carlotta Tonon, "Prove tecniche nel paesaggio," *Casabella* 767, Italy; "Architectural Practices," *El Croquis* 142, Spain; Various authors, "Fachadas," *Detail* 8, Spain; Various authors, "Iconic Headquarters," *AV Monografías* 129–130, Spain; "Small Architecture in Spain," *A+U* 456, Japan // Recent exhibitions 2008: *JAE (Spanish Young Architects)*, Arquería de los Nuevos Ministerios, Madrid; *The natural seduction of stone—Contemporary architecture of Spain*, IFEMA, Madrid; *Crudo 100%*, COAM Foundation, Madrid; 2007: *Avance de una Contingencia. Arquitectura Contemporánea en Galicia*, Galician Centre for Contemporary Art, Santiago de Compostela; *Architecture of Stone in Spain*, Marble Architecture Design 42nd Marmomacc, Verona, Italy; 2005: *Monoespacios COAM 7*, COAM, Madrid // Awards 2005: International Award for Architecture in Stone, Italy; Finalist, Spanish Architecture Prize, Spain; Finalist, European Union Prize for Contemporary Architecture Mies van der Rohe Award; Design Vanguard Prize, *Architectural Record*, USA; 2008: Spotlight: Rice Design Alliance Prize, USA; Best Architect of the Year, *Architectural Digest*, USA

Aranda\Lasch

www.arandalasch.com
Benjamin Aranda born in USA, 1973; Chris Lasch born in USA, 1972 // Both live and work in New York // Education Both M.Arch, Columbia University, New York, 1999 // Recent works 2005: Grotto, Young Architects Program, MoMA, New York; 2006: Baskets, with Terrol Dew Johnson, Artists Space, New York; OnSite: New Architecture in Spain exhibition design, MoMA, New York; 2008: Rules of Six, commissioned installation for MoMA, New York; Design Miami/ Temporary Structure, Miami // Recent publications 2005: Stephen Zacks, "Building: Digital Logic," Metropolis Magazine, USA; Peter Hall, Else/Where: Mapping, University of Minnesota Press, USA; 2006: Shumon Basar, "The 'Rithm Kings" TANK 4, UK; 2007: Thomas de Monchaux, "Math Appeal," I.D., USA; Julia Chaplin, "Design of the Times," Wallpaper, UK; 2008: Nick Clarke, "Form and Content is Collapsed Into One," ICON, UK; Markus Zehentbauer, "Rococo Rocks!" Form 219, Germany; Jonathan Lott, "Aranda/Lasch: Cabinet of Curiosity," Praxis 9: Expanding Surface, USA; Nicolai Ourosoff, "The Soul In The New Machines," New York Times, USA; Pilar Viladas, "Now Showcasing: Design Miami," New York Times Style Magazine, USA; Joseph Grima, "The Morning Line," Domus, Italy // Recent exhibitions 2005: Young Architects Program, MoMA, New York; 2006: Aranda/Lasch: Tooling, Knowlton School of Architecture, Columbus, USA; 2007: Terraswarm: Color Shift, Columbia University, New York; Young Architects Forum Exhibition, Architectural League of New York; Scripted by Purpose, FUEL Collection, Philadelphia; Figuration in Contemporary Design, Art Institute of Chicago; 2008: Design and the Elastic Mind, MoMA, New York; 11th International Architecture Exhibition, Venezia; 3rd Bienal Internacional de Arte Contemporario de Sevilla, Spain // Awards 2005: Finalist, MoMA / P.S.1 Young Architects Program, USA; 2006: Recipient, Graham Foundation Grant, USA; Recipient, NYSCA Architecture Independent Projects Grant, USA; 2007: United States Artists Fellow, Target Fellows in Architecture and Design, USA; Young Architects Forum Award, Architectural League of New York, USA

Arctangent Architecture & Design

www.arctangent.com
Kyle Chia-Kai Yang born in Taiwan, 1964 // Lives and works in Taipei // Education M.Arch, Columbia University, New York, 1992, M.S. Civil Engineering, Columbia University, New York, 1989 // Recent works 2006: Chong-ming Park, Taichung City, Taiwan; 2008: Far Eastern Telecom Building, Jhongli City, Taiwan; 2010: Stratus House, Aodi, Taiwan // Recent publications 2007: Kyle Chia-Kai Yang, "New Kung Dee Urban Instrument," Taiwan Architect 388, Taiwan; 2008: Chiakai Kyle Yang, "Children's Story Telling Park," Taiwan Architect 400, Taiwan; Chiakai Kyle Yang, "The Far Eastern Telecommunication Building," Taiwan Architect 405, Taiwan; Chiakai Kyle Yang, "The Stratus House," A+U 453, Japan; 2009: Bee Kuang-Chien, "Re-shuttle the Criteria," Taiwan Architect 410, Taiwan; Wen-Lin Fang, "Reverberation," Art Collection + Design, Taiwan // Recent exhibitions 2008: Taiwan pavilion, 11th International Architecture Exhibition, Venezia // Awards 2000 and 2004: Honorable Mention, Taiwan Architecture Award; 2008: Grand Prize, Taiwan Architecture Award

at 103

www.at103.net
Francisco Pardo born in Mexico, 1974; Julio Amezcua born in Mexico, 1974 // Both live and work in México D.F. // Education Francisco Pardo: B.Arch, Universidad Anahuac, México D.F., 1997, M.Arch, Columbia University, New York, 1999; Julio Amezcua: B.Arch, Universidad Anahuac, México D.F., 1999, M.S. Advanced Architectural Design, Columbia University, New York, 2001 // Recent works 2006: Fire Station, México D.F.; Romero House, Queretaro, Mexico; 2010: Ordos 100 House, Ordos, China // Recent publications 2008: Anya Eckbo, "Comprando una propiedad," Architectural Digest Mexico 9, Mexico; "Architects Directory 2008," Wallpaper, UK; Paolo Viloria, "Ordos 100," Celeste, Mexico; Arturo Emilio Escobar, "Bienal de Venecia 2008," Reforma-Entremuros 146, Mexico // Recent exhibitions 2005: GA Houses Project 2005, GA Gallery, Tokyo; 2007: Architecture lessons Vol. 1, Visions of Latin American Architecture, El Museo de Barrio, New York; 2008: 11th International Architecture Exhibition, Venezia; Ordos 9, Iberoamericana Gallery, México D.F. // Awards 2007: Honorary Mention, Bienal Miami+Beach, USA; Official Selection, 4th BIAU Ibero-American Biennial of Architecture and Urbanism, Lima; 2008: Selection, International Architecture Awards, Chicago Athenaeum, USA; The World's 50 Hottest Young Architecture Practices, Wallpaper, UK; Shortlist, World Architectural Festival, Barcelona, Spain; 2009: Emerging Voices lecture series, Architectural League of New York, USA

Atelier Kempe Thill

www.atelierkempethill.com
Andre Kempe born in German Democratic Republic (GDR), 1968; Oliver Thill born in GDR, 1971 // Both live and work in Rotterdam // Education Both Dipl.Ing. Arch., TU Dresden, 1996 // Affiliations both TU Delft, 1999–2003, Academie van Bouwkunst Arnhem, Netherlands, 2003–4, Academie van Bouwkunst Rotterdam, 2005–6; Andre Kempe: Young European Architects, 2003 // Recent works 2006: Franz Liszt Concert Hall, Raiding, Austria; 2007: Apartment block, Amsterdam-Ijburg, Netherlands; 2008: Museum for Traditional Crafts, Veenhuizen, Netherlands; Information Centre, Ministry of Justice, Rotterdam; Town Houses in Osdorp, Amsterdam; 2012: Remodeling 1100 Apartments Uithoorn, Netherlands // Recent publications 2004: Naomi Shibata, "Young Architects in the Netherlands," A+U, Japan; Phaidon Editors, The Phaidon Atlas of Contemporary World Architecture, Phaidon Press, UK; 2007: Dirk Meyhöfer, Made in Germany: Best of Contemporary Architecture, Verlagshaus Braun, Germany; Tracy Metz, "Atelier Kempe Thill finds ways to bring together continuity and innovation," Architectural Record, USA; 2008: Andre Kempe and Oliver Thill, "Klassizismus für die Ikea-Generation," Bauwelt, Germany; Francesca Chiorino, "Museo e centro espositivo, Veenhuizen," Casabella, Italy // Recent exhibitions 2004: Atelier Kempe Thill—Specific Neutrality, Aedes Galerie, Berlin; Europan 7—NOW, between past and future, NAI, Rotterdam; De Grote Verbouwing, NAI; 2005: Atelier Kempe Thill—prototypes, Architekten Akademie, Dresden; 2007: Holland—Italy, Maxxi, Roma // Awards 2003: Bauwelt Award, Germany; 2005: Detail Award, Germany; Rotterdam–Maaskant Prize for Young Architects, Netherlands; 2007: Design Vanguard Prize, Architectural Record, USA; 2008: Architekturpreis des Landes Burgenland, Austria

Bernaskoni

www.bernaskoni.com
Boris Bernaskoni born in USSR, 1977 // Lives and works in Moskva // Education M.Arch, Moskva Academy of Architecture, 2000 // Affiliations Founder and Co-Editor-in-Chief, Architectural Materials and A3, Russian Federation, 1999–present // Recent works 2000: Place Memorial on Lubyanskaya Square, Moskva; Urupinsk Word Development Project, Urupinsk, Russian Federation; 2001: Krasnaya Presnya Stadium, Moskva; 2002: Tetris Living Towers, Moskva; Karabikha Hotel, Yaroslavl, Russian Federation; 2003: BBDO Office, Moskva; Mediacity, Moskva; 2004: Ozerna village, near Moskva; 2008: Perm Museum, Perm, Russian Federation; Matrex Building, Moskva; Russia Pavilion, Shanghai // Recent publications 2004: Rob Gregory, "Young Architects in Moscow," The Architectural Review 1287, UK; Federica Patti, "Mosca: centro allargato," Abitare 444, Italy; Alexei Muratov, "From S to XL (Villandscape)," Project Russia 33, Russian Federation; 2008: Alessandro De Magistris, "Intervista a Irina Korobina," Area 96, Italy; Friederike Mayer, "Perm Museum XXI," Bauwelt 25, Germany // Recent exhibitions 2003: Presidents Cabinet 2020, 8th Arch-Moskva Exhibition; 2006: New Moscow 4, Mendrisio, Switzerland; 2008: 1st Moskva Biennale of Architecture; Russian pavillion, 11th International Architecture Exhibition, Venezia // Awards 2003: Winner, Best Work of Architecture, Moskva Review, Russian Federation; Nominee, Golden Section, Russian Federation

Bevk Perović Arhitekti

www.bevkperovic.com
Matija Bevk born in Slovenia, 1972; Vasa J. Perović born in Yugoslavia, 1965 // Both live and work in Ljubljana // Education Matija Bevk: B.Arch, University of Ljubljana, 1999; Vasa J. Perović: B.Arch, University of Belgrade, 1992, M.Arch, Berlage Institute of Architecture, Rotterdam, 1994 // Recent works 2006: Student Housing, Ljubljana; House H, Ljubljana; Faculty of Mathematics, Ljubljana; 2007: Congress Centre Brdo, Kranj, Slovenia; Non-profit Housing, Cesta v Gorice, Ljubljana; Non-profit Housing Poljane, Maribor, Slovenia; House HB, Pirnice, Slovenia; 2008: House D, Ljubljana // Recent publications 2006: Andrej Hrausky, "Connected," Architektur Aktuell 7/8, Austria; 2007: Hiroshi Kohno, "Timber Construction," Detail, Japan; Tadej Glazar, "Living and Learning," Mark 6, Netherlands; 2008: Luka Skansi and Francesca Chiorino, "Bevk Perović Un Profilo," Casabella 771, Italy // Recent exhibitions 2007: Sixpack, Galerija Mak, Ljubljana; Arhitektura Inventura 2004/2006, Cankarjev Dom, Ljubljana; 2008: Slovenia Architecture_The Masters & the Scene, Architektur im Ringturm XVII, Vienna; Contemporary Architecture in Croatia & Slovenia, Harvard University Graduate School of Design, Cambridge, USA; Balkanology: New Architecture and Urban Phenomena in South-Eastern Europe, Swiss Architecture Museum, Basel // Awards 2005: Plecnik Prize for Architecture, Slovenia; Preseren prize for architectural production in 2002–4, Slovenia; 2006: Kunstpreis Berlin, Germany; 2007: Emerging Architect Special Mention, European Union Prize for Contemporary Architecture Mies van der Rohe Award; Plecnik Prize for Architecture, Slovenia

BIG Architects

www.big.dk
Bjarke Ingels born in Denmark, 1974 // Lives and works in København // Education Architecture diploma, Royal Academy of Arts, København, 1999 // Affiliations Rice University School of Architecture, Houston, USA, 2005; Harvard University Graduate School of Design, Cambride, USA, 2007; MAA Danish Architecture Association, present; Jury of European 8 Norway and Cyprus, present; Danish Cultural Ministry Educational Council, present; Arkitektens Forlag Editorial Committee, present; Henning Larsen Prize Committee, present; København X Architectural Council, present // Recent works MAR Maritime Youth House, København, 2004; VM VM Houses, Ørestad, Denmark, 2005; MTN Mountain Dwellings, København, 2008; XPO Danish Pavilion, Shanghai, 2010; SØF Danish Maritime Museum, Elsinore, Denmark, 2011 // Recent publications 2008: Ulyana Olhovskaya, Sovremenny interior, Russian Federation; Lorenzo Covadonga, Arquitectura Viva, Spain; Jin Seon Park and Hyo Eun Yu, "Mountain Dwellings," Details, Korea; Maria Shollenbarger, "Ghetto Fabulous," Interior Design, USA; Sarah Balmond, "High Hopes," Monocle, UK // Recent exhibitions 2004: Italian pavillion, 9th International Architecture Exhibition, Venezia; 2007: Copenhagen Experiments, Storefront for Art and Architecture, New York; European Union Prize for Contemporary Architecture Mies Van Der Rohe Award Exhibition, Paris // Awards 2004: Golden Lion, 9th International Architecture Exhibition, Venezia, Italy; 2005: Forum AID Award, Sweden; European Prize For Urban Public Spaces, European Union

Tatiana Bilbao

www.tatianabilbao.com
Tatiana Bilbao born in Mexico, 1972 // Lives and works in México D.F. // Education B.Arch, Universidad Iberoamericana, México D.F., 1996 // Affiliations Colegio de Arquitectos de Mexico, 1999 // Recent works 2007: Casa Observatorio, Roca Blanca, Mexico; 2008: Estudio Explanada, México D.F.; Mexican pavillion design, Zaragoza Exhibition, Zaragoza, Spain; Exhibition design, Mexico Expected/ Unexpected, Maison Rouge, Paris; 2012: Housing and Cultural Center, Guadalajara, Mexico // Recent publications 2007: Joseph Grima, "Broken Topography," Domus 899, Italy; 2008: Robert Klanten and Lukas Feireiss, eds., Strike a Pose!: Eccentric Architecture and Spectacular Spaces, Die Gestalten Verlag, Germany; Cathelijne Nuijsink, "Viewpoint: The One and Only Tatiana Bilbao," Mark 17, Netherlands // Recent exhibitions 2008: Tlatelolco and the localized negotiation of future imaginaries, New Museum, New York; Mexican pavilion, 11th International Architecture Exhibition, Venezia // Awards 2007: Design Vanguard Prize, Architectural Record, USA

Ueli Brauen + Doris Wälchli architectes

www.bw-arch.ch
Ueli Brauen born in Switzerland, 1954; Doris Wälchli born in Switzerland, 1963 // Both live and work in Lausanne // Education Ueli Brauen: Diploma in civil engineering, École d'ingénieurs, Burgdorf, Switzerland, 1976, Diploma in architecture, Swiss Federal Institute of Technology (EPF), Lausanne, 1988; Doris Wälchli: Diploma in architecture, EPF, Lausanne, 1988 // Affiliations Ueli Brauen: École d'ingénieurs de Fribourg, Switzerland, 1990–95, Accademia di Mendrisio, Switzerland, 1999–2000, University of Pennsylvania, Philadelphia, 2000, École d'architecture de Strasbourg, 2002–3, Accademia di Mendrisio, 2004–5, École d'architecture de Nancy, 2005; Doris Wälchli: ETH Zürich, 1998–2000, University of Pennsylvania, 2000, Accademia di Mendrisio, 2004–5 // Recent works 2002: Headquarters of the Interparliamentary Union, Geneva; 2003: Swiss Embassy, La Paz; 2005: Swiss Embassy, Praha; 2008: Multifunctionnal Center for International Olympic Committee (IOC) Headquarters, Lausanne; 2009: Langensand Bridge, Luzern, Switzerland; 2012: Swiss Embassy, Moskva // Recent publications 2007: Heinz Wirt, ed., Brauen + Wälchli, Quart Verlag, Switzerland; 2008: Manuel Bieler, "Shopping mall, Lausanne," A10 new European architecture 23, Netherlands; Christoph Wieser, "Luftkissenarchitektur, Geschäftshaus 'La Miroiterie' in Lausanne von Brauen + Wälchli," Werk, bauen + wohnen 4, Switzerland; // Recent exhibitions 2007: Ueli Brauen + Doris Wälchli, 1999–2004 et projets récents, École nationale supérieure d'architecture de Grenoble, France, Espace Malraux, Chambéry, and Galerie Chambre Claire, Annecy; Carte Blanche, F'ar (Forum d'architectures), Lausanne; Distinction Romande d'Architecture, Architekturforum, Zürich; 2008: Ueli Brauen + Doris Wälchli 1999–2004 et projets récents, École d'ingénieurs et d'architectes, Fribourg // Awards 2000: Distinction Vaudoise d'architecture (Centre d'enseignement professionnel), Switzerland; ATU Prix, Regional Trains Maintenance Shed, Switzerland; 2003: European Parking Association Award, Germany; 2004: Best of (Swiss) Solar Prize, Switzerland

Brückner & Brückner

www.architektenbrueckner.de
Christian Brückner born in Germany, 1971; Klaus-Peter Brückner born in Czechoslovakia, 1939; Peter Brückner born in Germany, 1962 // Christian Brückner: lives and works in Würzburg; Klaus-Peter and Peter Brückner: live and work in Tirschenreuth // Education Christian Brückner: Architectural studies, Staatlichen Akademie der bildenden Künste Stuttgart, 2000; Klaus-Peter Brückner: Civil Engineering studies, University of Applied Sciences Regensburg, 1964; Peter Brückner: Architectural studies, TU München, 1990 // Affiliations Christian Brückner: University of Applied Sciences München (HM), 2003, Bund Deutscher Architekten (BDA), Stuttgart, 2005, FH Würzburg, 2006, Vitra Design Museum, Weil am Rhein, Germany, 2006–7, FH Regensburg, 2007; Peter Brückner: HM, 2003, BDA, 2004, TU Weimar, 2005, Vitra Design Museum, 2006–7, FH Regensburg, 2007, Deutsche Gesellschaft für christliche Kunst, München, 2008 // Recent works 2003: Addition to St. Peter's Church, Wenzenbach, Germany; 2004: Umbau der Spielbank, Bad Kissingen, Germany; Ongoing: Erweiterung Wallfahrtsmuseum/Neue Schatzkammer, Altötting, Germany; Neubau Standortkasino Siemens, Amberg, Germany // Recent publications 2005: Till Wöhler, Neue Architektur Sakralbauten, Verlagshaus Braun, Germany; Nicolette Baumeister, Architektur neues Bayern, Verlagshaus Braun; 2006: Architekten Profile 2006/2007, Birkhäuser, Switzerland; Architektur in Deutschland 2005, Karl Krämer Verlag, Germany; Best architects 07, Zinnobergruen, Germany; Ruth Slavid, Wood Houses, Laurence King, UK // Recent exhibitions 2004: German pavillion, 9th International Architecture Exhibition, Venezia; 2005: Architektur an der Grenze, UIA Congress Istanbul; Neue Architektur in Bayern, Ljubljana; 2007: Museen – u. Ausstellungsbauten in Bayern seit 2000, Kunsthaus Marktoberdorf and Luftmuseum Amberg, Germany // Awards 2006: BDA Regionalpreis Franken, Germany; 2007: Lobende Erwähnung Natursteinpreis, Germany; Deutscher Holzbaupreis, Germany; Best architects 08 Award Düsseldorf, Germany; 2008: Second Place, Offices/ Administration Buildings, contract-world.award, Germany

Bureau Alexander Brodsky

www.brod.it

Alexander Brodsky born in USSR, 1955 // Lives and works in Moskva // Education M.Arch, Moskva Architectural Institute, 1978 // Recent works 2005: Private House, Klyazminskoe Vodohranilishe Resort, Moskovskaya Oblast; 2006: Tarusa House, Kalugaskaya Oblast; 2007: Winzavod Arts Center, Moskva; 2008: IMHO VI Office, Moskva // Recent publications 2006: Bart Goldhoorn et al., "Alexander Brodsky," *Project Russia* 41, Russian Federation; 2007: "Alexandr Brodsky," *Lotus International* 130, Italy; 2008: Carlos Seoane, "Alexander Brodsky," *Obradoiro* 33, Spain; Umberto Zanetti, "Il te nero di Sasha," *Interni* 47, Italy; Ingerid Helsing Almaas and Einar Bjarki Malmquist, "Tegningens virke-lighet," *Arkitektur N* 4, Norway; Phaidon Editors, *The Phaidon Atlas of 21st Century World Architecture*, UK // Recent exhibitions 2005: *Office of the Future*, Red October, Moskva; 2006: Russian pavillion, 10th International Architecture Exhibition, Venezia; *Russia!* Guggenheim Bilbao, Spain; 2007: *Moscopolis*, Espace Louis Vuitton, Paris; *BornHouse*, Vhutemas Gallery, Moskva; 2008: Moskva Biennale of Architecture, Russian Federation; *Russian Palladianism*, Museum of Architecture, Moskva // Awards 2001: First Prize, Milano Europa 2000, Palazzo della Triennale, Italy; 2002: Best building, Grand-Prix of architectural critics, 7th Arch-Moskva Exhibition, Russian Federation; 2004: Best Interior, 9th Arch-Moskva Exhibition, Russian Federation; 2005: Grand-Prix of architectural critics, 10th Arch-Moskva Exhibition, Russian Federation

Candalepas Associates

www.candalepas.com.au

Evangelos Candalepas born in Australia, 1967 // Lives and works in Sydney // Education B.Arch, University of Technology, Sydney, 1992 // Affiliations University of New South Wales, 2004–present; Australian Institute of Architects, 1994–present // Recent works 2007: Lamia, Marrickville, Australia; Messy House, Glebe, Australia; Propylaea, Pyrmont, Australia; 2008: All Saints Grammar School, Belmore, Australia; 61 York Street, Sydney; Pindari, Randwick, Australia; Kensington House, Sydney; Paddington House, Sydney // Recent publications 2007: Davina Jackson, *Next Wave: Emerging Talents in Australian Architecture*, Thames & Hudson, UK; David Neustein, "Messy House," *Architectural Review* 101, UK; David Neustein, "Double Barrel," *Houses* 59, Australia; 2008: John de Manincor, "61 York Street," *The Architectural Review* 106, UK; Samantha Spurr, "Heaven in the Detail," *Monument* 82, Australia // Recent exhibitions 2005: *Young Architects Exhibition*, Customs House, Sydney; 2006: *Supermodels*, Surry Hills, Sydney; 2008: 11th International Architecture Exhibition, Venezia; *Venice Biennale New Australian Pavilion*, Di Stasio Ideas Competition, Bulleen, Australia // Awards 2005: Byera Hadley Travelling Scholarship, Australia; 2005, 2006, & 2007: AIA NSW Chapter Architecture Award, Australia; 2008: Shortlist, Commercial Category, World Architecture Festival Barcelona, Spain; AIA NSW Chapter Architecture Award, Australia; Commendation, AIA NSW Chapter Architecture Award, Australia; Shortlist, Di Stasio Ideas Competition, Australia

Cassandra Complex

www.cassandracomplex.com.au

Cassandra Fahey born in Australia, 1972 // Lives and works in Melbourne // Education B.A., RMIT University, Melbourne, 1995; B.Arch, RMIT University, 1999 // Affiliations Royal Australian Institute of Architects (RAIA), present // Recent works 2007: The Smith Great Aussie Home, Blackrock, Australia; New Gold Mountain, Melbourne, Australia // Recent publications 2006: Leon Van Schaik, *Design City Melbourne*, Wiley, Australia // Recent exhibitions 2006: *Pavilions for New Architecture*, Monash Museum of Modern Art, Clayton, Australia // Awards 2007: RAIA Marion Mahoney Award for Interior Architecture, Australia; RAIA National Commendation for Interior Architecture, Australia; RAIA Residential Architecture Award, Australia; 2006: RAIA Institutional New Architecture Award, Australia; RAIA Commercial Architecture Award, Australia; 2004: RAIA National Interior Architecture Award, Australia; RAIA Residential Architecture Award, Australia; Design Institute of Australia, Interior Design Award, Australia

CEBRA

www.cebra.info

Mikkel Frost born in Denmark, 1971; Kolja Nielsen born in Denmark, 1968; Carsten Primdahl born in Denmark, 1970 // All live and work in Århus // Education Mikkel Frost and Kolja Nielsen: M.Arch, Århus School of Architecture, 1996; Carsten Primdahl: M.Arch, Århus School of Architecture, 1998 // Affiliations Mikkel Frost: Danish Art Society, København, 1998–present, Danish Ministry of Culture, København, 1999, Danish architecture schools, academic censor, 2001–present, AA (Academic Architects union), 2001–present; Kolja Nielsen: Århus School of Architecture, 2002, External member of School council on the Århus School of Architecture, 2004–6, Danish architecture schools, academic censor, 2006–present; Carsten Primdahl: Århus School of Architecture, 1999– present, Danish architecture schools, academic censor, 2003–present, AA, 2003–present, Danish Art Society, 2005–present // Recent works 2007: Fuglsang Næs Apartments, Herning, Denmark; 2008: Multimedia House, Århus, Denmark; Gersonsvej, Gentofte, Denmark; Pinball House, Silkeborg, Denmark; 2010: Villa Strata, Kolding, Denmark; KKG School, Kristiansand, Norway; 2011: Isbjerget (Iceberg), in collaboration with JDS, SeARCH, and Louis Paillard, Århus // Recent publications 2005: Pablo Vallejo Urresta, "CEBRA," *ION+ Magazine*, Spain; 2006: "School Extension, Gentofte," *A10* 10, Netherlands; 2008: Kjeld Vindum, "Arkitekturbiennale," *Arkitekten* 12, Denmark; "JDS + CEBRA Win Competition for a Housing Complex in Aarhus, Denmark," *A+U* 454, Japan // Recent exhibitions 2006: Danish pavilion, 10th International Architecture Exhibition, Venezia; 2008: Danish pavilion, 11th International Architecture Exhibition, Venezia; Danish pavilion, EXPO2010 Shanghai, China, 2008 // Awards 2006: The Golden Lion, 10th International Architecture Exhibition, Venezia; Selected, European Union Prize for Contemporary Architecture Mies van der Rohe Award; 2008: Nykredit Architecture Prize, Denmark

CJ Lim/Studio 8 Architects

www.cjlim-studio8.com

CJ Lim born in Malaysia, 1964 // Lives and works in London // Education AA Dipl., Architectural Association, London, 1987 // Affiliations The Bartlett, University College London, 1993–present // Recent works 2007: Daejeon Urban Renaissance, Daejeon, Republic of Korea; Parkway Iconic Bridge, Sheffield Parkway, UK; Birnbeck Island Mixed-Use Development, Weston-Super-Mare, UK; Brockholes Wetland Vistor Centre, Lancashire, UK; Sustainable Office Building, Preston, UK; MOCAPE Museum of Contemporary Arts + Planning, Shenzhen, China; 2008: STU Campus, Shenzhen; Sichuan Earthquake Memorial, Sichuan; NanYu Shopping Park, Shenzhen; Magok Waterfront, Seoul; GuangMing Sustainable Centre Park, Shenzhen // Recent publications 2003: CJ Lim, *How Green is your Garden?*, Wiley Academy, UK and USA; 2005: CJ Lim, *Neo Architecture: CJ Lim*, Images Publishing, Australia; 2006: CJ Lim, *Virtually Venice*, The British Council, UK; 2008: Zhang HongXing and Lauren Parker, eds., *China Design Now*, Victoria and Albert Museum, UK; Howard Watson, "CJ Lim Profile," *New Urban China (Architectural Design)*, John Wiley & Sons; Annabela Chan, "Through the Looking Glass," *EastWest Hong Kong* 25, China // Recent exhibitions 2004: British pavilion, 9th International Architecture Exhibition, Venezia; 2006: *On The Threshold*, Victoria and Albert Museum, London; 2008: *New Trends in Architecture in Europe + Asia Pacific 2008 – 2010*, Art Front Gallery, Tokyo; *China Design Now*, Cincinnati Art Museum, USA, and Victoria and Albert Museum, London; *Summer Exhibition 2008*, Royal Academy of Arts, London // Awards 2006: Grand Architecture Prize, AJ/Bovis Lend Lease Awards for Architecture, UK

Dellekamp Arquitectos

http://dellekamparq.com
Derek Dellekamp born in Mexico, 1971 // Lives and works in México D.F. // Education B.Arch., Universidad Iberoamericana, México D.F., 1997 // Affiliations Mxdf Urban Research Center, México D.F., 2004–present // Recent works 2007: Hotel Hacienda De Cortes, Cuernavaca, Mexico; Ongoing: La Capital, México D.F.; Circle Sanctuary, Cerro del Obisco, Mexico; Gratitude Open Chapel, Lagunillas, Mexico; Villa No. 14, Ordos, China // Recent publications 2005: Elaine Louie, "Buildings That Don't Forget Air and Space," *New York Times*, USA; Choire Sicha, "Architects of Mexico City," *New York Times*, USA; 2008: Aaron Betsky et al., *Out There: Architecture Beyond Building*, Vol. 4, Marsilio, Italy; Josep Lluis Mateo, ed., *Global Housing Projects: 25 Buildings Since 1980*, Actar, Spain // Recent exhibitions 2005: *Mexico City Dialogues: New Architectural Practices*, Center for Architecture, New York; 2008: Mexico pavilion, 11th International Architecture Exhibition, Venezia // Awards 2004: Honorary mention, VIII Architecture Bienal Mexico; 2006: First place, Environmental and Education Park in Chapultepec, Mexico, with Taller de Operaciones Ambientales; 2008: Best New Global Design, International Architecture Awards, USA

Paulo David

http://paulodavidarquitecto.com
Paulo David born in Portugal, 1959 // Lives and works in Funchal // Education Architecture diploma, Technical University of Lisbon, 1989 // Recent works 2004: Casa das Mudas Art Center, Calheta, Madeira, Portugal; Salinas Swimming Pools and Promenade, Câmara de Lobos, Madeira; 2006: Salinas Restaurant and Garden, Câmara de Lobos; 2007: Casa Funchal 05, Funchal, Madeira; 2008: São Vicente Caves, São Vicente, Madeira // Recent publications 2007: David Cohn, *Centro Das Artes – Casa Das Mudas*, Architectural Record, USA; Jeong Seon Lee, "Creative Perspective," *C3*, Republic of Korea; Luis Fernández-Galiano, "Piedra al Límite," *Arquitectura Viva*, Spain; Nobuyuki Yoshida, "Size and Architects in Portugal," *A+U* 439, Japan; 2008: Francesco dal Co, "Abitazioni Unifamiliari," *Casabella* 765, Italy // Recent exhibitions 2008: 5th European Biennial of Landscape Architecture, Barcelona // Awards 2005: Enor Prize, Portugal; European Union Prize for Contemporary Architecture Mies van der Rohe Award; 2007: International Award for Architecture in Stone, Italy; FAD Award, Spain

Durbach Block Architects

http://durbachblock.com
Camilla Block born South Africa, 1966; Neil Durbach born in South Africa, 1954 // Both live and work in Sydney // Education Camilla Block: B.Arch, University of Sydney, 1991; Neil Durbach: B.Arch, University of Cape Town, 1978 // Affiliations Camilla Block: RAIA SA Chapter, 2001, North Sydney Design Excellence Awards, 2006; Neil Durbach: University of New South Wales, 2005 and 2008, Creative Director, International Architecture Exhibition, Venezia, 2008 // Recent works 2002: Commonwealth Place, Canberra; 2003: Spry House, Sydney; 2004: Holman House, Sydney; 2005: Brick Pit Ring, Sydney; 2006: Hrdlicka House, Sydney; 2007: Sussan Sportsgirl Headquarters, Melbourne; 2008: McHugh House, Browns Mountain, Australia // Recent publications 2006: Raul A. Barreneche, *Pacific Modern*, Rizzoli, USA; 2008: Phaidon Editors, *The Phaidon Atlas of 21st Century World Architecture*, Phaidon Press, UK; Joseph Buch, *Architecture Inspired by Australia*, Mint Publishing, UK // Recent exhibitions 2004: Australian pavilion, 9th International Architecture Exhibition, Venezia; *Process*, Danks Street Gallery, Sydney; *Changing Spaces*, Elizabeth Bay House, Sydney; 2008: Australian pavilion, 11th International Architecture Exhibition, Venezia // Awards 2003: RAIA ACT Urban Design Award, Australia; 2004: NSW AILA Excellence Award for Design in Landscape, Australia; The National Robin Boyd Award, Australia; 2005: RAIA Wilkinson Award for Housing, Australia; 2006: RAIA Lloyd Rees Civic Design Award, Australia

Durisch + Nolli Architetti

www.durischnolli.ch
Pia Durisch born in Switzerland, 1964; Aldo Nolli born in Italy, 1959 // Both live and work in Lugano // Education Pia Durisch: Architecture degree, ETH Zürich, 1988; Aldo Nolli: Architecture degree, ETH Zürich, 1983 // Affiliations Both Swiss Architects Federation, present; Swiss Society of Engineers and Architects (SIA), present; Ticino Corporation of Engineers and Architects, present // Recent works 2005: M.A.X. Museo, Chiasso, Switzerland; 2006: Riqualificazione Urbana, Spazio Officina, Chiasso; 2008: Ampliamento Scuola Media e Doppia Palestra, Riva San Vitale, Switzerland; 2009: SSIC Professional Center, Gordola, Switzerland // Recent publications 2006: Mercedes Daguerre, "Generare un luogo," *Casabella* 745, Italy; Alberto Alessi, "Architetture di passaggio," *Città*, Italy; 2007: Giuliano Tedesco and Shigeo Fukuda, "Il museo e il suocero giapponese," *Abitare* 469, Italy // Recent exhibitions 2000: *Living Architecture: The Architecture of Durisch + Nolli*, I-Space Gallery, Chicago; 2006: *Architetture di Pasaggio*, Istituto Svizzero di Roma, Italy; 2007: *Swiss Architecture*, University of Wuppertal, Germany // Awards 2004: Nomination for Best of Europe Office, AIT Intelligente Architektur, Germany; 2007: Best Public Building, SIA, Switzerland; 2008: First place, Nuovo Tribunale Federale Penale e Nuovo Pretorio, Switzerland

Keller Easterling

www.panix.com/~keller/
Keller Easterling born in the USA, 1959 // Lives and works in New York City // Education B.S., Princeton University, USA, 1981; M.Arch, Princeton University, 1985 // Affiliations Yale University School of Architecture, New Haven, USA, 1990–present // Recent works 2008: White House Redux, Competition, New York; 2010: Ordos 100 Villa, Ordos, China // Recent publications 2005: Keller Easterling, *Enduring Innocence: Global Architecture and its Political Masquerades*, MIT Press, USA; 2006: Thomas de Monchaux, "The Age of Innocence," *Architects Newspaper*, USA; 2007: Gregory Clancey, "Enduring Innocence," *Technology and Culture* 48, USA; Keller Easterling, "Zone," *Visionary Power*, NAI, Netherlands; 2008: Mimi Zeiger, "Ordos or Ardor," *Architects Newspaper*, USA; Keller Easterling, "Only the Many," *Log*, USA; Keller Easterling, "Absolute Submission," *Urban China*, China // Recent exhibitions 2007: *Envisioning Power*, "Corporate City," Internationale Architecture Biennale Rotterdam; 2008: *Some True Stories*, Storefront for Art and Architecture, New York; *13:100 Thirteen New York Architects Design for Ordos*, Architectural League of New York; *Cable*, Installation, Storefront for Art and Architecture; *Floor*, Installation, Storefront for Art and Architecture // Awards 2006: Fellowship, New York State Council for the Arts, USA; Gustav Ranis International Book Award, Yale University, USA; Grant, Graham Foundation for Advanced Studies in the Fine Arts, USA; 2009: Cornell Society for the Humanities Fellowship, USA

ecosistema urbano

www.ecosistemaurbano.com
Belinda Tato born in Spain, 1971; Jose Luis Vallejo born in Spain, 1971 // Both live and work in Madrid // Education Both Architectural diploma, The Bartlett, University College London, 1997; M.Arch, ETSAM, Madrid, 1999 // Affiliations Jose Luis Vallejo: ETSAM, Madrid, present // Recent works 2006: Eco Boulevard, Phase Two, Madrid; 2009: Meteorological Museum, Madrid; Master Plan for Fuencarral, Madrid; Water Park, Madrid; 2010: Madrid Pavilion design, Expo 2010, Shanghai // Recent publications 2005: Javier Arpa, "In Common II," a+t, Spain; 2006: ecosistema urbano, Monoespacios 8, Association of Architects of Madrid, Spain; 2007: "España 2007 Yearbook," AV Monografias 123–24, Spain; 2008: Emmie Vos, ed., Europan 9: The Sustainable City and New Public Spaces, Distributed Art Publishers, USA; 2009: a+t editors, "The Public Chance: New Urban Landscapes," a+t, Spain // Recent exhibitions 2008: Italian pavilion, International Architecture Exhibition, Venezia; Urban Ecologies, Spazio Gallery, Milan; Spanish pavilion, Expo Zaragoza, Spain; 2009: The Future Has Arrived: Architecture for a Sustainable World, Louisiana Museum of Contemporary Art, København; Silence, Biennial of the Canary Islands, Spain; Urban Hypothesis: Research About Contemporary Design, Circulo de Bellas Artes, Madrid // Awards 2005: European Acknowledgement Award, Holcim Foundation for Sustainable Construction, Switzerland; 2006: Ecology and Sustainability Research Cluster Award, Architectural Association and the Environments, UK; 2007: Nomination, Emerging European Architect, European Union Prize for Contemporary Architecture Mies van der Rohe Award; First place, AR Award for emerging architecture in London, UK; 2008: Arquia-Proxima Award, Best Young Office in Spain, Caja de Arquitectos, Spain; Silver Award for Europe, Holcim Foundation for Sustainable Construction, Switzerland

Estudio Teddy Cruz

Teddy Cruz born in Guatemala, 1962 // Lives and works in San Diego // Education B.Arch, California Polytechnic State University at San Luis Obispo, 1987; MDesS, Harvard University Graduate School of Design, Cambridge, USA, 1997 // Affiliations American Academy in Rome, 1991–present; University of California San Diego, 2005–present; Julius Shulman Institute, Los Angeles, 2005–present // Recent works 2005: Manufactured Sites, Tijuana, Mexico; 2007: Hudson 2+4, Hudson, New York; 2008: From The Global Border to the Border Neighborhood mural-narrative, New York and San Luis Obispo, USA; LA/SD/TJ Photo-construction, MoMA, New York; US pavilion, 11th International Architecture Exhibition, Venezia // Recent publications 2008: Michael Sorkin, ed., Indefensible Space : The Architecture of the National Insecurity State, Routledge, USA; Barry Bergdoll and Peter Christiansen, Home Delivery: Fabricating the Modern Dwelling, MoMA, USA; John Beardsley, "The Solution is not Architectural: Housing Problems of the Poor in Tijuana," Harvard Design Magazine, USA; Aaron Betsky, Out There: Architecture Beyond Building: 11th International Architecture Exhibition La Biennale di Venezia, Vol. 3, Marsilio, Italy // Recent exhibitions 2008: On Cities—Maps, Cars, People and Environments in the Urban Environment, Arkitekturmuseet, Stockholm; Home Delivery: Fabricating the Modern Dwelling, MoMA, New York; Worlds Away: New Suburban Landscapes, Walker Art Center, Minneapolis, USA; US pavilion, 11th International Architecture Exhibition, Venezia // Awards 2001: Young Architects Forum Award, Architectural League of New York, USA; Progressive Architecture Award, Architect Magazine, USA; 2004: Stirling Prize, Canadian Centre for Architecture, Van Alen Institute, New York, and London School of Economics and Political Science, UK; 2006: Emerging Voices National Design Award, Architectural League of New York, USA; 2007: Second Prize, International Architecture Biennale Rotterdam, Netherlands

FAR frohn&rojas

www.f-a-r.net
Marc Frohn born in Germany, 1976; Mario Rojas born in Germany, 1973 // Marc Frohn: Lives and works in Köln and Los Angeles; Mario Rojas: Lives and works in Santiago // Education Marc Frohn: M.Arch, Rice University, Houston, USA, 2004; Mario Rojas: Diploma, RWTH Aachen University, Germany // Affiliations Marc Frohn: SCI-Arc, Los Angeles, 2007–present; Mario Rojas: UNAB, Santiago, 2007–present // Recent works 2007: Wall House, Santiago; House in Heat, prototype; 2 in 1, Köln // Recent publications 2007: Beatrice Galilee, "Part Tent, Part Home," ICON, UK; "Beyond the Wall," The Architectural Review, UK; Laura Bossi, "An Interwoven Diamond," Domus 908, Italy; Marc Frohn, "Klimazwiebel," Arch+ 184, Germany; 2008: Jeannette Plaut, "Record Houses 2008," Architectural Record, USA; Marc Frohn, "Wall House," IW Magazine 62, Taiwan; Gae Aulenti and David Adjaye, "SOS Abitare," Abitare 482, Italy; "Casa Wall," Arquitectura Viva 127, Spain; Patricio Mardones Hiche and Marc Frohn, "Where the sun never sets," C3 283, South Korea; Luca Molinari, Y08 The Skira Yearbook of World Architecture 2007–2008, Skira, Italy; Robert Klanten and Lukas Feireiss, ed., Strike a Pose!: Eccentric Architecture and Spectacular Spaces, Die Gestalten Verlag, Germany // Recent exhibitions 2006: German pavillon, 10th International Architecture Exhibition, Venezia; 2007: AR Award for Emerging Architecture, Berlin, Köln, and Seoul; Emerging Architecture, RIBA, London; Convertible City (Formen der Verdichtung und Entgrenzung), KAP Forum, Köln; 2008: Chilean pavilion, 11th International Architecture Exhibition, Venezia; EUTOPIA, Chile, architecture and development, Museu da Casa Brasileira, São Paulo; 2009: DAM Preis für Architektur in Deutschland 2008, Deutsches Architektur Museum (DAM), Frankfurt am Main // Awards 2007: AR Award for Emerging Architecture, UK; Förderpreis des Landes Nordrhein-Westfalen für junge Künstlerinnen und Künstler, Germany; 2008: Reiners-Stiftung Architecture Award, Germany; 2009: DETAIL Prize, ArchitekturXport, Germany

FAT

http://fashionarchitecturetaste.com
Sean Griffiths born in the UK, 1966; Charles Holland born in the UK, 1969; Sam Jacob born in he UK, 1970 // All live and work in London // Education Sean Griffiths: Dip. Arch, Polytechnic of Central London, 1991; Charles Holland: Dip. Arch, The Bartlett, University College London (UCL), 1996; Sam Jacob: Dip. Arch, The Bartlett, UCL, 1995 // Recent works 2005: Museum of Croydon, London; 2006: San Gerado, Camber Sands, UK; Islington Square, Manchester; 2007: Sint Lucas Art Academy, Boxtel, Netherlands; Peyton & Byrne Bakery, London; Heals Restaurant, London; 2008: KesselsKramer Outlet, London; Heerlijkheid Hoogvliet, Netherlands; Paradise Pavilion, Liverpool 1, Liverpool // Recent publications 2007: Crimson Architectural Historians and Felix Rottenberg, WiMBY! Hoogvliet: Future, Past and Present of a New Town, NAi Publishers, Netherlands; Robert Klanten and Lukas Feireiss, eds., Strike A Pose!: Eccentric Architecture and Spectacular Spaces, Die Gestalten Verlag, Germany; Luca Molinari, Y08 The Skira Yearbook of World Architecture 2007–2008, Skira, Italy; Kieran Long, Hatch: The New Architectural Generation, Laurence King, UK // Recent exhibitions 2005: 40 Under 40, Victoria and Albert Museum, London; 2006: All You Can Eat, Stroom Den Haag; In a Lonely Place, RIBA, London; 2007: Gritty Brits: New London Architecture, Carnegie Museum of Art, Pittsburgh, USA; 2008: Summer Exhibition, Royal Academy of Arts, London; From Now to Eternity, Mother, London; 2008–9: Worlds Away: New Suburban Landscapes, Carnegie Museum of Art, Pittsburgh, Walker Arts Center, Minneapolis, Yale School of Architecture, New Haven, USA // Awards 2005: Best Public Building, FX Design Awards, UK; 2006: Regeneration Partnership of the Year, Regeneration Awards, UK; Best Public Housing Project, Brick Development Association Awards, UK; Next Generation Award, Architecture Foundation, UK; 2007: Best Museum, FX Design Awards, UK; European Award, RIBA, UK; 2008: Shortlist, World Architecture Awards, Spain

Didier Fiuza Faustino/Bureau des Mésarchitectures

www.mesarchitecture.org
Didier Fiuza Faustino born in France, 1968 // Lives and works in Paris // Education Architectural diploma, Paris-Villemin School of Architecture, 1995 // Recent works 2002: AMJ Floating Theater, Expo02, Switzerland; 2005: CCA Lab, Kitakyushu, Japan; 2006: Zentral Nerven System, Marseille; 2008: One Square Meter House, Paris; Sky is the Limit, Yang Yang, Republic of Korea // Recent publications 2003: Didier Fiuza Faustino, Stairway to Heaven, Onestar Press, France; 2004: Fiuza Faustino, Anticorps, Editions HYX, France; 2006: Fiuza Faustino, Plans & Directions, CCA Kitakyushu, Japan; 2007: Design Document Series_21: Didier Fiuza Faustino/ Bureau des Mésarchitectures, Damdi Architecture Publishing, Republic of Korea; 2008: Fiuza Faustino, Short Cuts, Monographik Editions, France; 2009: Vanessa Morisset, "Didier Faustino," 20/27, France // Recent exhibitions 2007–8: H-Box, multiple venues including Centre Georges Pompidou, Paris, MUSAC, Spain, Tate Modern, London; 2008: Opus Incertum, 11th International Architecture Exhibition, Venezia; (G)host in the (S)hell, Storefront for Art and Architecture, New York

Gramazio & Kohler

www.gramaziokohler.com
Fabio Gramazio born in Switzerland, 1970; Matthias Kohler born in Switzerland, 1968 // Both live and work in Zürich // Education Both M.Arch, ETH Zürich, 1996 // Affiliations Co-chairs for Architecture and Digital Fabrication (DFAB), ETH Zürich // Recent works 2005: Bahnhofstrasse Christmas Lights, Zürich; 2006: Facade for Gantenbein Winery, Fläsch, Switzerland; 2007: Tanzhaus, Zürich; 2008: House Riedikon 2, Riedikon, Switzerland // Recent publications 2007: Jeff Byles, "I Robot," *The Architect's Newspaper*, USA; 2008: Hubertus Adam, "Unbestimmtheit als Wirkungsbedingung," *Hochparterre*, Switzerland; Hira Se Yu Yin, "The Rebirth of Digital Materiality," *Nikkei Architecture*, Japan; Lilia Glanzmann, "Hase in Gold: Bauklötze staunen," *Hochparterre*, Switzerland // Recent exhibitions 11th International Architecture Exhibition, Venezia // Awards 2007: Daylight Award, Velux Foundation, Switzerland; 2008: Brick Award, Wienerberger AG, Austria; Golden Rabbit, Hochparterre, Switzerland

Guedes + de Campos

www.guedesdecampos.com
Cristina Guedes born in Macau, 1964; Francisco Vieira de Campos born in Portugal, 1962 // Both live and work in Porto // Education Cristina Guedes: Faculdade de Arquitectura da Universidade do Porto (FAUP), 1991; Francisco Vieira de Campos: FAUP, 1992 // Affiliations Cristina Guedes: Lusíada University, Porto, 1994–present; Universidade Autónoma de Lisboa, 2002–3; Francisco Vieira de Campos: Lusíada University, 1998–present // Recent works 2004: Renovation of Na SRa da Luz Fortress, Cascais, Portugal; 2006: INAPAL Metal Industrial Unit, Palmela, Portugal; 2009: Quinta do Vallado Winery, Peso da Régua, Portugal; 2010: Gaia Rope-way Teleferic, Vila Nova de Gaia, Portugal; Azores Contemporary Art Center, Ribeira Grande, Portugal // Recent publications 2004: *Casabella* 719 and 722, Italy; *Frame* 40, Netherlands; 2005: Ana Vaz Milheiro, *2G Dossier. Portugal 2000–2005: 25 Buildings*, Editorial Gustavo Gili, Portugal; 2006: "Portugal Panoramico, Geometria y 'Saudade' al Borde del Atlántico," *Arquitectura Viva* 109, Spain; "Contemporary Architecture & Landscape Architecture in Portugal," *World Architecture* 187, China; 2007: "Metal Skins," *A+U* 441, Japan; 2008: *Domus* 913, Italy // Recent exhibitions 2004: Portuguese pavilion, 9th International Architecture Exhibition, Venezia; 2006: V BIAU, Ibero-American Biennial of Architecture and Urbanism, Montevideo; 2007: VI BIAU, Lisbon; 7th International Architecture Biennial, São Paulo; Architecture Triennial of Lisbon; *Portugal Now: Country Positions in Architecture and Urbanism*, Cornell University College of Architecture, Art and Planning, Ithaca, USA // Awards 2003: Finalist, FAD Awards, Spain; 2006: Finalist, Secil Architecture Award, Portugal; 2008: European Union Prize for Contemporary Architecture Mies van der Rohe Award

Hiroshi Nakamura & NAP Architects

www.nakam.info
Hiroshi Nakamura born in Japan, 1974 // Lives and works in Tokyo // Education M.Arch, Meiji University, Tokyo, 1999 // Recent works 2006: Lotus Beauty Salon, Mie, Japan; 2007: Dancing trees, Singing birds, Tokyo; Hoya Tokyo; Gallery Sakuranoki, Nagano; 2008: Shibuya Publishing & Booksellers, Tokyo; Nihonbashi 1-1-1, Tokyo; House C, Chiba; 2009: Tokyo's Tokyo // Recent publications 2007: Hiroshi Nakamura, *Koisuru Kenchiku*, ASCII Media Works, Japan; 2009: *Modern Living* 183, Japan // Recent exhibitions 2007: *Kuuki no ie*, Living Design Center Ozone, Tokyo; Architecture Triennial of Lisbon // Awards 2006: Grand Prize, Interior Planning Award, The Japan Architectural Education and Information Center, Japan; Grand Prize, JCD Design Award, Japanese Society of Commercial Space Designers, Japan; 2007: Detail Prize, Germany; 2008: Gold Prize, Good Design Award, Japan; 2009: JIA Award, Japan Institute of Architects, Japan

Information Based Architecture (IBA)

www.iba-bv.com
Mark Hemel born in the Netherlands, 1966; Barbara Kuit born in the Netherlands, 1968 // Both live and work in Amsterdam // Education Both B.S., TU Delft, 1993; Mark Hemel: GradDiplDes, Architectural Association, London, 1996 // Affiliations Mark Hemel: Architectural Association, London, 1999–2008 // Recent works 2007: Zeeburgerdijk Lawyer Offices, Amsterdam; 2009: Guangzhou Television and Sightseeing Tower, Guangzhou, China; 2010: Multifunctional Complex, Cape Coast, Ghana; Canton Tower, Ghuangzhou; 2014: Office-Hotel Tower, Fushan, China // Recent publications 2005: *TANK* 1, UK; 2006: *De Ingenieur* 3, Netherlands; *Mark* 3, Netherlands; *Drenthe Magazine*, Netherlands; 2008: "Beton Kern Van Toren Voltooid," *De Ingenieur* 117, Netherlands; Liu Li Fang, *The Bund*, China; 2009: Zara Zhong, *Lifeweek*, China; Owen Hatherly and Shumon Basar, *Frieze* 120, UK // Recent exhibitions 2002: Nordic-Baltic Architecture Triennal, Estonia; 2004: Architectural Biennial Beijing; 2005: *Dutch Architects in Booming China*, Arcam, Amsterdam // Awards 2002: Shortlist, Young Architect of the Year Award (YAYA), *BD*, UK; 2003: Bronze Medal Tutor Award, RIBA, UK

International Festival

www.international-festival.org
Tor Lindstrand and Mårten Spångberg born in Sweden, 1968 // Both live and work in Stockholm // Education Tor Lindstrand: M.Arch, Royal Institute of Technology (RIT), Stockholm, 1997 // Affiliations Tor Lindstrand: RIT, present; Mårten Spångberg: University College of Dance, Stockholm, present // Recent works 2006: Piazza Taxingeplan, Stockholm; Your Space, Van Abbe Museum, Eindhoven, Netherlands // Recent publications 2007: Markus Miessen, "Mission Impossible. In conversation with International Festival," *Build*, Germany; Malin Zimm, "The Theatre," *Rum*, Sweden; Bea Galilee, "Confettification," *ICON*, UK; Kyra Kilston, "International Festival," *Modern Painters*, USA; 2008: Bea Galilee, "Activist Architects," *ICON*, UK // Recent exhibitions 2007: *Performa07*, New York; 2008: *Capitalism! Bring It On Again*, NAI, Rotterdam; Italian pavilion, 11th International Architecture Exhibition, Venezia; 2008–9: *Start Me Up*, Tate Liverpool, England // Awards 2007: Architect of the Year, Swedish Association of Architects, Sweden

Sebastián Irarrázaval

www.sebastianirarrazaval.com
Sebastián Irarrázaval born in Chile, 1967 // Lives and works in Santiago // Education B.Arch, Pontificia Universidad Católica de Chile, Santiago, 1991; Graduate Diploma, Architectural Association, London, 1994 // Affiliations School of Architecture, Pontificia Universidad Católica de Chile, 1994–present; Universidad Central de Caracas, Venezuela, 1996; University of Arizona, Tucson, USA, 2003; Massachusetts Institute of Technology, Cambridge, USA, 2004 // Recent works 2006: Ocho al Cubo House, Marbella, Chile; La Reserva House, Santiago; Pedro Lira House, Santiago; 2007: Indigo Patagonia Hotel, Puerto Natales, Chile; 2007–9: School of Design, Pontificia Universidad Católica de Chile, Santiago; 2009: Indigo Santiago Hotel, Santiago; Chilean Embassy Cultural Center, Buenos Aires // Recent publications 2003: Luis Fernández-Galiano, ed., "Ultimo Chile," *Arquitectura Viva* 85, Spain; 2006: Nobuyuki Yoshida, ed., "Deep South," *A+U* 7, Japan; 2007: Rob Gregory, "AR Awards Early Alert," *The Architectural Review*, UK; 2008: Giovanny Gerolla, "Cenografia Chilena," *AU Architectura & Urbanismo* 72, Brazil // Recent exhibitions 2003: Pontificia Universidad Católica de Chile pavilion, Internationale Architecture Biennale Rotterdam; 2002: Chilean pavillion, 8th International Architecture Exhibition, Venezia; 2008: Chilean pavillion, 11th International Architecture Exhibition, Venezia; Chilean Architecture Biennial, Santiago // Awards 2007: Instituto del Cemento Award, Chile; 101 World´s Most Interesting Emerging Practices, *Wallpaper*, UK; 2008: Chilean Architecture Biennial Award, Chile

James Carpenter Design Associates

www.jcdainc.com
James Fraser Carpenter born in the USA, 1949 // Lives and works in New York // Education BFA, Rhode Island School of Design (RISD), USA, 1972 // Affiliations American Institute of Architects (AIA); American Society of Civil Engineers (ASCE); Illuminating Engineering Society of North America (IESNA); International Society for Glass Technology; International Solar Energy Society (ISES); International Association for Bridge and Structural Engineering (IABSE); Buckminster Fuller Institute, Board of Trustees; RISD, Board of Trustees; Council on Tall Buildings and Urban Habitat (CTBUH); Institute for Urban Design // Recent works *Wall enclosure design*: 2007: 145 Penthouse, New York; Gucci Fifth Avenue, New York; 2008: Fulton Street Transit Center, New York; 2009: South Station, Boston; Israel Museum, Jerusalem; *Sculpture/structure*: 2006: Hearst Tower Ice Falls, New York; *Landscape*: 2006: Hoboken City Pier, USA; 2007: Brooklyn Bridge Park Soccer Field Enclosure, New York // Recent publications 2006: Sandro Marpillero, *James Carpenter: Environmental Refractions*, Princeton Architectural Press, USA; 2008: "Responding to Light—toward an architecture of engagement," *Intelligent Glass Solutions* 2, UK; Jeff Byles, "Studio Visit – James Carpenter Design Associates, *The Architect's Newspaper*, USA; Christine Killory and Rene Davids, *Detail in Process (AsBuilt)*, Princeton Architectural Press, USA // Recent exhibitions 2007: *Design Life Now: National Design Triennial*, Cooper-Hewitt National Design Museum, New York; *A Gathering of Contemporary Glass: Artists from Haystack and Pilchuk*, Farnsworth Art Museum, Rockland, USA; 2008: *Studio Glass in Providence: The Chihuly Years*, RISD Museum, USA // Awards 2004: National Engineering Award of Excellence, American Institute of Steel Construction, USA; MacArthur Foundation Fellowship, USA; 2006: MASterwork Best New Building Award (with Skidmore, Owings & Merrill), Municipal Art Society of New York, USA; AIA Architecture Merit Award (with SOM), USA; 2007: Paul Waterbury Award, IESNA, USA; 2008: Academy Awards in Architecture, American Academy of Arts and Letters, USA

Jan De Vylder Architecten

www.jandevylderarchitecten.com
Jan De Vylder born in Belgium, 1968; Inge Vinck born in Belgium, 1973 // Both live and work in Gent // Education Jan De Vylder: Architecture degree, Sint-Lucas Visual Arts (SLBK), Gent, 1992; Inge Vinck: Architecture degree, SLBK, 1997 // Affiliations Jan De Vylder: TU Delft // Recent works 2004: Studio 118, Gent; 2005: House 43, Gent; 2007: House Jef, Gent; House H, Oosterzele, Belgium; Kraakje Kindergarten, Ukkel, Belgium; 2008: HeL, Gent; House Alexis, Gent // Recent publications 2004 and 2006: *Flanders Architectural Yearbook*, Flemish Architecture Institute, Belgium; 2007: *Ons Erfdeel* 1, Belgium and Netherlands; 2008: *De Standaard* 1, Belgium // Recent exhibitions 2007: *35m*, deSingel International Arts Centre, Belgium; *Création architecturale et innovation urbaine dans le centre historique de Bordeaux*, Exhibition Arc en Rêve, Bordeaux; 2008: 11th International Architecture Exhibition, Venezia // Awards 2009: Nomination, European Union Prize for Contemporary Architecture Mies van der Rohe Award

Jarmund/ Vigsnæs

www.jva.no
Einar Jarmund and Håkon Vigsnæs born in Norway, 1962; Alessandra Kosberg born in Norway, 1967 // All live and work in Oslo // Education Einar Jarmund: Architecture diploma, Oslo School of Architecture (AHO), 1987, M.Arch, University of Washington, Seattle, 1989; Håkon Vigsnæs: Architecture diploma, AHO, 1989; Alessandra Kosberg: Architecture diploma, AHO, 1994 // Affiliations Einar Jarmund: AHO, 1992–93, Bergen School of Architecture, Norway, 1996–97, Washington University in St. Louis (WU), USA, 2004, University of Arizona, Tucson, USA, 2005; Håkon Vigsnæs: AHO, 1990–91, 1993–97, WU, 2004 // Recent works 2005: Svalbard Science Center, Longyearbyen, Norway; 2006: Norwegian Ministry of Defense, Oslo; White House, Strand, Norway; Triangle House, Nesodden, Norway; 2008: Edge House, Kolbotn, Norway; Farm House, Toten, Norway // Recent publications 2008: *Umran Magazine* 24, Saudi Arabia; *PUU Wood*, Finland; *a+u*, Japan; *Arquitectura y Diseõ*, Spain; *The Architectural Review* 1335, UK; *Details*, Korea; *Monocle*, UK; *Arkitektur N*, Norway; 2009: *Domus*, Russian Federation // Recent exhibitions 2007–8: *Lost in Nature*, La Galerie d'Architecture, Paris, Nordische Botschaften, Berlin, Casa dell'Architettura, Roma, Museo Nacional de Bellas Artes, Santiago, et al.

JDS Architects

www.jdsarchitects.com
Julien De Smedt born in Belgium, 1975 // Lives and works in København and Brussel // Education Architecture diploma, Superior Architecture Institute Saint Luc, Brussel, 1995; Architecture diploma, The Bartlett, University College London, 2000 // Affiliations Danske Arkitektvirksomheder, København, present // Recent works 2007: TRØ Bended Tower, Århus, Denmark; ALX Complex, Berlin; SLC High-Rise and Urban Planning, Shenzhen, China; KAI Housing and Retail, Berlin; DUB Dublin Harbour Bath, Ireland; ZAK Zakusala Entertainment Island, Riga; 2008: TAI Next Gene 20, Aodi, Taiwan, 2010: TAD Århus Docklands, Århus // Recent publications 2005: Shumon Basar, *TANK*, UK; 2006: Joseph Grima, *Domus* 896, Italy; *A+U*, Japan; 2007: *Concept*, Korea; 2008: *Architecture Note* 5, Japan; *WestEnd Magazine*, China; *Designers' Workshop* 157, Japan; "Twenty Essential Young Architects," *ICON*, UK // Recent exhibitions 2006: *The Good Life*, Van Alen Institute, New York; 2007: *The Street Belongs to All of Us!* City on the Move Institute, Paris; *New Trends of Architecture in Europe and Asia-Pacific 2006–2007*, FORM, Perth, Australia; Oslo Triennale; *PIXL to XL*, Danish Architecture Center, København; 2007–8: Shenzhen and Hong Kong Bi-City Biennale of Urbanism and Architecture, Shenzhen; 2008: 11th International Architecture Exhibition, Venezia // Awards 2004: Young Architect of the Year Award, Building Design, UK; European Prize for Best Urban Public Space, Centre de Cultura Contemporània de Barcelona, Cité de l'Architecture et du Patrimoine, France, et al.; The Golden Lion, Best Concert Hall Worldwide, International Architecture Exhibition, Venezia; European Union Prize for Contemporary Architecture Mies van der Rohe Award (also 2007 and 2008); 2008: Europe 40 Under 40, The European Centre for Architecture, Art, Design and Urban Studies, Ireland, Greece, and Chicago Athenaeum, USA; Best Interior and Best Architecture, Forum AID Award, Sweden

Johnston Marklee

www.johnstonmarklee.com
Mark Lee born in Hong Kong, 1967; Sharon Johnston born in USA, 1965 // Both live and work in Los Angeles // Education Mark Lee: B.Arch, University of Southern California, Los Angeles, 1991, M.Arch, Harvard University, Cambridge, USA, 1995; Sharon Johnston: B.S., Stanford University, Palo Alto, USA, 1988, M.Arch, Harvard University, 1995 // Affiliations Both UCLA Department of Architecture and Urban Design, Los Angeles, 1998–present; American Institute of Architects (AIA), present // Recent works 2007: Aohai Housing Master Plan, Tianjin, China; Honor Fraser Gallery, Culver City, USA; Helios House, Los Angeles; Mameg/Maison Martin Margiela, Beverly Hills, USA; 2008: Roberts + Tilton Gallery, Culver City, USA; View House, Rosario, Argentina; 2009: House House, Ordos, China; 2010: Poggio Golo Winery, Montepulciano, Italy // Recent publications 2007: Beate Engelhorn, *Young Americans: New Architecture in the USA*, DOM Publishers, Germany; Edie Cohen, "One Size Fits All: Mameg/ Maison Martin Margiela Boutiques," *Interior Design*, USA; Osamu Tsukihashi, "Scenery Spirals Up to Create Space: View House," *Kenchiku Note*, Japan; Phaidon Editors, *The Phaidon Atlas of 21st Century World Architecture*, Phaidon Press, UK; *In Sight USA: Shaping the Future: CityScapes/LandScapes/WaterScapes*, Aedes Pfefferberg, Germany // Recent exhibitions 2006: *Critical Mass at the Fringe*, UCLA, Los Angeles; 2007: *Fresh*, MOCA, Los Angeles; 2008: *One Variation in Five Parts*, Syracuse University, USA; *No Room*, Christopher Grimes Gallery, Santa Monica, USA; *One Shot: 100X100*, LaxArt, Los Angeles; *InSight USA*, Aedes AM Pfefferberg, Germany // Awards 2006: Design Honor Award, AIA, USA; 2007: Honor Award, Westside Urban Forum, USA; Design Award Citation, AIA, USA; American Architecture Award, Chicago Athenaeum, USA; 2008: Notable Project, *Architype Review*, USA; Design Distinction in Environments, *I.D. Magazine*'s Annual Design Review, USA; Best in Design, Clio Awards, USA; Design Award, Architectural Commission of the City of Beverly Hills, USA

Jun Igarashi Architects

http://jun-igarashi.web.infoseek.co.jp
Jun Igarashi born in Japan, 1970 // Lives and works in Hokkaido, Japan // Education Hokkaido Central Kougakuin Technical College, 1990 // Affiliations Hokkaido Institute of Technology, 2004–present; Nagoya Institute of Technology, 2007; Tohoku University, 2007 // Recent works 2006: Tea House; ANNEX; 2007: Rectangle of Light; Density; Room/Set; Corridor of the Waste; 2008: Layered House; Agricultural Burn; House of Trough all in Hokkaido // Awards 2006: AR Award for Emerging Architecture, UK; Best of Residential, American Wood Design Awards, USA; 2007: Excellence Prize, JIA Environmental Architecture, Japan; 3rd prize, Sapporo ADC Competition & Award, Japan

junya.ishigami+ associates

www.jnyi.jp
Junya Ishigami born in Japan, 1974 // Lives and works in Tokyo // Education MFA Architecture, Tokyo National University of Fine Arts and Music, 2000 // Recent works 2005: Lexus automobile exhibition design, Salone di Mobile, Milano; 2008: Kanagawa Institute of Technology (KAIT) Workshop, Atsugi, Japan; Yohji Yamamoto Flagship Store, New York // Recent publications 2007: Junya Ishigami, *Tables As Small Architecture*, Gallery Koyanagi, Japan; 2008: Naomi R. Pollock, "Kanagawa Institute of Technology Workshop," *Architectural Record*, USA; Junya Ishigami, *Small Images*, INAX Publishing, Japan; Taro Igarashi and Junya Ishigami, *Plants + Architecture*, junya ishigami+associates, Japan; Julian Worrall, "Junya Ishigami's Facility," *ICON*, UK // Recent exhibitions 2007: *Space For Your Future*, Museum of Contemporary Art, Tokyo; 2008: Japanese pavilion, International Architecture Exhibition, Venezia // Awards 2005: SD Prize, SD Review, Japan; Kirin Prize, Kirin Art Project, Japan; 2008: Iakov Chernikhov Prize, Iakov Chernikhov International Foundation, Russian Federation; Kanagawa Cultural Award, Japan; Highly Commended, AR Awards for Emerging Architecture, UK; 2009: Best of Offices/Administration Buildings, contractworld.award, Germany; Bauwelt Award, Germany

K2S Architects

www.k2s.fi
Kimmo Lintula born in Finland, 1970; Niko Sirola born in Finland, 1971; Mikko Summanen born in Finland, 1971 // All live and work in Helsinki // Education Kimmo Lintula: M.S. Architecture, Helsinki University of Technology, 2001; Niko Sirola: Helsinki University of Technology, Department of Architecture, 1992; University of Art and Design Helsinki, 1993; Mikko Summanen: M.S. Architecture, Helsinki University of Technology, 1999; Tokyo Institute of Technology, 1997 // Affiliations Kimmo Lintula: Helsinki University of Technology 1999–2000; Niko Sirola: Helsinki University of Technology, 2003–present; Mikko Summanen: Helsinki University of Technology, 2000–present // Recent works 2005: New Roof for Olympic Stadium, Helsinki; 2006: City Hall, Helsinki; 2007: ENTER Sipoo Upper Secondary School, Sipoo, Finland; City Center extension, Lahti, Finland; 2008: Villa Sarvilahti, Luumäki, Finland; 2011: Paasitorni Hotel, Helsinki // Recent publications 2006: Roger Connah and Esa Piironen, *Steel Visions–Millennium Steel Architecture in Finland*, Kustannusosakeyhtiö Avain, Finland; 2007: Daniel Golling "A school for its time," Forum AID 3.07, Sweden; Suneet Paul, "A laminar profile," *Architecture+Design India XXIV*, India; 2008: Maija Kasvio, ed., *Finnish Architecture 0607*, Museum of Finnish Architecture; "Villa Sarvilahti," *The Finnish Architectural Review 5/2008* // Recent exhibitions 2006–7: *From Wood to Architecture*, Scandinavia house, New York, Finnish Embassy, Washington D.C., and Felleshus, Nordic Embassies, Berlin; 2007: *Contemporary Finnish Architecture for Learning and Culture*, Deutsches Architektur Zentrum, Berlin; *44 young architects*, Praza da Quintana, Santiago de Compostela and Centre d'Art Santa Mònica, Barcelona; 2008: *London Festival of Architecture*, Finnish Embassy, London; *Finnish Architecture 0607*, Museum of Finnish Architecture; *Architecture Finlandaise—Séléction 2006–2007*, Cité de l'Architecture et du Patrimoine, Paris; *Wood with a Difference*, University of Technology, Vienna // Awards 2005: Steel Prize, Finland; II prize, RIL-prize (prize of the Finnish Association of Civil Engineers), Finland; Highly Commended, AR Award for Emerging Architecture, UK; 2008: Chicago Athenaeum International Architecture Award, USA

Kavakava

www.kavakava.ee
Katrin Koov born in Estonia, 1973; Kaire Nõmm born in Estonia, 1971; Heidi Urb born in Estonia, 1974; Siiri Vallner born in Estonia, 1972 // All live and work in Tallinn // Education Katrin Koov and Kaire Nõmm: Architecture diploma, Estonian Academy of Arts (EAA), Tallinn, 1997; Heidi Urb: M.A., EAA, 2003; Siiri Vallner: Architecture diploma, EAA, 1998 // Affiliations Katrin Koov: Architectural Association, London, 2001, EAA, 2000–present, Union of Estonian Architects (UEA), 2001–present; Kaire Nõmm: EAA, 2000–2006; Siiri Vallner: EAA, present; UEA, 2001–present // Recent works 2002: Concert Hall, Pärnu, Estonia; 2003: Lasnamäe Track and Field Center, Tallinn; Museum of Occupations, Tallinn; 2008: Kindergarten, Tartu, Estonia // Recent publications 2004: *A10*, Netherlands; 2005: *De Architect 3*, Netherlands; 2005: Kristen Ring: *Emerging Identities – EAST!* Jovis, Germany; 2006: *Estonian Architectural Review*; 2008: Phaidon Editors, *The Phaidon Atlas of 21st Century World Architecture*, Phaidon Press, UK // Recent exhibitions 2005: *Emerging Identities – EAST!* Berlin DAZ; 2008: *RoomBoom*, Estonian Architecture Museum, Tallinn; *100 Models 100 Rooms*, Hungarian Contemporary Architecture Center, Budapest; *Peacebuilding*, Casa dell'Architettura, Roma // Awards 2003: Building Prize, Estonian Culture Endowment; Special Award, Estonian Concrete Union; 2005: Accomplishment of the Year, Citizens of Pärnu, Estonia; 2008: Special Award, Estonian Concrete Union

Diébédo Francis Kéré

www.kere-architecture.com
Diébédo Francis Kéré born in Burkina Faso, 1965 // Lives and works in Berlin // Education Architecture diploma, TU Berlin, 1999 // Affiliations TU Berlin, 2004–present // Recent works 2005: Teachers' Housing, Gando, Burkina Faso; 2007: School addition, Dano, Burkina Faso; 2008: Primary School addition, Gando; 2009: Women's Center, Gando; 2011: Office Building, Ouagadougou, Burkina Faso // Recent publications 2007: "Diebedo Francis Kere: Primary School, Gando, Burkina Faso," *ume* 21, Australia; Alan Ford, *Designing the Sustainable School*, Images Publishing Group, Australia; *Atlas: Global Architecture circa 2000*, Fundación BBVA, Spain; 2008: "Architecture for a Sustainable World," *Architectura Viva*, Spain; Kristin Feireiss and Lukas Feireiss, *Architecture of Change: Sustainability and Humanity in the Built Environment*, Die Gestalten Verlag, Germany; Phaidon Editors, *The Phaidon Atlas of 21st Century World Architecture*, Phaidon Press, UK // Recent exhibitions 2008: *Africa Is Building His Future*, German Foreign Ministry, Berlin; *Architecture for a Sustainable World*, Zaragoza-Kyoto, Spain; German pavilion, International Architecture Exhibition, Venezia // Awards 2004: Aga Khan Award for Architecture, Switzerland; 2006: Chevalier de l'ordre national, Burkina Faso; 2007: Honorable Mention, Zumtobel Award for Sustainable Architecture, Germany

Klein Dytham architecture

www.klein-dytham.com
Mark Dytham born in the UK, 1964; Astrid Klein born in Italy, 1962 // Education Mark Dytham: B.Arch, Newcastle University School of Architecture, UK, 1985, M.Arch, Royal College of Art, London, 1988; Astrid Klein: BA Interior Design at Ecole des Arts Décoratifs, Strasbourg, France, 1986, M.Arch, Royal College of Art, London, 1988 // Affiliations Mark Dytham: Tokyo Science University, 1999, University of California, Berkeley, 2006; Astrid Klein: Nihon University, College of Science and Technology, Tokyo, 1997–2005, Keio University and Tsukuba University, Tokyo, 2002–3, University of California, Berkeley, 2006 // Recent works 2007: TBWA\ Hakuhodo office interior, Tokyo; Virgin Atlantic Airways Upper Class Lounge, Chiba, Japan; Narita International Airport Lounge, Chiba; Wonder Room, Selfridges, London; 2008: Alpha Resort Tomamu Towers, Hokkaido, Japan; Wilson House, Chiba // Recent publications 2001: *Klein Dytham Architecture: Tokyo Calling*, Frame/Birkhauser, Netherlands; 2002: "Klein Dytham architecture, Architect's Works File 2," *Xknowledge*, Japan; 2006: *Japan: The New Mix*, Graphic Sha, Japan // Recent exhibitions 2005: *KDa at the bath house*, Architectural Association, London; 2009: *20 Klein Dytham architecture*, Gallery MA, Tokyo // Awards 2000: MBE (Member of the British Empire) medal (Mark Dytham); 2002: AR Award for Emerging Architecture, *The Architectural Review*, UK; 2003: Finalist, *Business Week/Architectural Record* Awards, USA; JCD Design Award, Japan; 2004: First Prize, Annual Design Review, *I.D. Magazine*, USA; 2005: Environmental Design and Architecture, D&AD Awards, UK; 2006: Honorable Mention, Annual Design Review, *I.D. Magazine*, USA; 2007: Nikkei New Office Awards, Japan

Totan Kuzembaev Architectural Workshop

www.totan.ru/en/workshop/totan/index.html
Totan Kuzembaev born in USSR, 1953 // Lives and works in Moskva // Education M.Arch, Moscow Architectural Institute (MARHI), 1982 // Affiliations Union of Russian Architects, present // Recent works 2004: Côte d'Azur Restaurant, Pirogovo Resort, Moskovskaya Oblast, Russian Federation; Guest Houses, Pirogovo Resort; 2006: Yacht Club, Pirogovo Resort; 2007: Golf Club, Pirogovo Resort // Recent publications 2007: *Elle Decor* 60 and 64, USA; *Forbes Real Estate*, USA; *Interior Digest* 79, Russian Federation; *ARX* 11, Russian Federation // Recent exhibitions 11th International Architecture Exhibition, Venezia // Awards 2006: ARX Award, *ARX*, Russian Federation

LAR/Fernando Romero

www.l-a-r-fernandoromero.com
Fernando Romero born in Mexico, 1971 // Lives and works in México D.F. // Education Architectural degree, Universidad Iberoamericana, México D.F., 1996 // Affiliations CICSA (Carso Infraestructura y Construcción); AIA (American Institute of Architects); CAM (Mexican Chamber of Architects); Columbia University, New York // Recent works 2007: Bridging Tea House, Jinhua, China; 2008: Banco del Bajío Headquarters, Monterrey, Mexico; 2010: Soumaya Art Museum, México D.F.; Master Plan for Polanco, México D.F.; Zurich Building, México D.F.; Cervantes Complex, México D.F. // Recent publications 2005: Fernando Romero, *Translation*, Actar, Spain; 2007: Fernando Romero, *Hyperborder: The Contemporary U.S./Mexico Border and Its Future*, Princeton Architectural Press, USA; 2008: Alex Pasternack, "Being Constructive," *Time*, USA; Various authors, *AV Monografías 128/Twenty Emerging Teams*, Arquitectura Viva, Spain; Yukio Futagawa, ed., *GA Houses 103*, Japan; Interview, *ArchIdea* 37, Netherlands; Rafael Fernández Bermejo, "Fernando Romero/Estudio LAR: Vivienda en Chapultepec, México," *Diseño Interior* 189, Spain // Recent exhibitions 2007: Hong Kong & Shenzhen Bi-city Biennale of Urbanism\Architecture; 2008: *Exonome*, Mexican Embassy in San Francisco; Museum of Architecture (MUAR), Moskva; *Myths, Mortals, and Immortality: Works from Museo Soumaya de México*, Alameda Museum, San Antonio, USA; 2009: *Laboratory of Architecture/Fernando Romero*, Carnegie Museum of Art, Pittsburgh, USA // Awards 2002: Global Leader of Tomorrow, World Economic Forum (WEF); 2004: Recognition, International Bauhaus Award, Germany; 2005: Award of Honor, SARA (Society of American Registered Architects) Professional Design Award, USA; 2006: Recognition, International Bauhaus Award; Best of the Best, Red Dot Award, Germany

m3architecture

www.m3architecture.com
Michael Banney born in Australia, 1970; Michael Christensen born in New Zealand, 1969; Michael Lavery born in Australia, 1967; Ben Vielle born in Australia, 1979 // All live and work in Brisbane // Education Michael Banney: B.Arch, Queensland University of Technology (QUT), Brisbane, 1995, M.Arch, RMIT University, Melbourne, 2007–present; Michael Christensen: B.Arch, QUT, 1995, M.Arch, RMIT, 2007–present; Michael Lavery: B.Arch, QUT, 1999, M.Arch, RMIT, 2007–present; Ben Vielle: B.Arch, QUT, 2002, M.Arch, RMIT, 2007–present // Affiliations Michael Christensen, Michael Lavery, Ben Vielle: Royal Australian Institute of Architects (RAIA); Michael Lavery: Design Institute of Australia // Recent works 2005: Queensland University of Technology Human Movement Pavilion, Brisbane; 2006: Brisbane Girls' Grammar School (BGGS) Cherrell Hirst Creative Learning Centre, Brisbane; 2007: University of Queensland Chemistry Laboratories Levels 9 +10, Gatton // Recent publications 2004: Phaidon Editors, *The Phaidon Atlas of Contemporary World Architecture*, Phaidon Press, UK; 2007: Davina Jackson, *Next Wave: Emerging Talents in Australian Architecture*, Thames and Hudson, UK; N. de Monchauz, "Out From Under: Australian Architecture Now," *Architecture Australia* 96; 2008: S. Stutchbury and M. Wallace, *Place Makers: Contemporary Queensland Architects*, Queensland Art Gallery, Australia; Michael Hensel and Achim Menges, eds.,*Versatility and Vicissitude: Performance in Morpho-Ecological Design*, Wiley, USA // Recent exhibitions 2006: Australian pavilion, 10th International Architecture Exhibition, Venezia; *[v3]*, QPAC Forecourt, Southbank, Brisbane; *The Design Institute of Australia Awards & Exhibition*, Queensland Art Gallery, Brisbane; 2007: *Out From Under: Australian Architecture Now*, AIA, San Francisco; 2008: Australian pavilion, 11th International Architecture Exhibition, Venezia // Awards 2004: Design Innovation and Excellence Award and Award of Merit, The Design Institute of Australia (DIA); 2005: Award of Merit, DIA; 2006: State Commendation, RAIA Queensland Architecture Awards; 2007: State and regional awards, RAIA Queensland Architecture Awards; 2008: Sir Zelman Cowan Award for Public Architecture, RAIA National Awards

MAD Office

www.i-mad.com
Yansong Ma born in China, 1975; Yosuke Hayano born in Japan, 1977; Qun Dang born in China, 1969 // Yansong Ma and Qun Dang: Live and work in Beijing; Yosuke Hayano: Lives and works in Tokyo // Education Yansong Ma: M.Arch, Yale University, New Haven, USA, 2002; Yosuke Hayano: B.Arch, Waseda University, Tokyo, 2001, M.Arch Design, Architectural Association, London, 2003; Qun Dang: M.Arch, Iowa State University, Ames, USA // Recent works 2006: Hong Luo Clubhouse, Beijing; 2009: Absolute Towers, Mississauga, Canada; 2010: Ordos Museum, Ordos, China; 2012: Sinosteel International Plaza, Tianjin, China; // Recent exhibitions 2004: WTC Rebuilt–Floating Island and Fish Tank, Architectural Biennial, Beijing, and National Art Museum of China, Beijing; 2005: "Ink Ice," Chinese Calligraphy Art exhibition, The China Millennium Monument, Beijing; 2006: MAD in China, 10th International Architecture Exhibition, Venezia; MAD Under Construction, Tokyo Gallery, Beijing; 2007: MAD in China, Danish Architecture Center, København // Awards 2006: Young Architects Forum Award, Architectural League of New York, USA

Francisco Mangado

www.fmangado.com
Francisco Mangado born in Spain, 1957 // Lives and works in Pamplona // Education Architecture diploma, University of Navarra School of Architecture, Pamplona, 1981 // Affiliations University of Navarra School of Architecture, 1982–; University of Texas at Arlington, USA, 1986–87; Harvard University Graduate School of Design, 1998 and 2001; International University of Catalonia (UIC) 2001–4; Yale University School of Architecture, New Haven, USA, 2008–present // Recent works 2003: Congress Center Auditorium of Navarra (Baluarte), Pamplona; Pey-Berland Square, Bordeaux, France; 2006: Football Stadium, Palencia, Spain; 2008: Municipal Congress and Exhibition Center of Ávila, Ávila, Spain; Spanish Pavilion, Expo Zaragoza, Spain; 2009: Archaeology Museum of Álava, Vitoria–Gasteiz, Spain // Recent publications 2004: Jose Manuel das Neves, Francisco Mangado: Baluarte, Palacio de Congresos y Auditorio de Navarra, Editorial Caleidoscopio, Portugal; 2005: Luis Fernández-Galiano and Carlos Jimenez, Francisco Mangado. Works and Projects, Editorial Gustavo Gili, Spain; Francisco Mangado and Francesc Torres, Plaza Dalí, Madrid, Editorial Gustavo Gili; 2006: Francisco Mangado. Arquitectura 1998-2006, Tribuna de la Construcción, Spain; 2008: Luis Fernández-Galiano, ed., Pabellón de España, Arquitectura Viva, Spain; Francisco Mangado, Deados 4, Colegio Oficial de Arquitectos de Almeria, Spain. // Recent exhibitions 2006–7: On-Site: New Architecture in Spain, MoMA, New York, and Botanical Gardens, Madrid // Awards 1991: Special Mention, Andrea Palladio International Competition, Italy; 1993: City of Thiene Prize for Architecture, Italy; Architecti Prize, Portugal; 1997: CEOE Foundation Award, Spain; 2004: FAD Award, Spain; 2007: Enor Award, Spain; Saloni Architecture Prize, Spain

Matharoo Associates

www.matharooassociates.com
Gurjit Singh Matharoo born in India, 1966 // Lives and works in Ahmedabad // Education Diploma in Architecture, CEPT University, Ahmedabad, 1989 // Affiliations Council of Architecture, India 1991–present; CEPT University, 1991–present // Recent works 2005: OVaL Retail Outlet for ONGC, Mangalore, India; Cattiva Mobile Blood Van, India; 2006: Parag Shah Residence, Surat, India // Recent publications 2008: GA Document 101, Japan Awards 2002: Young Architect of the Year, J.K. Cement Ltd., India; 2003: Emerging International Architecture Award, The Architectural Review, UK; 2005: Emerging International Architecture Award, The Architectural Review, UK

McBride Charles Ryan

www.mcbridecharlesryan.com.au
Rob McBride born in Australia, 1960; Debbie Ryan born in Australia, 1959 // Both live and work in Melbourne // Education Rob McBride: B.Arch, RMIT, Melbourne, 1985; M.Arch, RMIT, 1994; Debbie Ryan: BA, Monash University, Melbourne; Arts, Monash University; Diploma of Interior Decoration, Melbourne College of Decoration; Certificate of Visual Merchandising, Melbourne College of Decoration; Interior Design, RMIT // Affiliations Rob McBride: Royal Australian Institute of Architects (RAIA), 1985; Debbie Ryan: Design Institute of Australia, 2008 // Recent works 2004: Narveno Court, Hawthorn, Australia; QVII Apartment Building, Melbourne; 2005: Pine Street, Camberwell, Australia; Kent Court, Toorak, Australia; 2007: Monaco House, Melbourne; 2008: Klein Bottle House, Rye, Australia // Recent publications 2007: Stephen Crafti, Details for Living, Images Publishing, Australia; Stephen Crafti, The Ultimate Urban Makeover 2007, Images Publishing; Clare Newton, "A Design Excursion," Architecture Australia, Australia; Stephen Crafti, "Message in a Bottle," MARK 10, Netherlands; Simon Drysdale, "Klein Bottle House," Architecture Review 103, Australia; 2008: Jacinta Le Plastrier Aboukhäter, "A House Less Ordinary," Belle, Australia; McBride Charles Ryan, "The Dome House," Builders Choice Magazine, Australia; Simon Drysdale, "Monaco House," Aa 97, no. 2, Australia; Dijana Satkute, "Nesumeltuota Intriga," Centras 02, Lithuania; Ha Ji-hae, "Klein Bottle House," Interior World Korea, 66, Republic of Korea; Li Miao, "Klein Bottle House," A+A China, China; Cécile Maury, "Bottle at Sea," Perspective China, China // Recent exhibitions 2006: Australian pavilion, 10th International Architecture Exhibition, Venezia; 2007: Living the Modern_Australian Architecture, Germany; 2008: Abundant, 11th International Architecture Exhibition, Venezia; Out of the Square, Mornington Peninsula Regional Gallery, Australia // Awards 2008: New Residential Architecture, Robyn Boyd Award, Australia; Commercial Architecture Award, Australia; New Residential Architecture, Harold Desbrowe-Annear Award, Australia; Commercial Architecture, Sir Osborn McCutcheon Award, Australia

Meixner Schlüter Wendt Architekten

www.meixner-schlueter-wendt.de
Claudia Meixner born in Germany, 1964; Florian Schlüter born in Germany, 1959; Martin Wendt born in Germany, 1955 // All live and work in Frankfurt am Main // Education Claudia Meixner: Architecture diploma, TU Darmstadt, Germany, 1991, Universita degli Studi, Florence, Italy, 1988; Florian Schlüter: Architecture diploma, TU Darmstadt, 1988, Universita degli Studi, Florence, 1986; Martin Wendt: Architecture diploma, FH Frankfurt am Main, 1981 // Affiliations Claudia Meixner: Advisory Council for Town and Country Planning, City of Frankfurt am Main, 2005–present; Florian Schlüter: Siegen University of Applied Science, 2001 // Recent works 2006: Dornbusch Church, Frankfurt am Main; 2007: Flohr House, Kronberg im Taunus, Germany; Lessing Secondary School, Frankfurt am Main; 2009: Reading Room, Museum of Modern Art (MMK), Frankfurt am Main; Town Clerk's Office, Frankfurt am Main // Recent publications 2006: Lilli Hollein, "The Void and the Volume," MARK 4, Netherlands; 2007: Enrico Santifaller, "Floating Snack Bar (Licht und Luftbad Niederrad)," werk bauen + wohnen 7/8, Switzerland; Robert Klanten and Lukas Feireiss, eds., Spacecraft: Fleeting Architecture and Hideouts, Die Gestalten Verlag, Germany; 2008: Christian Brensing, "Off the radar," The Architectural Review, UK; Peter Cachola Schmal, "Residence F.," German Architecture Yearbook 2007/08, Prestel Verlag, Germany // Recent exhibitions 2006: 10th International Architecture Exhibition, Venezia; konversion/transformation/umbau, Architekturgalerie am Weißenhof, Stuttgart; 2007: Neu Bau Land–Architecture and Urban Restructuring in the Former East Germany, Deutsches Architekturmuseum (DAM), Frankfurt am Main; 2008: Vertrautes Terrain–Contemporary Art in/about Germany, ZKM, Kahlsruhe, Germany // Awards 2003: Mention, German Architecture Prize; 2006: 1st Prize, Design Award of the Wüstenrot-Foundation "Umbau im Bestand," Germany; 2008: Winner and shortlisted, World Architecture Festival, Spain

Miller & Maranta

www.millermaranta.ch

Paola Maranta born in Switzerland, 1959; Quintus Miller born in Switzerland, 1961 // Both live and work in Basel // Education Paola Maranta: Architecture diploma, ETH Zürich, 1986; Quintus Miller: Architecture diploma, ETH Zürich, 1987 // Affiliations Both Swiss Federal Institute of Technology (EPF), Lausanne, 2000–2001; Accademia di Architettura University of Lugano (USI), Mendrisio, Switzerland, 2007–8; ETH Zürich 2008–present; Quintus Miller: Commission for Urban Planning and Architecture, Luzern, Switzerland, present; Commission for Historic Preservation, Zürich, 2005–present // Recent works 2002: Markthalle Färberplatz, Aarau, Switzerland; 2004: Villa Garbald, Castasegna, Switzerland; Wohnhaus Schwarzpark, Basel; 2006: Seniorenresidenz Spirgarten, Zürich-Altstetten // Recent publications 2000: Steven Spier and Martin Tschanz, *Swiss Made: New Architecture from Switzerland*, Thames & Hudson, UK and USA; 2004: Philippe Carrard and Sonja Hildebrand, *Villa Garbald: Gottfried Semper – Miller & Maranta*, gta Verlag, Switzerland; Hochbaudepartment der Stadt Zürich, ETH Zürich, eds., et al., *Schulhausbau: Der Stand der Dinge/School Buildings: The State of Affairs*, Birkhauser, Switzerland // Recent exhibitions 2006: *Miller & Maranta*, aut. architektur und tirol, Innsbruck, Austria; *Miller & Maranta*, Architekturforum, Zürich // Awards 2004: Goldener Hase für Architektur, Kulturpreis der Zeitschrift Hochparterre, Switzerland; 2005: Architektur Preis Beton, Germany; 2007: contractworld.award, Germany

Minsuk Cho/ Mass Studies

www.massstudies.com

Minsuk Cho born in Republic of Korea, 1966 // Lives and works in Seoul // Education B.Sc. in Architectural Engineering, Yonsei University, Seoul, 1988; M.Arch, Columbia University, New York, 1992 // Affiliations Graduate School of Architecture, Kyonggi University, Seoul, 1999 and 2001 // Recent works 2005: Nature Poem, Seoul; Torque House, Paju City, Republic of Korea; Seoul Commune 2026, Seoul; 2006: Chipped House, Paju City; Cracked House, Paju City; Bundle Matrix Building (S-Trenue), Seoul; Rethinking Towers in the Park, Seoul; 2007: Oktokki Space Center, Incheon, Republic of Korea; Xi Gallery, Busan, Republic of Korea; Ann Demeulemeester Shop, Seoul; Ring Dome, New York; 2008 Ring Dome, Kitakyushu and Yokohama, Japan, Milan, Italy; 2008: Boutique Monaco, Seoul // Recent publications 2008: "+Architect 00: Mass Studies," *SPACE*, Republic of Korea; "Tre progetti in Corea del Sud," *Abitare* 478, Italy; "Green Icon," *MARK* 13, Netherlands; "From Hab to Habitat," *DAM* 20, Belgium; Robert Klanten and Lukas Feireiss, eds., *Strike a Pose!: Eccentric Architecture and Spectacular Spaces*, Die Gestalten Verlag, Germany; Joseph Grima, *Instant Asia*, Skira, Italy; Phaidon Editors, *The Phaidon Atlas of 21st Century World Architecture*, Phaidon Press, UK // Recent exhibitions 2007: *Open House*, Pasadena, California; *The New Trends of Architecture*, Tokyo; *Korean Home–the Way of Living*, National Museum of Finland, Helsinki; *Ring Dome New York*, Temporary Pavilion for the Storefront for Art and Architecture, New York; *Open House*, Vitra Design Museum, Weil am Rhein, Germany; *Megacity Network*, Deutsches Architekturmuseum (DAM), Frankfurt; 2008: *Ring Dome Milan*, Temporary Pavilion in Galleria Vittorio Emanuele, Milan; *Air Forest*, Temporary Pavilion for Dialog: City and the National Democratic Convention, Denver, USA; *Ring Dome Yokohama*, Temporary Pavilion for the Yokohama Triennale, Japan; *NOW Jump!*, Nam June Paik Art Center, Yongin, Korea; *BIG INABA MAD MASS*, Gyeonggi Museum of Modern Art, Ansan, Korea // Awards 2003: Citation, Progressive Architecture Awards (with James Slade); 2008: Finalist, International Highrise Award (DAM), Germany; Silver Award, Emporis Skyscraper Award, Germany

Miró Rivera Architects

www.mirorivera.com

Juan Miró born in Barcelona, 1964; Miguel A. Rivera born in San Juan, Puerto Rico, 1964 // Both live and work in Austin, USA // Education Juan Miró: Professional Degree in Architecture, ETSAM, Madrid, 1987, M.Arch, Yale University, New Haven, USA, 1991; Miguel Rivera: BS in Environmental Design, University of Puerto Rico School of Architecture, San Juan, 1986, M.Arch, Columbia University, New York, 1989 // Affiliations Both American Institute of Architects (AIA), 1998–present; Juan Miró: Colegio Oficial de Arquitectos de Madrid (COAM), 1988–present, University of Texas at Austin School of Architecture (UTSOA), 2003–present; Miguel Rivera: UTSOA, 1997–2003 // Recent works 2007: Residence 1414 Renovation, Austin, USA; 2008: Trail Restroom, Austin; Residence 319, El Lago, USA; 2009: Garden Footbridge, West Surrey, UK // Recent publications 2007: "Pedestrian Bridge," *C3 Magazine*, Republic of Korea; 2008: Christine Killory and René Davids, eds., *Detail in Process (AsBuilt* series), Princeton Architectural Press, USA; "Pedestrian Bridge," *World Architecture Magazine*, China; Dror Baldinger, "Trail Restroom," *Texas Architect*, USA; *1000 x Architecture of the Americas*, Verlagshaus Braun, Germany; 2009: Jeff Turrentine, "Putting a Fresh Spin on Tradition," *Architectural Digest*, USA // Recent exhibitions 2007: *Young American Architects,* Deutsches Architekturmuseum (DAM), Germany; *AR Awards for Emerging Architecture*, RIBA, UK; 2008: *InSight USA–Shaping the Future: Cityscapes/Landscapes/Waterscapes*, AEDES Gallery, Germany; 2009: *Madrid 100% Arquitectura*, COAM, Spain // Awards 2006: Honor, Merit, and Firm Achievement Awards, AIA Austin, USA; Winner, AR Award for Emerging Architecture, UK; 2007: Merit Award, AIA Austin, USA; 2008: Honourable Mention, AR Award for Emerging Architecture, UK; Shortlist, World Architecture Festival Design Awards, Spain; Design awards, Texas Society of Architects, USA; Citation of Honor Award, AIA Austin, USA; Design Competition Merit Award, *Residential Architect*, USA; Grand and Merit awards, Custom Home Design Awards, USA

Mount Fuji Architects Studio

www14.plala.or.jp/mfas/fuji.htm

Masahiro Harada born in Japan, 1973; Mao Harada born in Japan, 1976 // Both live and work in Tokyo // Education Masahiro Harada: M.Arch, Shibaura Institute of Technology, Tokyo, 1997; Mao Harada: B.Arch, Shibaura Institute of Technology, 1999 // Affiliations Masahiro Harada: Keio University, 2005–present; Shibaura Institute of Technology, 2008–present // Recent works 2003: XXXX House, Yaizu, Japan; 2004: Secondary Landscape, Art-archives, Tokyo; Light-Light Shelter, Delica Shop, Shizuoka, Japan; 2006: Football Stadium, Okinawa, Japan; M3/KG, Tokyo; Sakura House, Tokyo; 2008: Architecture in the Climate, Tokyo; Yotsubako, Tenant Building, Yokohama, Japan // Recent publications 2007: *Wallpaper* 103, UK; 2008: Petra Schmidt, Barbara Glasner, Ursula Schondeling, eds., *Patterns 2: Design, Art and Architecture*, Birkhauser Verlag, Switzerland; *Casa Vogue Brazil* 272, Brazil; Phaidon Editors, *The Phaidon Atlas of 21st Century World Architecture*, Phaidon Press, UK; *The Architectural Review* 1342, UK // Recent exhibitions 2006: *Archilab 2006 Japan*, ArchiLab, France; Bucharest Architecture Biennial, Romania; 2007: Lisbon Architecture Triennale, Portugal; 2008: *Design Miami/Basel*, USA // Awards 2001: Selected project, Tokyo Designer's Block, Japan; 2003: Grand Prix, SD Review Japan; 2004: Honor Award, American Wood Design Awards, USA; 2007: Best International Works, Barbara Cappochin Prize for Architecture, Italy; 2008: Honourable Mention, AR Award for Emerging Architecture, UK

Nendo

www.nendo.jp

Oki Sato born in Canada, 1977 // Lives and works in Tokyo // Education B.Arch, Waseda University, Tokyo, 2000; M.Arch, Waseda University, 2002 // Affiliations Showa Women's University,Tokyo, 2006 // Recent works 2003: Drawer House, Tokyo; 2005: Book House, Tokyo; Fireworks House, Chichibu, Japan; 2008: Meguro office, Tokyo; Kenzo Parfums store, Paris; Moss House, Tokyo; Looking at TOD'S, Milan; ASOBIO store, Shanghai // Recent publications 2006: Naomi Saeki, "The Top 100 Respected Japanese," *Newsweek*1025, Japan; 2007: Naomi Saeki, "The Top 100 Small Global Companies," *Newsweek* 1078, Japan; 2008: Daab editors, *nendo*, Daab, Germany; Justin McGuirk, "nendo," *ICON* 60, UK; Merel Kokfuis and Cathelijne Nuijsink, "Mr. Smiley and Friends," *Frame* 64, Netherlands // Recent exhibitions 2007: *bloomroom*, National Art Center, Japan, and Hangaram Design Museum, Republic of Korea; *Interior Lifestyle*, Tokyo Big Sight, Japan; *Space for Your Future*, Museum of Contemporary Art Tokyo (MOT); *Material And Colour*, Triennale di Milano, Italy; 2008: *XXIst Century Man,* 21_21 Design Sight, Tokyo; *Design and the Elastic Mind*, MoMA, New York; *Lexus L-finesse*, La Permanente, Milano // Awards 2007: Best of Category, Annual Design Review, *I.D. Magazine*, USA; 2008: Red Dot Award, Germany; Grand Prize, Furniture Design Award, Singapore; Nomination, Best Contribution, 100% Design, UK; Nomination, Brit Insurance Design Award, UK; iF products design award, Germany

NEXT architects

www.nextarchitects.com
Bart Reuser born in Tanzania, 1972;
Marijn Schenk born in Netherlands, 1973; Michel Schreinemachers born in Netherlands, 1973; John van de Water born in Netherlands, 1974 // Bart Reuser, Marijn Schenk, and Michel Schreinemachers live and work in Amsterdam; John van de Water lives and works in Beijing // Education Bart Reuser and Marijn Schenk: Politecnico di Milano, 1996; Michel Schreinemachers: ETH Zürich, 1996; All: M.Arch, TU Delft, 1999 // Recent works 2007: House M&M, Amsterdam; Bridges Enschede, Enschede, Netherlands; Stadsmuseum, Rotterdam; 2008: Two Bridges, Nijverdal, Netherlands; Media Wharfe, Amsterdam; 40 Youth Dwellings, Zoetermeer, Netherlands; Wieden+Kennedy, Amsterdam; Villa Overgooi, Almere, Netherlands; 2009: Intense Lowrise, Groningen, Netherlands; Growth Monument, Tilburg, Netherlands // Recent publications 2005: Naomi Shibata, "An attitude towards the public domain," A+U, Japan; 2006: Valerio Paolo Mosco, Contemporary Public Space: Un-volumetric Architecture, Skira, Italy; Roberta Smith, "Is It Design? Art? Or Just a Dutch Joke?" New York Times, USA; 2007: Eva Schaap, "Message in a Box," Frame 46, Netherlands; 2008: David Keuning, "No Fooling About," Mark 13, Netherlands; Catja Edens, Facts and Forms, NAi Publishers, Netherlands; Kieran Long, Hatch: The New Architectural Generation, Laurence King Publishing, UK; David Sokol, "The Canal Zone," Interior Design (Nov), US // Recent exhibitions 2005: Laboratorium Rotterdam, Centrale Bibliotheek, Rotterdam; 2006: Dutch Architects in Booming China, ARCAM, Netherlands; 2007: Dry Tech 3, Droog Design, Netherlands; Density Studies, TU Delft, Netherlands; 2008: Actions: What You Can Do With the City, Canadian Center for Architecture, Montréal; 11th International Architecture Exhibition, Venezia; Dynamics of Density, Moskva Biennale of Architecture, Russian Federation // Awards 2004: European Regional and Urban Planning Achievement Award, European Union; 2008: First Prize, Lensvelt Architect Interior Award, Netherlands; Nomination, AMNAI Award, Netherlands; Nomination, Gouden Piramide Prize, Netherlands; First Prize, Best Foreign Presentation, Dutch Design Award, Netherlands

Neville Mars/ Dynamic City Foundation

www.dynamiccity.org
Neville Mars born in Netherlands, 1975 // Lives and works in Beijing // Education M.Arch, TU Delft, 2001 // Recent works 2005: Boloni Hotel and Flagship Store, Beijing; Gao Bei Dian, Sustainable Art District, Beijing; 2006: Beijing Boom Tower; D-Rail, Beijing; 2007: Solar Car Park and Shanghai Expo Living Diagram, Shanghai; 2008: Tianjin Green CBD Master Plan, Tianjin, China; Tanggu Exhibition Hall, Tianjin; Tanggu TV Tower, Tianjin; Taipei Performing Arts Center, Taipei; Interior China Pavilion, Shanghai // Recent publications 2004: Neville Mars, "Cities Without History," TANK, UK; 2007: Shumon Basar, ed., Cities from Zero, AA Publications, UK; Neville Mars, "The D-rail–a high-speed levitated people mover," Urban China, Utopia 28; 2008: Ma Xiao Wei, "Interview: Dreaming about the future," Archicreation, China; Neville Mars, "Urban Organics," in Sophie Wolfrum, Winfried Nerdinger, Susanne Schaubeck, eds., Multiple City, Jovis, Germany; Adrian Hornsby, Neville Mars, "Cracking Creativity," Urban China 33, China; Neville Mars and Adrian Hornsby, The Chinese Dream–A Society under Construction, 010 Publishers, Netherlands // Recent exhibitions 2005: Second Guangzhou Triennial, Guangdong Museum of Art, China; 798 International Art Festival, DCF Space, Beijing; The Chinese Dream, ARCAM, Amsterdam; 2006: Shiji Tan Exhibition, Millennium Museum, Beijing; 2007: In the line of fight, Millennium Museum, Beijing; DEAF Interactive Media Festival, V2_Institute for Unstable Media, Rotterdam; Hong Kong & Shenzhen Bi-city Biennale of Urbanism\Architecture, Shenzhen; 2008: Peking Fine Arts, High-rise for the Stars, Pekin Gallery, Beijing// Awards 2002: IFHP Documentary Film Award, Netherlands; 2008: Critics Choice Award, Hong Kong & Shenzhen Bi-city Biennale of Urbanism\Architecture, China; Annual Book Awards, China Architecture Readers Review, China

Nieto Sobejano Arquitectos

www.nietosobejano.com
Fuensanta Nieto and Enrique Sobejano born in Spain, 1957 // Both live and work in Madrid // Education Architecture diploma, ETSAM, Madrid, 1982 and 1981; M.Sc. Building Design, Columbia University, New York, 1983 // Affiliations Colegio Oficial de Arquitectos, Spain, 1983; ETSAM; European University of Madrid // Recent works 2007: National Sculpture Museum Extension, Valladolid, Spain; 2008: Moritzburg Contemporary Art Museum Extension, Halle, Germany; 2010: Córdoba Center for Contemporary Art, Córdoba, Spain; 2011: Kastner & Öhler, Graz, Austria // Recent publications 2006: Terence Riley, On Site: New Architecture in Spain, MoMA, USA; William J.R. Curtis, "Entre la lógica y la intuición: La arquitectura reciente de Fuensanta Nieto y Enrique Sobejano," Arquitectura COAM 343, Spain; 2007: A+U 437, Japan; María Gómez-Guillamon, "Spansk Saerpraeg," Arkitekten 04/07, Sweden; 2008: Bauwelt 27/08, Germany; Anne Isopp, "Spanish architects Nieto Sobejano's original design for radical intervention in an historical roofscape ran foul of UNESCO," A10 22, Netherlands // Recent exhibitions 2000: 7th International Architecture Exhibition, Venezia; 2002: 8th International Architecture Exhibition, Venezia; CAPLA University of Arizona, Tucson, USA; 2003: VII Bienal Española de Arquitectura y Urbanismo (BEAU); El Haz y el Envés, Galería Raquel Ponce, Madrid; 2005: Extreme Eurasia, Tokyo; Monoespacios, Fundación Cultural COAM, Madrid; 2006: On Site: New Architecture in Spain, MoMA, New York; 10th International Architecture Exhibition, Venezia; Interferencias: Arquitectura-Arte, Galería Astarté, Madrid; 2008: Arquitectura Concreta, AEDES Gallery, Berlin, Kunsthaus, Graz, Austria, and Moritzburg Contemporary Art Museum, Halle // Awards 2005: Finalist, FAD Award, Spain; Mention, COAM Prize, Spain; Mention, Prize of Implementations, Europan I to IV, Spain; 2007: Finalist, FAD Awards, Spain; Prize Arquinfad Members, Spain; National Prize for Conservation and Restoration of Cultural Patrimony, Spain

Kenichiro Niizeki/ Niizeki Studio

www.niizekistudio.com
Kenichiro Niizeki born in Japan, 1969 // Lives and works in Tokyo // Education M.Arch, Meiji University, Tokyo, 1995 // Recent works 2005: Residence in Kamogawa, Japan; 2006: Whole Earth Project, Shimokitazawa, Japan; Residence in Yoyogi-uehara, Japan; 2007: Residence in Nakano, Japan; Residence in Kuhonbutsu, Japan; Residence in Sendagi, Japan; 2008: Residence in Naruse, Japan; 2009: Office Building, Oyama-cho, Japan // Recent publications 2007: Masaki Uchino, "Whole Earth Project," Detail 12, Japan; Masahiro Toyoda, "Whole Earth Project," Japan Architect 253, Japan; Masaki Uchino, "Residence in Sendagi," Detail 20; 2008: Masahiro Toyoda, "Residence in Sendagi," Japan Architect 261; Kazuhiko Yamane, "A Tranquil Box," Detail 177; Marcia Iwatate and Geeta K.Mehta, Japan Living, Tuttle Publishing, USA; Mitsue Nakamura, "Residence in Nakano," Japan Architect 272 // Recent exhibitions 2007: Exhibition for 55 houses, Modern Living, Japan; Detail Symposium 2007, DETAIL, Germany // Awards 2007: Special Prize for Wood, DETAIL Prize, Germany

NO.MAD– Eduardo Arroyo

www.nomad.as
Eduardo Arroyo born in Spain, 1964 // Lives and works in Madrid // Education Architecture and Urbanism diploma, ETSAM, Madrid, 1988 // Affiliations Colegio Oficial de Arquitectos Vasco-Navarro (COAVN), 1988–present // Recent works 2002: Desert Square, Barakaldo, Spain; 2003: Lasesarre Football Stadium, Barakaldo, Spain; 2006: Levene House, San Lorenzo de El Escorial, Spain; 2008: Banco Arquia, Bilbao, Spain; 2009: Zafra-Uceda House, Aranjuez, Spain // Recent publications 2006: Terence Riley, On Site: New Architecture in Spain, MoMA, USA; 2007: Monica Gili, ed., 2G: Eduardo Arroyo, Editorial Gustavo Gili, Spain; 2008: Sports Buildings–A design manual, Birkhäuser, Germany; Architettura contemporanes, Motta Architettura, Italy; Spanish Architecture, CA, China; "Spain," A+U 456, Japan; Design of the Year, British Museum Catalogue, UK; DBZ 3/2008, Germany; Domus 910, Italy // Recent exhibitions 2005: +Durango, Museo de Bellas Artes, Bilbao, Spain; VII Bienal Española de Arquitectura y Urbanismo (BEAU), Spain; Extreme Eurasia, Tokyo; 2006: On Site: New Architecture in Spain, MoMA, New York; 2007: Architecture of everyday life, Museum of the Revolution, Hanoi; 2008: Best Architectural Design 2007, Design Museum, London // Awards 2000: 1st Prize, CEOE Foundation Award, Spain; 2005: 1st Prize, VIII Biennial of Spanish Architecture, Spain

Office Kersten Geers David Van Severen

www.officekgdvs.com
David Van Severen born in Belgium, 1978; Kersten Geers born in Belgium, 1975 // Both live and work in Brussel // Education Kersten Geers: Architect-Engineer diploma, Gent University, Belgium, and ETSAM, Madrid, 1999; David Van Severen: Architect-Engineer diploma, Gent University, and ETSAM, Madrid, 2001 // Affiliations Kersten Geers: Gent University, 2003–present, TU Delft, 2003–present; David Van Severen: Gent University, 2004–present // Recent works 2007: Exhibition Architecture, Bozar, Brussel; Cité de Refuge, Rotterdam; A Green Archipelago (Care City), Markemeer, Netherlands; Villa, Buggenhout, Belgium; Reconversion of Grain Silos, Leuven, Belgium; Lake Side Villa, Keerbergen, Belgium; 3 Villas, Ibiza, Spain; Masterplan Kortrijk Xpo, Kortrijk, Belgium; 2008: Water Silos, Beersel, Belgium; After the Party, Venezia, Italy; 25 Rooms (Villa in Ordos), Ordos, China; Central Park, Turnhout, Belgium // Recent publications 2007: Christine de Baan, Joachim Declerck, Veronique Patteeuw, eds., Visionary Power, NAi Publishers, Netherlands; 2008: Mihnea Mircan, Memosphere. Rethinking Monuments, Meta Haven, Netherlands; 2008: Guy Chatel, "De genoegdoening van een openluchtkamer," A+ 210, Belgium; Marc Verminck, ed., "De Compositie van het Beeld," in Over Schoonheid, A&S Books, Belgium; Benjamin Eggermont, "Summer House," A+U 458, Japan // Recent exhibitions 2004: Groepsportretten, Witte de With Center for Contemporary Art, Rotterdam; 2005: Wonderland: Young European Architects, multiple venues in Netherlands, France, Italy, Croatia, Slovenia; "35m³" deSingel International Art Center, Flemish Architecture Institute (VAi), Antwerp, Belgium; 2006: New Trends in Europe and South East, multiple venues in Japan, Greece, Australia, Luxembourg; 2007: Power, Internationale Architecture Biennale Rotterdam; 2008: Since We Last Spoke About Monuments, Stroom Den Haag, Netherlands; Seven Rooms, deSingel International Art Center, Antwerp, Belgium

Satoshi Okada architects

www.okada-archi.com
Satoshi Okada born in Japan, 1962 // Lives and works in Tokyo / Education M.Sc. Building Design, Columbia University, New York, 1989; Ph.D, Waseda University, Tokyo, 1993 // Affiliations Columbia University, 1997–8; Graduate School of Architecture, Chiba University, 2003–present // Recent works 2005: Gallery in Kiyosato, Hokuto City, Japan; House in Ogikubo, Tokyo; 2006: House with Gallery for Buddhist Arts, Nagano, Japan; House in Wakabadai, Kawasaki, Japan; Villa Atami, Shizuoka, Japan; 2008: Warszawa Gallery of Photography, Warszawa; House in Normafa, Budapest; Villa in Karuizawa, Nagano; House in Hiroo, Tokyo; House in Kakinokizaka, Tokyo // Recent publications 2007: Robyn Beaver, ed., The New 100 House x 100 Architects, Images Publishing, Australia; Alejandro Bahamón and Patricia Pérez, Analogias Arquitectura Mineral, Parramon Ediciones, Spain; Andrea Boekel, ed., Outdoor Living: Courtyards, Decks, Patios, Images Publishing; Almanac of Architecture & Design 2007 Edition, Greenway Group, USA; Architecture Water, Edizioni Gribaudo, Italy; "Dialogue with Satoshi Okada," FUTU Magazine 06-07, Poland; Grand Designs 043, UK; 2008: Casabella 771, Italy; HISE, Arhitektura Oblikovanje Interier Vrtovi Biointeligentno 47, Slovenia // Recent exhibitions 2006: Dedalo Minosse International Prize: World Tour Exhibition, multiple international venues; 2007: World Architecture Award: World Tour Exhibition, multiple international venues; 2009: Satoshi Okada architect–Intensity of Architecture, Casa dell'Architettura, Roma // Awards 2006: Grand-prix, Dedalo Minosse International Prize, Italy; "Present of Future" Design Award, Russian Federation; 2007: Winner, International Architecture Awards, Chicago Athenaeum, USA; 2008: Winner, International Architecture Awards, Chicago Athenaeum

Onix

www.onix.nl
Haiko Meijer born in Netherlands, 1961; Alex van de Beld born in Netherlands, 1963 // Haiko Meijer: lives and works in Groningen, Netherlands; Alex van de Beld: lives and works in Helsingborg, Sweden // Education Haiko Meijer: M. Arch, Higher Technical School (HTS), Groningen, 1985, M.Arch, Academy of Architecture, Groningen, 1991; Alex van de Beld: M.Arch, Higher Technical School (HTS), Leeuwarden, Netherlands, 1985, M.Arch, Academy of Architecture, Groningen, 1991 // Affiliations Haiko Meijer: Member of various architectural juries (Vredeman de Vries Prize 2008); Board of Platform, GRAS (Groningen architecture and town planning); Alex van de Beld: Member of various architectural juries (Europan 2007) // Recent works 2007: Searching House, Lemmer, Netherlands; 2008: Egenes Park, Stavanger, Norway (with HLM Architects); Timber House, Bosschenhoofd, Netherlands; Dike House, Wierumerschouw, Netherlands; Multifunctional Center, Nijehaske, Netherlands // Recent publications 2005: Onix: Awaiting Signification, NAi Publishers, Rotterdam // Recent exhibitions 2007: Tangible Traces, VII International Architecture Biennial, São Paulo // Awards 2000: School Building Prize, Netherlands; 2001: 1st Prize, Wood Architecture Prize, Netherlands; 2003: Second Prize, Wood Architecture Prize, Netherlands; 2004: 1st Prize, Dutch Design Awards; 2005: Honourable mention, Vredeman de Vries Prize, Netherlands; 2006: First Prize, Vredeman de Vries Prize; 2008: Nominated, Architect of the Year, Netherlands

Patkau Architects

www.patkau.ca
John Patkau born in Canada, 1947; Patricia Patkau born in Canada, 1950 // Both live and work in Vancouver // Education John Patkau: M.Arch, University of Manitoba, Winnipeg, Canada, 1972; Patricia Patkau: M.Arch, Yale University, New Haven, USA, 1978 // Affiliations Royal Architectural Institute of Canada (RAIC), 1976–present; American Institute of Architects (AIA), Honorary Fellowship, 1999; Royal Institute of British Architects (RIBA), Honorary Fellowship, 2001 // Recent works 2005: Central Library of Québec, Montréal; Winnipeg Centennial Library Addition, Winnipeg; 2008: Our Lady of the Assumption Parish Church, Port Coquitlam, Canada; 2009: UBC Biodiversity Research Centre, Vancouver; Pothier/Onetto House, Salt Spring Island, Canada; Peterson/Munck House, Quadra Island, Canada // Recent publications 2007: Virginia McLeod, Detail in Contemporary Residential Architecture, Laurence King Publishing, UK; Phyllis Richardson, Big Ideas, Small Green Buildings, Thames and Hudson, UK; 2008: Sascha Hastings and Esther E. Shipman, eds., Logotopia: The Library in Architecture, Art and the Imagination, Cambridge Galleries Publications, Canada; Canadian Who's Who, University of Toronto Press, Canada; Federico Bucci, "Patkau Architects: ampliamento della Centennial Library," Casabella 72, Italy; Rob Gregory, Key Contemporary Buildings, Laurence King Publishing, UK // Recent exhibitions 2005: Substance over Spectacle: Contemporary Canadian Architecture and 3 Teams: 3 Visions: University Boulevard Architectural Design Competition, Morris and Helen Belkin Art Gallery, Vancouver; Cabin, Cottage, and Camp: New Designs on the Canadian Landscape, Charles H. Scott Gallery, Vancouver; Living Spaces: 21 Contemporary Canadian Homes, Dalhousie Architecture Gallery, Halifax, and York Quay Gallery, Toronto; 2008: 11th International Architecture Exhibition, Venezia // Awards 14 Canadian Architect Awards of Excellence, Canada (1983–2008); 12 Governor General's Medals, Canada (1986–2008); 3 National Honor Awards, AIA, USA (2005 and 2007)

Paul Morgan Architects

www.paulmorganarchitects.com
Paul Morgan born in Australia, 1960 // Lives and works in Melbourne // Education B.Arch, RMIT, Melbourne, 1986; M.Urban Design, RMIT, 1992 // Affiliations Royal Australian Institute of Architects (RAIA) // Recent works 2006: Cape Schanck House, Cape Schanck, Australia; GippsTAFE Learning Centre, Leongatha, Australia; 2007: Chisholm Institute School of Business and Management, Melbourne; 2008: Lal Lal Cabin, Lal Lal, Australia; Northern Melbourne Institute of TAFE Epping, Melbourne // Recent publications 2007: Leon Van Schaik, "Cape Schanck House," Architectural Review 099, Australia; Jeanne Tan, "Climate Modeling," Metropolis, USA; Helen Kaiser, "Freshwater Creature," Mark 8, Netherlands; Davina Jackson, Next Wave, Thames & Hudson, UK; 2008: Lukas Feireiss, Architecture of Change: Sustainability and Humanity in the Built Environment, Die Gestalten Verlag, Germany; Phaidon Editors, The Phaidon Atlas of 21st Century World Architecture, Phaidon Press, UK // Recent exhibitions 2008: Australian pavilion, 11th International Architecture Exhibition, Venezia; World Architecture Festival, Emap group, Barcelona; Platforms for Living and Beach Architecture on the Mornington Peninsula, Mornington Peninsula Regional Gallery, Australia // Awards 2007: Winner, RAIA Robin Boyd Award for Residential Architecture; Winner, Residential Architecture–Houses Award, RAIA Awards; Nominated, Zumtobel Group Award for Architecture and Humanity, Austria; Overall Winner, IDEA 07 Design Excellence Awards, Australia; Winner, Best Residential Interior, IDEA 07 Design Excellence Awards; 2008: Winner, Built Form and Design category, Victorian Coastal Awards for Excellence, Australia

Pedrocchi Meier Architects

www.pedrocchi-meier.ch
Reto Pedrocchi and Beat Meier born in Switzerland, 1973 // Both live and work in Basel // Education Reto Pedrocchi: University of Fine Arts, Berlin 1997, College of Technology, Basel, 1998; Beat Meier: University of Fine Arts, Berlin 1999, College of Technology, Basel, 2000 // Recent works 2006: Meggen Single Family House, Luzern; MRG Communications Conversion, Basel; Seven Sisters Shop Conversion, Basel; Furnishing Comme des Garçons Guerrilla Store, Gare du Nord, Basel; 2007: Furnishing Comme des Garçons Guerrilla Store, Imprimerie, Basel; 2008: Rennweg Single Family House Conversion, Basel; Kulturbüro Conversion, Basel; 2009: Institute for Sports, University of Basel // Recent publications 2007: Katharina Marchal, "Light it Up," *Mark* 6, Netherlands; Janina Poesch, "Vetrauenssache," *AIT* 1|2, Germany; Tibor Joanelly, "Nonchalante Coolness and Die wohnliche Oberflaeche," *Baumeister B3*, Germany; Ralf F. Broekman, Olaf Winkler, "Inhalte Produzieren," *build 3*, Germany; Roderik Hoenig, "Gemuetlichkeit ist kein Thema," *Hochparterre* 3, Switzerland; *Wall Design Book*, Daab, Germany

Pezo von Ellrichshausen Architects

www.pezo.cl
Mauricio Pezo born in Chile, 1973; Sofia von Ellrichshausen born in Argentina, 1976 // Both live and work in Concepción, Chile // Education Mauricio Pezo: M.Arch, Catholic University of Chile, Santiago, 1998, Professional degree, Universidad del Bío-Bío, Concepción, 1999; Sofia von Ellrichshausen: Professional degree, University of Buenos Aires, 2002 // Affiliations Mauricio Pezo: School of Architecture at Universidad del Bío-Bío, 2001–9; Both: School of Architecture at Talca University, Chile, 2006–9; Cornell University, Ithaca, USA, 2009 // Recent works 2003: Rivo House, Valdivia, Chile; 2005: Poli House, Coliumo, Chile; Wolf House, Andalue, Chile; 2008: Parr House, Chiguayante, Chile; Hema Studio, Buenos Aires; 2009: Fosc House, Venado, Chile // Recent publications 2007: Luis Fernández-Galiano, "Dado Desnudo," *Arquitectura Viva* 112, Spain; 2008: Phaidon Editors, *The Phaidon Atlas of 21st Century World Architecture*, Phaidon Press, UK; Ariadna Cantis, ed., *Rivo and Poli: 2G Dossier Iberoamerica*, Spain // Recent exhibitions 2006: V BIAU Ibero-American Biennial of Architecture and Urbanism, Montevideo; 2007: *Chilean Architects in Belgrade,* Museum of Applied Arts, Belgrade; *Visions of Latin American Architecture,* El Museo del Barrio, New York; *44 Young Architects*, Centre d'Art Santa Mónica, Barcelona; 2008: *Building, Dwelling, Thinking*, Insitut Valencià d'Art Modern, Spain; *Triatlon*, National Museum of Fine Arts, Santiago; 11th International Architecture Exhibition, Venezia // Awards 2005: Commended, AR Award for Emerging Architecture, UK; 2006: Architectural Quality Prize, XV Chilean Architecture Biennial, Chile; Best Work of Young Architects Prize, V BIAU Ibero-American Biennial of Architecture and Urbanism, Uruguay

Bill Price

www.billpriceinc.com
Bill Price born in USA, 1965 // Lives and works in Houston // Education B.Arch, Virginia Polytechnic and State University, Blacksburg, USA, 1991; M. Arch, Virginia Polytechnic and State University, 1994 // Affiliations Prairie View A&M, USA; University of Houston; Virginia Polytechnic and State University // Recent works 2005: Translucent Concrete Pavilion, Chaumont-sur-Loire, France; 2008: Translucent Concrete Pavilion, Seoul; Inflatable Air Dome, Seoul; Reboot Recycle Reuse; Ordos 100, Ordos, China; 2009: 4 Houses, Texas // Recent publications 2006: Lucie Paye-Moissinac, *Jouer au Jardin*, Conservatoire International des Parcs et Jardins du Paysage, France; Jean-Louis Cohen, ed., *Liquid Stone–New Architecture in Concrete*, Princeton Architectural Press, USA; 2008: "Translucent Concrete Pavilion," *Design is Air*, Seoul Metropolitan Government, Republic of Korea // Recent exhibitions 2004: *Liquid Stone–New Architecture in Concrete*, National Building Museum, Washington, D.C.; 2005: Gwangju Biennale, Gwangju, Republic of Korea; *East West North South–Arc en Rêve*, Bordeaux, France; 2006: Le Musée du Conservatoire National des Arts et Métiers, Paris; 2008: Seoul Design Olympiad, Seoul; 2007: III Biennale of Architecture Veritas, San Jose, Costa Rica // Awards 2005: American Institute of Architects (AIA) Research Grant for Translucent Concrete; 2006: Hilton Research Grant, USA

Productora

www.productora-df.com.mx
Carlos Bedoya Ikeda born in Mexico, 1973; Wonne Ickx born in Belgium, 1974; Victor Jaime born in Mexico, 1978; Abel Perles born in Argentina, 1972 // All live and work in México D.F. // Education Carlos Bedoya Ikeda: Architecture diploma, Universidad Iberoamericana, México D.F., 1998, M.Arch, ETSAB, Barcelona, 2000; Wonne Ickx: Civil Engineering and Architecture diploma, University of Gent, Belgium, 1998, M.A. in Urbanism and Development, University of Guadalajara, Mexico, 2001; Victor Jaime: Architecture diploma, Universidad Iberoamericana, 2001; Abel Perles: Architecture diploma, University of Buenos Aires, 1999 // Affiliations Carlos Bedoya Ikeda: Colegio de Arquitectos de la Ciudad de Mexico, 2008–9; Tec de Monterrey, México D.F., 2007–9; Wonne Ickx and Victor Jaime: Centro de Diseño, México D.F., 2006–9 // Recent works 2006: Museum of Contemporary Art of Lima, Peru; 2007: CSI Corporate Headquarters, México D.F.; 2008: Hotel Tulum, Tulum, Mexico; Plaza San Sebastián, México D.F.; Villa in Ordos, Ordos, China // Recent publications 2007: "Limac, Museum of Contemporary Art," *Space* 480, Republic of Korea; "Guadalajara – Productora. Nuove prospettive per la cittá storica – New perspectives for the old city," *Domus* 900, Italy; 2008: Cathelijne Nuusink, "Casa Mixcoac," *Mark* 15, Netherlands; Bert de Muynck, "Ordos 100, 100 villa's voor Ordos," *A + 213*, Belgium // Recent exhibitions 2007: Young Architects Forum, Urban Center New York; 44 Young International Architects, Biennale of architecture Encontros d'arquitectura, Santiago de Compostela, Spain; 2008: Vacios Urbano, Museo de la Ciudad de Mexico, México D.F.; 11th International Architecture Exhibition, Venezia // Awards 2006: Honorable Mention, Concurso para jóvenes arquitectos, Mexico; 2007: Young Architects Forum Award, Architectural League of New York, USA

Project Meganom

Yury Grigorian born in USSR, 1965; Pavel Ivanchikov born in USSR, 1964; Il'ya Kuleshov born in USSR, 1968; Alexandra Pavlova born in USSR, 1965 // All live and work in Moskva // Education All Architecture diplomas, Moskva Architectural Institute; Yury Grigorian and Pavel Ivanchikov: 1990; Il'ya Kuleshov: 1993; Alexandra Pavlova: 1988 // Affiliations All Union of Moskva Architects, 1994–present; Moskva Architectural Institute, 2006–present // Recent works 2003: Moskva House of Theatre, Moskva; 2006: Hotel and Residential Complex, Yalta, Ukraine; Residential Building Sezam, Tel Aviv; Residential Complex Krasnaya Polyana, Sochi, Russian Federation; Luxury Village Shopping Complex, Moskva; 2008: Mercury Theatre in Luxury Village, Moskva; Butikovsky Center, Moskva // Recent exhibitions 2006 and 2007: *International Exhibition of Architecture and Design*, Arch-Mosvka; 2008: 11th International Architectural Exhibition, Venezia; Moskva Biennale of Architecture // Awards 2000: Best Interior Design Award, Arch-Moskva, Russian Federation; 2002: Best Architectural Project Award, Arch-Moskva; 2007: Architects of the Year, Arch-Moskva

Smiljan Radic

Smiljan Radic born in Chile, 1965 // Lives and works in Santiago // Education Architecture diploma, Pontificia Universidad Católica de Chile, Santiago, 1989 // Recent works 2007: FMMM Project, Santiago; Chilean House 1, Rancagua, Chile; Mestizo Restaurant, Santiago; 2008: House A, Talca, Chile; Vik Millahue Winery, VI Región, Chile // Recent publications 2008: Patricio Mardones, Smiljan Radic, and Alberto Sato, *2G N.44*, Gustavo Gilli, Spain; *Smiljan Radic Clarke*, Publicaciones 2G, Spain; Clifford A. Pearson, "Design Vanguard 2008," *Architectural Record*, USA // Recent exhibitions 2009: *Crossing: Dialogues for Emergency Architecture*, National Art Museum, Beijing // Awards 2001: Best Chilean Architect Under the Age of 35, College of Architects of Chile, Chile

Philippe Rahm Architectes

www.philipperahm.com
Philippe Rahm born in Switzerland, 1967 // Lives and works in Paris and Lausanne // Education Architecture diploma, Swiss Federal Institute of Technology (EPF), Lausanne, 1993 // Affiliations Ecole cantonale d'art de Lausanne (ECAL), 2004–present // Recent works 2008: Head Offices Building for VNF, Paris; Fitness Center on the Water, Lyon, France; Project for 28,000-sq.-m Office Building, Venezia; House for Dominique Gonzalez-Foerster, Île-de-France; 2009: Museography of *La Force de l'Art 02*," Grand-Palais, Paris // Recent publications 2005: Philippe Rahm and Marie Darrieussecq, *Ghost Flat*, CCA Kitakyushu, Japan; 2006: Giovanna Borasi, ed., *Gilles Clément/Philippe Rahm, Environment: Approaches for Tomorrow*, Skira, Italy; 2008: Javier Garcia German, *Con-textos 2008*, Escuela Superior de Arquitectura, Universidad Camilo José Cela, Spain; Markus Landert, ed., *Moral Imagination: Art and Climate*, Verlag für Moderne Kunst Nürnberg, Germany; Akos Moravánszky and Ole W. Fischer, *Precisions: Architecture Between Sciences and the Arts*, ETH Zürich/Jovis Verlag, Germany; Flavio Albanese, "Remember Venezia *2008*," *Domus* 919, Italy; Michael Wang, "On Ephemerization," *Artforum*, USA; Shumon Basar, "Digestible gulf stream," *TANK* 5, UK; Justin McGuirk, "The 20 Essential Young Architects," *ICON* 58, UK // Recent exhibitions 2008: *Biennale Internationale Design*, Saint-Etienne, France; *Acadia 2008*, University of Minnesota, USA; *Youniverse*, Sevilla Biennale, Spain; 11th International Architecture Exhibition, Venezia; *Manifesta 7*, Fortezza–Bolzano, Italy; *Moralische Fantasien*, Kunsthaus Thurgau, Switzerland; *Archilab*, Taipei Fine Arts Museum, Taipei // Awards 2003: Architecture Section, Swiss Art Awards, Switzerland; Winner, Villa Kujoyama Scholarship, Japan; 2008: Winner, Carte Blanche VIA, Industries françaises de l'ameublement, France

Randić-Turato

www.randic-turato.hr
Sasa Randić born in Croatia, 1964; Idis Turato born in Croatia, 1965 // Both live and work in Rijeka // Education Sasa Randić: Architect-engineer diploma, University of Zagreb, 1990, M.Arch, Berlage Institute, Amsterdam, 1992; Idis Turato: Architect-engineer diploma, University of Zagreb, 1991, M.Arch in Historical Building Preservation, University of Zagreb, 2004 // Affiliations Sasa Randić: President, Croatian Architects Association, 2003–7 // Recent publications 2000: Various authors, *Randić Turato–Architecture of Transition*, Arhitekts, Croatia; Sasa Randić and Idris Turato, *In-Between: A book on the Croatian coast, global processes, and how to live with them*, K.L.J.B, Croatia // Recent exhibitions 2005: Internationale Architecture Biennale Rotterdam; 2006: Croatian pavilion, 10th International Architecture Exhibition, Venezia // Awards 2004: Viktor Kovacić Award, Croatia; 2005: Piranesi Award, Slovenia; 2006: Vladimir Nazor State Prize, Croatia; 2007: Selected, European Union Prize for Contemporary Architecture Mies van der Rohe Award; 2008: Nominated, Swiss Architectural Award

raumlaborberlin

www.raumlabor-berlin.de
Markus Bader born in Germany, 1968; Andrea Hofmann born in Germany, 1969; Jan Liesegang born in Germany, 1968; Christof Mayer born in Germany, 1969 // All live and work in Berlin // Education Markus Bader: Architecture diploma, The Bartlett, University College London, 1996; Andrea Hofmann: Architecture diploma, FH Münster, 1995; Jan Liesegang: Architecture diploma, TU Berlin, 1997; Christof Mayer: Architecture diploma, TU Berlin, 1998 // Affiliations Markus Bader: Brandenburg Technical University Cottbus, Germany, 1998–2004; Jan Liesegang: Akademie der Künste, Stuttgart, 2001–present; Christof Mayer: Swiss Federal Institute of Technology (EPF), Lausanne, 2006–present // Recent works 2007: Pfefferbett Hostel, Berlin; Silver Pearl Congress Centre and Spa, Rostock, Germany; 2008: Overland Boat, Brandenburg, Germany; Moderato Cantabile, Graz, Austria; Megastructure Reloaded, Berlin; 2009: Eichbaum Opera, Eichbaum, Germany // Recent publications 2006: Benjamin Foerster-Baldenius, "Convertibility," *Pasajes arquitectura* 81, Spain; Amelie Deuflhard, *Urbane Performance*, Spielräume Produzieren, Germany; 2007: Robert Klanten and Lukas Feireiss, eds., *Spacecraft: Fleeting Architecture and Hideouts*, Die Gestalten Verlag, Germany; 2008: Jaap Jan Berg et al., *Houses of Transformation*, NAi Publishers, Netherlands // Recent exhibitions 2006: French pavilion, 10th International Architecture Exhibition, Venezia; Kitchen Monument in Sustainable Buildings, BDA Gallery, Berlin; 2008: "Glow-Lounge"Glow: Forum of light in Art and Architecture, Eindhoven, Netherlands; We are coming! 0047, Oslo; P2-Residence in House of Imagination, Berlin; Italian pavilion, 11th International Architecture Exhibition, Venezia; The System: The Work of raumlaborberlin, Heidelberger Kunstverein, Heidelberg, Germany // Awards 2004: Distinction, Hans Schäfers Prize, Germany; Erich Schelling Prize, Germany; 2005: Red Dot Award, Germany; International Forum Design Award, IF, Germany; 2008: Nomination, European Union Prize for Contemporary Architecture Mies van der Rohe Award

REX

www.rex-ny.com
Joshua Prince-Ramus born in USA, 1969 // Lives and works in New York // Education B.A., Yale University, New Haven, USA, 1991; M.Arch, Harvard University, Cambridge, USA, 1996 // Affiliations Yale University, 2007; TED Brain Trust, New York, present // Recent works 2009: Vakko Headquarters and Power Media Center, Istanbul; Dee and Charles Wyly Theater, Dallas, USA; 2011: Museum Plaza, Louisville, USA // Recent publications 2008: Jesse Green, "Enter the Boosters, Bearing Theaters," *New York Times*, USA; Justin McGuirk, "The 20 Essential Young Architects," *ICON*, UK; Aurora Fernandez Per and Javier Mozas, eds., "Museum Plaza," *a+t: Hybrids I*, Spain; Frederick Tang, "Diagrammatic Urbanisms: Museum Plaza and Wyly Theatre," *Praxis 10*, USA; 2007: Karrie Jacobs, "The New Tastemakers: Group Dynamics," *House and Garden*, USA // Recent exhibitions 2007: Canaries Bienal, Las Palmas de Gran Canaria, Spain // Awards 2006: 40 Under 40, *Wallpaper*, UK; 2007: New Tastemakers, *House and Garden*, U.S.A.; 2008: Best New American Architect, *Esquire*, U.S.A.; 20 Essential Young Architects, *ICON*, UK

Rojkind Arquitectos

www.rojkindarquitectos.com
Michel Rojkind Halpert born in Mexico, 1969 // Lives and works in México D.F. // Education B.A., Universidad Iberoamericana, México D.F., 1994 // Recent works 2007: Torre Axis High Rise, México D.F.; Phillips Stand, México D.F.; 2008: Singapore Marina South, Singapore; Code Horizon, Dubai; Huaxi City Center, Guiyang, China; Nestlé Mexico, Querétaro, Mexico; Pulse Mixed Use High Rise, Monterrey, Mexico; R432 Mixed Use High Rise, México D.F.; 2009: Centro Cultural Tamayo, México D.F. // Recent publications 2007: Javier Barreiro, "Renew or Die," Mark 10, Netherlands; Kwang-young Jeong , Architecture Annual, Archiworld, Republic of Korea; 2008: Rumi Fukasaku, "Windows of the World," Casa Brutus, Japan; "Michel Rojkind and his 'Rock'hitecture,'" Vision Magazine 5, Japan; Dan Rubinstein, "Eye Candy," Surface Magazine 69, USA; Caia Hagel, "From a Rock Star to Star Architect," POL Oxygen 20, Australia // Recent exhibitions 2007: Exceptional Houses: Alternative of Individual Housing, Centrum Architektury, Czech Republic; 2008: Brit Insurance Designs of the Year, Design Museum, London; Open House – Architecture and Technology for Intelligent Living, Vitra Design Museum, Oslo; Mexico pavilion, 11th International Architecture Exhibition, Venezia; New World Architecture, University of Florence, Italy, and the European Centre for Architecture Art Design and Urban Studies, Athens // Awards 2008: Best 10 Buildings 2007, British Museum Awards, UK; Best 100 Realized Designs Around the World, International Architecture Awards, USA

savioz meyer fabrizzi architectes

www.smfar.ch
Claude Fabrizzi born in Switzerland, 1975; François Meyer born in Switzerland, 1974; Laurent Savioz born in Switzerland, 1976 // All live and work in Sion, Switzerland // Education All Architecture diploma, École d'ingénieurs et d'architectes de Fribourg, Switzerland, 1998 // Affiliations All Union Technique Suisse, 1998; Groupement Professionnel des Architectes, Switzerland, 1998 // Recent works 2005: House Renovation, Chamoson, Switzerland; 2007: Hotel Renovation, Sierre, Switzerland; 2008: Disabled Home Renovation, Ardon, Switzerland; 2009: Primary School, Vollèges, Switzerland; 2010: Sports Hall, Visp, Switzerland // Recent publications 2007: Detail, Germany; AIT 1-2, Germany; 2008: Architecture Now! 6, Taschen, USA; New European Architecture 05/06, A10, Netherlands; C3, Republic of Korea; A+U, Japan // Recent exhibitions 2008: Transformations in Hotel Architecture, Serralves Museum of Contemporary Art, Porto // Awards 2006: Best Change and Recondition Award, Switzerland

SeARCH

www.search.nl
Bjarne Mastenbroek born in Netherlands, 1964; Uda Visser born in Germany, 1970 // Both live and work in Amsterdam // Education Bjarne Mastenbroek: Architecture diploma, TU Delft, 1989; Uda Visser: Architecture diploma, TU Darmstadt, 1996 // Affiliations Bjarne Mastenbroek: Netherlands Architecture Fund, present; Academie van Bouwkunst, Amsterdam; University of Cataluña, Barcelona; Uda Visser: University of Aachen, Germany // Recent works 2005: Dutch Embassy, Addis Ababa, Ethiopia; 2006: Scherf 13 Housing, Utrecht, Netherlands; 2007: Wijnruitstraat Housing and Urban Planning, Hoogvliet, Netherlands; Junior College, Den Helder, Netherlands; Blok 5 Housing + Shopper Hall, Almere, Netherlands; 2008: Cultuurcluster Museum, Housing and Studios, Enschede, Netherlands // Recent publications 2008: "Architectuur en Materiaal Cultuurcluster Enschede," Architectuur NL 4, Netherlands; "Easy Does It," Mark 14, Netherlands; "This Building Is Singing," ICON 60, UK; "Textilfabrik wird Museum," Bauwelt 23, Germany; "Cultural Therapy," Mark 15, Netherlands // Recent exhibitions 2004: Fresher Facts, NAI, Rotterdam; 2005: Een Vorstelijke tentoonstelling, NAI; 2006: SeARCH, RAS, Barcelona; 2007: Rietveld Award Selection, Architectuurcentrum Aorta, Utrecht; Europan Generation: The Reinterpreted City, Cité de l'Architecture et du Patrimoine, Paris // Awards 2004: Nomination, AM NAI Prize, NAI, Rotterdam; Gouden Piramide Prize, Netherlands government, Netherlands; 2005: Achterhoek Architecture Prize, Netherlands; 2006: Design Vanguard Prize, Architectural Record, USA; 2007: Gouden Piramide Prize; Aga Khan Award, with Dick van Gameren, Switzerland

selgascano

www.selgascano.com
Lucía Cano and José Selgas born in Spain, 1965 // Both live and work in Madrid // Education Both Architecture diploma, ETSAM, Madrid, 1992 // Recent works 2006: Conference Center and Auditorium, Badajoz, Spain; Silicon House, Madrid; 2009: Conference Center and Auditorium, Plasencia, Spain; 20 Garden Villas, Madrid // Recent publications 2008: Details 7, Republic of Korea; "La Lista del MoMA," Arquitectura Viva, Spain; 2007: md International Magazine of Design, Germany // Recent exhibitions 2006: On-Site: New Architecture in Spain, MoMA, New York; 10th International Architecture Exhibition, Venezia; 2007: IX Biennial of Spanish Architecture, Madrid; 2008: GA International Exhibition, GA Gallery, Tokyo // Awards 2002: Architecture Prize, Madrid City Council, Spain; 2007: Finalist, IX Biennial of Spanish Architecture, Spain

Shim+Sutcliffe Architects

www.shim-sutcliffe.com
Brigitte Shim born in Jamaica, 1958; Howard Sutcliffe born in England, 1958 // Both live and work in Toronto // Education Both Environmental Studies and Architecture diploma, University of Waterloo, Canada, 1983 // Affiliations Brigitte Shim: Yale University, New Haven, USA, 2001 and 2005, Swiss Federal Institute of Technology (EPF), Lausanne, 2002, University of Toronto, present; Howard Sutcliffe: American Institute of Architects (AIA), Royal Canadian Academy of Arts (RCA), Royal Architectural Institute of Canada (RAIC), Ontario Association of Architects, Toronto Association of Architects, all present // Recent works 2005: House on Hurricane Lake, Haliburton, Canada; 2006: Massey College, University of Toronto; Craven Road Studio, Toronto; 2008: Integral House, Toronto // Recent publications 2005: James Adams, "A Work of Art Fit for Works of Art, Globe and Mail, Canada; 2007: Ian Chodikof, "The Sum of Its Parts," Canadian Architect, Canada; John Flannery and Karen Smith, eds., Library Design, teNeues, Germany; 2008: Brigitte Shim, "Nature, Culture of the Local," A+U 458, Japan; Phaidon Editors, The Phaidon Atlas of 21st Century, Phaidon Press, UK // Recent exhibitions 2005: Cabin, Cottage and Camp: New Design on the Canadian Landscape, Emily Carr Institute of Art, Vancouver, Canada; 2006: Less and More: Extending the Rational in Architecture, Alvar Aalto Akatemia, Jyväskylä, Finland; 44 to 66: Regional Responses to Sustainable Architecture in Canada, Cambridge Galleries, Cambridge, Canada; 2007: Integral House – On Process. Shim-Sutcliffe Architects, Eric Arthur Gallery, Toronto // Awards 2006: Wood Design Award, North American Wood Award Program, Canada; 2005: Award of Merit, 31st Annual Heritage Toronto Awards, Canada; 2004: Good Design Award, Chicago Athenaeum and Museum of Architecture and Design, USA; Governor General's Medal in Architecture, Canada; Designers of the Year, Interior Design Show, Canada

Srdjan Jovanovic Weiss/NAO

www.thenao.net
Srdjan Jovanovic Weiss born in Serbia, 1967 // Lives and works in Philadelphia // Education M.Arch, University of Belgrade, 1995; M.Arch II, Harvard University, Cambridge, USA, 1997; Ph.D., Goldsmiths College University of London, pending // Affiliations University of Pennsylvania, 2000–present; Temple University, Philadelphia, 2008–present; Harvard University, 2008–present // Recent works 2007: *Yona Friedman: About Cities* exhibition design, The Drawing Center, New York; House for an Expatriate, California; Cemetery Crematorium, Novi Sad, Serbia; 2008: Slought Foundation Office, Philadelphia // Recent publications 2006: Markus Miessen and Shumon Basar, *Did Someone Say Participate?: An Atlas of Spatial Practice*, MIT Press/Revolver, USA; Peter Mortenbock and Helge Mooshammer, eds., *Networked Cultures: Parallel Architectures and the Politics of Space*, NAi Publishers, Netherlands; Detlef Mertins, *Work 2007/2008*, University of Pennsylvania, USA 2009: Srdjan Jovanovic Weiss, *Camp David: Spectacle of Retreat*, Tyler School of Art_Architecture, USA; Srdjan Jovanovic Weiss, Aaron Levi and Katherine Carl, *Evasions of Power: Architecture of Political Adjustment*, Slought Foundation, USA // Recent exhibitions 2005: *Lost Highway Expedition*, MIT Center for Advanced Visual Studies, Cambridge, USA; 2006: *The Good Life: New Public Spaces For Recreation*, Pier 40, Van Alen Institute, New York; *The Fall and Rise of the Balkan City*, Akademie Schloss Solitude, Stuttgart; 2008: *13:100 | Thirteen New York Architects Design for Ordos*, Architectural League of New York; *Balkanology*, Swiss Architecture Museum, Switzerland // Awards 2007: Merit Award, American Institute of Architects (AIA), USA; 2008: Nominee, Iakov Chernikhov International Prize for Young Architects, Russian Federation

Studio Gang Architects

www.studiogang.net
Jeanne Gang born in USA, 1964 // Lives and works in Chicago // Education B.S. in Architecture, University of Illinois, Chicago, 1986; M.Arch, Harvard University, Cambridge, USA, 1993 // Affiliations Illinois Institute of Technology, 1997–present; Harvard Univeristy Graduate School of Design, present // Recent works 2003: Bengt Sjostrom Starlight Theater, Rockford, USA; 2004: Chinese American Service League, Chicago; 2007: SOS Children's Village Lavezzorio Community Center, Chicago; 2009: Aqua Tower, Chicago // Recent publications 2006: Barbara Ballinger and Lisa Skolnik, "Green with Envy: Sustainable Architecture in Chicago," *i4design*, USA; 2007: Christine Killory and René Davids, eds., *Details in Process (AsBuilt series)*, Princeton Architectural Press, USA; Kira Gould and Lance Hosey, *Women in Green: Voices of Sustainable Design*, Ecotone Publishing, USA; 2008: Stephen Zacks, "Jeanne Gang: The Art of Nesting," *Metropolis Magazine*, USA; Judith Dupré, *Skyscrapers: A History of the World's Most Extraordinary Buildings*, 2nd ed., Black Dog and Leventhal Publishers, USA; Branko Kolarevic and Kevin Klinger, eds., *Manufacturing Material Effects: Rethinking Design and Making in Architecture*, Routledge, USA // Recent exhibitions 2003: *NASA: Aerospace Design Exhibition*, Pratt Institute, New York, National AIA Headquarters, Washington, D.C., Art Institute of Chicago; *Marble Curtain*, National Building Museum, Washington, D.C.; 2004: 9th International Architecture Exhibition, Venezia; 2008: *Hyderabad Tellapur*, Chicago Architecture Foundation, Chicago // Awards 2008: Special Commendation, World Architecture Festival, Spain; Distinguished Building Award, AIA Chicago, USA; Interior Architecture Award Citation of Merit, AIA Chicago, USA; 2009: Award for Architectural Excellence in Community, The Richard H. Driehaus Foundation, USA

studio mk27

www.marciokogan.com.br
Marcio Kogan born in Brazil, 1952 // Lives and works in São Paulo // Education Degree in Architecture and Urbanism, Mackenzie University, São Paulo, 1976 // Recent works 2006: Casa das Mirindibas, São Paulo; 2007: Micasa Store Vol.B, São Paulo; Prime Time Nursery, São Paulo; 2008: Corten House, São Paulo // Recent publications 2006: Elisa Urbanelli, ed., *Modern American Houses: Fifty Years of Design in Architectural Record*, McGraw-Hill, USA; Michael Webb, *Art Invention House*, Rizzoli, USA; Mercedes Daguerre, *Case Latino Americane*, Mondadori Electa, Italy; 2007: Nobuyuki Yoshida, "Architects' Homes," A+U, Japan; Ellie Stathaki, "Micasa Vol.B," *Wallpaper*, UK; 2008: Yoshio Futagawa, ed., "Six Points About the Contemporary Latin American Houses," *GA Houses*, Japan // Recent exhibitions 2008: *Architectural Sketches*, FAI- Fondo Ambiente Italiano, Milano // Awards 2004: Associação Brasileira dos Escritórios de Arquitetura (ASBEA) Award, Brazil; House Award, *Architectural Record*, USA; IAB Award, Brazil; 2005: Shortlist, Design Award, *Wallpaper*, UK; 2007: Bienal Barbara Cappochin, Italy; 2008: The Yellow Pencil, D&AD Awards, UK; Dedalo Minosse International Prize, Italy

Studio Mumbai

www.studiomumbai.com
Bijoy Jain born in India, 1965 // Lives and works in Alibag, India, and Mumbai // Education M.Arch, Washington University in St. Louis, USA, 1990 // Recent works 2006: Bungalow 8, Maharashtra, India; 2007: Palmyra House, Maharashtra; 2008: Leti 360 Resort, Utaranchal, India; House on Pali Hill, Mumbai; Research Centre, Maharashtra; Trinity Guest House, Kerala, India; Utsav House, Maharashtra; 2009: Belavli House, Maharashtra // Recent publications 2008: Paul Finch and Catherine Slessor, eds., "Cool Water: Studio Mumbai's Subterranean Sanctuary," *The Architectural Review*, UK; Prathima Manohar, "Studio Mumbai names two louvered boxes Palmyra House after a popular Indian tree," *Architectural Record*, USA; Laura Bossi, *Skilled Resistance*, *Domus* 914, Italy; Maria Vittoria Capitanucci, "Penombre Tropical," *Casa Grazia*, Italy; Christian Schittich, ed., *Beach House in Nandgaon*, *DETAIL*, Germany; "Original Ecology," *Interior Design China*, China; Sophy Roberts, "Himalayan Luxury," *Departures*, USA // Recent exhibitions 2008: *Technology & Tradition*, Japan Institute of Architects, and Architects Institute of Japan, Tokyo // Awards 2007: Design for Asia Design Excellence Award, Hong Kong Design Center, China; 2008: AR Award for Emerging Architecture, UK

SYSTEM architects

www.systemarchitects.net
Jeremy Edmiston born in Australia, 1964; Douglas Gauthier (co-founder and partner until 2007) // Jeremy Edmiston lives and works in New York // Education B.Arch, University of Technology, Sydney, 1989; M.S. Advanced Architectural Design, Columbia University, New York, 1992 Affiliations City University of New York, 2000–present // Recent works 2008: Burst*008, MoMA, New York, 2009: Palmer Hall, All Angel's Church, New York // Recent publications 2004: "What If," *Metropolis Magazine*, USA; 2005: Bill Saporito, "The Newest Cut at Prefab," *Time 23*, USA; 2006: Peter Hall, "Bursting Out of the Box," *Metropolis Magazine*, USA; 2008: Ariel Kaminer, "New House, Available for Delivery, Convenient to Museum," *New York Times*, USA; Martin Filler, "Fabrication and Bucky Fuller," *New York Review of Books*, USA // Recent exhibitions 2006: *City of the Future: A Design and Engineering Challenge*, Grand Central Station, New York; *Connective Corridor Urban Design Competition*, Syracuse University, Syracuse, USA; *OOZ, Inc. (...for the birds)*, Postmasters Gallery, New York; *RAIA Annual Exhibition*, Royal Australian Institute of Architects (RAIA), Australia; 2007: *ParaFab*, University of British Columbia, Vancouver; 2008: *Home Delivery: Fabricating the Modern Dwelling*, MoMA, New York // Awards 2006: Wilkinson Award for Residential Architecture, RAIA, Australia; Australian Timber Design Award

Terroir

www.terroir.com.au

Scott Balmforth born in Australia, 1971; Richard Blythe born in Australia, 1965; Gerard Reinmuth born in Australia, 1970 // Scott Balmforth: lives and works in Hobart; Richard Blythe: lives in Hobart and works in Melbourne; Gerard Reinmuth: lives and works in Sydney // Education Scott Balmforth: B.Env. Des, University of Tasmania (UT), Hobart, 1991, B.Arch, UT, 1996, M.Arch, RMIT, Melbourne, 2008; Richard Blythe: B.Env.Des, Tasmanian State Institute of Technology (TSIT), Hobart, 1986, B.Arch, TSIT, 1998, M.Arch, University of Melbourne, 1998; Gerard Reinmuth: B.Env.Des, UT, 1991, B.Arch, University of Sydney, 1996, M.Arch, RMIT, 2008 // Recent works 2007: Fish349 Restaurant and Café, Hobart; Maitland City Bowls Club, Rutherford, Australia; Commonwealth Place, Canberra; 2008: Tasmanian Museum and Art Gallery, Hobart; 2009: 86-88 George St., Sydney // Recent publications 2007: Davina Jackson, *Next Wave: Emerging Talents in Australian Architecture*, Thames and Hudson, UK; Luis Fernandez-Galiano, *AV Monographs Emergentes*, Architectura Viva SL, Spain; 2008: Phaidon Editors, *The Phaidon Atlas of 21st Century World Architecture*, Phaidon Press, UK // Recent exhibitions 2007: *Out from Under: Australian Architecture Now*, multiple locations, USA; *Living the Modern_Australian Architecture*, Deutsches Architektur Zentrum, Berlin; 2008: 11th International Architecture Exhibition, Venezia // Awards 2006: Best in State Commercial, Interior Design Awards, Australia; 2008: Energy Australia National Trust Heritage Award for Conservation, Energy Management, Australia; Dulux Colour Award, Commercial Exterior, Australia; Small Projects Architecture Award, Tasmanian Royal Australian Institute of Architects (RAIA) Awards, Australia

Thomas Heatherwick/Heatherwick Studio

www.heatherwick.com

Thomas Heatherwick born in UK, 1970 // Lives and works in London // Education M.A., Royal College of Art, London, 1991 // Affiliations Sheffield Hallam University, Sheffield, UK, 2005; Manchester Metropolitan University, Manchester, UK, 2007; University of Brighton, UK, 2007; University of Dundee, UK, 2007 // Recent works 2004: The Rolling Bridge, London; 2006: La Maison Unique, Longchamp flagship store, New York; 2007: East Beach Café, Littlehampton, UK; 2009: Paperhouse newspaper kiosks, London // Recent publications 2007: Christine Killory and René Davids, eds., *Detail in Process (AsBuilt* series), Princeton Architectural Press, USA; *Landscape Design: Urban Furniture*, Loft Publications, Spain; 2008: Phaidon Editors, *The Phaidon Atlas of 21st Century World Architecture*, Phaidon Press, UK; Barbara Glasner, Petra Schmidt, Ursula Schöndeling, and Anja Welle, *Patterns 2: Design, Art and Architecture*, Birkhauser, Germany; Clare Lowther and Sarah Schultz, *Beachlife: Interior Design and Architecture on the Seaside*, Frame Publishers, Netherlands; 2009: John Sorell, *Creative Island II*, Laurence King, UK // Recent exhibitions 2005: *The Good Life: Design For All*, Van Alen Institute, New York; 2006: *Love and Money*, The British Council, multiple locations worldwide; 2008: *Skin & Bones: Parallel Practices in Fashion and Architecture*, Somerset House, London; 2009: *Le Temps des Boutiques*, Fondation pour l'Architecture, Brussel; *Contemporary Westminster*, New London Architecture, London // Awards 2006: Interior Design Practice of the Year, FX Award, UK; Best of Year, *Interior Design* Awards, USA; Prince Philip Designers Prize, UK; Best of 2006 Retail, *New York Construction Magazine*, USA; Top Honor Award, American Institute of Architects (AIA), USA; 2007: Civic Trust Award, UK; Best Retail Interior, Design Week Awards, UK; 2008: Regional and National Awards, Royal Institute of British Architects (RIBA), UK; South Geoffrey Osborne Innovation Award, Institute of Civil Engineers, UK

Thomas Phifer and Partners

www.tphifer.com

Thomas Phifer born in USA, 1953 // Lives and works in New York // Education B.Arch, 1975, M.Arch, 1977, Clemson University, South Carolina, USA // Affiliations American Academy in Rome, 1995–96; American Institute of Architects (AIA), present // Recent works 2006: Salt Point House, Salt Point, New York; 2007: Raymond and Susan Brochstein Pavilion and Central Quadrangle, Houston, USA; Boulder Residence, Boulder, USA; 2008: 1099 New York Ave., Washington, D.C. // Recent publications 2007: Anne Guiney, "Here Comes the Sun," *The Architect's Newspaper*, USA; Vernon Mays, "Everything Is Illuminated," *Architect*, USA; Pilar Viladas, "Side Impact," *New York Times Magazine*, USA; 2008: Beth Brome, "Inspired Designs for Wooded Settings," *Architectural Record*, USA; Michael Webb, "Relighting New York," *Domus* 912, Italy // Awards 2003: American Architecture Award, Chicago Athenaeum, USA; 2004: Medal of Honor, New York Chapter of the AIA, USA; Design Award, U.S. General Services Administration, USA; 2006: National Honor Award, AIA, USA; 2007: Honor Award, New York Chapter of the AIA, USA

TNA Takei Nabeshima Architects

www.tna-arch.com

Chie Nabeshima born in Japan, 1975; Makoto Takei born in Japan, 1974 // Both live and work in Tokyo // Education Chie Nabeshima: Diploma in Habitation Space Design, Nihon University, Tokyo, 1998; Makoto Takei: Architecture diploma, Tokai University, Tokyo, 1997 // Affiliations Chie Nabeshima: Tokai University, 2006–present; Musashino Art University, Tokyo, 2008–present; Toyo University, Tokyo, 2008–present; Makoto Takei: Tokyo Institute of Technology, 1999 // Recent works 2005: Wood Wear House, Hayama, Japan; Color Concrete House, Yokohama, Japan; 2006: Ring House, Karuizawa, Japan; 2007: Wood Ship Café, Hayama; Mosaic House, Tokyo; Stage House, Karuizawa; Plaster House, Kofu, Japan; 2008: Forest Side, Tokyo; Figured Glass House, Tokyo; Passage House, Karuizawa // Recent publications 2006: *JA Yearbook 2006* 64, Japan; 2007: *The Architectural Review*, UK; *JA Yearbook 2007*, Japan; *DETAIL*, Germany; 2008: *Wallpaper*, UK; *GA Houses* 107, Japan; *JA Yearbook 2008* 72, Japan // Recent exhibitions 2007: *Gesture Architecture*, Prismic Gallery, Tokyo; 2008: Design Miami/Basel, Switzerland // Awards 2007: Commended, AR Award, UK; Jutaka-Kenchiku Prize, Japan; 2008: Design Award, *Wallpaper*, UK; Wooden Architectural Space Design Prize, Japan; 2009: Special Prize for Glass, DETAIL Prize, Germany; The 24th Shinkenchiku Prize, Japan

Werner Tscholl

www.werner-tscholl.com

Werner Tscholl born in Italy, 1955 // Lives and works in Morter, Italy // Education Architecture diploma, University of Architecture, Florence, 1981 // Recent works 2007: Museum of the Monastery of Marienberg, Mals, Italy; 2009: Museum of the Timmelsjoch Hochalpenstrasse, Italy-Austria // Recent publications 2003: Paolo Vocialta, Marco Mulazzani, and Marco Biagi, *Werner Tscholl Architetture 1993–2002, Progettocontemporaneo 1*, General Membrane, Italy; 2008: Bettina Schlorhaufer, ed., *WalterDietl/Arnold Gapp/Werner Tscholl: Portraits of Three Val Venosta Architects*, Springer, Austria and USA // Recent exhibitions 2002: 8th International Architecture Exhibition, Venezia; 2003: Personal exhibition, Galleria Progetto Contemporaneo, Italy; 2004: Personal exhibition, Dessa Gallery, Slovenia; 2007: Personal exhibition, ESC itinerary di arte e Architettura contemporanea, Rovigo, Italy // Awards 2006: Città Oderzo Award, Italy; Dedalo Minosse International Prize, Italy (also 2008)

UnSangDong Architects Cooperation

www.usdspace.com

Jang Yoon Gyoo born in Republic of Korea, 1964; Shin Chang Hoon born in Republic of Korea, 1970 // Both live and work in Seoul // Education Jang Yoon Gyoo: B.S., Seoul National University, Seoul, 1987, M.Arch, Seoul National University, 1990; Shin Chang Hoon: B.A., Youngnam University, Seoul, 1997, M.Arch, University of Seoul, 2006 // Affiliations Both Korean Institute of Architects, 2006–present // Recent works 2007: Culture complex of HongIk University, Seoul; Life & Power Press, PaJu Book City, Republic of Korea; 2008: Gallery ACOZA, Wonju, Republic of Korea; Flagship Tower, Seoul; House Linear Loop, Seoul; Eco-Community Housing, Seoul; Kring (Kumho Culture Complex), Seoul; 2009: Architectural Sculpture of Hi-Seoul Festival, Seoul // Recent publications 2006: Fred A. Bernstein, "Design Vanguard 2006," Architectural Record 12, USA; 2007: Catherine Slessor, "AR Awards for Emerging Architecture 2007," The Architectural Review 1330, UK; Mathias Remmele, "Korea: Fassadenraum," db deutsche bauzeitung 102007, Germany; "Design Seoul: Jang Yoon Gyoo & Shin Chang Hoon," Sumau 032, Japan; "Emergentes: Twenty Emerging Teams," Arquitectura Viva 128, Spain; 2008: Yen Ping Chua, "Promoting Harmony," Mark 17, Netherlands; 2009: Sergio Pirrone, "Grocce di vetro sulla citta," Interni 588, Italy // Recent exhibitions 2007: Architects' Furnitures, Lock Museum, Republic of Korea; Architects in PaJu Publisher City, Architects' Center, Austria; 2008: Architects Jang Yoon Gyoo, Gallery Lonchel, Republic of Korea; 2009: UnSangDong Architects, Kring (Kumho Culture Complex), Republic of Korea // Awards 2006: Design Vanguard Prize, Architectural Record, USA; 2007: AR Award, The Architectural Review, UK; 2008: Grand Prize, Korea Space Design Award, Republic of Korea

Guillermo Vázquez Consuegra

www.vazquezconsuegra.com

Guillermo Vázquez Consuegra born in Spain, 1945 // Lives and works in Sevilla // Education B.Arch, Universidad de Sevilla, 1972 // Affiliations Universidad de Buenos Aires, 1993; Universidad Complutense de Madrid, 1993–2004; Getty Center, Los Angeles, 1994–95; University of Lausanne, 1995–97; Syracuse University, USA, 2001; University of Bologna, 2002–3; Universidad de Sevilla, 2004; Università della Svizzera Italiana (USI), Mendrisio, 2007–present // Recent works 2004: Museum of the Sea, Genoa, Italy,; Waterfront Promenade, Vigo, Spain; 2008: Maritime Archaeology National Museum, Cartagena, Spain // Recent publications 2002: Guillermo Vázquez Consuegra, Introduzione Francesco Gulinello, Facoltà di Architettura di Bologna, Italy; 2005: Vázquez Consuegra, Saggio di V. Pérez Escolano, Documenti di Architettura, Electa, Italy; 2007: Tommaso Vecci, Trentotto domande a Guillermo Vázquez Consuegra (Saper Credere in Architettura), Clean Edizioni, Italy; 2008: Vázquez Consuegra: Frente Marítimo de Vigo, Editorial Gustavo Gili, Spain // Recent exhibitions 2007: Avance de una contingencia, Arquitectura Contemporánea en Galicia, Centro Galego de Arte Contemporánea (CGAC), Spain; Horizons: Madrid Social Housing 1981–2006, Royal Institute of British Architects (RIBA), UK, and Aedes Galerie de Berlin, Germany; Vázquez Consuegra, Universidad de Navarra, Spain; 2008: Premio Europeo Ugo Rivolta, Congreso Mundial de la UIA, Italy; I Premio Andalucía de Arquitectura, Real Alcázar de Sevilla, Spain // Awards 2001: Confederación Española de Organizaciones Empresariales (CEOE) Award, Spain; 2005: National Prize in Architecture, Spain

Wandel Hoefer Lorch + Hirsch

www.wandel-hoefer-lorch.de

Nikolaus Hirsch born in Germany, 1964; Andreas Hoefer born in Germany, 1955; Wolfgang Lorch born in Germany, 1960; Andrea Wandel born in Germany, 1963; Rena Wandel Hoefer born in Germany, 1959 // All live and work in Saarbrücken and Frankfurt am Main // Education Andreas Hoefer and Rena Wandel Hoefer: Architecture diploma, TU Darmstadt, 1985; Wolfgang Lorch and Andrea Wandel: Architecture diploma, TU Darmstadt, 1990 // Affiliations Nikolaus Hirsch: Städelschule, Frankfurt am Main, 2008–present; Wolfgang Lorch: TU Darmstadt, 2003–present; Rena Wandel Hoefer: Department of Building, City of Saarbrücken, 2008–present // Recent works 2007: Kindergarten, Wendel, Germany; Documentation Center, Ravensbrück, Germany; 2008: Landwehrplatz, Saarbrücken; The Great Pyramid Competition, Germany // Recent exhibitions 2007: Ready for Take Off, VII International Architecture Biennial, São Paulo; 2008: Germany Architecture Yearbook 2007/2008, Deutsches Architekturmuseum, Frankfurt am Main; Ready for Take Off, Deutsches Architekturmuseum // Awards 2006: Mention, Deutscher Stahlbaupreis, Germany; 2007: Preis des Deustchen Architekturmuseums, Germany; 2007: Deutscher Naturstein Preis, Germany; 2008: Recognition, Balthaser-Neumann Preis, Germany; Deutscher Städtebaupreis, Germany

Eyal Weizman

Eyal Weizman born in Israel, 1970 // Lives and works in London // Education AA Dipl., Architectural Association, London, 1998; Ph.D, The London Consortium/University of London, 2006 // Affiliations Director, Centre for Research Architecture, Goldsmiths College University of London, 2005–9 // Recent works 2003: Territories, multiple locations; 2004: Ashdod Museum of Art, Ashdod, Israel; Ungrounding, Psagot settlement, West Bank; 2008: Refitting of the evacuated Oush Grab military base, Beit Sahour, West Bank // Recent publications 2003: Eyal Weizman, A Civilian Occupation: The Politics of Israeli Architecture, Verso, UK; Weizman and Anselm Franke, eds., Territories 1, 2 and 3, Verlag Walter König, Germany; 2007: Weizman, 665: "The Lesser Evil," Manifesta7 Companion, Silvana Editoriale, Italy; Weizman, Hollow Land: Israel's Architecture of Occupation, Verso, UK; 2008: Weizman, Alessandro Petti, and Sandi Hilal, Future Archaeology, BOZAR, Belgium // Recent exhibitions 2003: Territories, Kunst-Werke, Berlin, Witte de With, Rotterdam, and Malmö Konsthall, Sweden; 2008: Decolonizing Architecture, 11th International Architecture Exhibition, Venezia, Gemak Gallery Den Haag, and BOZAR, Brussel; YouPrison–Reflections on Limitations of Space and Freedom, Sandretto Re Rebaudengo Foundation, Torino, Italy; "665: The Lesser Evil," Manifesta7, Trento, Italy // Awards 2006: James Stirling Memorial Lecture Prize, Canada

WORK Architecture Company

www.work.ac

Amale Andros born in Lebanon, 1973; Dan Wood born in USA, 1967 // Both live and work in New York // Education Amale Andros: B.Arch, McGill University, Montreal, 1996, M.Arch, Harvard University, Cambridge, USA, 1999; Dan Wood: M.Arch, Columbia University, New York, 1992 // Affiliations Both Princeton University School of Architecture, Princeton, USA, 2005–present; Ohio State University Knowlton School of Architecture, Columbus, USA, 2006 and 2008; Columbia University, GSAPP, 2009; Lawrence Technical University, Southfield, USA, 2008; Parsons The New School for Design, New York, 2009; Amale Andros: Harvard University Graduate School of Design, 2006–7; University of Pennsylvania, 2008; Architectural League of New York, 2008–present; Dan Wood: The Cooper Union School of Architecture, 2004–5 // Recent works 2007: Diane von Furstenberg Headquarters, New York; Anthropologie Dos Lagos, Corona, USA; 2008: Public Farm 1, New York // Recent publications 2008: Beatrice Galilee, "20 Essential Young Architects," ICON, UK; GiovannaDunmall,"Lightness=Fundamental," MARK 15, Netherlands; Eva Hagberg, "On the Cusp," Metropolis, USA; Phaidon Editors, The Phaidon Atlas of 21st Century World Architecture, Phaidon Press, UK; Braun Editors, 1000x Landscape Architecture, Verlagshaus Braun Vertrieb, Germany // Recent exhibitions 2008: 13:100 | Thirteen New York Architects Design for Ordos, Architectural League of New York; Proposals for Hudson Park and Boulevard, Architectural League of New York // Awards 2006: New York New Practices Award, American Institute of Architects (AIA) New York Chapter, USA; Design Vanguard, Architectural Record, USA; Design Award, AIA, USA; 2008: Best of Year, New York Construction, USA; Best of Year, Interior Design, USA; Winner, MoMA/P.S. 1 Young Architects Program, USA

Index

Photography Credits

Paul Adams: 120 t; Koichiro Aitani: 187 cl; Daici Ano: 136 tl, tr, bl, 137 tl, tr, bl, 138-39, 192, 244-46, 381; Satoshi Asakawa: 241 bl; Ryota Atarashi: 195, 241 t, br, 242; Reio Avaste: 184 tl; Iwan Baan: 56, 57 t, br, 202 tl, 254, 255 l, tr, br; © david baltzer/bildbuehne. de: 323 tr; Paul Bardagjy: 239 tr; Alessandra Bello: 128; Peter Bennetts: 78, 284-85, 287 t; Eva Beth: 323 b; Helen Binet: 360 tr, bl, br, 362 tl, cr, bl, bc; Patrick Bingham Hall: 98 tr, bl; Reiner Blunk: 96; Brett Boardman: 72-73, 74 t, bl, c, br, 75, 97 t, cr, 98 tl, br, 99 tl, r, 368-70; Anthony Browell: 97 bl, 99 bl, c; G. Bruneel: 265 br; Esben Bruun: 52 cr; Ed Burtynsky: 344 tl; Ed Burtynsky and Richard Johnson: 344 tr, bl; Gaia Cambiaggi: 232; Jean-Philippe Daulte: 63; Julien de Smedt: 52 t; Emilio P. Doiztua: 108-9, 111; James Dow: 346 tc, b, 347 t, bl; © James Dow/Patkau Architects: 280, 282-83; DPI: 338 tl; Siméon Duchoud: 188; Filip Dujardin: 156-57, 158 tr, bl, 159; Carlos Eguiguren: 149; Estúdio GOMA: 134 tl, tr, cr; Elizabeth Felicella: 404-5, 407; GeeLy: 288 cl; Jesus Granada: 340; Miguel de Guzman: 267; Ralph Feiner: 131; Paul Finkel: 236, 238, 239 tl, bl; Floto and Warnter: 364-65; Scott Frances: 376-79; Martin Friedli Fotografie: 288 tl, tr, br; Richard Glover: 74 bc; John Gollings @ Gollings Photography Pty. Ltd: 76-77, 79; Fernando Guerra: 132-33; Fernando Guerra & Sergio Guerra: 88-91; Bob Gundu: 346 tl, tr; Kaido Haagen: 185 bl, br, 186, 187 tl, tr, cr; Roland Halbe: 24-25, 27, 212, 213 tc, bl, 214 c, 215, 256-57, 264, 265 tl, tr, bl, 266, 396 tr, br, 399; Shu He: 210; Mads Hilmer: 52 cl, br; Arander Hoek: 10-11; Guy Holmes, J Toelle Construction: 281; Florian Holzherr: 12-13, 15; Image Fiction: 352 l; Thomas Jantscher: 332-33; Rob de Jong, SAPh: 277, 279; Ray Joyce: 371; Peter de Kan p278 tl, tr, bl, 276; Andreas Keller: 152, 154 l, tr, 155; Roman Keller: 130;

Jan Kempenaers: 158 tl, br; Katsuhisa Kida: 193; Woo Il Kim: 299 tr; Yong-Kwan Kim: 233, 235, 389; Florian Kleinefenn: 124; Raimund Koch: 347 br; Gertjan Kocken: 253; Nelson Kon: 356-58; Christoph Kraneburg: 224-27; Maarten Laupman: 123 tl; Hong Lee: 127 tl, r; Jens Lindhe: 54; Jon Linkins: 204-7; Andrius Lipsys: 286; Jason Lowe: 361; Felix Luong: 164 t, 165 b; Duccio Malagamba: 392-95; Trevor Mein: 287 bl, bc, br; Miguletz: 396 tl, bl; Gianpaolo Minelli: 100; Adam Moerk: 80, 82; Nikolaj Møller: 164 b; Jeroen Musch: 278 cr, 336 br; Nacasa & Partners: 247; Goong-Sun Nam: 388; Jaime Navarro: 37, 330; Finn O'Hara: 345; Cristobal Palma: 116-17, 292-95, 308-9, 310 tl, bc, 148, 150; Yury Palmin: 45, 68-70; Arnaldo Pappalardo: 359; Adolfo Pardo: 36; Rob Parrish: 123 tr, cl, cr, bl; Jens Passoth: 14; Pedrocchi Meier Architects/Philipp Schaerer: 289 t, br, 290 t, br; Pedro Pegenaute: 214 tl, tr, bl, bc; Sergio Pirrone: 390; Bas Princen: 271; Gonzalo Puga: 310 bl, br; Alexa Rainer: 384-85, 387 t, bl; Christian Richters: 336 t, bl, 338-39; Paolo Rosselli: 52 bl, 53 b; Rainer Schlautmann: 320 b; Ulrich Schwarz: 40-43; Vaclav Sedy: 387 br; Shinkenshiku: 154 br; Martin Siplane: 185 c; Gert Skærlund Andersen: 165 tl; Tim Soar: 120 bl, br; Steve Speller: 373; Studio Gang Architects/Conflux: 355 tl; Studio Gang Architects/Mike Graham: 355 tr; Studio Gang Architects/Greg Murphy [Greg Murphy Studios, Inc.]: 355 cl, br; Koze Takayama: 194; Helen Thomas: 374; Guido Torres: 328-29, 331; Karola van Rooyen: 8-9; Rauno Volmar: 184 bl, br; Ruedi Walti: 228-30; Adrian Wilson: 375; Patrick Wong: 237; Pablo Zuloaga Photos: 343